NICHOLAS OF CUSA
IN SEARCH OF GOD
AND WISDOM

STUDIES IN THE HISTORY
OF
CHRISTIAN THOUGHT

EDITED BY

HEIKO A. OBERMAN, Tucson, Arizona

IN COOPERATION WITH

HENRY CHADWICK, Cambridge

JAROSLAV PELIKAN, New Haven, Conn.

BRIAN TIERNEY, Ithaca, N.Y.

A.J. VANDERJAGT, Groningen

VOLUME XLV

G. CHRISTIANSON AND TH. M. IZBICKI

NICHOLAS OF CUSA
IN SEARCH OF GOD
AND WISDOM

NICHOLAS OF CUSA
IN SEARCH OF GOD
AND WISDOM

Essays in Honor of Morimichi Watanabe by the American Cusanus Society

EDITED BY

GERALD CHRISTIANSON

AND

THOMAS M. IZBICKI

E.J. BRILL
LEIDEN • NEW YORK • KØBENHAVN • KÖLN
1991

The paper in this book meets the guidelines for permanence and durability of the Committee on Production Guidelines for Book Longevity of the Council on Library Resources.

B
765
.N54
N48
1991

Library of Congress Cataloging-in-Publication Data

Nicholas of Cusa: in search of God and wisdom: papers from the
    American Cusanus Society / edited by Gerald Christianson and Thomas
    M. Izbicki.
        p.   cm.—(Studies in the history of Christian thought, ISSN
    0081-8607; v. 45)
    Papers delivered at several conferences sponsored by the American
Cusanus Society, 1981-1988.
    Includes bibliographical references and indexes.
    ISBN 90-04-09362-1 (Leiden; cloth)
    1. Nicholas, of Cusa, Cardinal, 1401-1464—Congresses.
2. Philosophy, Medieval—Congresses. 3. Theology—Middle Ages,
600-1500—Congresses. I. Christianson, Gerald. II. Izbicki,
Thomas M. III. American Cusanus Society. IV. Series.
B765.N54N48   1991
230'.2'092—dc20   90-22415
                                                             CIP

ISSN   0081-8607
ISBN   90 04 09362 1

PRINTED IN THE NETHERLANDS

DEDICATION

To Morimichi Watanabe on his 64th Birthday

This first volume of studies on Nicholas of Cusa in English is dedicated to Professor Morimichi Watanabe as he begins his 65th year. The editors and contributors offer it to him in recognition of his imaginative, effective, and tireless work as President of the American Cusanus Society and as founder and editor of its *Newsletter*. We value most highly not only his initiatives in shaping the annual sessions of the Society at the International Congress on Medieval Studies, but also his encouragement in planning the biennial Gettysburg conferences and his enthusiastic encouragement in preparing this book. We honor him for his long series of publications on Cusanus' career as a late medieval conciliarist, churchman, and political philosopher. We appreciate the international contacts he has established with the German Cusanus-Gesellschaft of whose Academic Advisory Board he is a member, and with the Japanese Cusanus Society (Nihon Kuzanusu Gakkai) of which he is an Honorary Adviser. Above all, we are pleased to count him as our friend. In an Appendix we list his awards, positions, and publications. Here we add our best wishes for health, prosperity, and abundant affection.

August 8, 1990

LIST OF CONTRIBUTORS

James E. Biechler
La Salle University
Department of Religion
Philadelphia, PA 19141

H. Lawrence Bond
Appalachian State University
Department of History
Boone, NC 28608

Edward J. Butterworth
University of Detroit
Detroit, MI 48221

Gerald Christianson
Lutheran Theological Seminary
Gettysburg, PA 17325

F. Edward Cranz
Connecticut College (Emeritus)
New London, CT 06320

Donald F. Duclow
Gwynedd-Mercy College
Gwynedd Valley, PA 19437

M.L. Führer
Augsburg College
Department of Philosophy
731 21ste Avenue South
Minneapolis, MN 55454

A. Richard Hunter
Gwynedd-Mercy College
Gwynedd Vallley, PA 19437

Thomas M. Izbicki
Johns Hopkins University
Milton S. Eisenhower Library
Baltimore, MD 21218

Thomas P. McTighe
Georgetown University (Emeritus)
Philosophy Department
Washington, DC 20057

Clyde Lee Miller
State University of New York, Stony Brook
Department of Philosophy
Long Island, NY 11794

Joachim Stieber
Smith College
Department of History
Northampton, MA 01063

Charles Trinkaus
University of Michigan (Emeritus)
Department of History
Ann Arbor, MI 48109

Morimichi Watanabe
Long Island University, C.W. Post Campus
Brookville, NY 11548

Pauline Moffitt Watts
Sarah Lawrence College
Bronxville, NY 10708

CONTENTS

PART TWO
COMPREHENDING THE COSMOS

PART THREE
DETERMINING THE POWERS AND LIMITS OF HUMAN THINKING

PART FOUR
CONSIDERING RELIGIOUS DIFFERENCE

EPILOGUE

APPENDICES

PREFACE

During the Sixteenth International Congress on Medieval Studies, which was held at Western Michigan University in Kalamazoo in May of 1981, a group of scholars interested in the life and thought of Nicholas of Cusa (1401-1464), under the leadership of Professor H. Lawrence Bond of Appalachian State University, started an informal organization called the Cusanus Society of America. Every year since its inception, the Society has sponsored at Kalamazoo sessions dealing with the many aspects of Cusanus' life, thought, and influence on later thinkers. Formally reorganized in 1983 as the American Cusanus Society, this Society has continued to sponsor sessions at Kalamazoo; but it also has held two "working conferences" at Gettysburg Lutheran Seminary, Gettysburg, Pennsylvania. The first, held in 1986, focused on Cusanus' *De pace fidei;* the second, in 1988, focused on his *De ludo globi.*

The articles presented in this collection have been chosen from among the papers which have been delivered in Kalamazoo or in Gettysburg. The Society hopes that these studies not only shed light on Cusanus' ideas and activities, but that they will stimulate, especially in English-speaking countries, further work on the famous German theologian, philosopher, lawyer, and ecclesiastical reformer, one of the leading figures of the fifteenth century. The comprehensive bibliography of all works in English, both studies on Cusanus and translations of his works, was compiled by Professor Thomas M. Izbicki, The Wichita State University, to help advance research on topics related to this rapidly expanding field of study.

It is my pleasant duty, as President of the American Cusanus Society, to thank Professor Heiko Oberman, the editor of this distinguished series and a "forerunner" of the current renaissance in late medieval scholarship, for accepting this volume for inclusion, and to salute Professor Gerald Christianson, Gettysburg Lutheran Seminary, and Professor Izbicki for their sustained and selfless efforts to bring this first publication of the Society to successful completion.

Morimichi Watanabe

EDITORS' NOTES

The gestation period for this volume almost exactly coincides with the period which began when the American Cusanus Society elected as its president Morimichi Watanabe, to whom we dedicate these offerings. The year was 1983 and for the two of us, both church historians, it was an auspicious moment. Not only did we meet one another and members of the Society for the first time, but as historians who had known Nicholas of Cusa mainly for his contributions to the Council of Basel and political theory, we were impressed--perhaps a bit awed--by the learning of our new colleagues, most of whom were specialists in Cusanus' speculative thought.

We began almost at once to discuss informally with each other, and later with members of the Society, the possibility of publishing essays from past Society meetings at the International Congress on Medieval Studies in Kalamazoo, Michigan. The response was hesitant. Rather than spade up old ground, we were encouraged to cultivate new materials specifically with publication in mind.

Thus within three years the Society was holding a working conference at Gettysburg Lutheran Seminary on *De pace fidei*. Charles Trinkaus, celebrating his 70th birthday, delivered the plenary address, and others gave papers. The result was a handsomely bound, computer-printed text of *De pace fidei* edited by James E. Biechler with translation by H. Lawrence Bond.

Two years later a second conference was held in Gettysburg with *De ludo globi* as the focal text. This conference, noted for its outstanding papers by guests from abroad and a plenary address by F. Edward Cranz, will also be remembered for the presentation of an unusual gift to the Society by Hans Gerhard Senger of Cologne: a playable "game of spheres" based on Nicholas' scheme. Some participants sat down immediately to play the game; others have since used it in their courses to illustrate Cusanus' thought. From the point of view of this volume, however, Gettysburg II solidified the conviction that the moment for publication had arrived. Final action was postponed, however, until the 24th International Congress in May, 1989. This time there was no hesitation. All who were invited to submit articles agreed without second thoughts.

The conferences at Gettysburg, and this book which is dependent upon them, would not have been possible without the support, both moral and financial, of Gettysburg Lutheran Seminary. We are grateful to its former president, Herman G. Stuempfle, Jr., for his genial hospitality and to Dean Gerhard Krodel, who exemplifies the twin Cusa-like gifts of scholarship and churchmanship, for arranging generous grants for the conferences. This volume owes much to them.

We also are indebted to two of the Society's most distinguished scholars, F. Edward Cranz and Charles Trinkaus, both of whom have stayed with us throughout the project, giving detailed critiques of the papers, offering helpful advice on matters great and small, entering into the give and take of editorial decisions, and never flagging in their patience.

We appreciate Richard Wood for two reasons: not only did he put Gettysburg College's Academic Computer Center at our service; he introduced us to Ms. Kim Breighner. She, in turn, introduced our project to a new world--the world of computers in scholarly publication. At the same time, she handled Nicholas' theological jargon and our most obscure footnotes with equal aplomb, and met all our requests with remarkable good cheer. Neal Kentch, Alice Kerr Laird, and Rachel Christianson also gave generously of their time to bring the manuscript to publication.

We are pleased that the frank and open dialogue that has marked the Cusanus enterprise at Kalamazoo and Gettysburg continues. This dialogue is represented here by a broad spectrum of essayists--some of established reputation, others relatively new to the field--and, to give only one example, is illustrated by the different perspectives in which *De pace fidei* is read.

We offer our contribution to this dialogue with gratitude to the members of the Society because they took us in, made us feel at home, expanded our horizons, and encouraged us in the task now brought to fruition, even as they have demonstrated two characteristics of *homo quaerens* which Nicholas of Cusa himself would greatly admire: creative thought and genuine humanity. May their enterprise grow and prosper.

Gerald Christianson

Thomas M. Izbicki

Note on the Citations to Cusanus' Works

The basic text used is the edition of the Heidelberg Academy:

> *Nicolai de Cusa Opera omnia iussu et auctoritate Academiae Litterarum Heidelbergensis* (Hamburg, 1932-   ) = h.

Works are cited by book, chapter, and section number; h by volume and page. For example, *De coniecturis* I, 1, #5 (h III, 7-8) refers to *De coniecturis,* Book One, Chapter One, Section Five (in the Heidelberg edition, Volume Three, pages 7-8).

Where volumes in h have appeared in more than one edition, both are cited, and the later editions are indicated by suprascript numbers, e.g. V and V².

De pace fidei (h VII, ed. R. Klibansky and H. Bascour) was first printed in: The Warburg Institute, Mediaeval and Renaissance Studies, Supplement 3 (London, 1956). Some small changes were made when this edition was incorporated into h; the pagination, however, is identical.

Several works have not yet appeared in h, and are cited in the following editions:

> *De visione dei.* Jasper Hopkins, *Nicholas of Cusa's Dialectical Mysticism: Text, Translation, and Interpretive Study of De* visione dei (Minneapolis, 1985).
>
> *De ludo globi.* Cited from Nicolaus Cusa, *Opera,* 3 vols. (Paris, 1514). I, 99-114 is reproduced photographically in *Nicholas de Cusa,* De ludo globi: *The Game of Spheres,* translation and introduction by Pauline Moffitt Watts (New York, 1986). When the Paris 1514 edition is cited in the pages below, the Latin has been standardized.
>
> *Sermones.* H contains the *Sermones* through *Sermo* XXXIX of 1444. Others may be found excerpted in the Paris 1514 edition under the title *Excitationum libri decem* (II, fol. 7ʳ-188ʳ [*sic,* for 190]).

The sources of the translations used are indicated in the notes to the individual articles.

Most of the works in h are also found, though not in a critical edition and with only minimal annotation, in: Nikolaus von Kues, *Philosophisch-theologische Schriften,* ed. Leo Gabriel, with a German translation by Dietlind and Wilhelm Dupré, 3 vols. (Vienna, 1967; reprinted Vienna, 1982).

The following is a summary of Cusanus' works cited in this book, preceded by volume number in h:

> I.   *De docta ignorantia,* ed. E. Hoffmann and R. Klibansky (1932).

II. *Apologia doctae ignorantiae*, ed. R. Klibansky (1932).
III. *De coniecturis*, ed. J. Koch and K. Bormann, with J. G. Senger (1972).
IV. *Opuscula* I, ed. P. Wilpert (1959):
De deo abscondito.
De quaerendo deum.
De filiatione dei.
De dato patris luminum.
Coniectura de ultimis diebus.
De genesi.
V. *Idiota de sapientia. Idiota de mente*, ed. L. Baur (1937); *Idiota de staticis experimentis*, ed. L. Baur (1937).
V^2. *Idiota de sapientia. Idiota de mente*, ed. R. Steiger (1983).
Idiota de staticis experimentis, ed. L. Baur (1983).
VII. *De pace fidei cum epistula ad Ioannem de Segobia*, ed. R. Klibansky and H. Bascour (1959).
VII^2. *De pace fidei cum epistula ad Ioannem de Segobia*, ed. R. Klibansky and H. Bascour (1970).
VIII. *Cribratio Alkorani*, ed. L. Hagemann (1986).
X, 2. *Opuscula* II:
Fasciculus 2. *De deo unitrino principio.*
b. *Tu quis es (De principio)*, ed. K. Bormann and A.D. Riemann (1988).
XI, 1. *De beryllo*, ed. L. Baur (1940).
XI, 1^2. *De beryllo*, ed. J. G. Senger and K. Bormann (1988).
XI, 2. *Trialogus de possest*, ed. R. Steiger (1973).
XI, 3. *Compendium*, ed. B. Decker and K. Bormann (1964).
XII. *De venatione sapientiae; De apice theoriae*, ed. R. Klibansky and J. G. Senger (1981).
XIII. *Directio speculantis seu de Non Aliud*, ed. L. Baur and P. Wilpert (1944).
XIV, 1, 2, 3, 4. *De concordantia catholica*, ed. G. Kallen (1959-1968).
XVI, 1, 2, 3, 4. *Sermones* (1430-1441), ed. R. Haubst, M. Bodewig, and W. Krämer (1970-1985).
XVII. *Sermones* (1443-1452), fasciculus 1, ed. R. Haubst and H. Schnarr (1983-   ).

INTRODUCTION

HOMO QUAERENS: NICHOLAS OF CUSA
IN SEARCH OF GOD AND WISDOM

Charles Trinkaus

Nearly sixty years ago the name of Nicholas of Cusa came to my notice for the first time. A fellow graduate student in Professor Austin Evans' seminar on medieval social and religious history was attempting to produce a paper on Cusanus. I remember the group pouring over the sixteenth-century folio volume of Cusanus' *Opera* with fascination. Nothing further came of this. My fellow student undoubtedly finished her paper, but it was never published. Thirty years later, with the publications of John Patrick Dolan's *Unity and Reform: Selected Writings of Nicholas de Cusa,* Paul Sigmund's *Nicholas of Cusa and Medieval Political Thought,* and Morimichi Watanabe's *The Political Ideas of Nicholas of Cusa* in 1962 and 1963,[1] I began including readings of Nicholas in my senior seminar, *Studies in Ancient and Renaissance Thought,* and commenced my own serious study of his works. I did not deal with Cusanus in my *In Our Image and Likeness*[2] (written in 1965/67, published in 1970) because it dealt with Italians and humanists, but my readings in him strongly influenced my thinking in this book. Sometime in the early 'seventies the late Myron P. Gilmore remarked to me that he considered Nicholas of Cusa and Lorenzo Valla to be the two most original thinkers of the Renaissance.

My personal contact with Cusanus studies is of incidental importance only. But it is illustrative of the fact that, apart from the essays of Lord Acton and E. F. Jacob on Cusanus' political thought, Henry Bett's little book of 1932 *(Nicholas of Cusa),*[3] and a number of encyclopedia-like articles, there was only sporadic interest in the Anglo-American scholarly world until the early 'sixties, with a marked increase in the 'seventies, and not quite a flood in the 'eighties. This book of essays by members of the American Cusanus Society is the first collective volume on Nicholas of

[1] Dolan (South Bend, 1962); Sigmund (Cambridge, Massachusetts, 1963); Watanabe (Geneva, 1963).

[2] *In Our Image and Likeness: Humanity and Divinity in Italian Humanist Thought* (London and Chicago, 1970).

[3] Bett (London, 1932); Acton, "Nicholas of Cusa", *The Chronicle* (September 7, 1867): 565-567; Jacob, "Nicholas of Cusa", *The Social and Political Ideas of Some Great Thinkers of the Renaissance and the Reformation,* ed. F.J.L. Hearnshaw (New York, 1925).

Cusa in English and is the fruit of the swelling interest in this powerful thinker. Together with the founding of the American Cusanus Society in 1983 (whose members read versions of these papers at its meetings), it is symptomatic of the growing importance accorded to Cusanus studies today.

Further indication of this importance is the extensive treatment given to Cusanus by Professor Charles H. Lohr in his chapter on "Metaphysics" in *The Cambridge History of Renaissance Philosophy* of 1988.[4] Lohr sees Cusanus as the most important Renaissance elaborator of a medieval tradition centered around the work of Ramon Llull. According to Lohr, Cusanus was influenced by Llull's efforts to formulate Christian thought in a way that would simultaneously communicate Christian understandings of religious truth to the Islamic and Jewish co-inhabitants of the Mediterranean basin, and project a new dynamic conception of human activity and creativity flowing from an equally dynamic vision of the Godhead as characterized by will and power. As will be seen, some of these themes are taken up in the articles below. Moreover, Lohr sees Cusanus as closely linked in his ideas and aspirations to the contemporary Renaissance ideal of the dignity of man through his contacts with humanists at Padua, the Council of Basel, and the Roman Curia. He attributes to Cusanus a leading role in stimulating the revival of Platonism and Neoplatonism through his association with Cardinal Bessarion at the Curia and through his influence on thinking about the varieties of Platonism manifested in his dialogue *De non aliud.* Lohr also sees Cusanus as drawing on the elaboration by Nicole Oresme and others of the conceptions of the Nominalist school of the latitude, or intention and remission of forms, for his own conception of degrees of perfection. Although Lohr is aware, as Ernst Cassirer originally was not,[5] that Cusanus had no direct influence on Marsilio Ficino or Giovanni Pico della Mirandola, he sees the importance of the three Renaissance Platonists for the advancement of the idea of a dynamic God as exemplar for mankind. This was, according to Lohr, set back in the sixteenth century by the growing fascination with magic and the diversion of intellectual and philosophical energy into the religious controversies of the Reformation. Cusanus' major historical influences on modern thinkers were to come later.

[4] Ed. Charles B. Schmitt, Quentin Skinner, Eckhard Kessler, and Jill Kraye (Cambridge, 1988).

[5] Ernst Cassirer, *The Individual and the Cosmos in Renaissance Philosophy,* trans. Mario Domandi (Oxford, 1963), chap. 2, "Cusanus in Italy," esp. pp. 63-72. Trans. from Cassirer's *Individuum und Kosmos in der Philosophie der Renaissance,* Studien der Bibliothek Warburg, vol. 10 (Hamburg, 1927), one of the great classics of German Cusanus studies which culminated in the founding of the Heidelberg *Opera omnia.* See Watanabe's essay below.

Lohr's concerns for establishing Cusanus' religious philosophy as a kind of "harvest" for the medieval Platonic tradition (*pace* Heiko Oberman's claim for Gabriel Biel and the scholastic tradition), and Lohr's view of Nicholas as the most striking representative of Renaissance "dynamism", were oriented toward the elucidation of the pre-Reformation philosophy of the Renaissance and were not explicitly directed toward establishing Cusanus' modernity. However, Hans Blumenberg in *The Legitimacy of the Modern Age*[6] features Cusanus as a key figure in the transition from the medieval to the modern epochs. It is Blumenberg's view of history that large time blocks of many centuries are dominated and their unspoken assumptions are determined by a fundamental idea complex such as Christian/Ptolemaic/Aristotelian for the medieval period and secular/ Copernican/empirical for the modern. Despite the condition that, at least to this historian, this method of periodization seems no longer tenable, Blumenberg contributes a range of compelling insights concerning Cusanus, among a number of misperceptions and some mistakes. Since Cusanus undermined the prestige of centrality and enhanced that of the circumference, and thought that inhabitants of the sun or the other planets would see things from a different perspective than earth-dwellers, but, on the other hand, retained an essentially Ptolemaic cosmos and Aristotelian physics, Blumenberg makes of him only a "threshold" figure who, although there is no evidence of conscious intention, was effectually striving to preserve the medieval world system facing ruin. Amidst a floodtide of premonitions of modernity let loose by such internal fissures and contradictions in the medieval world system as the Nominalist movement, Cusanus stalwartly defended the intellectual structure of medievalism in a last ditch effort at preservation before the whole system collapsed. So Blumenberg sees him.

This melodramatic posture assigned to Cusanus, which is nevertheless characterized by Blumenberg's dazzling perceptual virtuosity, has been seriously impugned by Hans-Georg Gadamer[7] and more recently by Jasper Hopkins.[8] For Gadamer, Cusanus' relaxed manner of philosophizing, his

[6] Hans Blumenberg, *The Legitimacy of the Modern Age*, trans. Robert M. Wallace (Cambridge, Massachusetts, 1983). Trans. from *Die Legitimatät der Neuzeit*, 2nd rev. ed. (Frankfurt, 1973, 1974, 1976).

[7] In his review of Blumenberg, *Philosophische Rundschau* 15 (1966): 208.

[8] *Nicholas of Cusa's Dialectical Mysticism: Text, Translation, and Interpretive Study of* De visione dei (Minneapolis, 1985). See Hopkins' "Interpretive Study," pt. 6: "Nicholas of Cusa and the Modern Age," pp. 50-93. Forty-three of the ninety-seven pages of the "Interpretive Study" are devoted to Blumenberg. In his Notes Hopkins also includes criticisms of Jacques Doyon (n. 232, 3 pages), Donald F. Duclow (n. 334, 4 pages), Richard Campbell (n. 334, 6 pages), and Marcia Colish (n. 334, 15 pages). My direct citation of Hopkins is from pages 93 and 96-97.

Leichtigkeit, belied Blumenberg's notion of pessimism and sense of impending ruin, of an urge to frantic defense, in Cusanus. (We shall see below that Cusanus indeed had his dark and desperate moments, but also a genuinely optimistic vision of man's and God's working.) For Hopkins, who in his defensively sensitive concern over the precision of his own understanding of Cusanus leaps upon every conceivable flaw in Blumenberg's treatment, the problem is that Blumenberg ignores Cusanus' own insistence on the innovative character of his discovery of "learned ignorance," which is undeniably so. Hopkins calls him, if not "the Father of modern philosophy" [who would be Descartes], "the first modern philosopher," but also in "his pre-Modern standpoint" as retaining "the conception of a hierarchical world."

Thus the three of them, Blumenberg, Gadamer, and Hopkins agree at least on this: Cusanus was almost but not quite "modern." For me (and I suspect for several of the authors of this book) the problem is somewhat different. A self-consciously European culture takes its start around 1100, give or take a century. The scholastic culture of the High Middle Ages, as that of the nominalistic *via moderna,* the Renaissance, the Reformation, the Counter-Reformation, the Scientific Revolution (all of them "so-called") are interacting, overlapping, interdependent parts of a regionally and otherwise differentiated cultural whole in a continuous historical flow. Cusanus by heritage, affinity, or influence is related in some way to all six of them. He knew that Anselm, Albert, Llull (among many others) had wrestled with the problems that drove him; he knew and drew on Augustine and the other Christian Fathers of later antiquity and especially upon the Pseudo-Dionysius. He was familiar with the more recent philosophers of his own times and reacted to them: to Aquinas, Scotus, and those of the *via moderna* such as Ockham, Buridan, Oresme, and others. He knew of the world of pagan antiquity both before and after the Advent enough to disagree in part with Plato and Aristotle as well as to agree in part, to promote and procure translations of Proclus and Plato, to collect manuscripts of the ancients. He was certainly aware of history in the larger sense as well as understanding the historical dynamics of his own time extremely well. And in his *De pace fidei* and *Cribratio Alkorani* he reveals himself to be strongly conscious of religious and cultural difference. Yet it may be argued that his consciousness was more vertical than horizontal, more theocentric, cosmic, and mental than historical.

Nicholas was also a reformer. His personal career was deeply embedded in the politics of conciliarism and papalism to both of which he at some time adhered. His legations to Germany were devoted to efforts to purify the ecclesiastical institutions and to free them from subservience to the powerful. His disastrous efforts to accomplish the same in his episcopate of Brixen had the same purpose; as did his service as governor of the city of

Rome for Pius II. Let us listen to Pius' own report in his *Commentaria* of Nicholas' complaint:

"I have long suspected, your Holiness, that I was hateful to you. Now I am certain of it since you ask me what I cannot grant without incurring Heaven's reproach. You are preparing to create new Cardinals without any pressing reason merely at your own whim, and you have no regard for the oath you swore to the Sacred College in the Conclave before and after your election: namely that you would on no account create Cardinals unless with the consent of the majority of the College and according to the decrees of the Council of Constance. Now you ignore the ordinance of the Synod and do not ask the consent of the College, and you wish to make me a tool of your ambition. I cannot do it. I do not know how to flatter. I hate adulation. If you can bear to hear the truth, I like nothing which goes on in this Curia. Everything is corrupt. No one does his duty. Neither you nor the Cardinals have any care for the Church. What observance of the Canons is there? What reverence for laws? What assiduity in divine worship? All are bent on ambition and avarice. If I ever speak in a Consistory about reform, I am laughed at. I do no good here. Allow me to withdraw. I cannot endure these ways. I am an old man and need rest. I will return into seclusion, and since I cannot live for the commonweal, I live for myself." With these words he burst into tears.[9]

Such was the man whose personal sincerity and zeal for the right was matched by the mental intensity of his search for God and for truth and wisdom. Cusanus belonged to no school or sect or *via* in his own time. But he shared with proponents of the *via moderna* (among whom he was listed on one contemporary document) their conviction of the absolute power and omnipotence of the deity and of man's duty to adhere to the ordinances of nature, scripture, and church which flowed from God's own command and commitment to order. Nothing strange for a Christian of those times, and present also in the outlook of Thomas Aquinas and others of the so-called *via antiqua*.[10]

But one matter in the thinking of Nicholas stood apart: "educated ignorance." Nicholas' famous doctrine was obviously far more elaborate

[9] *The Commentaries of Pius II,* trans. Florence A. Gragg, notes by Leona C. Gabel (bks. 6-9, *Smith College Studies in History,* vol. 35, Northhampton, Massachusetts, 1951), p. 500.

[10] See William J. Courtenay, "Nominalism and Late Medieval Religion," *The Pursuit of Holiness in Late Medieval and Renaissance Religion,* ed. Charles Trinkaus with Heiko A. Oberman (Leiden, 1974), p. 38, n. 1.

than these two words. It meant (with the aid of the Pseudo-Dionysius'
negative theology) that there was in his view an absolute disproportion
between God's reality and power, and human knowledge, imagination,
conjecture. It was an impenetrable screen that was far more strict in its
denial of anthropomorphic projections of humanly conceived qualities upon
the deity than the other theologies (including that of the *via moderna*) to
which Nicholas was exposed. As Nicholas insisted, not even the law of
non-contradiction could be imposed on God, as those of the *via moderna*
had argued (i.e., that the only limit on God's omnipotence was that He was
subject to that law). Rather in God there was a coincidence of opposites
whereby, for example, the greatest and the least that man could conceive
could exist together. Cusanus was trying to express by this how far beyond
anything humanly conceived God necessarily had to be. In this teaching
Nicholas inferred that the thought and vision of all men was derived from
and limited to their individual perspectives which depended on their place and
time and all their other particular qualities within which each single mind
was encapsulated. Therefore God was not subject to perspective and could
be thought of as simultaneously center and circumference of the universe, as
everywhere, all powerful, eternal, seeing all, and knowing all. Thus for
Cusanus these traditional attributes of divineness ought to be newly seen
perspectivally by men from their perspectival points of vision. By knowing
his own ignorance, which was the invincible consequence of his
perspectivality, man can see God (or rather cannot see) more truly by no
longer projecting any part of his own limitations upon Him.

But paradoxically "educated ignorance" served only to enhance man's
cognitive pursuit of understanding of the spiritual and physical universe
within which he lived and of mankind itself. Driven by his knowledge of
his own ignorance, *homo quaerens* will hunt for wisdom even more
intensively and for that vision of God that had been denied to man by the
very fact of his humanness. Yet having faith in the divine word, and so
believing that man was created in the divine image and likeness, he would
continue to strive to discover that vision of the divine exemplar upon which
man's truly human life had been founded. Thus it is that we are calling this
collection of studies *Nicholas of Cusa: In Search of God and Wisdom,* for so
it was that Cusanus saw man, *homo quaerens,* engaged in what was his own
personal quest for God and wisdom.

Nicholas in his search for wisdom was very concerned with the mode of
the human thought process itself--not epistemology but the ways of the
mind in shaping a reality for itself within the whole of which it is a part.
The mind imagines the nature of the whole or postulates it by some mode
of the thought process. Nicholas presents us with many such modes in
various of his writings. We have mentioned the hunt for wisdom which in

his treatise of that name seeks it by partition of the territory over which the hunter roams according to discipline or field. He invents the "game of spheres" and finds an entire arsenal of analogies that can teach us concerning what we are searching. In the *Idiota de mente* it is the invention and shaping of a spoon that provides the *exemplum*. The icon with the omnivoyant eye in *De visione dei* teaches us about God's vision of us and our vision of God. In *De beryllo* it is a lens through which we can find our sought-for truth. All of these examples are familiar to anyone who has attempted to study Cusanus. Here they support the centrality of the search for knowledge and the thought process in Nicholas' philosophy.

Nicholas also describes *homo quaerens* as *homo cosmographicus* or map-maker in his *Compendium* of 1464. The cosmographer is assembling data brought to him by messengers coming into the city, who are the five external senses. With this data he makes his map.

> Finally when he has made a comprehensive description of the sensible world in his city, he collects it in a well-ordered and proportionally measured map, so that he will not lose it. He turns more towards this map, dismisses the messengers, and transfers his internal view to the creator of the world, who is none of all these things which are understood and noted by the messengers, but is the creator and cause of all things. He thinks him (the creator) to relate to the world in an anterior way, as he the cosmographer relates to the map, and from the relation of the map to the true world, the cosmographer speculates within himself like the creator of the world, by contemplating in his mind the truth in an image, the signified in a sign.[11]

It is this search for the truth in an image and the signified in a sign that Nicholas engages in and that, in a variety of ways, is the subject of the essays in this volume. *Nicholas of Cusa: In Search of God and Wisdom* begins with a very revealing essay on the historiography of the study of Cusanus: "The Origins of Modern Cusanus Research in Germany and the

---

[11] *Compendium* VIII, #23 (h XI, 3, 18-19). Trans. Pauline Moffitt Watts in *Nicolaus Cusanus: A Fifteenth-Century Vision of Man* (Leiden, 1982), p. 214 and n. 50: "Demum quando in sua civitate omnem sensibilis mundi fecit designationem, ne perdat eam, in mappam redigit bene ordinatam et proportionabiliter mensuratam convertitque se ad ipsam nuntiosque amplius licentiat clauditque portas et ad conditorem mundi internum transfert intuitum, qui nihil eorum est omnium, quae a nuntiis intellexit et notavit, sed omnium est artifex et causa. Quem cogitat sic se habere ad universum mundum anterioriter, sicut ipse ut cosmographus ad mappam, atque ex habitudine mappae ad verum mundum speculatur in se ipso ut cosmographo mundi creatorem, in imagine veritatem, in signo signatum mente contemplando."

Foundation of the Heidelberg *Opera omnia*" by Morimichi Watanabe.
Whereas today there is a major concentration of research on Cusanus in
Germany, especially in connection with the Heidelberg *Opera,* in the early
years of the twentieth century the most important studies were by Pierre
Duhem and Edmond Vansteenberghe in France and Paolo Rotta in Italy.
Watanabe's story tells how German scholarship eventually came to claim
Cusanus as one of Germany's greatest philosophers.

The studies on Cusanus himself begin with a first section on "Seeking
the Roads to God." M. L. Führer shows how Nicholas paralleled the
mystical theology of Albert the Great in setting forth the stages by which
the intellect moves toward a transcendent vision of God. Donald Duclow
contributes a close analysis of Cusanus' interpretations of the works of
Eckhart in his marginal annotations to these works and in his discussions of
Eckhart's theology in other writings. H. Lawrence Bond presents a more
extended commentary on the way Cusanus utilizes the complications of the
"game of spheres" which he had invented as a metaphorical device for
discussing the search for roads to God.

The "game of spheres" was clearly also a metaphorical vehicle for
discussing the universe and its relationships with its Creator, God, and his
image, man. Hence a second section on "Comprehending the Cosmos"
shows that knowledge of the external world cannot be separated from the
search for the divine in Cusanus' thinking. Edward J. Butterworth sees in
Nicholas' discussion of the cosmic sphere an effort to relate God and the
material creation by means of this metaphor. This essay, as well as Bond's,
arose out of a Cusanus Society conference at Gettysburg on the implications
of *De ludo globi.* A. Richard Hunter considers Cusanus' own efforts to
comprehend the natural world in this and other works, and asks whether they
might in any sense be considered science or contributed to future scientific
developments.

Inextricable from Cusanus' speculations concerning God and the cosmos
was his preoccupation with "Determining the Powers and Limits of Human
Thinking," the subject of the third section. Clyde Lee Miller explores the
meanings of Nicholas' usage of the term *coniectura* both as a mode of
knowing and as the content of what is known or thought. He is also
concerned with assessing whether Cusanus' *De coniecturis* should be
considered "medieval" or "Renaissance." An illuminating essay by F.
Edward Cranz on the late works of Cusanus follows. Behind this bibliographical topic is the story of what Cranz sees as Nicholas' triumphant
solution to the problem of the barrier that "educated ignorance" imposed on
man's reasoning about God and the world. Cranz, who during much of his
career has been concerned with a structural contrast between the ancient and
the western Christian conceptions of human knowledge, has long regarded

Cusanus as a central figure in these developments. As a consequence Cranz finds a special satisfaction in Cusanus' final vision of the mode of transcending the perspectival limits on human thought processes. Finally, Thomas P. McTighe, in an essay leading into the succeeding section, ponders the question of why Cusanus' dialectic of *complicatio/explicatio* cannot be applied to Christianity as *religio una in rituum varietate*.

The fourth section on "Considering Religious Difference" evolved from the Cusanus Society conference at Gettysburg on Nicholas' *De pace fidei*, a work searching the possibilities of religious concord. Thomas M. Izbicki examines whether the actual cultural and political conditions of the mid-Quattrocento rendered such a dialogue between representatives of Islam and Christianity a realistic possibility. James E. Biechler then presents a definitive analysis of the ideas and methods of Cusanus and John of Segovia in attempting to understand and convert the followers of Islam to Christianity. And Pauline Moffitt Watts discusses the different ways of addressing the spiritual other in Ramon Llull, Nicholas of Cusa, and Diego Valadés.

As a kind of epilogue Joachim Stieber reviews Cusanus' life and career, emphasizing the novelty of a man of humblest origins rising to positions of influence and power within the ecclesiastical hierarchy and becoming at the same time one of the most profound thinkers of his own time, if not in the entire Christian west. As an Appendix Thomas Izbicki has prepared a bibliography of the literature in English on Nicholas of Cusa through the year 1988.

It is our hope that we will have displayed not only our "learned ignorance" but something of our vision of Nicholas' "power itself."

PROLOGUE

THE ORIGINS OF MODERN CUSANUS RESEARCH
IN GERMANY AND THE ESTABLISHMENT OF
THE HEIDELBERG *OPERA OMNIA*

Morimichi Watanabe

It is apparent that in order to discuss modern Cusanus studies we must discuss publications and research activities not only in Germany but also in other European countries, especially France and Italy. In France, for example, Pierre Duhem (1861-1916), the noted historian of science, published two important studies at the beginning of the twentieth century in which he discussed Cusanus; one dealing with Cusanus and Leonardo da Vinci and another discussing Cusanus' relationship with Thierry of Chartres.[1] The most important and influential modern studies of Cusanus in French were those written by Edmond Vansteenberghe (1881-1943). Beginning with his study of *De ignota litteratura* of Johannes Wenck against Cusanus, which was published in 1910, Vansteenberghe's intensive and careful research culminated in the famous monograph, *Le cardinal Nicolas de Cues (1401-1464): L'action--la pensée* of 1920.[2]

Italian studies on Cusanus published in the late nineteenth and early twentieth centuries are much more numerous than those published in French. Giuseppe Rossi's study of Cusanus' philosophy and Enrico Constanzi's work on Cusanus as a precursor of Galileo appeared at the end of the nineteenth century.[3] Remigio Sabbadini's inquiry into the manuscript

---

[1] Pierre Duhem, *Études sur Léonard de Vinci* II (Paris, 1909): 97-279 and his "Thierry de Chartres et Nicolas de Cues," *Revue des sciences philosophiques et théologiques* 3 (1909): 525-531.

[2] Vansteenberghe's works include: *Le "De ignota litteratura" de Jean Wenck de Herrenberg contre Nicolas de Cues* [Beiträge zur Geschichte der Philosophie und Theologie des Mittelalters (=BGPhThM)] VIII, 6 (Münster, 1910); *Autour de la docte ignorance: Un controverse sur la théologie mystique au XVᵉ siècle,* BGPhThM XIV, 2-4 (Münster, 1915); *Le cardinal Nicolas de Cues (1401-1464): L'action--la pensée* (Paris, 1920; reprint, Frankfurt a.M., 1963); "Le cardinal-légat Nicolas de Cues et le clergé de Liége," *Leodium* 15 (1922): 98-123; *La vision de Dieu,* Museum Lessianum (Paris-Louvain, 1925); "Quelques lectures de jeunesse de Nicolas de Cues," *Archives d'histoire doctrinale et littéraire du moyen âge* 3 (1928): 275-284; "Un petit traité de Nicolas de Cues sur la contemplation," *Revue des sciences religieuses* 9 (1929): 376-390.

[3] Giuseppe Rossi, *Nicolò da Cusa e la direzione monistica della filosofia nel Rinascimento* (Pisa, 1893); Enrico Costanzi, "Un precursore di Galileo nel Sec. XV: il Cardinale Niccolò da Cusa," *Rivista internazionale di scienze sociali e discipline ausiliarie* (Rome, 1898).

studies done by conciliarists at the Council of Basel, which was published
in 1910, included interesting materials on Cusanus.[4]   Beginning with his
La filosofia dei valori nel pensiero di Nicolò da Cusa of 1910, Paolo Rotta
published four studies in the following decade, including his edition of *De
docta ignorantia* (1913).[5]   In the 1920's, Rotta continued to publish studies
of Cusanus, and his translation of *De docta ignorantia* into Italian appeared
in 1927.   His *Il cardinal Nicolò da Cusa: La vita ed il pensiero*, which was
published in Milan in 1928, can be regarded as a milestone in his research
on Cusanus.[6]

Since, however, the purpose of this article is to examine the beginnings
of Cusanus studies in modern Germany and show how the so-called
Heidelberg edition of Cusanus' *Opera omnia* began to be published, we shall
deal exclusively with studies of Cusanus published in the nineteenth and
early twentieth centuries in Germany.

Perhaps it is well to remember at the outset that the first contemporary
critic of Cusanus' philosophy was Johannes Wenck of Herrenberg (d. 1460),
a professor at the University of Heidelberg.[7]   Although there were some
notable publications on Cusanus which appeared before and in the eighteenth century, such as Caspar Hartzheim's *Vita Nicolai de Cusa* and

---

[4] See Remigio Sabbadini, "Niccolò da Cusa e i conciliari di Basilea alla
ricerca dei codici," *Rendiconti della R. Accademia dei Lincei* 20 (Rome, 1911):
3-41.

[5] Paolo Rotta, "La filosofia dei valori nel pensiero di Nicolò da Cusa,"
Rivista di Filosofia neo-scolastica [=RFNs] 2 (giugno, 1910): 244-261; *De
docta ignorantia* (Bari, 1913); *Il pensiero di Nicolò da Cusa nei suoi rapporti
storici* (Turin, 1915).

[6] "Il Cusano e la lotta contro gli Ussiti ed i Maomettani," RFNs 18
(settembre-dicembre, 1926); "La biblioteca del Cusano," RFNs 21 (gennaio-
febbraio, 1927), 22-47; Nicolò Cusano, *Della dotta ignoranzia, prima
traduzione italiana* (Milan, 1927); *Il cardinal Nicolò da Cusa: la vita ed il
pensiero* (Milan, 1928); "La nozione di misura nella concezione metafisico-
scientifica di Nicolò da Cusa," RFNs 23 (1931): 518-524; "Un manoscritto del
Cusano nell'Ambrosiana di Milano," *Rendiconti del R. Istituto Lombardo di
Scienze e Lettere* 74, 2 (1941-1942): 478-480; *Nicolò Cusano* (Milan, 1942).

[7] For recent discussions of Johannes Wenck and his attack on Cusanus, see
Rudolf Haubst, *Studien zu Nikolaus von Kues und Johannes Wenck*, BGPhThM
38, 1 (1955); Jasper Hopkins, *Nicholas of Cusa's Debate with John Wenck: A
Translation and an Appraisal of* De Ignota Litteratura *and* Apologia Doctae
Ignorantiae (Minneapolis, 1981; 3rd ed., 1988).

Johannes Semler's study and translation of Cusanus' *De pace fidei* ,[8] it was not until the beginning of the nineteenth century that serious research on Cusanus' life and thought began in German-speaking countries. No doubt the Romantic movement helped revive interest in his works.[9]

How what some historians called a Cusanus Renaissance occurred at the University of Tübingen in the 1820's under the influence of Johann Adam Möhler (1796-1838) has already been discussed in detail by Jochen Köhler in his article published in the *Mitteilungen und Forschungsbeiträge der Cusanus-Gesellschaft* 10 (1973).[10] We shall touch on some of the points in the article which have a direct bearing on our main concern in this paper and comment on them with a view to clarifying the contributions of the University of Tübingen to the later development of the Heidelberg edition of Cusanus' works.

Founded in 1477 by Count Eberhard of Württemberg, the University of Tübingen initially established fifteen chairs: three in theology, five in law, two in medicine, and five in arts. When the Reformation was introduced into Württemberg in 1534, the Protestant Theological Faculty obtained the leading position at Tübingen and retained its position into the nineteenth century. In 1809 Württemberg, which included areas of heavy Catholic population, became a kingdom. As a result, the University of Tübingen created a Faculty of Catholic Theology in 1817. Here the so-called "Catholic School of Tübingen" was quickly formed, with Johann Sebastian Drey (1777-1853) as its head. The development of historical and speculative theology at the School, which occurred under the influence of German Idealism and Romanticism, was of great importance in the history of

[8] Casparus Hartzheim, *Vita Nicolai de Cusa S.R.E. Presbyteri Cardinalis ad Vincula S. Petri* (Trier, 1730; reprint, Frankfurt a.M., 1968); Johannes Semler, *Des Kardinals Nicolaus von Cusa Dialogus von der Übereinstimmung oder Einheit des Glaubens* (Leipzig, 1787). About the influence of the philosophy of Cusanus from the fifteenth to the eighteenth century, see a recent study, Stephan Meier-Oeser, *Die Präsenz des Vergessenen: Zur Rezeption der Philosophie des Nicolaus Cusanus vom 15. bis zum 18. Jahrhundert* (Münster, 1989).

[9] For a general survey of the intellectual and theological response of Roman Catholics in Europe to the French Revolution and its aftermath, see Kenneth Scott Latourette, *Christianity in a Revolutionary Age*, vol. 1: *The Nineteenth Century in Europe--Background and the Roman Catholic Phase* (New York, 1958). See also Georg Schwaiger, ed., *Kirche und Theologie im 19. Jahrhundert* (Göttingen, 1975); Manfred Weitlauff, "Kirche und Theologie in der ersten Hälfte des 19. Jahrhundert," *Münchener Theologische Zeitschrift* 39, 3 (1988): 155-180.

[10] Jochen Köhler, "Nikolaus von Kues in der Tübinger Schule," *Mitteilungen und Forschungsbeiträge der Cusanus-Gesellschaft* [=MFCG] 10 (1976): 191-206.

theological study in modern Germany.[11]

Möhler,[12] who was ordained a priest in 1819, became a *Privatdozent* in 1822 in the Catholic Theological Faculty at Tübingen and was then sent on a six-month tour of central European universities (Würzburg, Göttingen, Braunschweig, Magdeburg, Berlin, Breslau, Prague, Vienna, Munich, and others), at which he made the acquaintance of leading professors, among them some prominent Protestant scholars.[13] He was particularly impressed with the deep and precise scholarship of Johann August Wilhelm Neander (1789-1850), a professor of church history since 1813 at the University of Berlin. While speaking with Neander, Möhler said that he intended to study a great historical subject: the period of the decline of the papacy from the removal of its seat to Avignon to the Councils of Constance and Basel.[14] He was clearly one of the notable supporters of the church, but his work on

[11] For a recent study of the Catholic School of Tübingen, see Thomas F. O'Meara, *Romantic Idealism and Roman Catholicism: Schelling and the Theologians* (Notre Dame, 1982). The School should not be confused with the (Protestant) Tübingen School of Historical Study. See R.W. Mackay, *The Tübingen School and Its Antecedents* (Hestford, 1869); Eduard Zeller, "Die Tübinger historische Schule," *Vorträge und Abhandlungen,* 2nd ed., 1 (Leipzig, 1875), 294-389; Peter C. Hodgson, *The Formation of Historical Theology: A Study of Ferdinand Ch. Baur* (New York, 1966); Horton Harris, *The Tübingen School* (Oxford, 1975).

[12] There are many studies of Möhler. To mention some important ones, A. Knöpfler, *Johannes Adam Möhler: Ein Gedenkenblatt zu dessen hundertsten Geburtstag* (Munich, 1896); Edmond Vermeil, *Jean-Adam Möhler et L'École catholique de Tubingue (1815-1840)* (Paris, 1913); Josef Rupert Geiselmann, *Johann Adam Möhler: Die Einheit der Kirche und die Wiedereinigung der Konfessionen* (Vienna, 1940); J.R. Geiselmann, *Lebendiger Glaube aus geheiligter Überlieferung: Der Grundgedanke der Theologie Johann Adam Möhlers und der katholischen Tübinger Schule* (Mainz, 1942; 2nd ed., Freiburg, 1966); Hans Geisser, *Glaubenseinheit und Lehrentwicklung bei Johann Adam Möhler* (Göttingen, 1971). In commemoration of the 150th anniversary of Möhler's death, the *Münchener Theologische Zeitschrift* published a special issue [39, 3 (1988)] dedicated to Möhler and his significance. See especially Georg Schwaiger, "Vorwort: Johann Adam Möhler (1796-1889): Zum 150. Todestag," pp. 153-154, and Peter Stockmeier, "Johann Adam Möhler und der Aufbruch der wissenschaftlichen Kirchengeschichtsschreibung," pp. 181-194.

[13] Weitlauff, "Kirche," p. 177.

[14] Stockmeier, "Johann Adam Möhler," p. 183.

the unity of the church, which he published in 1825,[15] received both enthusiastic appraisals and severe criticisms because of his ardent desire to reach
an understanding with Protestants and to accomplish the reunion of the
churches. In 1806 he became a full professor.

Möhler's later works, especially *Symbolik* (1832),[16] caused offense to
many of his more conservative Catholic colleagues because he attempted to
make a comparison between the Catholic and Protestant dogmas. His
sympathy for the theses of Protestantism regarding the invisible character of
the church and its mystical elements became increasingly strong. In his
early academic years he had studied the period of church fathers intensively,
but he began to take great interest in the conciliar period of the fifteenth
century and first studied the philosophical and theological ideas of conciliarist writers, such as Pierre d'Ailly (1351-1420), Nicholas de Clamanges
(ca. 1360-1437), and Jean Gerson (1363-1420). Although Möhler did not
refer to Cusanus specifically in his lectures and writings before 1829, there
is reason to believe that by 1829 he was studying the works of Cusanus.[17]

In 1829 the Catholic Theological Faculty of the University of
Tübingen sponsored an essay contest. Entrants were asked to submit an
essay on "A Description of the Life and the Ecclesiastical and Literary Work
of Cardinal and Bishop of Brixen, Nicholas of Cusa." Judging from the
extant draft of the official announcement, it is clear that the choice of
Cusanus as the subject for the contest was made and supported by Professor
Möhler.[18]   Three major essays submitted for consideration were all written
by Möhler's students, Franz Anton Scharpff (1809-1879), Karl Joseph
Hefele (1809-1893), and Ludwig Schmitt (1807-1877). When the decision
on the best essay was announced on November 6, 1831, Scharpff was the

---

[15] *Die Einheit in der Kirche oder das Prinzip des Katholizismus. Dargestellt
im Geiste der Kirchenväter der drei ersten Jahrhunderte* (Tübingen, 1825; critical
ed., Cologne and Olten, 1957). It is perhaps worth noting that Hans Küng, who
also taught in the Catholic Theological Faculty of Tübingen, cited Möhler's
work, *Die Einheit,* in his *Structures of the Church,* trans. S. Attanasio (New York,
1964), pp. 318-319. Concerning the controversy that arose as a result of the
book between J.A. Möhler and F.C. Baur, see Hodgson, *The Formation;* Joseph
Fitzer, *Moehler and Baur in Controversy, 1832-38* (Tallahassee, Florida, 1974).

[16] *Symbolik oder Darstellung der dogmatischen Gegensätze der Katholiken
und Protestanten nach ihren öffentlichen Bekenntnisschriften* (Mainz, 1832;
critical ed., Cologne and Olten, 1960-61).   It is interesting to note that Lord
Acton, a liberal Catholic, who wrote in 1867 one of the earliest studies of
Cusanus in English ["Nicholas of Cusa" in Lord Acton, *Essays on Church and
State* (London, 1952), pp. 246-250], cited Möhler's *Symbolik* in his essays.

[17] Köhler, "Nikolaus von Kues," pp. 192-195.

[18] Köhler, "Nikolaus von Kues," pp. 195-198.

winner of the first prize for his essay.[19]

Scharpff published a part of the essay as *Das kirchliche und literarische Wirken des Nicolaus von Cusa* in *Theologische Quartalschrift* (1837).[20] After intensive archival research in Kues and Brixen, he was able to publish in 1843 *Der Cardinal und Bischof Nicolaus von Cusa*, I. Theil, *Das kirchliche Wirken--Ein Beitrag zur Geschichte der Reformation innerhalb der catholischen Kirche in fünfzehnten Jahrhundert* (Mainz, 1843). With the publication of this study, serious modern research on Cusanus can be said to have begun in Germany. About this time, Mathias Martini (1794-1868), rector of St. Nicholas Hospital in Kues from 1827 to 1842, also published two articles on various documents related to Cusanus and his life, and wrote a guide book to St. Nicholas Hospital.[21] It is known that Martini was encouraged to study these topics and publish his findings under Möhler's influence.[22] We must also note that in 1843 F. J. Clemens published the cosmological statements of Cusanus which he had found in Codex Cusanus 211 in St. Nicholas Hospital.[23]

A detailed two-volume study of Cusanus and the church of his time, published in 1847 by Johann Martin Düx (1806-1875),[24] is the only major work on Cusanus from the first half of the nineteenth century which was not directly inspired by Möhler. Head of the Diocesan Priestly Seminary in Würzburg, Düx spoke of his research in the past eleven years and referred to Scharpff's book published in 1843. But he did not mention any of Möhler's works. Köhler has pointed out, however, that Düx was born in Simmringen, which was close to Möhler's hometown, Igersheim, Württemberg, and that Düx was in correspondence with Möhler.[25]

In the second half of the nineteenth century Scharpff and many other scholars published numerous studies of Cusanus not only dealing with his

[19] In his *Der Cardinal und Bischof Nicolaus von Cusa* (Mainz, 1843), pp. 3-4, Scharpff cited word for word from Möhler's lectures on church history.

[20] *Theologische Quartalschrift* 9 (1837): 2-35, 201-258, 687-763.

[21] Martini's publications include: "Nachträge zu Sinnachers Geschichte der Bischöflichen Kirche Säben und Brixen, enthaltend Urkunden, den Cardinal Nicolaus Cusanus betreffend," *Theologische Quartalschrift* 12 (1830): 171-179; "Berechtigungen und Zusätze zu den Lebensbeschreibungen des Cardinal Cusanus," *Theologische Quartal.* 13 (1831): 386-390; *Das Hospital von Cues und dessen Stifter* (Trier, 1841).

[22] Köhler, "Nikolaus von Kues," p. 198.

[23] Friedrich Jakob Clemens, *Giordano Bruno und Nicolaus von Cusa: Eine philosophische Abhandlung* (Bonn, 1847).

[24] Johann Martin Düx, *Der deutsche Cardinal Nicolaus von Cusa und die Kirche seiner Zeit*, 2 vols. (Regensburg, 1847).

[25] Köhler, "Nikolaus von Kues," p. 202.

life, but also with his philosophical and scientific ideas.[26]   One of the
notable writers in this period was Johannes Uebinger (1854-1912). Starting
with his dissertation of 1880, completed at the University of Würzburg,[27]
he published at least six other major studies of Cusanus, including his

---

[26]   Some of the important works published in the second half of the 19th
century are listed below chronologically: Franz Anton Scharpff, *Des Cardinals
und Bischofs Nicolaus von Cusa wichtigste Schriften in deutscher Übersetzung*
(Freiburg i.B., 1862); F.X. Kraus, "Die Handschriften-Sammlung des Cardinals
Nicolaus von Cusa," *Serapeum* 25, 23 (1864): 353-365; 24 (1864): 369-383;
26, 2 (1865): 24-31; 3 (1865): 33-42; 4 (1865): 49-59; 5 (1865): 65-76; 6
(1865): 81-89; 7 (1865): 97-104; Theodor Stumpf, *Die politischen Ideen des
Nicolaus von Cues: Zum Gedächtnis seines vierhundertjährigen Todestages* (11.
August 1464) (Coblenz, 1864); Joseph Klein, *Über eine Handschrift des
Nicolaus von Cues, nebst ungedruckten Fragmenten Ciceronischer Reden*
(Berlin, 1866); Clemens F. Brockhaus, *Nicolai Cusani de Concilii Universalis
Potestate Sententia explicatur* (Leipzig, 1867); F.A. Scharpff, *Der Cardinal und
Bischof Nicolaus von Cusa als Reformator in Kirche, Reich und Philosophie des
15. Jahrhunderts* (Tübingen, 1871); Rudolf Eucken, "Nicolaus von Cues,"
Philosophische Monatshefte 14 (1878): 449-470; Richard Falckenberg,
Aufgabe und Wesen der Erkenntnis bei Nicolaus von Kues (Breslau, 1880); R.
Falckenberg, *Grundzüge der Philosophie des Nicolaus Cusanus, mit besonderer
Berücksichtigung der Lehre vom Erkennen* (Breslau, 1880); Karl Grube, "Die
Legationsreise des Cardinals Nikolaus von Cusa durch Norddeutschland im Jahre
1451," *Historisches Jahrbuch* 1 (1880): 393-412; Jacob Schaefer, *Des Nicolaus
von Kues Lehre vom Kosmos* (Mainz, 1887); H. Schedel, *Die Gotteslehre des
Nicolaus von Kues* (Münster, 1888); Michael Glossner, *Nikolaus von Cusa und
Marius Nizolius als Vorläufer der neuern Philosophie* (Münster, 1891); Franz
Falk, "Cardinal Nicolaus von Cusa in Rom und Cues an der Mosel," *Der
Katholik* LXXII, 1 (1892): 88-96; H.V. Sauerland, "Notizien zur
Lebensgeschichte des Kardinals Nicolaus von Cues," *Römische Quartalschrift* 9
(1893): 192; Aloys Meister, "Die humanistischen Anfänge des Nikolaus von
Cues," *Annalen des Historischen Vereins für Niederrhein* 63 (1896): 1-21;
Hermann Grauert, "Nicolaus von Cues als Humanist, Handschriftenforscher und
Staatsphilosoph," *Literarische Beilage der Kölnischen Volkszeitung* 28, 29
(1897); Siegmund Günther, "Nikolaus von Cusa in seiner Beziehungen zur
mathematischen und physikalischen Geographie," *Abhandlungen zur
Geschichte der Mathematik* (Leipzig, 1899); J. Guttmann, "Aus der Zeit der
Renaissance: Nicolaus von Cusa, Jacobus Faber Stapulensis, Bonet de Lattes,
Carolus Bovillus," *Monatsschrift für Geschichte und Wissenschaft des
Judenthums*, N.S., 7 (Berlin, 1899): 250-266.

[27] Johannes Uebinger, *Die Philosophie des Nicolaus Cusanus* (Würzburg,
1880).

detailed study of Cusanus' mathematical ideas published in 1895-1897.[28] In his book, *Die Gotteslehre des Nikolaus Cusanus*, he published the text of *Tetralogus de non aliud*, which he had discovered during his archival research.[29] It is well to remember that some Cusanus scholars like Clemens, Kraus, and Uebinger had begun to realize by this time how important it was to obtain reliable, authentic texts of Cusanus' writings. After all, the published editions of his works, the Strassbourg edition of 1488 by Martin Flach, the Milan edition of 1502 by Benedictus Dolcibelli, the Paris edition of 1514 by Jodocus Badius Ascensius, and the Basel edition of 1565 by Henricus Petri, were at least three hundred years old.

The Strassbourg edition was rare, and the Milan edition, which was a slavish reprint of the first, was rarer still. The Paris edition by the famous French humanist Jacques Lefèvre d'Étaples was notable for the fact that it had important additions, the *De concordantia catholica libri tres* and the *Excitationum libri decem*, but was not very reliable because the humanist made many emendations of the text. The Basel edition added some mathematical treatises to the third. As a result, the Basel edition was regarded by many as the most useful of the printed editions.[30] Clearly there was a great need to establish an authentic, critical modern edition of Cusanus' works.

Düx and Uebinger, two prominent Cusanus scholars of the nineteenth century, were not members of the Catholic School of Tübingen, but members of the Tübingen School, such as Paul Schanz (1841-1905), Johann Storz (1839-1895), and Maximilian Birck (1841-1903), also made significant contributions to Cusanus studies in the second half of the

---

[28] "Kardinallegat Nikolaus Cusanus in Deutschland 1451 bis 1452," *Historisches Jahrbuch* 8 (1887): 629-665; *Die Gotteslehre des Nikolaus Cusanus* (Münster, 1888); "Zur Lebensgeschichte des Nikolaus Cusanus," *Historisches Jahrbuch* 14 (1893): 549-561; "Die philosophischen Schriften des Nikolaus Cusanus," *Zeitschrift für Philosophie und phil. Kritik* 103, 105, 107 (1894); "Der Begriff docta ignorantia in seiner geschichtlichen Entwicklung," *Archiv für Geschichte der Philosophie* 8 (1895): 1-32, 206-240; "Die mathematischen Schriften des Nicolaus Cusanus," *Philosophisches Jahrbuch* 8 (1895): 301-317, 403-422; 9 (1896): 54-66, 391-410; 10 (1897): 144-159; "Nikolaus Treverensis," *Philosophisches Jahrbuch* 19 (1906): 451-470.

[29] Uebinger, *Die Gotteslehre*, pp. 150-193.

[30] The edition printed at present-day Cortemaggiore is usually called the Milan edition. About various editions, see Vansteenberghe, *Le cardinal*, pp. 465-468; Gerd Heinz-Mohr and Willehad Paul Eckert, eds., *Das Werk des Nicolaus Cusanus: Eine bibliophile Einführung* (Cologne, 1963; 2nd ed., 1975), pp. 164-165; W.P. Eckert, "Der Stand der Cusanus-Edition," *Schweizer Rundschau* 63, 7/8 (1964): 443-448.

nineteenth century.[31]   The articles on Cusanus which were published in encyclopedias and lexica during the period were written mostly by the members of the Catholic School of Tübingen.[32]

To summarize, modern Cusanus research in nineteenth-century Germany was chiefly advanced by members of the Catholic School of Tübingen under the influence of Johann Adam Möhler. Not only did they study the life, philosophical ideas, and influence of Cardinal Cusanus, but some of them began to pay attention to his mathematical ideas and also to the importance of discovering reliable texts.

What we must now attempt to clarify is how nineteenth-century Cusanus scholarship which was initiated and prompted by the Tübingen School was related to the Cusanus research which began at the University of Heidelberg in the late 1920's and which resulted in the publication of a modern critical edition of Cusanus' works under the auspices of the Heidelberg Academy of Sciences (*Heidelberger Akademie der Wissenschaften*).

Who were the scholars that were directly and indirectly responsible for this development? What was the philosophical and intellectual milieu that gave rise to the ambitious, enormously complicated, and still continuing academic and literary enterprise? What was the role played by Dr. Felix Meiner of the Felix Meiner Verlag in Leipzig? These are some of the important questions which we must answer as we turn to the second period of modern Cusanus studies. In the transition to this period, certain prominent leaders of Neo-Kantian schools took great interest in the ideas of Cusanus and paved the way for the launching of the Heidelberg edition of Cusanus' works. These scholars include Hermann Cohen (1842-1918), Heinrich Rickert (1863-1936), and Ernst Cassirer (1874-1945).

In 1911 Dr. Felix Meiner (1883-1965) purchased from the Dürrsche Buchhandlung in Leipzig the *Philosophische Bibliothek,* which had been founded by Dr. Julius Hermann von Kirchmann (1802-1884) in 1868 and

---

[31] Their studies are: Paul Schanz, *Der Cardinal Nicolaus von Cusa als Mathematiker* (Rottweil, 1873); idem, *Die astronomischen Anschauungen des Nikolaus von Kues und seiner Zeit* (Rottweil, 1873); Johann Nepomak Storz, "Die spekulative Gotteslehre des Nicolaus Cusanus," *Theologische Quartalschrift* 55 (1873): 3-57, 220-285; Maximilian Birck, "Nikolaus von Cues' Auftreten auf dem Basler Konzil," *Theologische Quartalschrift* 73 (1891): 335-370; idem, "Hat Nikolaus von Cues seine Ansicht über den Primat geändert?," *Theologische Quartalschrift* 74 (1892): 617-642; idem, "Nikolaus von Cusa auf dem Konzil zu Basel," *Historisches Jahrbuch* 13 (1892): 770-782.

[32] Some of them are Carl von Prantl, "Cusanus," *Allgemeine Deutsche Biographie* 4 (Leipzig, 1876): 655-662; F.X. (von) Funk, "Nicolaus von Cusa," *Wetzer und Welte's Kirchenlexikon,* 2nd ed., 9 (1895): 306-315; R. Schmid, "Cusanus," *Realenzyklopädie für protestantische Theologie und Kirche* 4 (Leipzig, 1898): 360-364.

which had published many important German texts of prominent philosophers. The publishers of the *Philosophische Bibliothek* had changed hands many times, but the *Philosophische Bibliothek* was by 1911 a well-established library known to generations of German scholars and students.[33]

A list of forthcoming books, which Dr. Meiner received as he took over the *Philosophische Bibliothek* from the Dürrsche Verlag, contained two volumes of Cusanus' works to be edited by Hermann Cohen, the leader of the Marburg School of Neo-Kantianism.[34] Together with Paul Natorp (1854-1924), Hermann Cohen had made Marburg a great center of Neo-Kantian studies.[35] In addition to the Marburg School of Neo-Kantianism under Hermann Cohen and Paul Natorp, there was the South-West German School of Neo-Kantianism in Heidelberg which had been led by Wilhelm Windelband (1848-1915) and then by Heinrich Rickert.[36] Starting with Kant's premise that an unbridgeable gulf separated thought from existence, the Neo-Kantians of both schools rejuvenated the study of philosophy in the

[33] See Richard Richter, *Hundert Jahre Philosophische Bibliothek 1868-1968: Zeittafel und Gesamt-Verlagsverzeichnis* 1968 (Hamburg, 1968); *Hundert Jahre--Philosophische Bibliothek* 1868-1968 (Hamburg, 1968).

[34] Type-written notes entitled "Die Cusanus-Ausgabe" kept by Dr. Felix Meiner which are dated 19 May 1945 [=*Notes*], p. 1. The author wishes to thank Mr. Richard Meiner of the Felix Meiner Verlag, Hamburg, for permission not only to use the *Notes* but also to cite passages from them in this article.

[35] There are numerous books and articles on Hermann Cohen. Interest in him seems to be growing in recent years. See, for example, Walter Kinkel, *Hermann Cohen: Eine Einführung in sein Werk* (Stuttgart, 1924); J. Ebbinghaus, "Hermann Cohen als Philosoph und Publizist," *Archiv für Philosophie* 6 (1956): 109-122; Joseph Klein, *Die Grundlegung der Ethik in der Philosophie Hermann Cohens und Paul Natorps: Eine Kritik des Marburger Neukantianismus* (Göttingen, 1976); Helmut Holzhey, *Cohen und Natorp*, 2 vols. (Basel, 1986); William Kluback, *Hermann Cohen: The Challenge of a Religion of Reason* (Chicago, 1984); idem, *The Idea of Humanity: Hermann Cohen's Legacy to Philosophy and Theology* (Lanham, Maryland, 1987). About the Marburg School, see Henri Dussort, *L'École de Marbourg* (Paris, 1963); Bernard Tucker, *Ereignis: Wege durch die politische Philosophie des Marburger Neukantianismus* (Frankfurt a.M., 1984).

[36] See Heinrich Rickert, *Die Heidelberger Tradition und Kants Kritizismus* (Berlin, 1934); Franz Josef Brecht, "Die Philosophie an der Universität Heidelberg seit 1803," *Ruperto Carola* 5. Jhrg. Nr. 9/10 (June 1953): 55-67; H. Rickert, *Science and History: A Critique of Positivist Epistemology* (Princeton, 1962); Guy Oakes, *Weber and Rickert: Concept Formation in the Cultural Sciences*. Studies in Contemporary German Social Thought, ed. Thomas McCarthy (Cambridge, Massachusetts, 1988).

1860's by critically re-examining Kant's works.[37]

Cohen, who had become the leader of the Marburg School of Neo-Kantianism by 1876, developed the position which became known as the logistic *a priori* school "because it attempted to derive its ideas of truth and of philosophical science from mathematics and logic."[38] He defended this mathematical perception of reality because he felt it was rooted in the nature of reason itself. In mathematics, he believed, the work of our intellect could be observed and studied in an unadulterated form. In many of his writings, Cohen tried to make the infinitesimal and ordinal numbers the intellectual basis of any comprehension of reality.[39] As Dr. Meiner himself wrote in his *Notes* of May 18, 1945, the prominent leader of the Marburg School was not himself directly engaged in the editorial work for the projected two volumes on Cusanus. Following the prevailing German academic practice, one of his students had assumed the task of preparing the edition.[40] But the inclusion of the two volumes under the editorship of the noted Marburg philosopher undoubtedly reflected a deep interest which the followers of the school had taken in the thought of Cusanus.

Already in 1883, Hermann Cohen referred to Nicholas of Cusa and Giordano Bruno in his *Das Prinzip der Infinitesimal-Methode und seine Geschichte* (Berlin, 1883).[41] He tried to prove that the concept of the "infinitely small" is an indispensable and basic intellectual means for any scientific cognition of reality. In his famous book, *Logik der reinen Erkenntnis,* which was published by Bruno Cassirer in Berlin in 1902, Cohen also spoke of Cusanus' great interest in systematic philosophy, as well as in religion and ethics.[42] Since, as we saw before, there were many studies of Cusanus that had been published in the second half of the

[37] On Neo-Kantianism in general, see Thomas E. Willey, *Back to Kant: The Revival of Kantianism in German Social and Historical Thought, 1860-1914* (Detroit, 1977).

[38] David R. Lipton, *Ernst Cassirer* (Toronto, 1978), p. 21.

[39] See especially his *Das Prinzip der Infinitesimal-Methode und seine Geschichte: Eine Kapitel zur Grundlegung der Erkenntnis Kritik* (Berlin, 1883).

[40] Meiner, *Notes,* p. 1: "Cohen hatte die textliche Arbeit einem Schüler übertragen."

[41] *Das Prinzip,* p. 76, n. 8: "Es wäre der Vorwurf einer wichtigen und anziehenden Untersuchung, nachzuweisen, wie das theologische Interesse am Unendlichen mit diesem Grundbegriff der wissenschaftlichen Renaissance sich verbündet, um wie bei Nicolaus von Cues und Giordano Bruno die Diskussion des Infinitesimal zu fördern."

[42] Cohen, *Logik,* p. 29: "Nicolaus von Kues umfasst in seinem modernen Geiste alle Interessen der systematischen Philosophie, nicht zum mindesten auch die der Religion und der Ethik. . . ."

nineteenth century, it is easy to assume that Cohen was familiar with the growing literature on Cusanus. After all, one did not have to be a Neo-Kantian to take interest in Cusanus. But what is important for us to note here is that the Marburg School of Neo-Kantianism, as represented by Hermann Cohen, seems to have taken special interest in the mathematical and scientific ideas of Cusanus because of its penchant for studying philosophy in mathematical terms.

When we turn from Hermann Cohen to Ernst Cassirer, Cohen's most renowned student, it becomes clear that he also shared this preoccupation with Cusanus' mathematical and scientific ideas.[43] Born in Breslau in 1874 as the fourth child of a well-to-do merchant, Eduard Cassirer, Ernst Cassirer was studying at the University of Berlin in 1895 when in a lecture given by Georg Simmel (1858-1918) he heard the professor announce: "Undoubtedly the best books on Kant are written by Hermann Cohen, but I must confess that I do not understand them."[44] On hearing these words Cassirer made up his mind to go to Marburg and to study philosophy under Cohen's guidance. Immediately after the lecture, Cassirer went to his bookstore to purchase Cohen's books. He studied Kant's and Cohen's works thoroughly, as well as those of other philosophers essential for the understanding of Kant, such as Plato, Descartes, and Leibniz. Moreover, he devoted a considerable amount of time to the study of mathematics, mechanics, and biology which were indispensable for a clear understanding of Cohen's interpretation of Kant. Thus equipped, he arrived in Marburg in the spring of 1896 to hear Cohen's lectures.[45]

Known for his phenomenal memory and his vast knowledge on philosophical matters and admired for his kindly but somewhat aloof and unsociable attitudes because of his intensive study, Cassirer demonstrated in the first seminar under Cohen that he towered above all other Cohen's students because of his clear understanding of the most intricate problems of

---

[43] Of numerous recent studies of Cassirer, the following few may be mentioned in addition to Lipton's work cited in note 37 above. Carl H. Hamburg, *Symbol and Reality: Studies in the Philosophy of Ernst Cassirer* (The Hague, 1956); Seymour W. Itzkoff, *Ernst Cassirer: Philosopher of Culture* (Boston, 1977); John M. Krois, *Cassirer: Symbolic Forms and History* (New Haven, 1987); Massimo Ferrari, *Il giovane Cassirer e la scuola di Marburgo* (Milan, 1988). Paul A. Schlipp, ed., *The Philosophy of Ernst Cassirer* (Evanston, 1949), which is a collection of essays on Cassirer's life and ideas, as well as Cassirer's response, is a particularly useful publication.

[44] Schlipp, *The Philosophy,* p. 6.

[45] Schlipp, *The Philosophy,* p. 6.

Kantian and Cohenian philosophy.[46] His doctoral dissertation, completed in 1899 under Cohen, was entitled *Descartes' Kritik der mathematischen und naturwissenschaftlichen Erkenntnis* and received the highest possible mark from the Philosophical Faculty of the University of Marburg.[47] In the dissertation, which was published in 1899, Cassirer spoke of Cusanus' deep understanding of the idea of the common measure of straight and curved lines.[48] The dissertation was again published in 1902 as an "Einleitung" to a larger book, *Leibniz' System in seiner wissenschaftlichen Grundlagen.*[49]

Cassirer's keen interest in Cusanus was clearly manifested in his widely acclaimed book, *Das Erkenntnisproblem in der Philosophie und Wissenschaft der neueren Zeit,* Vol. 1, which was published by his cousin Bruno Cassirer of Berlin in 1906.[50] He wrote: ". . . only in exact science-- in its progress which, despite all vacillation, is continuous--does the harmonious concept of knowledge obtain its true accomplishment and verification; everywhere else this concept still remains a demand."[51] As one commentator put it, "[N]atural science Cassirer always looked upon as the highest and most characteristic expression of the power of the human mind."[52] In Chap. 1 of *Das Erkenntnisproblem,* which is entitled "Nikolaus Cusanus," Cassirer discusses Cusanus' concepts of God, the world, understanding, and sensitive faculty *(Sinnlichkeit),* his symbolic use of mathematics, objects, and natural philosophy, and other topics.[53] Already in this book, mostly in Chap. 2, Cassirer dealt with other notable thinkers of the fifteenth and sixteenth centuries, such as Georgius Gemistos Plethon, Pietro Pomponazzi, Lorenzo Valla, Giacomo Zabarella, Giovanni Pico della Mirandola, and Marius Nizolius.

In 1919, Cassirer accepted a call to become Professor of Philosophy at the University of Hamburg, which had been established as a result of the

[46] Schlipp, *The Philosophy,* p. 7: "'I felt at once,' said Cohen, 'that this man [Cassirer] had nothing to learn from me'."

[47] Schlipp, *The Philosophy,* p. 12. Ernst Cassirer, *Descartes' Kritik der mathematischen und naturwissenschaftlichen Erkenntnis* (Marburg, 1899).

[48] Cassirer, *Descartes' Kritik,* p. 97: "Der Gedanke des 'gemeisamen Masses' von Gerade und Krumm, den Nicolaus Cusanus bereits so tief erfasst hatte, ist hier bei Descartes also wiederum zurückgedrängt."

[49] Ernst Cassirer, *Leibniz' System in seinen wissenschaftlichen Grundlagen* (Marburg, 1902; reprint, Hildesheim, 1962).

[50] Ernst Cassirer, *Das Erkenntnisproblem in der Philosophie und Wissenschaft der neueren Zeit,* Vol. I (Berlin, 1906).

[51] Schlipp, *The Philosophy,* p. 218.

[52] Schlipp, *The Philosophy,* p. 693.

[53] Cassirer, *Das Erkenntnisproblem,* 2nd. ed. (Berlin, 1911), pp. 21-72.

birth of the Weimar Republic in Germany after the end of World War I. In a book published in 1921, which dealt with Einstein's theory of relativity, Cassirer described Cusanus' contribution as follows:

> It was one of the founders of modern philosophy, Nicolas Cusanus, who, with true speculative profundity, anticipated and announced "a relative minimum of measure" as the function of the concept of the atom, which was to be actually realized only in the history of natural science. Cusanus' fundamental doctrine of the infinite and of the unity of opposites in the infinite rested entirely on this insight into the relativity in principle of all determinations of magnitude, on the coincidence of the "greatest" and the "smallest".[54]

Then, in 1927, one of Cassirer's most famous books, *Individuum und Kosmos in der Philosophie der Renaissance* (Leipzig: B.G. Teubner, 1927), was published.[55] Chap. 1, entitled "Nikolaus Cusanus," was devoted to a discussion of Cusanus' ideas, and in Chap. 2, called "Cusanus und Italien," he discussed Cusanus' influence in Italy.

It is worth noting here that the book was published as No. 10 in a series called the *Studien der Bibliothek Warburg* (Warburg Library) and was dedicated to Aby Warburg (1866-1929) on his 60th birthday, June 13, 1926. Aby Warburg was the scion of a prominent banking family in Hamburg. Independently wealthy and devoted to scholarly research, he spent most of his time traveling, writing essays on the Renaissance and Reformation, and amassing an enormous collection of books on a wide range of subjects. After his physical and mental health declined from 1918 to 1920, his collection of books, known as the Warburg Library, was entrusted to Fritz Saxl.[56] The Library had become a place where Cassirer often did his research

[54] Ernst Cassirer, *Zur Einstein'schen Relativitätstheorie: Erkenntnistheoretische Betrachtungen* (Berlin, 1921). An English translation was published as *Substance and Function, and Einstein's Theory of Relativity*, trans. William C. Swabey and Marie C. Swabey (Chicago, 1923; reprint, New York, 1953).

[55] An English translation was published as *The Individual and the Cosmos in Renaissance Philosophy*, trans. Mario Domandi (New York, 1963).

[56] On Prof. Aby Warburg and his Warburg Library, see E.H. Gombrich, *Aby Warburg: An Intellectual Biography* (London, 1970); David Farrer, *The Warburgs: The Story of a Family* (New York, 1975); Aby Warburg, *Ausgewählte Schriften und Würdigungen,* ed. Dieter Wuttke and C.G. Heil, 2nd ed. (Baden-Baden, 1980); Ulrich Raulff, "Aby M. Warburg, un inconnu," *Préfaces* 11 (Janvier-fevrier, 1989): 105-106; Salvatore Settis, "Warburg *continuatus.* Description d'une bibliothèque," *Préfaces* 11 (Janvier-fevrier, 1989): 107-122 (bibliography, 122).

for his books on symbolic forms.[57] *Individuum und Kosmos* was published by B.G. Teubner, the publisher in Leipzig which had published many studies sponsored by the Warburg Library.

Examining Cassirer's books, mentioned above, it is not easy to determine which printed edition or editions of Cusanus' works he used in his study of Cusanus. Judging by the quotes in the books, he seems to have used the Basel edition. We must also note that in discussing Cusanus' ideas, Cassirer cited not only Vansteenberghe, but also some German authorities, such as Uebinger and Falckenberg. The results of the studies promoted by the Catholic School of Tübingen were absorbed into his research. His reliance, however, is mostly on primary sources and not much on secondary materials.

When we turn our attention from Cusanus research done by Cohen, Cassirer, and others in the Marburg School to the project of publishing Cusanus' works under the auspices of the Heidelberg Academy, we learn that after the death of Hermann Cohen in 1918, Dr. Felix Meiner sought a successor to Cohen as editor of Cusanus' works in the *Philosophische Bibliothek*.[58] The scholar whom Meiner approached was the noted historian of medieval philosophy at the University of Munich since 1912, Clemens Baeumker (1853-1924).[59] Baeumker was very much interested in the project and emphasized the importance of studying original manuscript sources if the planned edition was to be reliable and accurate.[60] He was anxious to undertake the task himself, but unfortunately was not able to gain access to Cusanus' library in St. Nicholas Hospital at Kues because the Hospital was at that time being used as an officers' club. The serious editorial work for the edition based on manuscripts could not be initiated until 1919 after the end of World War I.[61]

When favorable social and economic conditions returned after World War I, B.G. Teubner, the publisher of Cassirer's *Individuum und Kosmos*,

[57] Schlipp, *The Philosophy*, p. 26.

[58] Meiner, *Notes*, p. 1.

[59] Baeumker's writings included the following: *Abhandlungen zur Geschichte der Philosophie des Mittelalters* (Münster, 1923); *Studien und Charakteristiken zur Geschichte der Philosophie, insbesondere des Mittelalters* (Münster, 1928). See also "Clemens Baeumker" in Raymund Schmidt, ed., *Die deutsche Philosophie der Gegenwart in Selbstdarstellungen* 2 (Leipzig, 1927): 31-60.

[60] Meiner, *Notes*, p. 1: "Jedoch könne eine deutsche Ausgabe in wissenschaftlich befriedigender Form erst veranstaltet werden, wenn ein zuverlässiger lateinischer Text vorläge. Die bisherigen Drucke müsstenanhand [sic] der Handschriften revidiert werden."

[61] Meiner, *Notes*, p. 1.

approached Dr. Meiner with a proposal to publish a new edition of Cusanus'
Opera omnia. When informed by Prof. Eugen Kühnemann (1868-1946) of
the University of Breslau that Meiner had been making preparations for the
edition for some time, Teubner abandoned his plan and gave free rein to Dr.
Meiner.[62] Although Meiner told Kühnemann during his visit to Breslau on
July 2, 1926, about the preparations he had made for the edition, he heard
nothing from Kühnemann thereafter. The initiative for the edition had to be
taken by others.[63]

Besides Cassirer, the two scholars who were most directly responsible
for the initiation of a modern critical edition of Cusanus' works were Ernst
Hoffmann (1880-1952) and Raymond Klibansky (1905-) of the University
of Heidelberg. Born in Berlin in 1880, Ernst Hoffmann taught at the
Mommsen-Gymnasium in Berlin after graduating from the University of
Berlin. His field of interest was the classics. While teaching at the Gymnasium, the diligent scholar published two books on Aristotle's physics, a
third one on Plato, and other studies related to classical times.[64] It was
probably in 1919 or 1920 that Hoffmann, who regarded himself as Cassirer's
student, heard Cassirer's lecture in Berlin and learned of Cusanus.[65]

After moving to Heidelberg in 1922 as *Privatdozent,* Hoffmann pursued
his study of Platonism in the Middle Ages and began to do research on
Cusanus.[66] The Department of Philosophy at the University of Heidelberg

[62] Meiner, *Notes,* p. 1: "Sie (Teubner) verzichteten und träten [*sic*] zu
meinen Gunsten zurück." Dr. Meiner speaks then of receiving a letter from Prof.
Ludwig Baur (1871-1943), which prompted him to apply to the *Deutsche
Akademie* in Munich for support, but the contents of the letter are not clearly
indicated. See n. 93 below.

[63] Meiner, *Notes,* p. 2. Kühnemann had published *Grundlehren der
Philosophie: Studien über Vorsokratiker, Sokrates und Platon* (Berlin, 1899). He
was to visit the United States six times to teach at Harvard, the University of
Wisconsin, and others. See *Festschrift für Eugen Kühnemann.* Blätter der
Volkshochschule Breslau 7 (1928-1929); E. Kühnemann, *Mit unbefangener
Stirn: Mein Lebensbuch* (Heilbronn, 1937).

[64] *De Aristotelis Physicorum libri septimi origine et auctoritate* (Berlin,
1905); *De Aristotelis Physicorum libri septimi duplici forma* I-II (Friedenau,
1908-1909); *Methexis und Metaxy bei Platon* (1919); *Die Sprache und die
archaische Logik* (Tübingen, 1925). One of his pupils at the Gymnasium was
Paul Oskar Kristeller. See *Philosophy and Humanism: Renaissance Essays in
Honor of Paul Oskar Kristeller,* ed. Edward P. Mahoney (Leiden, 1976), p. 1.

[65] Thea Hoffmann, "Wie die Cusanus-Ausgabe begann," MFCG 5   (1965):
164.

[66] Hoffmann, "Wie," 164: "Als er nun 1922 als Dozent für Philosophie nach
Heidelberg berufen wurde, beschloss er, diesen unbekannten Philosophen näher
zu lernen."

was, since 1916, under the chairmanship of Heinrich Rickert, who as successor to Wilhelm Windelband had made Heidelberg ever more famous as the center of the South-West German School of Neo-Kantianism. Hoffmann's lectures at the Warburg Library on *Platonismus und Mittelalter,* which were published in 1926 as Vol. 3 of the Warburg Library series, shows how intensely he was engaged in research on medieval Platonism.[67] It was perhaps in 1926 that Ernst Cassirer told Heinrich Rickert and Ernst Hoffmann about what Felix Meiner had been doing in preparation for the critical edition of Cusanus' works.[68]

The next year, in 1927, Hoffmann taught a seminar on Cusanus at the University of Heidelberg. One of the students taking the seminar, Raymond Klibansky, was given the assignment to present a report on the works of Cusanus.[69] Thus the preparatory stage for the initiation of the project was set in 1927. As we mentioned above, Cassirer's work, *Individuum und Kosmos,* was published in 1927. It provided another occasion for advancing the publication plans. In the book, Cassirer published a text of Cusanus' *Liber de mente (Idiota de mente)* which was edited by Dr. Joachim Ritter, his student at Hamburg, and translated by his son, Heinrich Cassirer, a doctoral candidate at Heidelberg. The text of *Idiota de mente* was based on Codex Cusanus 218 in St. Nicholas Hospital Library with a few orthographical changes.[70] Klibansky, who was also a doctoral candidate in philosophy at the University of Heidelberg, told Cassirer that the publication of the text of *Idiota de mente* without appropriate scholarly apparatus did not contribute to

[67] The lecture was published as *Platonismus und Mittelalter*. Vorträge der Bibliothek Warburg 3 (Leipzig, 1926).

[68] Meiner, *Notes,* p. 2: "Von Cassirer waren inzwischen Geheimrat Rickert und Professor Ernst Hoffmann in Heidelberg von der Entwicklung der Dinge verständigt worden."

[69] "Besprechung mit Herrn Prof. Klibansky in Bernkastel-Kues am 12. August 1964," one-page document type-written by Mr. Richard Meiner on August 18, 1964. The author wishes to thank Mr. Meiner for giving him permission to use the document in this article.

[70] R. Meiner, "Besprechung": "Einen neuen Anstoss, sich mit Cusanus innerhalb der Philosophie zu beschäftigen, gab Ernst Cassirer, als er in seinem 1927 erschienenen Buch *Individuum und Kosmos in der Philosophie der Renaissance* einen Abdruck von *Idiota de mente* nach der Pariser Ausgabe vornahm." The text of *Liber de mente (Idiota de mente)* is found in Cassirer, *Individuum,* pp. 204-297. Carolus Bovillus' *Liber de sapiente,* ed. R. Klibansky, follows on pp. 299-412. Hans Joachim Ritter published his dissertation at Hamburg later as *Docta ignorantia: Die Theorie des Nichtwissens bei Nicolaus Cusanus* (Leipzig, 1927). Heinrich Cassirer's dissertation was published as *Aristoteles' Schrift "Von der Seele" und ihre Stellung innerhalb der aristotelischen Philosophie* (Tübingen, 1932).

the advancement of Cusanus research and that what was needed was a
thorough study of Cusanus' texts based on extant manuscripts in and outside
the Library at St. Nicholas Hospital.[71]

   Critical of what he considered the non-historical approaches of two
dominant intellectual schools of thought in Heidelberg at that time, that
is, the South-West School of Neo-Kantianism and Karl Jaspers'
Lebensphilosophie, Klibansky, whose main quest in Heidelberg was to
answer the question *Qu'est-ce que l'homme?*,[72] had decided to study the
history of philosophy.[73] He believed that despite Michelet, Burckhardt, and
Huizinga, there was no "rupture" between the Middle Ages and the
Renaissance, that Nicholas of Cusa, who was no radical, demonstrated the
continuity of medieval ideas, and that certain Neo-Kantians who called
Cusanus "the first modern philosopher" were mistaken.[74]

   After investigating where important Cusanus manuscripts and their
copies were located, Klibansky then drew up an outline for a critical edition
of the works of Cusanus. Visiting Cassirer in Hamburg soon thereafter,
Klibansky presented the outline to Cassirer and discussed the publication of

   [71] R. Meiner, "Besprechung."

   [72] Michèle Le Doeuff, "Raymond Klibansky--Périple d'un philosophe
illustre," *Préfaces* 13 (Mai-juin, 1989): 128-129. The author is indebted to Prof.
Klibansky for reference to this issue of the French publication.

   [73] "Raymond Klibansky, philosophe et historien--entretien avec Yves
Hersant et Alain de Libera," *Préfaces* 13 (Mai-juin, 1989): 137: "R.K.-- Lorsque
j'étudiais la philosophie à Heidelberg, la scène était occupée par l'affrontement
d'une philosophie traditionnelle, celle de l'école kantienne du sud-ouest
(*südwestdeutsche Schule*) menée par Heinrich Rickert, avec, de l'autre côté du
Neckar, l'école de la Lebensphilosophie de Karl Jaspers. J'ai connu les deux
intimement. Malgré leurs dissensions ils approchaient les problèmes de la même
manière: ils négligeaient l'histoire. C'est cette méconnaissance qui m'a décidé à
étudier l'histoire de la philosophie."

   [74] "Raymond Klibansky, philosophe et historien," pp. 138-140. Perhaps
one of the most famous books which shows these ideas of Prof. Klibansky is
*The Continuity of the Platonic Tradition during the Middle Ages: Outlines of a
Corpus Platonicum medii aevi* (London, 1939; new, expanded ed., Millwood,
New York, 1982). Also worth mentioning here is his famous study, "Ein Proklos-
Fund und seine Bedeutung," *Sitzungsberichte der Heidelberger Akademie der
Wissenschaften, Philosophisch-historische Klasse* [=HSB], Jhrg. 1928/29, 5.
Abh. (Heidelberg, 1929), which showed clearly that Cusanus was very much
influenced by Proclus. Klibansky's edition of Meister Eckhart's works appeared
as *Magistri Eckardi Opera Latina* (Leipzig, 1934-1935). The first volume edited
by Klibansky was *Super oratione dominica* which was published in Leipzig in
1934. It carried a list of fifteen planned volumes. But the second volume
published in 1935, which contained *Opus tripartitum*, seems to be the only
additional one edited and published by him.

a modern, critical edition with him.[75]   The outline was then submitted to Professor Hans von Schubert (1859-1931), the famous Protestant church historian at the University of Heidelberg and President of the Heidelberg Academy of Sciences. The prestigious Academy had been founded in 1909. Although independent of the University of Heidelberg administratively, many of its members were professors at the University. Schubert found the project important and strongly supported all attempts to initiate the publication of the critical edition under the auspices of the Heidelberg Academy.[76] Meanwhile, in September, 1927, Dr. Meiner visited Professors Heinrich Rickert and Ernst Hoffmann and discussed with them how the project for publishing the edition, if accepted by the Academy, could be entrusted with them.[77]   As a result of this conversation, it was decided to ask Professor Gerhard Kallen (1884-1973) of the University of Cologne to become another co-worker for the edition.[78]   Kallen had already signed a contract with the Verlag Ludwig Röhrscheid in Bonn to publish a facsimile edition of Cusanus' *De concordantia catholica,* using the Paris edition of 1514 as its text.[79]

In December, 1927, the Heidelberg Academy gave its final approval to the whole project. As a result, a Cusanus Commission was organized within the Academy. The Commission members included not only those scholars already familiar to us, Ernst Hoffmann, Raymond Klibansky, Heinrich Rickert, and Hans von Schubert, but also Heinrich Liebmann (1874-1939), who was famous for his mathematical and geometrical studies, and Friedrich Wilhelm Panzer (1870-1956), who was a noted philologist at the University

[75] R. Meiner, "Besprechung."

[76] In his letter of June 29, 1989, to the author, Prof. Klibansky wrote: "I first presented the plan of a critical edition of the *Opera omnia* to Ernst Hoffmann and Hans von Schubert; it was this plan which was submitted to the Heidelberg Academy and accepted by it. I insisted that there should be an 'Apparatus fontium' (for which, as is indicated in the Praefatio to vol. I) I alone was responsible and in which I proved (against E. Hoffmann's thesis of the rupture between Cusanus and mediaeval Platonism) the strong links between Nicolaus and the Platonists of Chartres, as well as his indebtedness to Proclus." Thea Hoffmann reports, p. 164, that Hans von Schubert and Karl Hampe, the medievalist, were interested in the study of Cusanus.

[77] Meiner, *Notes,* p. 2.

[78] Meiner, *Notes,* p. 2.

[79] *Nicolai de Cusa De concordantia catholica libri tres.* (Paris: Jodocus Badius Ascensius, 1514; reprint, Bonn, 1928).

of Heidelberg.[80]   Klibansky was made an assistant of the Heidelberg
Academy in charge of carrying out basic research for the edition.[81]

Thus began the serious preparatory work for an ambitious enterprise to
publish a modern critical edition of Cusanus' works under the aegis of the
Heidelberg Academy of Sciences. It was intended to supersede the defective,
often distorted, Strassbourg, Milan, Paris, and Basel editions. Judging by
the testimony of those familiar with the beginning phase of the project, the
Commission was indeed fortunate to have as its assistant the young, bright
scholar Klibansky who was sent to numerous libraries and archives to
examine and copy many extant manuscripts for the edition.[82]

Completing his doctoral work in 1928 under Hoffmann, Klibansky,
together with Hoffmann, published in 1929 the first study of Cusanus in the
Sitzungsberichte der Heidelberger Akademie. It was entitled *Cusanus-Texte,
I: Predigten 1: Dies Sanctificatus vom Jahre 1439* (with the text in Latin
and German with commentary).[83]   This was an important study which attempted to clarify the relationship between Cusanus' sermon of 1439 and his
major philosophical work, *De docta ignorantia*, which was completed in

[80] Liebmann later published "Über drei neugefundene mathematische
Schriften des Nikolaus von Cues und dessen Bedeutung," *Forschungen und
Forschritte* 5, 22 (1929): 261.

[81] Prof. Klibansky has often emphasized that contrary to the widely held
view that he became Hoffmann's assistant, he was made assistant at the
Heidelberg Academy. See R. Meiner, "Besprechung."

[82] Meiner, *Notes*, p. 2: "Für die ganze Ausgabe war Klibansky ein
unschätzbarer Mitarbeiter"; Hoffmann, *Wie*, 163: ". . . ein junger, hochbegabter
Student, Raimund Klibansky . . . der schon nach wenigen Jahren das Amt eines
Assistenten an der Cusanus-Ausgabe ausüben konnte."

[83] *Cusanus-Texte, I: Predigten 1, Dies Sanctificatus vom Jahre 1439* (HSB,
Jhrg. 1928/29, 3. Abh.; Heidelberg, 1929). Another student who completed his
doctoral work on Plotinus in 1928 under Hoffmann's guidance was Paul Oskar
Kristeller who had followed Hoffmann from Berlin to Heidelberg in 1923. Prof.
Kristeller's dissertation was published as *Der Begriff der Seele in der Ethik der
Plotin* (Tübingen, 1929). See Mahoney, ed., *Philosophy and Humanism*, p. 2.

1440.[84]   Another study, published by Hoffmann in 1930, dealt with Cusanus' concept of the universe and was accompanied by a Latin text by Cusanus on his cosmological ideas. The Latin text was edited by Klibansky.[85] This study shows that Hoffmann and Klibansky took special interest in Cusanus' cosmological thought which had found expression especially in Bk. II, Chaps. 1 and 2 of *De docta ignorantia.* On March 16, 1932, the *Apologia doctae ignorantiae,* which had been edited by Klibansky as Vol. II of the Heidelberg edition, was published.[86] On December 24 of the same year the *De docta ignorantia,* which Hoffmann and Klibansky worked on together, followed as Vol. I in the edition.[87]

In announcing the publication of these two important works of Cusanus and appealing to prospective subscribers, a 1932 prospectus stated that the unfavorable condition of the time made it necessary, at least for the time being, to limit the scope of publication to Cusanus' philosophical and political writings. They were scheduled to appear in fourteen volumes. The prospectus went on to say, almost innocently, that these volumes would be available by 1939, the year which would mark the 500th anniversary of the completion of *De docta ignorantia.*[88] Even the editors familiar with the complexity of the task which they had assumed could not fully appreciate the enormity of their undertaking and clearly forsee what the future held for them. The task of determining the authentic, reliable, and accurate texts for the edition turned out to be much more difficult and complex than originally

[84] Prof. Kugai Yamamoto (1903-   ) of Hiroshima University of Arts and Sciences in Japan, who studied in Heidelberg in 1929 and visited Hoffmann's home frequently to read books and articles together, including *Dies Sanctificatus,* stated in his special lecture delivered at the 6th Annual Meeting of the Japanese Cusanus Society on November 23, 1987, that Hoffmann was in the habit of saying "Wer hat Cusanus gelesen?", expressing his scepticism and wonder about other writers who could discuss and write about Cusanus without having read his works in their reliable, original sources. See *The Report of the Japanese Cusanus Society* 10 (1988): 35-49; "First Cusanus Scholar in Japan?," *American Cusanus Society Newsletter* V, 2 (September 1988): 15-16.

[85] Ernst Hoffmann, *Das Universum des Nikolaus von Kues* (HSB, Jhrg. 1929/30, 3. Abh.; Heidelberg, 1939), with Textbeilage, pp. 41-45, by Raymond Klibansky.

[86] Meiner, *Notes,* p. 2.

[87] Meiner, *Notes,* p. 2.

[88] The prospectus was entitled *Einladung zur Subskription: Nicolai de Cusa Opera omnia iussu et auctoritate academiae litterarum Heidelbergensis ad codicum fidem edita. Lipsiae: In aedibus Felicis Meiner 1932.* It has no page numbers. "Bis zum Jahre 1939, in welchem 500 Jahre seit der Erstveröffentlichung der *Docta ignorantia* verflossen sein werden, sollen diese Bände, auf die diese Subskription begrenzt ist, vorliegen" [(p. 7)].

anticipated.

A detailed, very favorable review of the first two published volumes in the edition, written by a leading medievalist, Martin Grabmann, and published in the *Deutsche Literaturzeitung,* greatly encouraged both the editors and the publisher.[89] Grabmann welcomed the initiation of a monumental editorial enterprise and praised in glowing terms Klibansky's thorough, competent work and superb scholarly accomplishments. He especially emphasized the importance of the scholarly apparatus in the edition, which not only contained comparisons of manuscript variants, but also gave sources *(fontes)* used by Cusanus and information about later writers who quoted Cusanus in their writings *(testimonia).*[90]

The publisher, the Felix Meiner Verlag, considered it a great honor to publish the edition under the auspices of the Heidelberg Academy of Sciences and made every effort to produce handsome volumes with accurate texts which were worthy of an academic edition and which could be regarded as a model for modern critical editions.[91] The use of high-quality paper certainly made the volumes attractive, but the task of establishing accurate texts and the printing of three kinds of scholarly apparatus in the footnotes proved to be not only expensive but difficult and time-consuming. As a result of anti-Semitic measures adopted and various threats made on his person, Klibansky had to depart from Heidelberg in early April, 1933, to seek, as he himself put it, a *"festen Boden"* for the continuation and promotion of

[89] Review of *Nicolai de Cusa Opera omnia . . . I, De docta ignorantia,* ed. Ernst Hoffmann and Raymond Klibansky (Leipzig, 1932) and II, *Apologia doctae ignorantiae,* ed. Raymond Klibansky (Leipzig, 1932) in *Deutsche Literaturzeitung,* Heft 15 (April 9, 1933), cols. 685-692 by Martin Grabmann. See also Meiner, *Notes,* p. 4: "Für den wissenschaftlichen Erfolg der Ausgabe war entscheidend eine Besprechung durch Grabmann in der Deutschen Literatur-Zeitung."

[90] Grabmann, cols. 688-689.

[91] Meiner, *Notes,* p. 3: "Die Druckausführung wurde nach Vorschlägen von Jakob Hegner festgelegt, wobei der Verlag seinen Ehrgeitz darein setzte, ebenso Vorbildliches auf diesem Gebiete zu leisten, wie die Herausgeber im Hinblick auf die Gestaltung einer Akademie-Ausgabe."

threatened humanistic studies in Germany.[92] It meant that the Cusanus Commission lost an indispensable worker. The pace of later publications became necessarily slow. In fact, it was not until September 27, 1937, that the Felix Meiner Verlag was able to publish a third volume (Vol. V of the *Opera), Idiota* (three books), which was edited by Ludwig Baur (1871-1943). Professor at the University of Tübingen since 1913, Baur became a connecting link between the initial period of modern Cusanus research in Germany as represented by the Catholic School of Tübingen and the second period of modern Cusanus scholarship which was based on the Heidelberg edition.[93]

The great care with which the publisher produced the edition was bound to attract the attention of other publishers. Dr. Meiner recalled in 1945 with pride and satisfaction that the famous Catholic publisher in Münster, the Aschendorff Verlag, approached him with the request that they be permitted to use the format of the Heidelberg edition in producing their own forthcoming edition of the works of Albertus Magnus, edited by Bernhard Geyer.[94] Father Ludger Meier, OFM, of the Duns Scotus Commission in Rome, Meiner also reported, sought advice from him about technical points in preparation for the Commission edition of the works of Duns Scotus.[95] It was clear that the Heidelberg *Opera* had established itself as a reliable,

[92] For a careful study of the exiled *Dozenten* and professors from the University of Heidelberg after 1933, see Dorothee Mussgnug, *Die vertriebenen Heidelberger Dozenten: Zur Geschichte der Ruprecht-Karls-Universität nach 1933* (Heidelberg, 1988). The author is grateful to Prof. Klibansky for reference to this book and to Mr. Richard Meiner for having a copy quickly sent to him. Mussgnug discusses Klibansky and his case on pp. 40-43, 67-68, 148, 175, 182-184, 271-280. She states on p. 184: "Klibansky empfand sich als 'Bewahrer des anderen Deutschland'." The book also discusses the fate of other members of the Cusanus Commission after 1933: E. Hoffmann, pp. 60-70, 115-117, 129-130, 206-207, 278; F. Panzer, pp. 67-68, 116, 278; H. Liebmann, pp. 70, 90, 115. About the role which Prof. Klibansky played in the removal of the Warburg Library from Hamburg to London, see Le Doeuff, "Raymond Klibansky," 125-126.

[93] Baur had published the following: "Die Lehre vom Naturrecht bei Bonaventura" in: *Festgabe zum 60. Geburtstag Clemens Baeumker* I (Münster, 1913): 217-239; "Der Einfluss des Robert Grosseteste auf die wissenschaftliche Richtung des Roger Bacon" in: A.G. Little, ed., *Roger Bacon Essays* (Oxford, 1914), pp. 35-54; *Die Philosophie des Robert Grosseteste, Bischof von Lincoln (†1253)* (Münster, 1917).

[94] Meiner, *Notes*, p. 4.

[95] Meiner, *Notes*, p. 4. See also Hans-Georg Gadamer, "Das Cusanus-Unternehmen der Heidelberger Akademie der Wissenschaften," *Ruperto Carola* 6, 15/16 (December, 1954): 78-79.

handsome edition of a medieval philosopher's works.

What happened after World War II can briefly be stated here. Of the fourteen announced volumes, only four had been published by the outbreak of World War II *(De docta ignorantia,* 1932; *Apologia doctae ignorantiae,* 1932; *Idiota,* 1937; and *De concordantia catholica,* Pt. 1, 1939). Since many subscribers to the edition were outside Germany, the war placed a heavy burden on the publisher. It also made it difficult for editors to travel to libraries and archives in and outside Germany where manuscripts were kept. Besides, in an air-raid of December 3/4, 1944, the entire establishment of the Felix Meiner Verlag in Leipzig, including the plates of the Heidelberg edition, was completely destroyed. It was a great setback for the project. Many difficulties had to be overcome to resume the work of publication. For example, Gerhard Kallen's edition of *De concordantia catholica,* which had been published before the air-raid as Vol. XIV, Pts. 1 and 2, in 1939 and 1941, had to be started all over again. Kallen was first able to bring out Pt. 3 in 1959. A new, revised edition of Pt. 1 was published in 1964. Pt. 2 appeared in its revised form in 1965 and was followed in 1968 by a register for the three parts. In the meantime, the Felix Meiner Verlag moved from Leipzig to Hamburg in 1951 for financial and political reasons, and in 1964 merged with the Richard Meiner Verlag, which had existed in Hamburg since 1948 under the leadership of Richard Meiner, Dr. Felix Meiner's son and present head of the Felix Meiner Verlag in Hamburg.[96]

Of the original fourteen volumes in the edition announced in 1932, all have thus far been published with the exception of *De visione dei* (original Vol. VI) and *De ludo globi* (original Vol. IX). A new, ambitious phase of the edition began in 1970, when *Sermones* 1, Fasc. 1, edited by Rudolf Haubst and his associates, was added as Vol. XVI, Pt. 1 of the series. Thus far Vol. XVI, Pts. 1-4 and Vol. XVII, Pt. 1 have been published in the *Sermones* series.[97] Entirely independent of the critical edition of the works of Cusanus, but in parallel with it, a new series called *Acta Cusana: Quellen zur Lebensgeschichte der Nikolaus von Kues* was launched in 1976

---

[96] The role played by Mr. Richard Meiner in the development of the publishing house is described by many scholars in: *Ceterum censeo . . . Bemerkungen zu Aufgabe und Tätigkeit eines philosophischen Verlegers: Richard Meiner zum 8. April 1983* (Hamburg, 1983).

[97] Vol. XVI, 1: *Sermones* I (1430-1441) Fasc. 1 (Sermones 1-4), ed. R. Haubst *et al.* (Hamburg, 1970); vol. XVI, 2: *Sermones* I (1430-1441) Fasc. 2 (Sermones 5-10), ed. R. Haubst *et al.* (Hamburg, 1973); vol. XVI, 3: *Sermones* I (1430-1441) Fasc. 3 (Sermones 11-21), ed. R. Haubst and M. Bodewig (Hamburg, 1977); vol. XVI, 4: *Sermones* I (1430-1441) Fasc. 4 (Sermones 22-26), ed. R. Haubst and M. Bodewig (Hamburg, 1984); vol. XVII, 1: *Sermones* II (1443-1452) Fasc. 1 (Sermones 27-39), ed. R. Haubst and H. Schnarr (Hamburg, 1983).

under the joint editorship of Erich Meuthen and Hermann Hallauer. It will include all extant deeds, documents, letters, and other materials in which Cusanus or his activities are mentioned. Two installments of Vol. 1, edited by Meuthen, have been published to date.[98] The Heidelberg edition of Cusanus' works, which began in 1932, is thus "in progress" in an expanded form.

In his critical study of Cusanus and his ideas, Karl Jaspers wrote:

> An attack on him by Wenck, a professor at Heidelberg, might have led to his condemnation. . . . However, the Church paid no attention to Cusanus' ideas. In the nineteenth century, a few Catholic theologians took up the old attack again and amplified it, but the Church remained silent. . . . After 1565 (date of the Basel edition of his works), neither the Church nor any monastery arranged for a new edition. The Heidelberg *Akademieausgabe* (begun in 1932) was initiated by non-Catholics.[99]

Our previous discussion shows clearly that Jaspers gives us only a half-truth.

Initiated and promoted by the Catholic School of Tübingen under the influence of religious Romanticism and under the guidance of the brilliant and controversial church historian Johann Adam Möhler, modern Cusanus research in Germany brought about what is sometimes called a "Cusanus Renaissance." It was the philosophers of the Neo-Kantian persuasion, especially Ernst Cassirer, who took special interest in Cusanus' mathematical and scientific ideas and labeled him as the "first modern philosopher."[100]

As the knowledge of Cusanus and his works became widespread and deepened, it was apparent to all serious students of Cusanus that the available editions of his works printed in the fifteenth and sixteenth

[98] *Acta Cusana: Quellen zur Lebensgeschichte des Nikolaus von Kues,* vol. 1, pt. 1: 1401-1437 Mai 17, ed. Erich Meuthen (Hamburg, 1976); vol. 1, pt. 2: 1437 Mai 17-1450 December 31, ed. E. Meuthen (Hamburg, 1983).

[99] Karl Jaspers, *Nikolaus Cusanus* (Munich, 1964), p. 74; Karl Jaspers, *Anselm and Nicholas of Cusa,* ed. Hannah Arendt and trans. Ralph Manheim (New York, 1974), pp. 64-65.

[100] Cassirer, *Individuum,* p. 10; Cassirer, *The Individual,* p. 10. It is interesting to note that Cassirer, a Neo-Kantian, did use the phrase "the first modern philosopher," of which, as we saw above, Klibansky is critical. Klibansky's closeness to Cassirer is shown especially by the fact that with H.J. Paton, he edited a collection of essays dedicated to Cassirer: Raymond Klibansky and H.J. Paton, eds., *Philosophy and History--Essays Presented to Ernst Cassirer* (Oxford, 1936; reprint, New York, 1963; Gloucester, Massachusetts, 1975).

centuries were often not only unreliable but also misleading. Ernst Hoffmann, a noted student of Plato and Platonism, and Raymond Klibansky, his bright and multi-lingual student, were instrumental in initiating the so-called Heidelberg edition in 1932 under the auspices of the Heidelberg Academy of Sciences and with the support of the publisher, the Felix Meiner Verlag. The edition has not been brought to an end and is likely to take some years to complete. It is perhaps significant to note that the project has been supported and carried on by scholars of various theological, philosophical, and religious backgrounds. Cusanus, who emphasized *pax* and *concordantia* so much in his writings, would probably give an approving nod to this joint enterprise for the promotion and propagation of his ideas.

PART ONE

SEEKING THE ROADS TO GOD

THE THEORY OF INTELLECT IN ALBERT THE GREAT
AND ITS INFLUENCE ON NICHOLAS OF CUSA

M.L. Führer

It is common knowledge among students of the writings of both Nicholas of Cusa and St. Albert the Great that a link exists between these two giants of German thought. Manuscripts of the works of St. Albert remain in the collection at Bernkastel with marginal notes in Nicholas of Cusa's own hand. The intellectual interests of the two men are remarkably similar. Cusanus studied at the University of Cologne, the very University that Albert helped to found out of the *studium generale* he developed for the Dominican house of studies in that city. Cusanus numbered several noted Albertists among his personal friends. It is also clear that he was deeply influenced by Albertist ideas that passed to him through students of the thought of St. Albert the Great, including Dietrich of Freiberg, Ulrich of Strasbourg, and Meister Eckhart.

In spite of this wealth of information about the connection of Albert the Great and Nicholas of Cusa, not much study has been devoted to the specific influences that the *Doctor universalis* had on Cusanus. The purpose of the present paper, therefore, is to provide a brief outline of the direction such a study should follow by focusing narrowly upon one specific influence.

When one compares both St. Albert and Cusanus with respect to their philosophical and theological interests, it becomes immediately apparent that striking similarities exist. Both men were deeply influenced by the writings of the Pseudo-Dionysius, both founded their respective theologies squarely upon the *triplex via*, i.e. purgation, illumination, and perfection, and similar Neoplatonic themes are interwoven throughout the entire fabric of their systems. However, a word of caution must be advanced. As every student of medieval thought knows, writers who share such common structures tend to look a great deal alike. Indeed, the differences that distinguish them are so subtle that the utmost care must be exercised in order to discern them at all.

It would appear then that this complex of ideas proves to be too common and consequently is a poor place to look in the attempt to study the influence of St. Albert upon Cusanus. This certainly would be true but for two points: first, that there is evidence to support the thesis that both writers did the bulk of their thinking within the framework of theological speculations that focused upon themes devoted to the threefold way, and second, that St. Albert grounded his speculations concerning the theology of contemplation upon a unique analysis of the role of the human intellect in knowing God. The rudiments of this theory can be discovered in the writings of Cusanus. Furthermore, they are used in almost the same manner in Cusanus as in St. Albert. To be sure, Cusanus develops several aspects of St. Albert's theory in his own fashion. Nonetheless, the theory is Albertist. Because of this uniqueness it seems profitable to begin the pursuit of the connection between Albert and Cusanus precisely in respect to their philosophical and theological speculations devoted to the topic of contemplation.

Since both writers ground their concept of the vision of God in the psychology of the intellect, it is best to begin the analysis with a comparison of their respective assumptions about the intellect and its general role in knowing God which they both equate with its perfection. It will then be possible to see how Cusanus follows St. Albert in the development of the *triplex via*.

Both Albert the Great and Cusanus hold a Neoplatonic view of the intellect. As the highest faculty in the hierarchy of the soul, it is marked by a spontaneity and a structural bias toward return to its source, God. Neoplatonist psychology speaks of a *reditus* tendency in spiritual or intellectual beings whereby they strive to return to their originating principle. Albert and Nicholas both agree that only when this tendency is put into act does the soul, and hence the whole man, begin to move toward his perfection--the vision of the divine exemplars in the divine mind. They further agree that the vision of the divine exemplars is as far as man can progress while in this life.

St. Albert, responding to the challenge of Latin Averroism's view of a pan-intellect, which is the theory that all men share a common but transcendental intellect, carefully distinguished the human intellect into two functions. The lower function, oriented toward the senses, tends toward the practical life of man. The higher function, which he identifies by several names including *intellectus adeptus, intellectus assimilativus,* and *intellectus agens,* is oriented towards man's metaphysical source, the divine mind. This dualism is thus useful in developing a functional psychology adapted to the vision of the divine exemplars. In addition, Albert colors his analysis with certain distinctive hues. The higher portion of the intellect "flows" into the lower, thus ensuring the continuity and integrity of man as intellect. At least this is what happens in "natural intellection," that is, the intellection focused on a created object. It is another matter when the higher portion of the intellect is focused on the very source itself of all ideas in the speculative as well as the practical orders. Here a separation or suspension from the lower portion of the intellect must precede the activation of the higher portion. In his treatise on the intellect, however, Albert insists that in the contemplation of its source the higher portion must be identified with its lower portion which contains the abstracted and lower forms. In this identity the human intellect literally becomes a microcosm reflecting the entire formal macrocosm as it exists in the mind of God. The perfection of the intellect *in via* is thus cosmological. All of creation over which Adam was given lordship in the Garden of Eden is now returned to God in this higher, contemplative vision of the mind of man. And this is another point that is uniquely developed by Albert: while admitting that illumination and perfection are works of grace and to that extent passively received by the intellect, he asserts what becomes the leitmotif of his entire philosophical-theological program, namely the doctrine that grace only perfects what nature develops. Thus in his mysticism the mystical faculty of the intellect is active in recreating the cosmos formally as it was given to Adam. Only on this condition can there be any infusion of grace. Nature and grace always cooperate.

Turning to Cusanus' theory of intellect, one notices at once its Albertist characteristics. In the twelfth chapter of his *Idiota de mente* Cusanus affirms anti-Averroism when he declares that the intellect is proportioned to the body in such a way that the identity of mind and body is unique:

> Because the mind has an operation by which it is called the soul, it demands an appropriate relation to a body adequately proportioned to it. This relation is found in one body, but not in another in the same way. Just so the identity of proportion cannot be multiplied.[1]

The principle of hylomorphism supporting Cusanus' position is apparently grounded in his reading of either Thomas Aquinas or Albert the Great.

In addition to fundamental agreement with respect to the question of the unity of the intellect, Cusanus' insight into the assimilative nature of the intellect reflects Albert's doctrine of the *intellectus assimilativus*. As Albert describes it in his treatise on the intellect, this faculty, which is a species of the agent intellect, is as close to a mystical power of the soul as Albert ever got. It is "divine," he claims, because it has the ability to know the divine ideas that exist apart from material reality. Through this faculty the soul experiences the gift of prophesy because it is so closely assimilated to future

---

[1] *Idiota. De mente* XII, #142 (h V, 102; h V^2, 195): "Nam cum mens habeat officium, ob quod anima dicitur, tunc exigit convenientem habitudinem corporis adaequate sibi proportionati, quae sicut in uno corpore reperitur, nequaquam in alio est reperibilis. Sicut igitur identitas proportionis est immultiplicabilis ita nec identitas mentis."

events in the divine order.[2]   Cusanus also echoes Albert's view on the
divinity of the assimilative intellect. First, he argues that the mind is a
"living divine number" proportioned to the resplendence of the divine harmony: "I believe that no one would be able to deny that the mind is a kind
of living, divine number that is well suited for the reflection of divine harmony."[3] In its operation of assimilation the human mind is a mirror of the
divine mind:

> The divine mind creates by conceiving, our [mind] in conceiving
> assimilates ideas or makes intellectual visions; the divine mind is
> the power of creating being, our mind is the power of assimila-
> tion.[4]

Nicholas is clearly carrying forward the Albertist idea that the
assimilative intellect operates as a microcosm in this mirror-like operation
of assimilation. What is more, this operation bears the Neoplatonic
hierarchical relationship expressed by Albert in terms of the assimilative
intellect "flowing" into the lower faculties of the soul. The relationship is
expressed by Nicholas as one of "imaging." The sensitive soul is not the
intellect, he claims, but rather its image or likeness: "Et ut videas animam
sensitivam non esse intellectum, sed eius similitudinem seu imaginem."[5]
Through the intellect all things flow out from God and ultimately
return to Him.[6] In explicating this operational relationship Cusanus
proceeds in a distinctly Albertist fashion, employing not only the language
of illumination but in a fashion identical to Albert. The light of the intellect
descends into the shadows of the senses through the superior part of reason

---

[2] Albertus Magnus, *Opera omnia, De intellectu et intelligibili* (Paris, 1890-
1899) IX; 2, i, 9 p. 516: "Est autem intellectus assimilativus, in quo homo
quantum possibile sive fas est proportionabiliter surgit ad intellectum divinum,
qui est lumen et causa omnium"; and p. 517: ". . . ita quod a quibusdam
prophetizare putantur." References to Albert will be to this edition by volume,
book, tractate, chapter, and page.

[3] *Idiota. De mente* VII, #98 (h V, 74; h V², 148): "Arbitror omnes non posse
dissentire mentem esse vivum quendam divinum numerum optime ad aptitudinem
resplendentiae divinae harmoniae proportionatum. . . ."

[4] *Idiota. De mente* VII, #99 (h V, 75; h V², 149-150): "Divina mens
concipiendo creat, nostra concipiendo assimilat notiones seu intellectuales
faciendo visiones; divina mens est vis entificativa, nostra mens est vis
assimilativa."

[5] *Compendium* XI, #35 (h XI, 3 p. 27).

[6] *De dato patris luminum* V, #114 (h V, 83): "Intellectualia autem sunt, per
quae inferiora fluunt a deo et refluunt ad ipsum."

which interacts with its inferior part, the imagination.[7] St. Albert argues that *portio superior* has been impressed with the image of creation and is the source for the *lumen sapientiae divinae* for the soul: "Hoc enim est officium superioris partis mentis in qua impressa est homini imago creationis, signata lumine vultus Dei per exemplum iustitiae aeternae, quae est lumen sapientiae divinae."[8]

The intellect in its assimilative function is like a separated light, he argues. "For the intellectual soul," he writes in his treatise on the intellect, "has from its assimilation to the first cause a universally active intellect which is like a separated light."[9] It is interesting to notice in passing that Albert's language can be read in an Eckhartian sense, arguing that the separateness and light of divine wisdom is evidence that the agent intellect is a spark of divinity in man. Cusanus, in a way, has yielded to this interpretation. As has already been seen, he calls the assimilative intellect a "living divine number."

Rather than follow Meister Eckhart, however, Nicholas prefers to adopt Albert's view of the assimilative intellect as a crucial agent in the cosmos facilitating the *exitus* and *reditus* of the divine ideas. Along with Albert, Cusanus develops a doctrine of man as microcosm based upon the assimilative intellect's being the image of God in man. In a crucial passage in which he brings together the doctrines of divine illumination, the exemplars in the mind of God, and the assimilative nature of the intellect as the *imago dei,* Nicholas grounds the cosmological function of the human intellect:

> The mind employs itself in this highest mode as it is the image of God. And God, who is all things shines forth [*relucet*] in it. Insofar as it is as a living image of God, it turns toward its exemplar assimilating itself with all its force. In this mode it intuits everything as one and itself the assimilation of this one, by means

[7] *De coniecturis* II, 16, #157 (h III, 156): "Descendente igitur lumine intelligentiae in umbram sensualem atque ascendente sensu in intellectum per gradus ternos medio loco duo exoriuntur, quae rationis nomen habere suppono. Superior autem huius rationis portio, quae intellectui prior reperitur, apprehensiva, inferior vero phantastica seu imaginativa, si placet, his aut aliis vocentur nominibus." For the equivalent idea of the descent of the light of intelligence into the shadow of the sensible in Albert, cf. *De intellectu,* treatise I, chap. 5.

[8] Albertus Magnus, *Summa theologiae,* II, tr. 15, q. 93, m. 3, sol. 33, 204.

[9] Albertus Magnus, *De intellectu et intelligibili,* ix, i, I, 6, 486: "Ex huius enim assimilatione causae primae habet intellectum universaliter agentem, qui sicut lux est separata."

of which it produces ideas about the one that is everything.[10]

Since it can assimilate all that pertains to the manifold of ideas, both in the sensible and the intelligible worlds, the human intellect is a cosmological fulcrum, or a microcosm, according to both Albert and Nicholas.[11]

Having completed the survey of both writers with respect to the intellect, it is now possible to inquire into their respective analyses of the *triplex via* that they ground in their theory of the intellect. In this regard primary attention must be paid to Albert the Great's commentary on the Pseudo-Dionysius' *Mystical Theology*. Not only does this commentary contain Albert's observations on the threefold way, but there is concrete proof that Cusanus actually studied this work to the point of making marginalia in his personal copy of the text. The method of inquiry will be to outline Albert's analysis of major themes while noting the repercussions of these themes in Cusanus' writings. No attempt will be made formally to explicate Cusanus' mystical theology.[12]

At the root of the threefold way in Albert's mystical theology is the doctrine of proportionality that he adopted from Aristotle. In his commentary this doctrine is expressed in his prayer of silence. God's quiddity cannot be expressed by us, so from an absolute point of view, the only speaking we can do about God is the prayer of silence.[13] Albert specifically defends the Dionysian concept of superessential predication on the grounds of this doctrine. The passage is rendered into English as:

> He calls "unlearned" those who are informed according to both affection and intellect by beings from which we receive knowledge. Consequently, they refuse to believe that anything exists supersubstantially above beings, that is, without proportion to them. Thus even the philosophers claim that the

[10] *Idiota. De mente* VII, #106 (h V, 78-79; V², 158-159): "Utitur autem hoc altissimo modo mens seipsa, ut ipsa est Dei imago; et Deus, qui est omnia, in ea relucet, scilicet quando ut viva imago Dei ad exemplar suum se omni conatu assimilando convertit. Et hoc modo intuetur omnia unum et se illius unius assimilationem, per quam notiones facit de uno, quod omnia."

[11] For the doctrine of the microcosm in St. Albert, cf. *De intellectu,* treatise I, chap. 6. In Cusanus, cf. *De docta ignorantia* III, 3, #198 (h I, 126- 127).

[12] Here the reader is advised to consult the author's article, "Purgation, Illumination and Perfection in Nicholas of Cusa," *The Downside Review* 98 (1980): 169-189.

[13] Albertus Magnus, *Super Dionysii mysticam theologiam* ed. P. Simon *Opera omnia* (Aschendorff, 1978), p. 456: ". . . silentium est simpliciter, quia de deo non potest dici 'quid', . . ."

first mover is proportionate to the first thing moved.[14]

Cusanus seems to begin his mystical theology in exactly the same place. Indeed, his doctrine of proportion introduces the purgative phase of the threefold way in terms of his famous teaching on learned ignorance. The concept of *docta ignorantia* was Nicholas' response to the problem of superessential predication. It is essentially a method for approaching God as the absolute who is beyond all comparison with the finite. He deliberately identifies purgation with this method of learned ignorance when he writes:

> Nothing seems to be left when I remove from my mind *(ab animo removeo)* all that has participated being. For this reason the great Dionysius says that an understanding of God is closer to nothing than to something. Sacred ignorance, however, teaches me that what seems to be nothing to the intellect is the incomprehensible Maximum.[15]

Purgation for Cusanus is the direct logical result of his doctrine of proportionality. Like Albert's prayer of silence, the realization of the non-proportionality of the finite and the infinite leads Nicholas to a state of sacred ignorance. For Albert, too, the disproportion between the human and the divine casts man into the condition of ignorance. But like the learned ignorance of Cusanus, Albert's silence is informing and hence he can refer to it as a "secret cloud of supersplendent learned silence." Using an analogy that Cusanus often favored, Albert likens this condition to the effect on the human eye of sunlight. The excessiveness of the sun's light casts the eye into darkness. A writer such as Albert does not lightly mix his metaphors. He means his readers to equate mystic silence, which is informed, with the darkness in the intellect when it realizes the overwhelming object of the mystic quest. To Cusanus this was learned ignorance. For both writers then there is a double effect of the doctrine of proportionality. First, there is the purgative effect--ignorance for Cusa, silence for Albert. Second, there is illumination, at least in a nascent stage. Thus the ignorance as well as the silence is "learned."

There is another interesting parallel between Albert and Cusanus with respect to the purgative phase of the mystical way. Albert, in developing his

---

[14] *Ibid.,* p. 458: "Dicit enim illos indoctos qui, cum sint informat et secundum affectum et secundum intellectum existentibus, a quibus scientiam accipimus, nihil credunt esse super entia supersubstantialiter, idest sine proportione ad ipsa. Unde etiam philosophi dicunt, quod motor primus est proportionatus mobili primo."

[15] *De docta ignorantia* I, 17, #51 (h I, 35).

idea that the purgative mode of thinking follows the divine *exitus* of creation in reverse by denying first those attributes that are least like God before moving on to deny those that are most like Him, suggests what will become the doctrine of contraction in Cusanus. He writes:

> Therefore, insofar as we ascend, our discourse contracts, that is becomes briefer, because the things by means of which we comprehend are few. Accordingly, as we finally remove all things, the entire discourse will be without voice because it will be united to that which is ineffable, namely God.[16]

Although creation for both Albert and Cusanus is a hierarchically ordered contraction of God, creatures in themselves are theophanic. That is, by themselves creatures are an expression of the manifestation of divine goodness. If there is one theme that forms a leitmotif in Albert the Great's writings, especially regarding natural philosophy, it is this one: creatures are a manifestation of divine light. Cusanus himself remarks in *De dato patris luminum*, "Our God is absolutely the infinite power, entirely in actuality, who wishes at the same time to reveal himself out of the nature of his goodness, making from himself various lights to descend, which are called 'theophanies'."[17] The doctrine of illumination is found throughout Albert's writings. His commentary on the *Mystical Theology*, however, presents a highly integrated version of illumination due to the matrix of the threefold way that directs the entire commentary.

Albert begins his analysis of illumination by observing that the divine light that God showers upon the soul not only illuminates the intellect, but elevates it at the same time. He uses the language of ecstatic mysticism. Divine light, he says, "overcomes" the human intellect *(convincens intellectum)* and "elevates" it to that which exceeds it.[18] On the surface this

[16] Albert, *Super mysticam theologiam*, p. 471: "Et ideo, secundum quod ascendimus, sermo noster contrahitur, idest breviatur, quia pauca sunt, quae de illis comprehendimus; et ad ultimum, quando omnia removerimus, totus sermo erit sine voce, quia unietur ei qui est ineffabilis, scilicet deo."

[17] *De dato patris luminum* IV, #109 (h IV, 80): "Absolute enim deus noster est infinita virtus penitus in actu, quae dum ex natura bonitatis se vult manifestare, facit a se varia lumina, quae theophaniae dicuntur, descendere."

[18] Albert, *Super mysticam theologiam*, p. 455: "Huismodi autem doctrina non procedit ex talibus principiis, sed potius ex quodam lumine divino, quod non est enuntiatio, per quam aliquid affirmetur, sed res quaedam convincens intellectum, ut sibi super omnia adhaereatur. Et ideo elevat intellectum ad id quod excedit ipsum, propter quod remanet intellectus in quodam non determinate noto."

position appears to be a form of ecstatic mysticism. And although there is no denying that within very strict limits he does advocate such a position, what is important to notice is that ecstatic illumination is functionally related to the doctrine of proportionality. Divine light must "overcome" the finitude of the human intellect by "elevating" it to the divine modes of knowing. Ecstasy for Albert is thus not an affective experience but a subtle incursion into the intellectual life of the soul. The result of this elevating illumination is not a vision of God, but an understanding of the manifestations of divinity in creation. The vision is therefore of the theophanies: "Moses did not see God himself in himself, but in his noblest effects, namely the effects of grace and of the theophanies that are expressed likenesses of divine goodness."[19]

Cusanus follows Albert very closely with regard to the theory of theophanic illumination. Both writers agree that divine light is neither sensible, rational, nor even intellectual. It does not belong to the epistemological order. It exists for its goodness and is manifested ultimately according to the order of beauty. Precisely because he maintains a metaphysics of an incomprehensible God, Cusanus needs theophanic illumination in order to reveal this God. Parallel to St. Albert, Cusanus maintains that this revelation is hierarchic. "The grades of intellectual nature," Cusanus writes, "are therefore ten. The first is more abstract and clearer in the act of apprehending God, the last is immersed in corporeal shadow and is called 'human'."[20] Cusanus' position differs from Albert's, however, in that Cusanus eschews any form of ecstatic mysticism. And so while he agrees with Albert in the rather unique position that divine light is a created theophany, not to be identified with the essence of its divine source, he prefers not to emphasize its supernatural nature nor insist on its supernatural effects upon the intellect. For Cusanus this divine light is manifested to the intellect through creatures, while for Albert it operated directly on the intellect while the lower faculties are suspended. It is Cusanus' interpretation that is more Neoplatonic on this point. Illumination becomes the principle of the soul's return to God in the mode of natural contemplation. As Cusanus explains, "Man sees that various creatures exist, and he is illuminated by the variety itself so that he might proceed to the essential

[19] Albert, *Super mysticam theologiam*, p. 464: "Moyses non vidit ipsum deum in se, sed in nobilissimis suis effectibus, scilicet gratiae et theophaniarum, quae sunt similitudines expressae divinae bonitatis."

[20] *De dato patris luminum* V, #114 (h IV, 83-84): "Decem igitur sunt gradus intellectualis naturae, et primus abstractior atque clarior multum in actu apprehendendi deum, ultimus immersus umbrae corporeae, qui et humanus dicitur minime in actu sed in virtuali potentia multum."

light of creatures."[21] Actually, Cusanus' position on the procession to the
essential light of creatures reflects Albert the Great's view, as expressed in
his *De intellectu,* that the function of the *intellectus assimilativus* was the
perception of the divine ideas as they exist in the mind of God.

The last stage of the mystical quest is perfection, or union. There are
many points here where Cusanus and Albert touch. They tend to be
commonplaces, however. But there is one complex of the analysis of
mystical union that is unique to Albert and which is a pronounced factor in
those mystical theologians who are aligned with his school. In his
commentary on Dionysius he developed the position that mystical union
requires perfection, and perfection in turn requires deification in some sense.
In trying to clarify this sense Albert concludes that it is by similitude, and
not by identity, that the soul is deified in the perfective stage. Similitude in
turn is grounded in the traditional doctrine of the creation of man according
to the image and likeness of God. While a factor in his own school, this
doctrine of deification by similitude is not adhered to strictly by all of
Albert's followers. The most notorious example of deviation is Meister
Eckhart. He accepted the Albertist thesis that perfection implies deification
but tended to opt for identity rather than similitude. Cusanus, however,
expresses all of the reservations that Albert does concerning identity. To be
sure, his doctrine of union has marked differences from that of Albert.
Nonetheless, he retains intact the perfection-deification-similitude complex.

It is significant that Albert writes that it is the mind that is deified:
mens deificatur et illuminatur.[22] His doctrine of the intellect as we have
reviewed it shows that Albert identifies the human person with his intellect.
Cusanus of course does exactly the same thing, and so it is not surprising
that he, too, speaks exclusively of the deification of the mind in the state of
mystical union. The soul must rise to the imitation of God, Albert writes,
insofar as the mind is made a reformed image of God by the action of glory,
or grace, upon it: "Sic debet consurgere ad imitationem dei, qui est super
omnem substantiam et cognitionem, secundum quod mens, in qua est imago
reformata per habitum gloriae vel gratiae, actu deum imitatur."[23]

Cusanus' account of mystical union is ambiguous to a certain extent.
Like Albert he has difficulty deciding whether union is an act of the intellect
or, conditioned by the language of Dionysius, a state of the soul "beyond
mind." But this ambiguity tends to dissolve when Cusanus directs his
attention to the nature of mystical union and away from his anthropological

---

[21] *De dato patris luminum* V, #115 (h IV, 84): "Videt homo varias creaturas
esse, et in ipsa varietate illuminatur, ut ad essentiale lumen creaturarum pergat."

[22] Albert, *Super mysticam theologiam,* p. 457.

[23] Albert, *Super mysticam theologiam,* p. 457.

concerns. He employs the traditional language of the *Brautmystik* when he describes the union of the soul with God as a "blissful union" *(nexum ac unionem felicissimam).*[24] He explicitly appeals to the doctrine of similitude as the necessary condition for union with God. "I know that the capacity that makes union possible is nothing other than similitude," he writes.[25] Metaphysically, the principle of similitude requires that the soul be similar to the divine nature in order to be assimilated to it. It is this application of the principle that saves Cusanus from the excessive language of Meister Eckhart, a caution which he may very well have gleaned from reading Albert's commentary on Dionysius. For it is very clearly set forth in Cusanus that deification must be construed in terms of similitude. Confident about similitude being the condition for union, he writes in *De dato patris luminum:*

> The one Spirit, who effects all things, is the blessed God, so that every creature in so far as the condition of its nature is brought forth might more nearly ascend through perfection to deification, that is, to the end of its repose.[26]

Cusanus' language is important because it is reminiscent of Dionysius' description of hierarchy as the assimilation of creatures to the likeness of God according to their capacities to imitate divinity. The capacity of the creature, no matter what it is, cannot exhaust the divine nature. As Cusanus argues, each creature "insofar as the condition of its nature is brought forth" truly reflects the deity.

The possibility thus exists for the soul to become deified, meaning to reflect the condition of its created nature as it proceeds from the divine mind, without becoming God.

Both Albert and Cusanus seem to have conditioned this view of the final mystical state with their doctrine of the assimilative nature of the intellect. The mind becomes like God, and thus fulfills the condition for mystical union, because it is the perfect reflection of the divine mind, recreating or reflecting exactly the ideas that the divine mind creates. *Splendere* becomes *resplendere* and *lucens* becomes *relucens.* The threefold

---

[24] Cf. *De visione dei* XVIII, #82, ed. Jasper Hopkins, *Nicholas of Cusa's Dialectical Mysticism* (Minneapolis, 1958), p. 216.

[25] *De visione dei* IV, #12 (Hopkins, p. 126): "Scio autem quod capacitas, quae unionem praestat, non est nisi similitudo."

[26] *De dato patris luminum* IV, #113 (h IV, 83): "Haec omnia operatur unus spiritus, qui est deus benedictus, ut omnis creatura per perfectionem propinquius ascendat, quantum naturae suae patitur condicio, ad deificationem, hoc est ad quietis terminum."

way in both authors is, therefore, a unique structuring of the assimilative nature of the intellect, allowing it to fulfill its destiny in ascending to its particular form of deification. There can be no doubt that the influence of Albert the Great was continuous and deep on Nicholas of Cusa's mystical thought. The debt he owed to Albert was profound. Not only did the consistency of Albert's theory of the intellect provide Nicholas with a ground for nearly all of his mystical writings, but the conservative interpretation of the perfection of this intellect saved him from excesses that could have rendered his message autotheistic and extravagant.

NICHOLAS OF CUSA IN THE MARGINS OF MEISTER ECKHART: CODEX CUSANUS 21

Donald F. Duclow

Several approaches are open to us for discussing Nicholas of Cusa's relation to Meister Eckhart. We can explore broad thematic and historical connections between these late medieval thinkers. Or we can search Nicholas' writings for passages reflecting Eckhart's influence, as Koch has done for Cusanus' sermons "in the spirit of Eckhart" and Wackerzapp for his earlier philosophical writings.[1] Yet a third approach, more modest and barefoot, will be followed here. I shall examine Nicholas' references to Eckhart in the *Apologia doctae ignorantiae* and his marginalia to his own manuscript of the German Dominican's works. These sources may tell us most directly how Cusanus viewed Eckhart and what interested him in the latter's writings. My primary focus will be on Cusanus as a reader of Eckhart. I shall first sketch Eckhart's place in Johannes Wenck's and Cusanus' dispute over learned ignorance, and then turn to Codex Cusanus 21, Nicholas' annotated manuscript of Eckhart's Latin writings. Finally, on this basis, I shall conclude with suggestions concerning the larger questions of influence and thematic comparison between these thinkers.

1. Eckhart in the Cusanus-Wenck Controversy

In 1442 Johannes Wenck invoked Eckhart in his polemic against Cusanus, *De ignota litteratura (On Unknown Learning)*. A Heidelberg theologian, Wenck saw Nicholas' *De docta ignorantia* (1440) threatening basic orthodox teaching on God, the natural universe, and Christ.[2] He sharply criticized

---

[1] Nicholas of Cusa, *Vier Predigten im Geiste Eckharts,* ed. and German trans. Josef Koch, *Cusanus-Texte* I, Sitzungsberichte der Heidelberger Akademie der Wissenschaften (1937); and Herbert Wackerzapp, *Der Einfluss Meister Eckharts auf die ersten philosophischen Schriften des Nikolaus von Kues (1440-1450),* ed. Josef Koch, *Beiträge zur Geschichte der Philosophie und Theologie des Mittelalters* 39, 3 (1962). See also Josef Koch, "Nikolaus von Kues und Meister Eckhart," *Mitteilungen und Forschungsbeiträge der Cusanus-Gesellschaft* 4 (1964): 164-173; and Rudolf Haubst, "Nikolaus von Kues als Interpret und Verteidiger Meister Eckharts," *Freiheit und Gelassenheit: Meister Eckhart heute,* ed. U. Kern (Munich, 1980), pp. 75-96.

[2] Johannes Wenck, *De ignota litteratura,* ed. and trans. Jasper Hopkins, *Nicholas of Cusa's Debate with John Wenck* (Minneapolis, 1981), p. 21. See Rudolf Haubst, *Studien zu Nikolaus von Kues und Johannes Wenck,* Beiträge zur Geschichte der Philosophie und Theologie des Mittelalters 38 (1955).

Cusanus for, among other things, identifying God and creation: "All things coincide with God. . . . God--on account of an absence of division--is the totality of things."[3]   He then sought to tar Cusanus with the brush of heresy by linking his doctrine to Eckhart and the condemned fourteenth-century "Beghards and sisters." For they too had proclaimed an identity of creatures, particularly of the human soul, with God. These claims would abolish both the Trinity and "the individual existence of things within their own genus."[4]   The implication of Wenck's charges is clear: *De docta ignorantia*, too, deserves condemnation.

In his *Apologia doctae ignorantiae* (1449), Cusanus replies that Wenck is a falsifier or forger *(falsarius)* who has read neither *De docta ignorantia* nor Eckhart accurately. He says that the thesis of all things coinciding with God is nowhere in *De docta ignorantia,* and that "he had never read that Eckhart taught the creation to be the creator."[5]   Interestingly, when accused of heresy Nicholas here takes up Eckhart's defense rather than distancing himself from the controversial Dominican. In so doing, Nicholas gives important evidence of his knowledge and views of Eckhart. He tells us that

> in various libraries he had seen Eckhart's many expository works on very many books of the Bible, many sermons, and many disputations. Furthermore, he had read many articles extracted from Eckhart's writings on John--articles which were criticized and rejected by others. And he had seen at Mainz, at the home of the teacher John Guldenschaf, Eckhart's short writing where he replies to those who tried to reproach him, and where he sets forth his own views and shows that the critics have not understood him.[6]

This passage suggests that Cusanus may have seen more of Eckhart's works than survive today. For we have Eckhart's commentaries on only four books of the Bible, and fragments on two others; taken together these seem fewer than Cusanus' *multa eius expositoria opera . . . super plerisque libris Bibliae.* Similarly, only five Parisian questions survive, which contrasts with the *disputata multa* that Nicholas mentions. It is also noteworthy that Cusanus knows suspect articles from the *Commentary on John* and Eckhart's *Defense.* This list of Johannine articles has not been found, but the *Defense* remains a basic document for interpreting the German

[3] Wenck, *De ignota litteratura,* pp. 25-26.

[4] Wenck, *De ignota litteratura,* pp. 26-27.

[5] Nicholas of Cusa, *Apologia doctae ignorantiae,* trans. Hopkins, in *Nicholas of Cusa's Debate with John Wenck,* p. 59 (h II, 25).

[6] *Apologia,* pp. 58-59 (h II, 25). Translation modified.

Dominican's trial and condemnation.[7]

Eckhart's *Defense* and condemnation hover over the Wenck-Cusanus debate and color Nicholas' view of Eckhart. For in Wenck Cusanus, too, faces a hostile critic who, he claims, does not understand him. And the memory of Eckhart's controversial history perhaps tempers Cusanus' admiration for him. In the *Apologia* Nicholas praises the Dominican's "genius and ardor," but wishes that

> his books would be removed from public places; for the people are not suited for [the statements] which Eckhart often intersperses, contrary to the custom of the other teachers; nevertheless, intelligent men find in them many subtle and useful [points].[8]

Cusanus here concedes a major point in Eckhart's condemnation--namely, the danger in making his works public. Pope John XXII's bull condemning Eckhart emphasizes this danger when it singles out "things which he put forth especially before the uneducated crowd in his sermons."[9] But while Cusanus elsewhere chooses an uneducated layman or *idiota* as his spokesman, he clearly considered himself among the *intelligentes* who can read Eckhart's works privately for their subtle and useful doctrine.

2. Cusanus' Eckhart Manuscript

Concerning Nicholas' reading of Eckhart, Codex Cusanus 21 supplies additional, invaluable information. This volume, one of four major manuscripts of Eckhart's Latin works, is dated 1444 (fol. 134) and is the only manuscript in this scribe's hand in Cusanus' library. It is written in a

[7] See Gabriel Théry, "Édition critique des pièces relatives au procès d'Eckhart contenues dans le manuscrit 33b de la Bibliothèque de Soest," *Archives d'histoire doctrinale et littéraire du moyen âge* 1 (1926): 129-268; and Bernard McGinn, "Eckhart's Condemnation Reconsidered," *The Thomist* 44 (1980): 390-414.

[8] *Apologia,* p. 59 (h II, 25).

[9] Pope John XXII, "In agro dominico," in Meister Eckhart, *The Essential Sermons, Commentaries, Treatises and Defense,* ed. and trans. Edmund Colledge and Bernard McGinn (New York, 1981), p. 77.

bastarda currens script[10] which, despite this designation, is quite legible. It contains nearly all of Eckhart's surviving Latin works: the prologues to the *Opus tripartitum,* both the literal and the "parabolic" commentaries on Genesis, the commentaries on Exodus, Wisdom, and the Gospel of John, brief sermons and *lectiones* on Ecclesiasticus, a short treatise on the Lord's Prayer, and an extensive series of sermons. In the midst of the manuscript is a list of seventeen condemned and eleven suspect articles (fol. 78). While Cusanus' *Apologia* indicates that this manuscript is not his only source for knowledge of Eckhart, it clearly deserves our attention. For here we have a copy of Eckhart's works that Nicholas both owned and read with care, as his textual corrections, marginal markings, and comments attest. Here I shall focus on the sermons for two reasons: first, it is in this section of the manuscript (fol. 137-172) that Cusanus' comments and markings are most frequent and concentrated; and second, because these sermons discuss many different topics, Nicholas' marginalia give us his response to a wide range of Eckhart's teaching.

Josef Koch remarks that in these Latin sermons we find ourselves "in Eckhart's workshop and can follow all the stages of his work from a short sketch or gathered notes to the completed sermon."[11] The sermons range from a few lines citing authorities to extensive, probing commentaries on biblical texts. They also seem designed for Eckhart's own use in the pulpit, as the repeated performance cues suggest: *Expone!* or "Explain and talk about the connection of the virtues."[12] Except for a few sermons for saints' feasts, they comment on lectionary readings for approximately half of the liturgical year, from immediately before Trinity Sunday to the First Sunday of Advent. The manuscript contains some repetition, as Eckhart comments on the same text more than once, and the scribe copies a small section of the sermons a second time. While there are some connections between the Latin and German sermons,[13] these Latin works are primarily academic

[10] Bernard Bischoff, quoted by Josef Koch, "Zur Einführung" to Eckhart's *Sermones, LW* IV, xiii. Heinrich Denifle discovered the manuscript and signaled its importance in "Das Cusanische Exemplar Meister Eckeharts lateinische Schriften in Cues," *Archiv für Literatur und Kirchengeschichte des Mittelalters* 2 (1886): 673-687. The critical edition of Eckhart's works is *Die deutschen und lateinischen Werke* (Stuttgart, 1936-   ); the Latin works will be cited as *LW,* and the German as *DW. LW* IV will be cited for the Latin sermons and Cusanus' marginalia by sermon number (e.g. S. VII), page, and paragraph. For a microfilm copy of Cod. Cus. 21, I thank the Hill Monastic Manuscript Library, St. John's University, Collegeville, Minnesota.

[11] Koch, "Zur Einführung," pp. xxix-xxx.

[12] S. VII, p. 90, n. 95; and S. XVIII,2, p. 262, n. 294.

[13] For example, compare S. XXI,1 with *Predigt* 18 (*DW* I, pp. 294-307); and S. XXXVII and XXXVIII with *Predigt* 21 (*DW* I, pp. 353-370).

sermons with clear links to Eckhart's biblical commentaries. The sermons are heavy with authorities, distinctions, and speculative argument, and as we shall see, they present many of Eckhart's basic themes.

If the Latin sermons bring us into Eckhart's workshop, their corrections and marginalia lead us into Cusanus' study where we can read over his shoulder. Koch and his colleagues have signaled the importance of Nicholas' corrections and marginalia by publishing them in the apparatus to their critical edition of Eckhart's Latin works. The marginalia include vertical lines alongside a column of text and occasionally a sketched hand with the index finger pointing to a passage. There are also written comments, often simply *nota* or *exemplum,* and transcriptions of phrases or sentences from Eckhart's text itself. These markings and comments make it easy for us to see what attracts Cusanus' attention. For example, at the beginning of a sermon on the soul and its "transformation" into God's being, Nicholas writes, *totus notandus.*[14]   On two other occasions he praises Eckhart's "genius" when the Dominican clarifies a difficult biblical text by altering a word within it. In this practice, notes Cusanus, "this master is exceptional in all his writings."[15]   Nicholas' comments occasionally announce the sermons' principle themes, as when he writes, "Note well concerning the interior man," and "Concerning mercy," and more elaborately, "Because the soul is an image of God, it is able to receive him; if four [qualities] come together, it is the house of God."[16]   Other marginalia relate to issues of speculative interest to Cusanus. For instance, Eckhart writes, "God is unnameable to us on account of the infinity of all being *(esse)* in him. But every concept and name of ours introduces something definite."[17]   Nicholas marks off this passage and comments, *cur deus innominabilis.* He isolates another basic feature of his learned ignorance when he writes elsewhere, "Note that nothing is known perfectly."[18]   But as we would expect, most of Cusanus' comments depend directly on Eckhart's texts and can be understood only in connection with their accompanying sermons.

[14] S. LV,4, p. 458, n. 547.

[15] S. II,2, p. 14, n. 13, where Eckhart changes *deus* to *esse*, Nicholas writes *nota ingenium scriptoris;* and S. XXIII, p. 205, n. 219, where Eckhart alters *spiritus sanctus* to *veritas,* Cusanus' note repeats his justification for the change, "alternatio dictionum multa obscura declarat," and adds, "et in hoc iste magister est in omnibus scriptis suis singularis."

[16] S. VII, p. 79, n. 83; S. XII,2, p. 119, n. 125; and S. XXIV,1, p. 218, n. 234: "anima quia imago dei capax est eius; si quattuor concurrunt domus dei est."

[17] S. VIII, p. 80, n. 84.

[18] S. XII,2, p. 133, n. 142.

3. Eckhart's *Sermon* XXIX

To focus our discussion, let us examine one sermon and Nicholas'
marginalia to it in some detail. *Sermon* XXIX is a virtual treatise on divine
unity, as Eckhart preaches on the text "God is one" (Gal. 3:16) and presents
many of his most distinctive themes. Eckhart scholars have emphasized the
importance of this sermon, an importance that Cusanus acknowledges with
his numerous markings and comments. Lossky scarcely exaggerates in
saying that the manuscript here is "covered" with marginal notes.[19]
Nicholas sets off much of the text with vertical lines, and draws a finger
toward a passage about love: "Whoever loves something totally does not
want it to be more than one."[20]   He further emphasizes this point by
transcribing it in the margin.
     Eckhart begins the sermon by citing Anselm's *Proslogion:* "Anselm
says 'God is that than which nothing better can be thought'." Here Nicholas
writes, *quid deus*.[21] When Eckhart describes the reciprocity between infinity
and simplicity in God, Cusanus repeats the point, and marks off the following section where Eckhart says that "God alone flows into all beings
. . . He alone 'is one'." Noting the sermon's turn toward love, Nicholas
writes that "God is loved because [He is] one." Eckhart discusses eleven
reasons explaining the connection between love and unity, including the
previously mentioned point that Cusanus put his finger on. Among others
that Nicholas marks off is the seventh: "The One is indistinct from all
things, and hence all things and the fullness of existence *(esse)* are found in
it by reason of indistinction or unity." Throughout this discussion Eckhart
outlines a metaphysic of unity and views love as the drive toward divine
unity, beyond God's distinct attributes of omnipotence, wisdom, and goodness. (It is, we may suspect, precisely the kind of argument to make Wenck
wince.)
     The sermon then explores a new theme. "Unity or the one," writes
Eckhart, "pertains to and is a property of the intellect alone." Nicholas' note

     [19] Vladimir Lossky, *Théologie négative et connaissance de Dieu chez
Maître Eckhart* (Paris, 1973), p. 165.

     [20] S. XXIX, p. 265, n. 298; Cod. Cus. 21, fol. 150ᵛ; trans. in *Meister
Eckhart: Teacher and Preacher*, ed. Bernard McGinn *et al.* (New York, 1986), p.
224.

     [21] Citations from *Sermo* XXIX and Cusanus' marginalia will follow in
sequence the text and apparatus in *LW* IV, pp. 263-270, nn. 295-305; and Cod.
Cus. 21, fol. 150-151. With slight modifications, I shall quote the sermon's
translation in McGinn, *Meister Eckhart: Teacher and Preacher*, pp. 223-226.
Eckhart cites Anselm, *Proslogion,* chap. 2 and 3, *Opera omnia*, vol. 1, ed. F. S.
Schmitt (Edinburgh, 1946), pp. 101, 103.

repeats this theme: *unitas proprietas intellectus*. Intellect thus becomes Eckhart's focus for conceiving divine unity, where existence or being *(esse)* and understanding *(intellectus)* coincide. Eckhart argues "that God alone properly exists, that he is intellect or understanding, and that he is purely and simply understanding with no other existence." Cusanus' annotations again follow the Dominican's argument closely. He notes that "In God there is no other being except understanding," and "God alone properly exists." The sermon then addresses the issue of creativity. Cusanus restates Eckhart's text: "God brings things into existence through intellect because existence is understanding in him alone." Everything but God has existence distinct from intellect, or it would not be a creature; it would instead exhibit the simple, intellectual unity of God. Further, God's intellect *creates* being. For as Cusanus notes, "understanding is uncreatable," while existence becomes "the first of created things."[22] No longer simply identifying understanding and being in God, Eckhart now exalts intellect above being as the uncreated over the created. This priority reflects Eckhart's preoccupation with the eternal, creative Word in the Gospel of John. As he tells us in the first Parisian question, "The evangelist did not say: 'In the beginning was being, and God was being,' but wrote instead, 'In the beginning was the Word'."[23] And of course "Word" means understanding and intellect.

Once the sermon has established the intellectual character of divine unity, Nicholas notes *(nota)* Eckhart's corollary that "all things that follow upon the One or unity (equality, likeness, image, relation, and the like) in the universal sense exist properly only in God or the Godhead." Eckhart supports this corollary with five arguments that emphasize the imprecision of all qualities outside of the divine intellect's unity. Cusanus marks both sides of the column for the fourth and fifth arguments. He summarizes the fourth, that in the created universe *non dantur duo aequalia,* and notes (*nota*) the fifth, that outside intellect there is always diversity.

Eckhart concludes the sermon by calling his audience to unity with God. Not surprisingly, this unity occurs in the intellect because--as Nicholas paraphrases--"God as God is only in the intellect." Citing Augustine's authority, Eckhart demands that we "Rise up then to intellect; to be attached

---

[22] Eckhart here quotes the *Liber de causis,* ed. A. Pattin (Louvain, 1966), p. 54, proposition 4: "prima rerum creatarum est esse."

[23] Eckhart, *Parisian Questions and Prologues,* trans. Armand Maurer (Toronto, 1974), p. 45; *LW* V, p. 40, n. 4. See also Eckhart's extensive commentary on the Gospel's prologue, *Expositio sancti Evangelii secundum Ioannem, LW* III, pp. 3-137, nn. 1-166; trans. in Eckhart, *Essential Sermons,* pp. 122-173.

to it is to be united with God."[24]   As Cusanus comments, Eckhart then repeats that "all being outside of intellect is creature." Nicholas also marks off the following sentence where Eckhart states what was to become a familiar Cusan theme, God as *non aliud* or not-other. Eckhart writes, "For in God there is no 'other' (*In deo enim non est aliud*)." The sermon then ends with a rhetorical praise of intellect as the locus for detachment and overcoming the oppositions and contrasts of being and this created world.

4. Variations on Eckhartian Themes

Sermon XXIX's themes occur elsewhere in Eckhart's Latin sermons, and Cusanus duly takes note of them. For example, he notes several passages exalting the intellect: "In virtue of intellect man is outside the here and now, and thus [is] always and everywhere"; "blessedness is in the intellect"; and "we are good in charity, blessed in intellect."[25]   Yet Eckhart occasionally qualifies this praise of intellect when he locates unity with God in the soul's hidden depth or essence, beyond the powers of will and intellect. Here one example may suffice. *Sermon* XXIV argues that because the intellect receives God under the garment of truth, a further ascent into God himself is necessary. For "God properly dwells in the soul's substance," which "is higher than intellect." Cusanus notes this argument's conclusion. He writes *quae domus dei* beside Eckhart's provocative text, "The house of God is the very essence of the soul into which God, alone and naked, flows."[26] The relation of intellect to the soul's essence remains a controversial issue in Eckhart scholarship, and one that we cannot resolve here. Let us simply note that Cusanus has read some of Eckhart's conflicting texts on this question, but that he consistently views union with God in intellectual terms. For example, Nicholas' *De filiatione dei* takes up a theme that Eckhart had often proclaimed: becoming "sons of God." For Cusanus this process involves "the removal of all otherness and diversity" and a return to God's unity. Yet it remains intellectual since

[24] Eckhart quotes Augustine, *Confessiones* 10,24,35 (CSEL 38, p. 254): *Ubi inveni veritatem, ibi inveni deum meum, ipsam veritatem.*

[25] S. XXVI, p. 245, n. 269; S. XI,2, p. 110, n. 117; and S. VI,3, p. 62, n. 64.

[26] S. XXIV,2, pp. 226-227, nn. 247-249; Eckhart, however, immediately goes on to discuss "Quomodo ratio superior est domus dei." See also S. XI,2, pp. 113-114, n. 120; and S. IX, pp. 93-94, nn. 98-99, where Nicholas comments, "Nota deus non illabitur animae nisi nudus." Concerning this and the related theme of the "spark of the soul," see Eckhart, *Predigt* 2, *DW* 1, pp. 21-45, trans. in *Essential Sermons*, pp. 177-181; and Frank Tobin, *Meister Eckhart: Thought and Language* (Philadelphia, 1986), pp. 126-140.

God, although He is not reached as He is, is nevertheless seen without any imaginative, enigmatic figure in the purity of the intellectual spirit; and for the intellect this is clear and face to face vision. This mode of appearance of absolute truth . . . is God, without whom the intellect cannot be happy.[27]

Here as elsewhere, Nicholas echoes the intellectualist theme of Eckhart's Sermon XXIX rather than his occasional claims about a more radical union with God in the soul's ground, or essence. On this point, Cusanus thus seems to pull back from Eckhart's more extreme views, and to develop a consistent account of intellect's role in mystical vision.

Nicholas' Eckhart manuscript suggests another difference between the two thinkers. For Eckhart's Latin sermons are richer in moral themes than Cusanus' marginalia suggest. While Nicholas consistently notes Eckhart's metaphysics and intellectualist spirituality, he shows less interest in the Dominican's moral and pastoral concerns. Sermon XXVII is a case in point. Here Cusanus' marginalia highlight a technical discussion of causality, being, and becoming in great detail, but abruptly disappear when Eckhart begins to criticize ildeness (otium).[28] More basically, Eckhart's characteristic theme of detachment and self-denial appears frequently in these sermons,[29] but is seldom noted by Cusanus. We may, indeed, wonder whether Eckhart would share Nicholas' strong affirmation of the self, as in De visione dei's prayer, "Unless I am my own, You [Lord] are not mine."[30] In a vernacular sermon, Eckhart urges us to desire nothing, to know nothing, to have nothing, and finally to be nothing distinct or created; only then, he says, may I "come to be free of will of myself and of God's will and of all his works and of God himself."[31] For all his reflection on coincidence and unity, Nicholas never makes so bold a claim. In De visione dei, mutual vision unites and distinguishes God and the soul, as each sees and is seen by the other. Cusanus' slighting of detachment may thus reflect his affirmation of the self's enduring role within this process of reciprocal seeing.

[27] Cusanus, De filiatione dei, III, #70 and #62 (h IV, 51 and 47). For a comparison of Cusanus and Eckhart on the mind, see M.L. Führer, "The Evolution of the Quadrivial Modes of Theology in Nicholas of Cusa's Analysis of the Soul," American Benedictine Review 36 (1985): 325-342.

[28] S. XXVIII,2, pp. 254-262, nn. 280-294.

[29] E.g., S. XIX, p. 175, n. 187; and S. XL,2, p. 342, n. 402; and especially S. XXV,2, p. 242, n. 266: "Abnegatio proprii est abnegatio creaturae sive huius et huius. Hoc enim et hoc proprium est, creatura est."

[30] Cusanus, De visione dei VII, 27, ed. and trans. Jasper Hopkins, Nicholas of Cusa's Dialectical Mysticism (Minneapolis, 1985), p. 147.

[31] Eckhart, Predigt 52, DW II, pp. 486-506; trans. in Eckhart, Essential Sermons, pp. 199-203.

66   DONALD F. DUCLOW

These differences between Eckhart and Cusanus may reflect the broader historical relation between the two men. The condemnation of Eckhart's teachings--and of other fourteenth-century figures like Marguerite Porete--was ample practical reason for later thinkers to temper their descriptions of the soul's relation to God. We may therefore expect Cusanus to emphasize reciprocal vision rather than radical detachment and the soul's "breakthrough" into the Godhead. Another, more specific historical issue is a reversal that occurs in Eckhart's own influence. His immediate Dominican heirs, Tauler and Suso, distanced themselves from his metaphysics and intellectualist spirituality, and developed distinctive moral and pastoral theologies. Suso in particular produced an intensely affective devotion to Christ's passion. In contrast, Cusanus retrieves precisely Eckhart's metaphysical and intellectualist themes. In the *Apologia* and *De visione dei,* he develops a spirituality linked to an "intellectual" logic of coincidence that transcends reason and its oppositions.[32] He also takes great pains to correct the Tegernsee monks' attempt to interpret learned ignorance in exclusively affective terms akin to the *devotio moderna*.[33] Turning from the path of Tauler and Suso, Nicholas thus returns directly to Eckhart's more speculative concerns.

Cusanus' retrieval of Eckhart could have been costly, since the Dominican's teachings were still considered dangerous enough to invoke charges of heresy. Hence, we have seen Wenck's polemic against Cusanus link him with the condemned Dominican. Codex Cusanus 21 confirms this association, as we witness Nicholas highlighting doctrines that Wenck found objectionable. Whether Wenck interprets these doctrines correctly is, however, another question. He differs most sharply from Eckhart and Cusanus about divine unity and the relation between God and creatures. On Wenck's view, Eckhart and Cusanus identify creatures with God, and thereby destroy "the individual existences within their own genus."[34] In the *Apologia,* Cusanus replies that Wenck ignores key distinctions. When Wenck says that for Cusanus "all things coincide with God," he overlooks the distinction between *complicatio,* or enfolding, and *explicatio,* or unfolding. A mathematical example illustrates this contrast. Unity enfolds or contains all number within itself, while numbers unfold into multiplicity from unity. Similarly, God enfolds or contains all things in unity, so that

[32] Coincidence is essential for Nicholas' approach to God, who is nevertheless "beyond the coincidence of contradictions" (*Apologia,* p. 52; h II, 15). See D.F. Duclow, "Mystical Theology and Intellect in Nicholas of Cusa," *American Catholic Philosophical Quarterly,* forthcoming (Spring, 1990).

[33] See Edmond Vansteenberghe, *Autour de la docte ignorance,* Beiträge zur Geschichte der Philosophie des Mittelalters 14 (1915); especially relevant are Cusanus' letters of 14 September 1453 (p. 115) and 18 March 1454 (p. 135).

[34] Wenck, *De ignota litteratura,* pp. 25-27.

all things are one in God; but as they unfold into creation, things become distinct from one another and from God. Hence, "in the mode of enfolding [God] is all things, but . . . in the mode of unfolding He is not any of these things."[35] Nicholas thus affirms both an identity and difference between God and creatures, as God simultaneously is and is not all things. He also cites Eckhart who says that God--as being *(esse)* itself--establishes the existence of individual creatures as "this or that being."[36] In addition, Cusanus has read passages where the Dominican clearly distinguishes between God and creation: "God is not all things, but the *ratio* [reason or cause] of all things"; and "God is indistinct in his own nature, but most distinct from all things."[37]

The last point highlights Eckhart's dialectic of identity and difference.[38] Considered as unity, God is simple and thus "indistinct" within himself; yet this very indistinction distinguishes God from all creatures, which are com- posite and "distinct" both within themselves and from each other. God's *distinction* from creatures preserves divine transcendence, while *indistinc- tion* also guarantees his immanence throughout creation, since in virtue of it God is indistinct from all things. Cusanus recalls this Eckhartian dialectic when he includes "indistinct distinction" among the *Apologia's* paradoxical descriptions of God.[39] Nicholas develops a similar dialectic between the terms *non aliud*/not-other and *aliud*/other. The *non aliud* is the "absolute concept" that all thinking and being presuppose, because it defines both itself and everything else. It defines itself as follows: *Non aliud est non aliud quam non aliud.*[40] As in Eckhart, the *non aliud* is transcendent as the "indistinct" unity prior to all difference; it is clearly *not* bound by otherness

---

[35] *Apologia*, p. 63 (h II, 31). See Thomas P. McTighe, "Meaning of the Couple *Complicatio-Explicatio* in the Philosophy of Nicholas of Cusa," *American Catholic Philosophical Society Proceedings* 32 (1958): 206- 214.

[36] *Apologia*, p. 59 (h II, 26); citing Eckhart, *Prologus in opus propositionum, LW* I, pp. 175-176, n. 15.

[37] S. XXV,1, p. 231, n. 253; and S. IV,1, pp. 27-28, n. 28: "deus indistinctus in sui natura, tamen ab omnibus distinctissimus." See also S. II,2, p. 15, n. 14.

[38] See Eckhart, *Expositio libri sapientiae, LW* II, pp. 481-491, nn. 144- 156; Tobin, *Meister Eckhart*, pp. 54-55; and Bernard McGinn, "Meister Eckhart on God as Absolute Unity," *Neoplatonism and Christian Thought*, ed. D.J. O'Meara (Albany, 1982), pp. 132-134.

[39] *Apologia*, p. 49 (h II, 10); and in a Trinitarian context, p. 58; (h II, 24).

[40] Cusanus, *Directio speculantis seu de non aliud*, chap. 1 (h XIII, 4). See D.F. Duclow, "The Analogy of the Word: Nicholas of Cusa's Theory of Language," *Bijdragen: Tijdschrift voor Filosofie en Theologie* 38 (1977): 293- 299.

or distinction. Yet it also defines difference: "the other is not other than the other"--e.g., the heavens are not other than the heavens. Here the *non aliud* becomes immanent in varied concepts and things as their defining principle. Cusanus therefore considers the *non aliud* well suited to guide our speculation toward God who is "all in all, although nothing of all things."[41] In a sermon, Cusanus cites Eckhart on just this point. Discussing "where" God is, the Dominican says that it is easier to see where he is not, and Cusanus adds, "God is in all things and in none. For he is in each thing insofar as it is being *(ens)*, but in none insofar as it is this being *(hoc ens)*."[42] With Eckhart, Cusanus thus develops a Neoplatonic dialectic that respects both God's immanence and transcendence. By contrast, Wenck relies on Aristotelian logic where non-contradiction is the rule, and opposites cannot coincide; he therefore misses the subtle interplay of identity and difference in Nicholas and Eckhart's teachings on God and creation. Hence, although Wenck perceives Cusanus' debt to Eckhart, he seriously misinterprets both thinkers.

In conclusion, while Cusanus' familiarity with Eckhart has been clear since the controversy with Wenck, we are still learning the details of Nicholas' knowledge and use of the Dominican's works. Koch and Haubst have shown that Cusanus' sermons from the 1450's quote Eckhart directly, and Wackerzapp has outlined textual and thematic parallels in the two thinkers' metaphysics.[43] This essay has explored Nicholas' *Apologia* and Codex Cusanus 21. Because they enable us to identify which of Eckhart's works Cusanus read, these documents offer essential evidence for comparing these two thinkers. We should nevertheless use this evidence with restraint. For Cusanus was not a man of one book, as his library in Bernkastel-Kues amply testifies.[44] Indeed, it is remarkable that so much of Nicholas' personal library survives, and that it contains such clear evidence of his reading. This situation is rare--and perhaps unique--for a medieval thinker. His Eckhart manuscript and marginalia occupy a place in a lifetime of book collecting and reading, thinking, and writing. The question of Eckhart's

[41] *De non aliud* VI (h XIII, 14). Nicholas is quoting Pseudo-Dionysius, *De divinis nominibus* V,8 and VII,3 (*Patrologia Graeca,* 3, 824a-b, 872a).

[42] Cusanus, *Ubi est qui natus est rex Iudaeorum?* in Koch, *Vier Predigten,* p. 100; see also p. 104. Cusanus quotes Eckhart's *Expositio sancti Evangelii secundum Johannem, LW* III, pp. 174-175, nn. 206-207; at this point in Cod. Cus. 21, Nicholas writes in the margin, "quomodo deus in omnibus et tamen in nullo."

[43] Koch, *Vier Predigten;* and Haubst, "Nikolaus von Kues als Interpret und Verteidiger Meister Eckharts," pp. 86-87. For Wackerzapp, see n. 1 above.

[44] See Jakob Marx, *Verzeichnis der Handschriften-Sammlung des Hospital zu Cues* (Trier, 1905).

influence thus becomes complicated as Cusanus reads, among others, Proclus, Pseudo-Dionysius, Eriugena, and Albert the Great. Hence, even where Eckhart speaks most directly to Nicholas' metaphysics and spirituality, we should be wary of claiming too direct a connection between their teachings. For example, Cusanus claims the *non aliud* as his own invention, and credits not Eckhart but Pseudo-Dionysius with having come closest to this discovery.[45]   He similarly invokes Dionysius' authority for emphasizing intellect in mystical theology, and his doctrine of intellect also owes much to the Albertist school that includes Dietrich of Freiburg and Ulrich of Strasbourg as well as Eckhart himself.[46]   As these instances suggest, we must recall that Eckhart and Cusanus are late medieval thinkers within a common Platonizing tradition, whose vocabulary and themes they share with many others.   This tradition, moreover, has had a way of encouraging highly idiosyncratic thinkers--for example, Meister Eckhart and Nicholas of Cusa.   It would therefore be a mistake to look simply for recycled Eckhart in Cusanus' works. We should expect Nicholas' reading of Eckhart to yield something at once more general as part of a shared tradition, and more specific and novel as a product of his own thought.

---

[45] *De non aliud* I (h XIII, 5).

[46] See Duclow, "Mystical Theology and Intellect"; and M.L. Führer, "Ulrich of Strasbourg and Nicholas of Cusa's Theory of Mind," *Classica et Mediaevalia* 36 (1985): 225-239.

I thank Professors James Biechler, F. Edward Cranz, Mark Führer, and Frank Tobin for their suggestions during the article's revision.

THE JOURNEY OF THE SOUL TO GOD
IN NICHOLAS OF CUSA'S *DE LUDO GLOBI*

H. Lawrence Bond

Nicholas of Cusa devoted one of his last works, *De ludo globi* (1462-1463),[1] to a series of meditations on a contemporary game involving a small wooden ball, partly hollowed out so that it is concave on one side and convex on the other. A spot is marked off from which to roll. A large circle is drawn on a flat surface of ground. Nine other circles are inscribed within it, one within the other, as can be found today on a conventional archery target. Each circle fits inside the next largest and is assigned a different value, from *one* to the region outside the perimeter of the largest circle and farthest from the center of the target to *ten* at the center itself. With the rounded convex side fitting in the palm of the hand, the ball is rolled into the nine concentric circles. Because of its shape, it travels in a heavy and determined spiral motion until it comes to rest on its convex side as near to the center as possible. Each player takes his turn, and the winner is the one who is the first to reach a score of *thirty-four*, the years of Christ's life on earth. The game suggests to Cusanus a range of theological and philosophical implications. He presents his meditations in the form of two successive

[1] I have utilized the text in the 1514 Paris edition reprinted in *Nicholas de Cusa,* De ludo globi: *The Game of Spheres,* trans. with intro. by Pauline Moffitt Watts (New York, 1986) [hereafter Watts]. This paper, therefore, cites the Paris edition in Watts' book (with appropriate folio and page number). I have consulted Watts, and although there are verbal similarities, the translations are my own.

However, let the reader be aware that the 1514 Paris edition of *De ludo globi* is flawed. The Strasbourg edition of 1488 more faithfully follows the manuscript in Cusanus' own library at Kués, Cod. Cus. 219. It is reprinted in Paul Wilpert (ed.), *Nikolaus von Kues Werke,* vol. 2 of *Quellen und Studien zur Geschichte der Philosophie,* vol. 5 (Berlin, 1967). Watts includes a valuable list of significant variants between Lefèvre's edition and the more reliable text ed. by Leo Gabriel in *Nikolaus von Kues. Philosophisch-theologische Schriften,* vol. 3 (Vienna, 1967), pp. 222-355. Gabriel also uses the two extant manuscripts: Cod. Cus. 219 (fol. 138^r-162^v) and Krakow 682 (fol. 3r-33r). Watts' translation is based on the Paris 1514 edition, but occasionally uses Gabriel's text (with indications in the notes).

dialogues, which comprise the work.[2]

I am bringing to the text a special interest in the history of spirituality. *De ludo globi* is particularly intriguing. Its gross metaphor of a game of rolling balls has levels of contemplative application. The author draws inferences from it for a variety of considerations, e. g., (1) God in relation to creation, to creatures, to the individual and to the soul; (2) the parts of the universe in relation to the whole; (3) the parts of the human in relation to one's entire being; and (4) the soul in relation to the body and to whatever else comprises a person, to earthly and heavenly things, to what is knowable and known, and to all that the soul enfolds and unfolds. The game also allows interpretation according to the different "senses" of reading scripture, similar to the fashion in which Dante directs the reader to consider his *Commedia*.[3] At one level the game is symbolic of the soul's journey, and at every level it is play.

The soul's journey as play is the theme I would like to pursue in this paper. The soul at play is its life-work. The soul reaches to God in play. This is the soul's essential and ultimate story. Everyone's story is at root, at the outer and innermost limits, the soul's story. Time, as Nicholas states in the treatise, is subject to soul, is its instrument, and does not contain the soul but is enfolded by it; soul stands outside and explains time, time in some sense is the image of soul, and time's story is the unfolding of the soul's story.

Moreover, the soul alone among creation is free to play. This is its condition, the *fortuna* in which it finds itself. That is why its motion, unlike that of the rest of creation, is journey.

In some ways Cusanus' treatise calls to mind Bonaventure's *Itinerarium mentis in deum*, inspired by his meditation on Francis' vision of

---

[2] Wolfgang Breidert, "Rhythmomachie und Globusspiel," *Mitteilungen und Forschungsbeiträge der Cusanus-Gesellschaft* 10 (1973): 155-171, sketches the game's origin and development. For an illustrated description of the game and of the shape and motion of the ball, see Gerda von Bredow's notes to her translation of *Vom Globusspiel*. De ludo globi (Hamburg, 1952), pp. 98-99, and the introduction to Watts' translation of *De ludo globi*, pp. 22-26. See also Gerd Heinz-Mohr, *Das Globusspiel des Nikolaus von Kues*. Kleine Schriften der Cusanus-Gesellschaft, vol. 8 (Trier, 1965). Cusanus describes the game in the first dialogue or I, fol. CLVIII, p. 78.

[3] Dante describes the two traditional levels of reading, that is, (1) the literal and (2) the mystical, which, in turn, is comprised of the allegorical, the tropological, and the anagogical: *Epistola ad Canem Grandem,* usually attributed to Dante and accompanying the first canto of the *Paradiso*. See Epistola X in Dante, *Le opere,* ed. E. Moore and rev. Paget Toynbee (Oxford, 1924), pp. 414-420.

the six-winged Seraph.[4] It, too, is story. Bonaventure's treatise came out of his own journey, which traced Francis' footsteps up Mount La Verna in Tuscany to the same place Francis had experienced the vision and received the Stigmata.[5] Bonaventure's work intends to direct the reader by steps or stages to union with God. It is clearly and determinedly mystical theology, part treatise, part memoir, and part manual. It is intended to be meditative and evocative in an immediate way. The work's explicit inspiration and model is Francis' vision, and although the genre, on the surface, seems pedagogical, yet the intent is to effect experience.[6] Cusanus' purpose, however, is more descriptive and analytical as well as playful. It is meditation on a game, delivered as part of two separate conversations. It is cosmology and epistemology in service to mystical theology rather than to mystical experience. The model or metaphor is a game of rolling balls, which is experiential, but the intended effect of the dialogue is pedagogy. Unlike Bonaventure, Cusanus does not intend to effect the soul's union with God but to analyze its journey and to do so in the context of "play."

It should be noted that Cusanus' two dialogues are also narrative. They unfold as a tale while at the same time rehearsing the story of the soul's pilgrimage. They are fictive and theological and intend to engage the listener or reader in a meditative instruction on his own journey. In them Cusanus constructs a premise and a story-world for the reader, as well as an image to orient and direct the reader in the real world.

The conversations themselves and their progression are story, and so are the figure or symbolism of the game and the procedure of play. The soul's effort and play in its quest for God are story. There is an inner narrative at work in the dialogues, at both the cosmic and microcosmic levels. At the deepest level the various rolls of the ball possible in the game represent the various life stories possible to all human souls. The game proves to be a

---

[4] Cusa was well aware of Bonaventure's *Itinerarium*. A copy in his possession dates from his student days at Heidelberg or Cologne. It is included in Cod. Strassburg 84. For dating the manuscript, see Rudolf Haubst, "Die Thomas- und Proklos-Exzerpte des 'Nicholaus Treverensis' in Codicillus Strassburg 84," *Mitteilungen und Forschungsbeiträge der Cusanus-Gesellschaft* 1 (1961): 18-20.

[5] See Bonaventure's *Prologus* in *Works of Saint Bonaventure,* vol. 2: *Itinerarium mentis in deum* (Saint Bonaventure, New York, 1956).

[6] See especially the prologue and the concluding chap. of the *Itinerarium.* As Bonaventure enjoins the reader, chap. 7 in *Works,* p. 100: "Moriamus igitur et ingrediamur in caliginem, imponamus silentium sollicitudinibus, concupiscentiis et phantasmatibus; transeamus cum Christo crucifixo ex hoc mundo ad Patrem." For the influence of Bonaventure on Cusanus, see Francis N. Caminiti, "Nikolaus von Kues und Bonventura," *Mitteilungen und Forschungsbeiträge der Cusanus-Gesellschaft* 4 (1964): 129-144.

model of the soul's game and has universal and timeless applications. It
embraces every human soul's journey and every possible variation of soul-
journey and soul-play. It is no exaggeration to say that *De ludo globi* has a
certain mythic quality, or the savor of myth, and the repetition of
oxymoronic playfulness, as does much of Cusanus' other theologizing.

I am looking at three elements in the dialogues that comprise Cusanus'
treatise: (1) *the soul at play,* i.e., the soul's journey to God; (2) *the play in
the soul,* i.e., what is present and what occurs in the soul at play; and (3)
the soul at rest, i.e., the soul at journey's end, at the completion of the
game.

1. The Soul At Play

One may consider that every effort of the rational soul is a form of play.
Gaming or play frequently has several components: participants, practice,
rules, goals, tries, intent, effort, tactics, strategy, scores, something to move
or to be acted upon, and a special environment.

The game of the soul is comprised of its own special features. Perhaps
all other games are enfolded in the soul and all are unfoldings of the soul's
game. The literal game of the dialogue, Nicholas explains, represents the
movement of the soul from its own realm to the realm of Eternal Peace and
Happiness.[7]

The first dialogue's premise is that the elderly Cusanus and John, the
young Duke of Bavaria, have just finished the game in which they took
turns rolling the ball onto the playing surface marked off by the ten circles,
or rings, each conveying a score of certain points. John describes the game
as "new and delightful." He suggests that its appeal may lie in some deeper
speculation that it seems to provoke. Cusanus announces that the game
represents not an insignificant philosophy.[8] John begs him to explain.
Later John's relative, Albert, initiates the second dialogue.[9] The two had
met, and Albert found John engrossed in reading "the little book on the
game of the ball," i. e., the first dialogue, and still fascinated with the game
itself. Albert desires further information. He has had trouble grasping its
full meaning. He asks Cusanus to set forth the mystical significance of
"the circles of the region of life."[10]

---

[7] *De ludo globi* I, fol. CLVIII; Watts, p. 78.

[8] *De ludo globi* I, fol. CLII; Watts, p. 54.

[9] John, Duke of Bavaria, was the oldest son of Duke Albert III, who had died
in 1460. On the question of the relationship of John and Albert and the
connection of the entire family with Nicholas of Cusa, see von Bredow, *Vom
Globusspiel,* pp. 108-109.

[10] *De ludo globi* I, fol. CLXv; Watts, p. 89.

In both dialogues an aging teacher, the Cardinal Cusanus, who will in fact die in the near future,[11] guides a young disciple in exploring hidden dimensions of an ordinary game, mining the activity of play for the deepest meanings it can yield. Conversation is the means of delivering and receiving light on the soul's motion toward God, the game behind all other games and playing. Cusanus sets world and soul in fresh light for his youthful associates by comparing the soul's journey to the motion of a ball in play traveling toward its ultimate designation. They in turn, by questions, provoke their teacher to further extensions and larger explanations, while providing additional insights of their own.

Cusanus playfully bemoans his aging mental condition as he deftly leads his apprentice philosophers into increasingly subtler and more ambitious realms. The game, however, he says, is easy to understand and invites laughter because of the ball's varied and unpredictable course.[12] Because it is both convex and concave, as it rolls, it cavorts and then wobbles and blunders to a stop where its odd shape and the playing surface bring it. The player who rolls the ball toward the circles is helpless once the ball is released. No roll is alike, no two players roll the same. The game is fraught with uncertainty and also with philosophical and theological implications. In the middle of the target is the circle of circles symbolizing "the seat of the ruler whose kingdom is the kingdom of life."[13] The game's strategy is to keep rolling the ball as close to the center as possible.

This, Nicholas explains in the first dialogue, is the soul's play. Christ is the center. He became center that the soul might have reachable destination, and he is the unique center in at least two ways: (1) as the one and only center in whom the soul can find its rest and (2) as each individual soul's unique center to whom no two souls ever stand in exactly the same relation.[14] There are "infinite places and mansions" within the center for each to reside.[15] Moreover, Christ is a living and willful center, for on our behalf he "moved the sphere *(globus)* of his person so that it came to rest in the middle of life."[16]

---

[11] Cusanus completed the work sometime during 1462-1463 and died in August, 1464. For the composition of *De ludo globi,* see von Bredow, *Vom Globusspiel,* pp. 108-109 and Edmond Vansteenberghe, *Le cardinal Nicolas de Cues (1401-1464): L'action--la pensée* (Paris, 1920), pp. 275-276.

[12] *De ludo globi* I, fol. CLVIII; Watts, p. 78.

[13] *De ludo globi* I, fol. CLVIII; Watts, p. 78.

[14] *De ludo globi* I, fol. CLVIII; Watts, p. 78.

[15] *De ludo globi* I, fol. CLVIII; Watts, p. 78. See John 14:2: "In domo Patris mei mansiones multae sunt."

[16] *De ludo globi* I, fol. CLVIII; Watts, p. 78.

The soul's journey is akin to the motion of the ball. One's life is a sphere. Each sphere is off-center, "declined downward according to its own nature," and must be moved and curved downward, though more for one life sphere than for another.[17] This is the soul's story: "after many variations and unstable revolutions and curvings" the soul may come to rest in the Kingdom of Life.[18] At least this is the journey set before the soul. It may choose otherwise.

The human is free but he is not free not to make choices, for that is part of the disposition given him which he cannot resist and stay human. Cusanus describes the human soul as "regal and imperial" and unrestricted by nature's structure, unlike the rest of creation.[19] He is also given moral judgment over choices. This power of moral discretion and the soul's free choosing are his and are subject to his will whatever extrinsic or fortuitous things may happen to him. His realm is his own to do with. Though the soul's journey to Life is set before him, he may choose not to acquiesce.[20]

Some choose to move their sphere only along an earthly path and deny themselves the soul's rest in eternal life. Others retain the hope of eternal life but proceed by the power of their own capacity and precepts apart from Christ, and their sphere is never able to reach the Kingdom of Life.[21] The soul's journey is impelled by choice, but in the case of the journey to the center, choice is shaped by faith.[22] To be chosen as the soul's destination the center first has to be seen; that is not the case with those who perceive only an earthly journey. Then it has to be believed and entrusted with the soul's life, and that is not so with those who persist entirely by their own efforts. Choice alone, however, is impotent without the spirit of faith to set the sphere of one's soul in motion. The soul may be self-moving, but it has no capacity to move itself in the eternal direction apart from faith even if it desires the journey's happiest end.[23] Without trust in God's intervention, regardless of choice, like the ball's motion after it is released, the human's sphere rolls whimsically and irregularly and as with the game the player can only stand by helplessly.[24]

[17] *De ludo globi* I, fol. CLVIIIv; Watts, p. 80.

[18] *De ludo globi* I, fol. CLVIIIv; Watts, p. 80.

[19] *De ludo globi* I, fol. CLVI; Watts, p. 70.

[20] *De ludo globi* I, fol. CLIX; Watts, p. 82.

[21] *De ludo globi* I, fol. CLVIII; Watts, p. 78.

[22] *De ludo globi* I, fol. CLIX; Watts, p. 82.

[23] *De ludo globi* I, fol. CLVIIIv; Watts, p. 80. For Cusanus this explains the tragic error of those who seem to "have the hope of happiness but strive to attain that life by their own powers and laws without Christ," fol. CLVIII; Watts, p. 78.

[24] *De ludo globi* I, fol. CLIXv; Watts, p. 84.

Cusanus likens the movement of the ball to one's earthly pilgrimage and the ball to the human condition on earth. The ball's weight and deflected surface causes its motion to resist the straight line and to fluctuate and decline variously and inconsistently.[25] Each player intends to reach the center of the circle, but none has the power to carry out his will, for after the ball is set in motion, he cannot modify its course by an additional effort.[26] The lesson for our earthly journey is severalfold: we are to take special care at the start, for the beginning and origin of the motion is critical;[27] we move our soul as we wish, but after it is set in motion inevitable consequences follow, and we can only do what is in us and trust God's help to provide the power we lack;[28] moreover, the soul's journey benefits from practice as does performance in the game.[29]

Cusanus ends the first dialogue by summarizing the application of the mystery of the game: to become proficient in the motion of one's soul and to arrive at the center, which is peace with Christ in the Kingdom of Life. The practice of the soul's quest for God is a constant venturing in order to learn the path and to master one's self. Faith is accompanied by persistence. As in the game players learn to correct "the inclinations and natural curvings by studious practice," in human existence it is necessary that each come "to master the inclinations of his own sphere and its affections" *(passiones)* through persistence.[30] None can master another's sphere. None can replicate another's motion. Notwithstanding the model of Christ's life, each has his own turn, each's sphere is his own responsibility, and each's motion and its rest is uniquely his own. "For each one's sphere comes to rest on its own point and atom, which no other could ever attain."[31] Cusanus declares the game's mystical power: "that through studious practice the sphere's curve can be regulated, so that after unstable fluctuations, its motion comes to rest in the kingdom of life." The practice of the soul is to find the path which is unimpeded by the curvature of one's sphere and down which one can make

[25] *De ludo globi* I, fol. CLIXv; Watts, p. 84.

[26] *De ludo globi* I, fol. CLIX; Watts, p. 82.

[27] *De ludo globi* I, fol. CLIX; Watts, p. 82.

[28] *De ludo globi* I, fol. CLIXv; Watts, p. 84. Cusanus speaks of bad habit as a motion disallowing good deeds until one initiates a new and different motion. One cannot change the bad habit's motion but can only set it aside and replace it with virtue: fol. CLIX; Watts, p. 82.

[29] *De ludo globi* I, fol. CLVIIIv; Watts, p. 80.

[30] *De ludo globi* I, fol. CLVIIIv; Watts, p. 80.

[31] *De ludo globi* I, fol. CLVIII; Watts, p. 78. Here I have followed Gabriel, *Nikolaus von Kues* 3:272, and Watts, p. 122, n. 16, who correct the *locus* of the Paris edition and of Cod. Cus. 219 to *globus*. Both cite the use of *globus* in Cod. Krakow 682.

one's way to the circle of Life.[32] The soul, therefore, makes its way to God by faith and practice.

2. The Play in the Soul

What is the soul and what is contained within it that enables it to journey? And what propels and sustains the soul in its journey? First, the soul is self-moving. Not even God directly moves the human soul in this sense. The soul is an intellectual substance, and its motion is self-subsistent and substantial.[33] Its nature is motion, and motion cannot happen to it, for it is by intellectual motion that the intellect is intellect. The ball in the game represents one's earthly life and is to be compared more to the body, for, Cusanus believes, motion best symbolizes the soul.[34]

The soul is at play because motion is of the essence of soul. The soul does not move by participation in motion. It is more properly speaking intellectual motion itself. Soul as motion is joined to the body through itself, is affected by the body and its environs but remains separable and a substance. It exists as power in the body, infuses the body and resides fully and simultaneously throughout different places in the body.[35] The soul is power, perpetually moving itself. But it is intellectual power, notional power and movement. It moves itself and therefore discerns, abstracts, divides, and assembles. Its power is to reason, and it possesses the power to shape itself to all that it would know. Moving itself, it knows by making itself the likeness of all knowable things. It is itself and is more truly power and best exercises its power when it detaches itself from the body and, as it can, exists entirely within its own freedom.[36] The soul's power is three and one: thinking, consideration, and determination. They are distinct but triune powers. Consideration proceeds from thought and determination from them both; yet together, as Cusanus has John observe, they are "one living motion moving itself perfectly."[37]

The soul is also life, or *ratio*, which is a living motion, moving itself in circular motion, perpetual, turning back on itself.[38]

Cusanus speaks of the traditional threefold distinction of the powers of the soul: vegetative, sensible, and intellective. The soul itself, however, is of one substance, enfolding *(complicans)* all the functions in its intellective

---

[32] *De ludo globi* I, fol. CLVIIIv; Watts, p. 80.

[33] *De ludo globi* I, fol. CLIIIv; Watts, p. 64.

[34] *De ludo globi* I, fol. CLV; Watts, p. 66.

[35] *De ludo globi* I, fol. CLV; Watts, p. 66.

[36] *De ludo globi* I, fol. CLVv; Watts, p. 68.

[37] *De ludo globi* I, fol. CLVI; Watts, p. 70.

[38] *De ludo globi* I, fol. CLVI; Watts, p. 70.

power, i.e., the vegetative, sensible, and the imaginative, which he distinguishes from the intellective. He cites the dictum that "inferior things are in superior things according to the nature of the superior thing."[39] Therefore, all these are perpetual through enfolding *(complicatio)*, through unitive residency in the intellectual nature which alone is itself perpetual.[40] The soul is simple, yet enfolding, and the human a microcosm in journey, "a little world which has a soul."[41]

In the second dialogue, he speaks of the soul as unity but not as God is unity. The soul's unity is notional, while God's unity is also being, enfolding all that is and all that can be as well as all that is known and all that can be known. The soul's unity is not absolute but proper to the soul itself and is enfolded in the unity that is God.[42] The soul, therefore, is a notional substance and power that enfolds. It enfolds all within itself notionally and is the enfolding power of all notional enfoldings. It unfolds *(explicat)* as well as enfolds, and in its simplicity it enfolds every notional unfolding *(explicatio)*, e. g., multitude, magnitude, number, point, motion, rest, time. It discerns all things in an unfolded way and is the inventor and measure of motions, disciplines, categories, universals, time, and all other conceptions.[43] God is the creator of beings, but the soul creates only *notionalia*. It owns the power and craft to create instruments with which to distinguish and to know and is not subject to its creations but stands outside them, in one way absolved from them, and in another seeing them all within itself, and at no time will it fail or cease to exist.[44]

Everything attained by sense and imagination are accidents[45] and are first enfolded in intelligible substance, which contains all accidents and is contained in them as they are unfolded. The soul is the intelligible substance of all powers and of their potentialities.[46]

The soul journeys, therefore, because it is in essence motion. But it moves notionally, and it moves toward God as it intends. "In the rational soul," Cusanus has Albert say, "intention is nothing other than the soul intending."[47] The soul moves but is not changed. Just as the sculptor moves his hands and instruments in fashioning a statue but his intention remains

[39] *De ludo globi* I, fol. CLVIv; Watts, p. 72.
[40] *De ludo globi* I, fol. CLVIv; Watts, p. 72.
[41] *De ludo globi* I, fol. CLVIv; Watts, p. 72.
[42] *De ludo globi* II, fol. CLXIIIIv; Watts, p. 104.
[43] *De ludo globi* II, fol. CLXIIIIv; Watts, p. 104.
[44] *De ludo globi* II, fol. CLXV; Watts, p. 106.
[45] *De ludo globi* II, fol. CLXI; Watts, p. 90.
[46] *De ludo globi* II, fol. CLXIv; Watts, p. 92.
[47] *De ludo globi* II, fol. CLXVv; Watts, p. 108.

steady, the soul notionally moves all things while its intention persists unchanged within it. The soul's intention is its *ratio*, or word, in which all the exemplars are enfolded. The one perpetual and final intention of the soul is to know God.[48]

Can the soul veer from its primary intent? Can it ignore it? Can other intentions override it? Cusanus states unequivocally that the soul's intent is to have in itself notionally this final good, the knowledge of God, "which all things desire," and that "the rational soul as it is rational never changes this intention."[49] Intent and attainment, however, are not the same. First the soul must see, the soul must perceive and contemplate the goal of its intent. Then the soul must return to the center which is also its cause.

Cusanus goes on to analyze intention as it operates at every level. To intend is to move and to see. When one intends to look at a visible object, one moves the eyes; when one intends to hear or walk, one moves the senses; when one intends to see what one perceives, one moves one's imagination or memory. But the soul's intent is toward the incorporeal. This entails a version of the negative way. When one intends to know what is incorporeal, one detaches from corporeal things, and the more one truly intends to know the incorporeal the more one withdraws from the corporeal. So when one intends to see the reason and cause of all things, he removes everything else and turns himself toward "the simplest and strongest intellectible power of the soul."[50] As the soul is drawn to see the Divine Exemplar of all things through his exemplifications *(exemplata)* so it is also directed to look within.[51] It proceeds by remotion or withdrawal to the world within.

The play in the soul, therefore, is its motion, which is substantial, perpetual, natural, and notional. This motion, which is self-motion, is the soul's intent to behold the cause of all things and of itself through its rational power and to perceive that the cause and reason of all things resides in its living reason. The soul's nature is to desire to know its cause, and it is restless until it knows. But it can know only when it sees and perceives its own desire of knowing, and it can contemplate "the eternal cause of its own reason in itself, that is, in the rational power."[52]

---

[48] *De ludo globi* II, fol. CLXVv; Watts, p. 108.

[49] *De ludo globi* II, fol. CLXVv; Watts, p. 108.

[50] *De ludo globi* II, fol. CLXVI; Watts, p. 110.

[51] *De ludo globi* II, fol. CLXI; Watts, p. 90.

[52] *De ludo globi* II, fol. CLXVI; Watts, p. 110.

3. The Soul At Rest

There is the question of the relation between motion and sight, between the soul's moving and the soul's seeing. The second dialogue provides a series of connections. Life is motion and the end of motion is life's cause and end. The end of the soul's motion is to know and to reside in its cause. The soul knows by seeing. In the realm of the soul seeing is living. Without sight there is darkness and also death. To know is to see and to live is to see. There is no rest for the soul apart from knowing and seeing. But there is no knowing or seeing without light, and there is no reachable destination of life without the light of Truth.[53]

What is the state of the soul at its journey's end? When and under what circumstances does the soul reach its destination? And what happens to the soul when it reaches God?

The soul's destination is rest at its journey's end. Its journey's end is residency in its center. This is discussed at more length in the second dialogue in which Cusanus explains the mystic meaning of the circles. Here the dialogue also presents the reader with a succession of complexities. The residency of the soul in its end follows and embraces seeing, trusting, and knowing. Its center is the center of all else--of circles, centers, motion, and every individual soul. Its center is like a single point that has an infinite spaciousness. The center is also circumference, is stationary but infinitely moving, invisible but can be seen, is the soul's intent and desire but can be missed, is found within and outside the soul, is maximum and minimum, is universal but in this life can best be seen in the very depths of the individual soul itself.

Albert raises the question of the soul's supreme desire and its relation to contemplation. He describes the desire as the yearning for discernment and knowledge. The soul longs to know the cause of its deepest longing and thereby find its own cause. The soul desires by nature to know, and what belongs to the soul is uniquely the soul's and is to be uniquely satisfied within the soul's being. The case for contemplation is concisely stated. First, the soul has knowledge within itself of the giver of its desire. It uses its discretive power to behold within itself the cause of its ultimate desiring. Second, what the soul does not see within itself it cannot desire. Third, it attains its desire's end when it contemplates in itself the knowledge of its cause.[54]

The soul's end is a kind of contemplation, for the ascent to God is an ascent within.

The soul's journey to God is, at the last, the journey to its center. But what is the center? How can the center be seen and how does sight occur? Christ is the center to be seen. When the soul seeks its center, it is seeking

[53] *De ludo globi* II, fol. CLXII; Watts, p. 94.

[54] *De ludo globi* II, fol. CLXVI; Watts, p. 110.

Christ, for the center of life is Christ. The circles of the game, understood
at one level, symbolize the circles or the regions of life. All circles are
representations of roundness. Roundness itself, however, is no mere
abstraction for Cusanus, it is substance and an absolute. It is the exemplar
of which the roundness of the world is image.[55] As name or metaphor,
roundness stands for "the circulation of the motion of perpetual and endless
life." Every circle, in order to be circle, has to have circularity. The presence
of circularity, or roundness, gives the circle being. All circles have the same
center. They receive being from the same center that is Life. This is the
center of centers, the center than which there can be nothing greater or lesser.
Without this center all other circles or regions of life cannot be known or
exist. The center of all is the circle of circles. This is the circle that is also
the center. Moreover, it is the center that is fixed but is also infinite motion.
This is the absolute and infinite center that is circularity or roundness itself.
It is a fixed point but embracing maximum and minimum motion. It is the
point in which center and circumference are the same. In its fixed eternity
all possible motion of life is enfolded, unfolds, and comes to rest.[56]

Cusanus also speaks of the circles as symbolic of grades of wisdom.
Again Christ is the center. The wisdom that God gives is invisible apart
from Christ. The purpose of every living rational motion is to receive the
wisdom of the cause of its life and to be fed by such wisdom. The soul,
however, languishes, for on its own it lacks the light to see and to live.
The manifesting light of Christ alone feeds the soul's intellectual sight, just
as illuminating physical light supplies vision to sensible sight. Divine
wisdom, therefore, is hidden to everyone unless Christ shows it. Christ, in
whom the filiation of God manifests itself, is the truth and is the light by
which we see the divine. Christ is the center of the circles or regions of
wisdom. In him wisdom is savory and, therefore, is apprehensible by us.
He is the center common to all, present in every circle but himself seen
only in the circle. Similarly his circumference is "of the circumferential
nature of all circumferences." If God may be spoken of as center and the
soul, or rational creature, as circumference, Christ, therefore, is both center
and circumference. As the center and the circumference, he is both the end
of the journey through the gradations of circles and the means by which we

---

[55] In *De ludo globi* I, fol. CLIIII; Watts, p. 62, Cusanus explains that
although the roundness of the world is the maximum roundness than which
nothing is *actually* greater, it is not absolute roundness but its image: "Non est
tamen ipsa absoluta verissima rotunditas. Ideo est imago rotunditatis absolutae."
He reiterates his careful distinction between the world's maximum roundness and
absolute roundness: "Rotundus enim mundus non est ipsa rotunditatis qua maior
non est: sed qua maior non est actu."

[56] *De ludo globi* II, fol. CLXIv; Watts, p. 92.

progress and see God.[57]

The soul in its journey, consequently, learns to see what is hidden. It sees with the eye of the mind, detached from corporeal vision, and therefore sees things and the structure of things as unfolded. By the motion of its rational power, which is its nature, it sees things unfolded and enfolded hierarchically, with each degree or level of being embracing what is below it and also containing what stands above. For example, the soul "virtually" possesses "the reason and knowledge of knowable things." The truth of this, however, is lost without what Nicholas calls "attentive reflection" (attenta cogitatio), without which one does not "perceive" intelligible things. The soul does not "perceive" what is within, i. e., "all the things comprehended in the reason" unless the soul's power is "roused and unfolded by attentive reflection."[58]

Cusanus also describes the circles as power. He calls this a mystical reading of the symbolism of the circles.[59] Albert asks about the hidden and the revealed and remarks that all power is hidden in the center. Cusanus cites Scripture to agree: God is hidden even from the eyes of the wise.[60] The cosmos itself is such that the invisible is hidden within the visible. He then offers a kind of meditation on power. He proclaims power to be spiritual and invisible and present in a hierarchical structure. In ascending order, the lowest power, the elemental, is hidden in chaos; the sensible is hidden in the elemental; in the sensible is the vegetative; in the vegetative is the imaginative; in the imaginative the logical, or rational; in the rational the intelligential; in the intelligential the intellectible; and in the intellectible is hidden the highest power of the hierarchy, "the power of powers."[61]

Albert begins to reflect on the principle of ascent and progression in the universe. He comes to the insight that the human experiences in himself an ascent "from the corporeal nature toward the spiritual" and therefore knows himself as miniature cosmos.[62] It is within and through the grades of being that the soul sees, and it is from its own power and within its own being that the soul finally beholds its center and its end. The journey is an ascent within.

Bonaventure's Itinerarium has the soul see in and through successive levels of being to a contemplation of God. So too Cusanus' De ludo globi has the soul move successively in and through levels, but these are levels

[57] De ludo globi II, fol. CLXII-CLXIIv; Watts, pp. 94 and 96.

[58] De ludo globi II, fol. CLXVI; Watts, p. 110.

[59] De ludo globi II, fol. CLXVIv; Watts, p. 112.

[60] De ludo globi II, fol. CLXVI; Watts, p. 110. See Matthew 11:25 and Luke 10:21.

[61] De ludo globi II, fol. CLXVI; Watts, p. 110.

[62] De ludo globi II, fol. CLXVIv; Watts, p. 112.

inside the soul, as notions enfolded in the soul and as images or assimilated reality contained in the soul itself, for the soul knows by conforming itself to what it can contemplate and know.

Cusanus concludes the treatise with a farewell discourse *(vale)* on value *(valor)*.[63] He provides a new analogy in place of the game: the analogy of the mint-master and the coin-broker. He likens God to an omnipotent king and mint-master, or coiner, who alone can produce all money but chooses to endow the coin-broker with the power to discern and distinguish the relative value of all coins. Each coin, however, bears the mint-master's image or likeness of his face.[64] Cusanus describes a son as a living image, or sign. In other words, a son is the image, substantial form, and appearance of his father. The living sign is the unique exemplar and formal cause. Through the coiner's substantial form, which is the same as the son, the creator and coiner is in all coins, just as a single signified thing is present in many signs. When one beholds the quiddity of that which is in all coins, one sees the coiner. When one sees only the signs, one sees a plurality of coins.[65]

Cusanus then considers what the soul can see when it concludes its contemplative journey. He now likens the intellect to a living coin, for it enfolds within itself all intelligible things. The soul, or intellect, looks through the individual to contemplate quiddity. But when the intellect contemplates, "it looks inside itself mentally" and speculates within itself.[66] This is so because the soul's life is intellectual, and it "discovers all things intellectually." But not everything knowable is known. Even some visible things exceed sight. Some have to be seen negatively. The sun, for example, possesses light too excellent to be seen and therefore can be said to be seen only negatively. So also the intellect "negatively" sees "infinite actuality or God and infinite possibility or matter." But "in its intelligible and rational power," it can "affirmatively" see all that resides in between. It contemplates within itself the modes of being that are intelligible as in a living mirror.[67]

Albert extends the analogy in a summary statement. If a coin were as the intellect, that is, had an intellectual life, it would have the power of the intellect, it would (1) know itself to be coin; (2) know itself to be the money of the coiner whose sign and image it bore; (3) know that it did not possess the being of coin from itself but from the one who stamped his image upon it; and (4) know that all coins would be of the same source by

[63] *De ludo globi* II, fol. CLXVII; Watts, p. 114.

[64] *De ludo globi* II, fol. CLXVIIv; Watts, p. 116.

[65] *De ludo globi* II, fol. CLXVIII; Watts, p. 118.

[66] *De ludo globi* II, fol. CLXVIII; Watts, p. 118.

[67] *De ludo globi* II, fol. CLXVIII; Watts, p. 118.

seeing "a similar image in all living intellects."[68]

The soul looks in and through all available to its sight and looks most deeply within itself and sees what otherwise is hidden from sight. It beholds one face, just as a living coin would see one face in the images of all coins. It sees "one true precise and most sufficient form forming all things, shining variously in various signs," just as the intellectual coin would, by seeing itself as a coin, know its truth and essence to be from "the truth which is in the sign, not from the sign imprinted in matter." It would contemplate its being "previously coinable before having been actually minted."[69] By contemplation in itself of its own form the soul would come to see itself as a signified thing and its cause as the one thing signified in all things.[70] It would know its cause, the end of its desire. Just as the coin would behold "in itself the matter which the impression of the sign determined to be a florin,"[71] the soul would see in itself its end, which is its center, its own truest self, the form of forms, one might even say the soul of souls. But unlike the soul, however deiform *(deiformis)* the soul may be, its center is not the creator of ideas only but of being, for it is the center that is all and within all and in whom are all that have being and can have being.[72]

The journey of the soul is a kind of contemplation within and through itself, seeing the means affirmatively and the end negatively, in mediation, whose highest mediation is that of the Son, the image of images, the center and circumference, the origin and end, in whose center all have dwelling at the journey's end. God, as Cusanus suggests in both *De docta ignorantia* and *De ludo globi,* is a circle whose center is everywhere and whose circumference is nowhere.[73]

It is the same concept with which Bonaventure brings Chapter Five of *Itinerarium* to an end.[74]   This is the chapter which describes the Divine

[68] *De ludo globi* II, fol. CLXVIIIv; Watts, p. 120.

[69] *De ludo globi* II, fol. CLXVIIIv; Watts, p. 120.

[70] *De ludo globi* II, fol. CLXVIII; Watts, p. 118.

[71] *De ludo globi* II, fol. CLXVIIIv; Watts, p. 120.

[72] *De ludo globi* II, fol. CLXVIIv; Watts, p. 116.   This distinction is essential to the second dialogue and its concluding analogy.

[73] In *De docta ignorantia* II, 12, #162 (h I, 104), Cusanus speaks of God as everywhere and nowhere, the circumference and center of the *machina mundi,* as if having its center everywhere and its circumference nowhere, and in *De ludo globi* II as a circle whose center is everywhere, fol. CLXIIIv; Watts, p. 100. The notation in the Heidelberg edition quotes the dictum from Hermes Trismegistus: "Deus est sphaera infinita, cuius centrum est ubique, circumferentia nullibi."

[74] Bonaventure quotes Alan of Lille, *Theologicae regulae* 7: the absolute and purest Being "est sphaera intelligibilis, cuius centrum est ubique et circumferentia nusquam." *Itinerarium,* chap. 5, in *Works,* p. 86.

Unity whose primary name is Being. The context is a discussion of the contemplation of God *supra nos*. Bonaventure cites two contemplative ways. In the first, considered in Chapter Five, the soul beholds the essential attributes of God, i.e., Being Itself. In the second, discussed in Chapter Six, the soul gazes at the attributes proper to the Persons of the Trinity, i.e., the Good Itself. Bonaventure's final chapter is a revery on spiritual and mystical rapture in which the intellect comes to rest and "affection entirely passes over into God."[75]

The vision by which Cusanus ends his treatise, however, is intellectual not affective. It is a contemplation of Being in the soul. Its means is not so much the life of prayer and affection as the mind's attentive reflection (*attenta cogitatio*). This attentiveness, however, is not entirely philosophical. It suggests a speculative mysticism. Cusanus speaks of seeing and attaining but not of union. But the seeing does not occur apart from a spiritual life and a spiritual journey. The soul's ascent is within, moving upward to God by moving more deeply into itself.

In the *De ludo globi* the soul, therefore, reaches to God (1) through contemplation, in the center of Life, which is also the center of one's soul, and (2) by faith and practice, not through effort alone, but trusting God to use its bumbling attempts. Though the human's sphere rolls "capriciously and inconstantly," God will not forsake those who place their hope in him.[76] The soul's journey sketched here in Nicholas of Cusa's dialogues is comedic and divine play, propelled by nature and overtaken by grace.

[75] *Itinerarium*, chap. 7, in *Works*, p. 96.

[76] *De ludo globi* I, fol. CLIXv; Watts, p. 84.

PART TWO

COMPREHENDING THE COSMOS

FORM AND SIGNIFICANCE OF THE SPHERE IN
NICHOLAS OF CUSA'S *DE LUDO GLOBI*

Edward J. Butterworth

The whole of Cusanus' *De ludo globi*[1] is understood as an extended metaphor in which the game of spheres, like the six-winged seraph in Bonaventure's *Itinerarium mentis in deum*, signifies the goal of the quest as well as the means of attaining it.[2] For Cusanus, the goal is transcendent truth, and the means is the observed structure of the cosmos. Both are aptly signified by the form of the Sphere and by the dynamics of circular motion when considered as derivative of that form. His work is preceded by a thirteenth-century treatment, the *Theologicae regulae* of Alan of Lille,[3] in which this approach is termed mathematical as distinguished from both literal and metaphorical. While Cusanus does not cite Alan, the congruence of their respective uses of language is sufficient to justify a comparison.

My purpose in this article is to explore the role of the Sphere as a mediating form between the cosmological scheme and the divinity in *De ludo globi*. I will show that this approach engenders a particular vision of the cosmos as *imago dei* and that such a vision is implicitly present in *De ludo globi*. Since the methodological tools for the examination of this vision are the very principles that Alan introduces in the *Theologicae regulae*, it is fitting that this work be treated as a foundation for the study of *De ludo globi*.[4]

---

[1] The edition used here is that translated and introduced by Pauline Moffitt Watts, *Nicholas de Cusa*, De ludo globi: *The Game of Spheres* (New York, 1986). (Hereafter Watts.)

[2] This work appears in the Quaracci edition of Bonaventure's *Opera omnia* (Ad Claras Aquas, 1882) 5:295-313, reproduced in *Obras de San Buenaventura* (Madrid, 1968) 1:474-534.

[3] This work, dated to the late twelfth century, is reproduced in J. P. Migne, *Patrologia latina* (1855) 210:621-684. All quotations will be from this edition, cited hereafter as PL. All translations are mine.

[4] The question of the relationship between Cusanus and Alan of Lille on the meaning of the sphere has been studied by Karsten Harries, "The Infinite Sphere: Comments on the History of a Metaphor," *Journal of the History of Philosophy* 13 (1975): 5-15. Harries sees its history as a continual (and necessary) transition from the sphere as model of God to model of cosmos. My approach focuses more on the continual tension between these two images which, I am convinced, struggle with each other in Alan, Cusanus, and anyone else who addresses the intelligible Sphere.

1. The Sphere in the Mathematical Methodology of Alan of Lille

One of the most remarkable methodological principles introduced in the
Theologicae regulae, both in the universality of its applicability and the
depth of its implications, is given in Rule XXXI: "Every mathematical
name is less improperly said of God than is a concrete name."[5] This principle is set forth within the context of statements concerning God ". . . which
refer to the divinity without reference to the person . . ."[6] This negative
qualification does not completely specify a *nomen mathematicum;* Alan provides a set of rules for the proper use of this category. These begin with a
categorical distinction between *mathematicum* and *concretivum* in which
Alan makes these two categories into a "partition"[7] of the possible ways of
referring to God insofar as they are exhaustive and mutually exclusive. The
dividing line between them is delineated as follows: "For mathematics aims
at simplicity, and the simpler something is the more accurately it looks toward God."[8] This makes the attribute of simplicity normative for any
human reference to God and, in so doing, raises the ancient philosophical
problem of the one and the many.[9] Alan's attempted resolution of this prob-

---

[5] Reg. XXXI: "Omne nomen mathematicum minus improprie dicitur de Deo,
quam concretivum" (PL 210:636). Alan uses the word "mathematical'" in a somewhat unfamiliar but, nevertheless, well-defined sense. In keeping with this specialized sense, he does not list *mathematica* as one of the *scientiae* described in
the prologue of the work (PL 210:621-622). In fact, he does not introduce the
word until Reg. XXX, although it can be argued that the method implied pervades
the whole of the work. The reference to '"person" here is not specifically to the
Persons of the Trinity, which are discussed earlier (Reg. XXIII-XXIX; PL
210:631-635), but to the grammatical persons, which then apply indirectly to
the Trinity. Terms used *quasi mathematice* are the "formal," or "essential" in contrast to "personal," attributes of God: "ut deitas, divinitas, natura, usia, essentia,
substantia" (Reg. XXX; PL 210:635-636). These terms apply to God as absolute
rather than in relatedness.

[6] Reg. XXX: ". . . quae significat deitatem nullo habito respectu ad person-
am . . ." (PL 210:636).

[7] The word "partition" is used here in a sense directly analogous with the
"partition function" of mathematical theory.

[8] Reg. XXXIIII: "Mathematica enim magis tendunt ad simplicitatem, quanto
autem aliquid simplicius, tanto ad Deum spectat competentius" (PL 210: 636).

[9] This is considered by some to be the fundamental question in Western philosophy. Good discussions of it are found in the following sources: Arthur O.
Lovejoy, *The Great Chain of Being* (Cambridge, 1957), pp. 75-99; John M.
McDermott, "A New Approach to God's Existence," *Thomist* 44 (1980): 230-
236; Frederick Copleston, *Religion and the One* (New York, 1980), pp. 15-40.

lem is expressed in his use of *concretivum* to refer to any means of expression that moves the underlying thought in the direction of multiplicity while terms used *quasi mathematice* are used whenever the underlying tendency of thought is in the direction of unity. In principle, all use of language can be divided into these two categories.

The use of this categorical scheme implies a relationship between thought and reality that is very different from those implied in most modern descriptions of how language is used. Nevertheless, Alan proceeds with a methodological rigor equal to any modern counterpart. This method leads to an explicit designation of God that fully retains its remarkable force: "God is the intelligible Sphere, the center of which is everywhere, the circumference is nowhere."[10] This axiom builds entirely upon the difference between *quasi mathematice* and *concretivum* delineated above: God is the termination point of the arrow that points from the *concretivum* to the *mathematicum*. With this in mind, Alan contrasts the two spheres: "How great the difference between the corporeal sphere and the intelligible Sphere!"[11] The corporeal sphere is the reflection, in the realm of multiplicity, of its Exemplar, the intelligible Sphere, which is absolutely singular.

The vast difference between the corporeal and the intelligible Sphere is made to serve as the mathematical reconstruction of the relationship between creation and God:

> The creature is called the center because, as time, compared to eternity, is thought a [fleeting] motion, so the creature, compared to God, is a central point. Therefore, the immensity of God is said to be the circumference, because it disposes all things in such a way that it encompasses them and enfolds all things within its

---

[10] Reg. VIIII: "Deus est spaera intelligibilis, cuius centrum ubique, circumferentia nusquam" (PL 210:627). (The scribe regularly used *spaera* for *sphaera*.) There is evidently a relationship between Alan's expression here and that found in the *Liber XXIV Philosophorum* of Pseudo-Hermetic origin. They differ only in the latter's use of *infinitus* where Alan uses *intelligibilis*. This has been studied by Harries (see n. 4 above) and by Michael Keefer, "The World Turned Inside Out: Revolutions of the Infinite Sphere from Hermes to Pascal," *Renaissance and Reformation* 24 (1988): 303-313. Both treat Alan's use as derivative of Hermes. Given their closeness in time, however, this is not obvious; they both may have derived the image from a common source. Keefer considers Alan's use of "intelligible" to remove intelligibility from an already paradoxical image (pp. 303-304), but Alan's exposition of *nomen mathematicum* provides one with an alternative interpretation.

[11] Reg. VII: "O magna inter spaeram corporalem, et intelligibilem differentia!" (PL 210:627).

immensity.[12]

The tone of this passage suggests strongly the absolute character and uncompromised transcendence of God; but the use of mathematics, as Alan understood it, reveals that the same image can be made to represent both God and creation. The intelligible Sphere may differ infinitely from the corporeal sphere but they can be related, through the *nomen mathematicum*, by the figure of the Sphere. This passage introduces two contrasting sets of images: the intelligible Sphere is contrasted with the corporeal sphere and the center (of which sphere?) is contrasted with the circumference.

The fact that Alan juxtaposes these sets of contrasting images without explicitly distinguishing between them raises some perplexing questions. If the first image (God=intelligible Sphere:creature=corporeal sphere) is taken as the norm, what basis exists for the second image (God=circumference:creation=center)? A rather naive juxtaposition makes the corporeal sphere the center of the intelligible Sphere rather than its image or opposite number. Can this be read literally as a figure in which the created cosmos is the center of God? A consistent use of the *nomen mathematicum* as theological method makes such a reading unnecessary. Center need not be accorded the prevailing cultural connotation as point of maximum importance, but, rather, may be viewed strictly in terms of its definition through relationship to circumference. Hence, as is the case with the earth-centered cosmology of Dante's *Commedia divina,* the center may be no more than the first, and therefore lowest, in a series of ordinals. In this sense, creation can indeed be the center of the Sphere which is God, since it is a point whose reality is determined by relation to the circumference. But by virtue of this same relationship, creation must reflect God--an obvious prerequisite to any possibility of creaturely knowledge of God. There can be no *Theologiae regulae* if there is no *theologia.*[13]

Hence, what is absolutely simple must be represented through an image of subtle complexity which tends toward simplicity as its formal object.

---

[12] Reg. VII: "Centrum dicitur creatura, quia sicut tempus collatum aeternitati reputatur momentum, sic creatura immensitati Dei comparata, punctum, vel centrum. Immensitas ergo Dei circumferentia dicitur, quia omnia disponendo quodam modo omnibus circumfertur, et omnia infra suam immensitatem complectitur" (PL 210:627).

[13] There is a very pointed significance behind Alan's title. In the opening paragraph of the *Theologicae regulae,* he explains that he is using the word *regula* to indicate a type of principle that functions in theology in a manner analogous to the rules of grammar, the commonplaces of rhetoric, aphorisms of physics, axioms of music, theorems of geometry, maxims of astronomy, etc. While the modern meanings of some of these words has shifted somewhat, Alan's intention is quite clear.

The attributes of God are reflected, however dimly, in the corporeal sphere which is the created cosmos, and the *nomen mathematicum* provides a way of describing that reflection. This raises another interesting question: if *centrum ubique* refers to the created cosmos, does this suggest that Alan held that this cosmos was spatially infinite?[14]

2. Cusanus' *De ludo globi* in the Light of Alan's Methodology

The ideas discussed here were familiar to Nicholas of Cusa, although he does not explicitly credit Alan as a source. Cusanus' operative concept is encapsulated in the abstract noun *rotunditas* which is used to indicate the mediation (one could almost say the medium of interaction) between God and creation. This *rotunditas* is characterized by its relationship to an absolute norm of perfection which Cusanus identifies as "The roundness which could not be rounder . . ."[15] The most important observation about this expression is its similarity to Anselm's famous formula identifying God in the *Proslogion*: "Something nothing greater than which can be thought."[16] The similarity is not merely one of verbal form since Cusanus acknowledges that this *rotunditas* has a normative role in the ordering of reality: "Since the surface of the [invisible] sphere [is] everywhere equidistant from the center of the sphere, the outer edge of the roundness is terminated in an indivisible point. . . ."[17]

The ordering in question emerges unforced once this *rotunditas* is established and evokes the recognition that *rotunditas quae rotundior esse non posset* must be identical with the intelligible Sphere of Alan of Lille. For how can roundness have a comparative degree? In a strictly geometric sense, all spheres are equally round. Differences in the radius of curvature do not entail differences in degree of roundness. Any change in the mathematical equation identifying a sphere $(x^2 + y^2 + z^2 = R^2)$ other than one of magnitude or position will produce a figure that cannot be identified formally as a sphere. Yet Cusanus, like Anselm, gives the comparative degree a place of fundamental importance in his identifying formula.

His doing so is necessitated by the nature of the relation between singularity and multiplicity. Without the comparative, this relation cannot even

[14] Speculation of this kind is, of course, always dangerous, and it would be injudicious to read a seventeenth-century dispute into Alan's work. What we can conclude is that a spatially infinite cosmos poses no logical or theological contradictions from the standpoint of the *Theologicae regulae*.

[15] *De ludo globi* I, fol. CLIII (Watts, p. 59): "rotunditas quae rotundior esse non posset."

[16] *Proslogion* II: "aliquid quo nihil maius cogitari potest."

[17] *De ludo globi* I, fol. CLIII (Watts, p. 59): "Cum enim superficies a centro spherae undique aeque distet: extremitas rotundi in indivisibili puncto terminita manet penitus nostris oculis invisibilis."

be described, and Cusanus intends not only to describe it but so specify it:

> Roundness cannot be composed out of points for, since a point is indivisible and does not have quantity or parts or a front and back or other differences, it cannot be joined to another point.[18]

For Cusanus, this does not exclude the comparative degree from the realm of *rotunditas*. Rather, it assures that the normative referent of that term lies outside the realm of description. "Therefore, the ultimate spherical roundness of the world, which I believe is the most perfect roundness, never is visible."[19] Since pure *rotunditas* is invisible, the visible sphere can at best be a reflection of the invisible sphere. But this does not yet identify the invisible sphere uniquely, apart from its having the fullness of the perfection termed *rotunditas*. It is significant that Cusanus does not use Alan's term, intelligible Sphere, since his development here runs roughly parallel to that used by Alan in *Regula* VII, and, like Alan, he appears to treat pure form as something that transcends the laws of space, proportion, and distance intrinsic to Euclidean geometry. This is already present in his identification of the circumference with the point,[20] a logical impossibility if extension is given absolute value. "Therefore the edge of the world is not composed of points, but its edge is roundness, which consists in one point."[21]

The circumference of the world, both more extensive and more perfect than anything within it, is an indivisible point. This apparent paradox seems to express the same idea as the *punctum vel centrum* in Alan of Lille.[22] But Cusanus' relativizing of spatial dimension does not end here; he proceeds to treat *rotunditas* as the absolute principle according to which this

---

[18] *De ludo globi* I, fol. CLIII (Watts, p. 59): "Non enim rotunditas: ex punctis potest esse composita, punctus enim cum sit indivisibilis et non habeat aut quantitatem aut partes sive ante sive retro et alias differentias: cum nullo alio puncto est componibilis."

[19] *De ludo globi* I, fol. CLIII (Watts, p. 59): "Ultima igitur mundi spherica rotunditas quam puto perfectissimam: nequaquam est visibilis."

[20] See n. 17 above. This passage clearly identifies the largest of all things, the circumference, with the smallest, a single point. This cannot be meaningful if "length" or "distance" is assumed to have absolute significance, as it does in the physics of Isaac Newton.

[21] *De ludo globi* I, fol. CLIII (Watts, p. 59): "Non est igitur extremitas mundi ex punctis composita: sed eius extremitas est rotunditas quae in puncto consistit."

[22] See n. 10 above. Infinite space is as a point when compared with the divine immensity, and yet the divine singularity is itself best represented by a point.

relativizing must take place:

> Only length and width can be seen. But in roundness nothing is
> long or wide or straight. Roundness is a kind of circumference, a
> certain convexity led around from point to point whose top is ev-
> erywhere. And its top is the atom, invisible because of its tini-
> ness.[23]

Rotunditas, equated here with circumference, is also equated with the
vanishing smallness of punctitude. The circumference is pointlike. The significance of the elaborate image developed here is not immediately evident,
since it requires that the most expansive of all things also be the most focused. Spatially, this would require that the largest also be the smallest,
which is impossible. It is as if Cusanus were trying to turn Alan's image
inside out.

Indeed, approaching Cusanus' sphere as just such an inversion may provide the clearest access to its significance.[24] The circumference of the world
can be taken, to put it simply, as the dividing line between God and the
world. All that is on this side of the circumference, in all its expansiveness
and complexity, is created; all that is beyond is uncreated. But since all
things are ordered with respect to that circumference, it must be singular and
indivisible as well as invisible and thus pointlike, the point at which God
touches the world. What is beyond the circumference is therefore also within the point, an orientation incapable of conception in spatial terms. One
could dismiss this as a bizarre mixing of metaphors, but there is an inner

---

[23] *De ludo globi* I, fol. CLIII-CLIIIv (Watts, p. 59): "Solum enim longum
latum et videri potest, sed in rotunditate nihil longum et latum seu directum: sed
circumductio quaedam et circunducta quaedam de puncto ad punctum convexitas
cuius summum est ubique et est atomus sua parvitate invisibilis."

[24] The inversion bears comparison with the interplay of distance and time
found in Einstein's special theory of relativity. No implication is contained
herein that Cusanus anticipated Einstein; more likely, this is simply a case in
which two unrelated avenues led to convergent conclusions. Nevertheless, the
mechanics of the theory of relativity can aid in one's understanding of this idea.
For the theory leads to the conclusion that there exists no absolutely fixed way
to define either a distance or an elapsed time in the absence of the other. Given
the observed invariance of the speed of light in a vaccuum, these quantities can
be defined consistently only with respect to each other, and thus cannot form an
absolute framework. Cusanus arrives at the relativizing of these quantities in an
entirely different way: his logic of perfection demands that the largest coincide
with the smallest. For more on Einstein's development of the theory of relativity, see Abraham Pais, *"Subtle Is the Lord . . .": The Science and the Life of
Albert Einstein* (Oxford, 1982).

logic which supports the identity of the Beyond with the Within. It is as if everything in the cosmos converges on the point which is also the circum-ference, pregnant with the possibility of encountering, but never seeing or grasping, what lies hidden beyond it. The point as circumference signifies such an encounter with what is of infinite depth.

This interpretation is supported by Cusanus' use of the formula *rotun-ditas quae rotundior esse non posset* in harmony with Anselm's formula. The foremost difference between them is that Anselm's *aliquid* is the horizon of intellectual activity while Cusanus uses the geometric aspect of the world to mediate between the concrete and the pure form. Nowhere is it more evi-dent that Cusanus, intentionally or not, has made Alan's method of *nomen mathematicum* his own. This interpretation returns in Cusanus' discussion of time and eternity[25] and in his numerological study.[26] The relationship between the roundness of the world and the absolute roundness of the singu-larity is explained in the following manner:

> The round world is not that roundness itself than which no round-ness can be greater, but that roundness than which nothing can ac-tually be greater. Absolute roundness is not of the nature of the roundness of the world, but is its cause and exemplar; the absolute roundness of which the roundness of the world is the image. I see the image of eternity in a circle where there is nether a beginning nor an end since there is no point in it which would be the begin-ning rather than the end.[27]

This leads into a discussion of time and eternity, in which the theme of God's relationship to the world and the manner in which God created the world are developed. God and the world relate to each other as absolute and relative; but, by using the image of the Sphere for both God and the world, Cusanus places the emphasis upon the world as a reflection of God and upon the possibility of knowing God through the world. Absolute *rotunditas* is

[25] On the question of time and eternity, see *De ludo globi* II, fol. CLXIII (Watts, p. 103). This treatment should be compared with Augustine's writing on the subject in the *Confessions*.

[26] For Cusanus' treatment of numerology, see *De ludo globi* II, fol. CLXIII-CLXIII (Watts, pp. 99, 101); II, fol. CLXV (Watts, p. 107); II, fol. CLXVIv-CLXVII (Watts, pp. 113, 115).

[27] *De ludo globi* I, fol. CLIIII (Watts, p. 63): "Rotundus enim mundus non est ipsa rotunditas qua maior non est: sed qua maior non est actu. Absoluta vero rotunditas non est de natura rotunditatis mundi: sed eius causa et exemplar cuius rotunditas mundi est imago. In circulo enim ubi non est principium nec finis cum nullus punctus in eo sit qui potius sit principium quam finis: video imaginem trinitatis." (For *qua maior non est*, Gabriel has *qua maior esse nequit*.)

invisible, but *rotunditas* as a perfection is grasped readily. We cannot imagine the Reality hidden within the point-singularity that at the same time cir-
cumscribes the world, but we can approach it asymptotically through the
way geometric entities resolve themselves into the point. The language is
not that of sheer, unmediated paradox, but of opposition mediated by the hierarchy of being. Thus, the *coincidentia oppositorium* entails the *nomen
mathematicum*.

Even more interesting is Cusanus' development of the theme of the
imago trinitatis. It is built around the same image in which the center coincides with the circumference. But here it is taken further. Cusanus finds in
the mystery of the Trinity the inner dimension of both point and world, or
that which is more singular than undifferentiated unity itself:

> Moreover unity is more perfect and simple to the degree that it is
> more uniting. Hence the Trinity, which is one in such a way that it
> is also in three persons, each of which is one, is more perfect.
> And unity would not be most perfect in any other way.[28]

The point-singularity contains the unity between God and the world.
On the inner side of it, God remains hidden and yet present to the world. It
is clear that Cusanus has identified a hierarchy of value among the things of
the world and that roundness, punctitude, simplicity, and circumference are
his preferred images for the apex of hierarchy. It is equally clear that, while
God is the term of this progression, God is not one element in a series, but
rather is that which gives the progression its orientation. Therefore, God
must remain distinct from elements of the progression considered both indi-
vidually and *in toto*.

In the light of this, the occasional suggestion that Cusanus was a pan-
theist becomes untenable. His own words explicitly identify a hierarchical
scheme of progression:

> Since in round things it is necessary to arrive at one actually exis-
> tent maximum, just as in hot things it is necessary to arrive at fire,
> which is the maximum in heat, there will therefore be only one

---

[28] *De ludo globi* I, fol. CLVI (Watts, p. 71): "Unitas autem quanto magis
uniens: tanto simplicior et perfectior. Hinc unitrina perfectior, quae sic est una
quod etiam in tribus personis quarum quaelibet est una ipsa est una. Et non esset
aliter perfectissima unitas." This constitutes an argument for the appropriateness
of God's being Trinity, and as such it is almost identical to that proposed by
Bonaventure in his *Quaestiones Disputatae de Mysterio Trinitatis*, II, 2. Critical
edition: Quaracci (1882-1902) 5:45-115. These works form part of a larger tradition that sees in the Trinity not unresolved paradox, but truth that is most emi-
nently fitting.

world. And this one world is so round that it comes closest to maximally eternal roundness itself.[29]

The context requires that *rotunditas* be treated as a perfection--perhaps the highest perfection. The *rotunditas* of material objects, the least perfect,[30] reflects the intelligible *rotunditas* of pure geometry, and leads up to the point that is also the circumference which in turn reflects its divine Exemplar. This progression is presented even more explicitly in his discussion of the hierarchical ordering of the heavenly spheres:

> The division of the heavens can also be hunted to some extent, for certain saints have understood there to be a visible heaven and an intelligible heaven and an intellectual heaven and three divisions in each heaven, so that a ninefold of heavens is completed inside the tenth where the seat of God is, above the cherubim.[31]

Each of these spheres in turn possesses a higher degree of the normative perfection of *rotunditas* than that which preceded it, and accordingly manifests a higher degree of unity, simplicity, and singularity. This can conclude only at the point which is also the circumference, beyond which is God.

3. Some Inferences

In *De ludo globi* Cusanus offers neither a theological treatise on God nor a handbook of natural philosophy, but sets forth a vision of the relationship between God and the world, a vision which is expressed in terms quite compatible with the *nomen mathematicum* of Alan of Lille. Sphericity in the material cosmos gives way to the *rotunditas* of the purely intelligible, which in turn gives way to the absolutely singular. The hierarchy of beings reflects the hierarchy of intelligibles, which in turn reflects the unity in Trinity which is God. The problem of the one and the many is resolved by

---

[29] *De ludo globi* I, fol. CLIIII (Watts, p. 63): "Nam cum in rotundis ad unum maximum actu necesse sit devenire: sicut inter calida ad ignem qui est maxime calidus: erit igitur unus tantum mundus, et hic tantum habet rotunditatis: quod ad ipsam rotunditatem aeternam maxime accedit."

[30] Cusanus compares the heavenly spheres with those produced by the woodworker's art. See *De ludo globi* I, fol. CLV (Watts, p. 67).

[31] *De ludo globi* II, fol. CLXIIII (Watts, p. 103): "possunt et coelorum discretione: aliquatenus venari, nam coelum visibile et coelum intelligibile et coelum intellectuale: quidam sancti esse comprehenderunt, et in quodlibet trinam distinctionem: ut novenarius coelorum in denario (ubi est sedes dei super cherubim) perficiatur." (Gabriel has *discretiones* for *discretione* and *quodlibet* for *in quodlibet*.)

finding in God a unity even greater than the unity of the number one itself:

> Consequently you must open up the gaze of your mind, and you will see that God is in all multitude because he is in the number one, and in every magnitude because he is in the point. From this it is established that divine simplicity is more subtle than the number one and the point which gives the unfolding power of multitude and magnitude. Hence God is a greater enfolding power than that enfolding power of the number one or of a point.[32]

The nature of this resolution is found in the exploration of the dynamics of *rotunditas*, once it is recognized as a perfection. It is indeed comparative, but the greater *rotunditas* is not as accessible as the lesser (which is to be expected in such an order), and the highest *rotunditas* is invisible. Hence for Cusanus as well as for Alan of Lille, the Sphere is the representation of God, of the world, and of the relationship between God and the world. Here one must take issue with Karsten Harries who sees a gradual transition (and one which he deems necessary) from the infinite sphere as a metaphor for God to a metaphor for the created cosmos.[33] I do not find evidence for such an evolution, since it seems that as early as Alan of Lille, the world as sphere is treated as a reflection of God as Sphere. Cusanus appears to be placing himself solidly within this tradition in which the geometry of the sphere represents that which is most perfect in the cosmos and which, therefore, is best suited to revealing the presence of God in that cosmos.

In Thomistic terms, *rotunditas*, like Being itself, both unites and distinguishes God and the world. God is joined to the world by this perfection, and yet the *rotunditas* of God is invisible to the world because it is more a point than the point itself. God and the world clearly do not possess this perfection in the same manner. Yet this very fact gives understanding to the point which is both center and circumference, and this, in turn, relativizes the reality of spatial extension so as to give transcendent significance to the sense of order and direction of the world. In the absence of the latter, no truly human activity is possible. Both thought and love presuppose a directedness in human affairs which is not an arbitrary creation of human activity, but which is, nevertheless, manifest in human activity. It is precisely such

---

[32] *De ludo globi* II, fol. CLXIIIv-CLXIIII (Watts, pp. 101, 103): "Consequenter aperi mentis obtutum et videbis deum in omni multitudine esse quia est in uno et in omni magnitudine: quia est in puncto, ex quo constat ut quod divina simplicitas subtilior est uno et puncto: quibus dat virtutem complicativam multitudinis et magnitudinis, quare deus est virtus magis complicativa quam unius et puncti."

[33] See n. 4 above.

a directedness which is enfolded in the perfection of *rotunditas*. This makes sense only when it is recognized that Cusanus treats *rotunditas* in a manner analogous to the way the transcendental attributes of Being (unity, truth, goodness, beauty) are treated by Thomists. Instead of the analogy of Being, we have here the analogy of *rotunditas*.

While this entire discussion can be treated as purely metaphorical, our study of the work of Alan of Lille suggests a different interpretation. In his *Theologicae regulae*, the mathematical manner of connotation is neither literal, nor metaphorical, nor symbolic. It is irreducible to any other form. While Cusanus does not directly refer to Alan, application of the method of the *nomen mathematicum* to the *De ludo globi* does emphasize the special role played by the Sphere in Cusanus' thought. There is, on the one hand, the material cosmos in which spherical structures and forms are very much in evidence. Even though it has become a cliche of the scientific world to discredit the medieval notion of the Sphere as a perfect form, that notion seems to re-emerge under other guises.[34] But, on the other hand, there is the absolute perfection of God whom Alan calls the "intelligible Sphere." Here it is not a question of geometry but of pure perfection---absolute unity, truth, goodness, beauty. What is at issue is the relationship between God and the world. Alan sees the mathetical sphere as the mediant of this relationship, expressing the visible sphere of the world as the image of the intelligible Sphere which is God. While Cusanus does not use this terminology, his work implies it. Furthermore, he expands the concept by placing the cosmos on the near side of *rotunditas*, which is both point and circumference, and God on the far side. In this way there is room for intellectual mediation of the relationship between God and the world, while God remains beyond the world.

---

[34]   Perhaps the most striking example is the emphasis on various forms of "symmetry" in the search for a unified field theory in physics. Other principles invoked, such as that of simplicity ("Among competing theories, the simplest is to be preferred"), also require non-empirical criteria that bear more than a coincidental resemblance to the medieval fascination with circular and spherical forms. The similarity lies in the simplicity of description necessary for the spherical form, a consequence of its symmetry.

WHAT DID NICHOLAS OF CUSA CONTRIBUTE TO SCIENCE?

A. Richard Hunter

Perhaps one should qualify the title to say "What--if anything--did Cusanus contribute to science?" The status of the Cardinal in the history of science is, at best, paradoxical and dubious. On the one hand, it has been minimized by many from Copernicus to McTighe.[1] On the other hand, Cusanus has tantalized philosophers of science who have been unable to ignore him, explain him away, or give a satisfying assessment of his thought.

We should not avoid the most obvious fact at the outset: Nicholas is not doing science primarily to advance our knowledge of nature, but rather to advance our knowledge of God and to explore the limitations of our knowledge and wisdom. His work shares this characteristic with that of most medieval contributors to science such as Roger Bacon and Robert Grosseteste. Many of these contributors were members of religious communities (Bacon) or bishops (Cusanus and Grosseteste). Often the purpose of their writing was theological or metaphysical, and Cusanus was firmly in this tradition.

We may well ask whether this is a positive or negative factor regarding his contribution to science. It would seem negative in determining the primary application of his energy and intelligence. Science was not his main concern, so it should not surprise us if his contributions are minor. However, if his thought alters ways of thinking, making scientific thinking more "modern" than it was before, then it may not matter so much what his discipline was, but rather who read his works. In that case, the prestige of the author and also of the subject may matter more than the purpose of the work. Theology and philosophy were, after all, very respectable in those days, not to mention cardinals.

Therefore, we must investigate not only Cusanus' purely scientific ideas but, perhaps more importantly, his "philosophy of nature." Did he alter the scientific mentality and world view of later thinkers? It is here, I think, that we shall discover Nicholas' main contribution. We can only mention in passing the related task of finding out more specifically which thinkers he influenced.

[1] See the important study by Thomas P. McTighe, "Nicholas of Cusa's Philosophy of Science and its Metaphysical Background," *Nicolò Cusano agli inizi del mondo moderno* (Florence, 1964), pp. 317-338. Raymond Klibansky has demonstrated that Copernicus did know Cusanus' *De docta ignorantia* II (McTighe, p. 317). We shall say more below regarding McTighe's estimate of Cusanus' contribution.

1. Scientific Ideas

Several of Cusanus' scientific notions are found in Book II of *De docta ignorantia* and are well known to historians of science. First is the so-called "infinity," or limitlessness, of the world.

> The Absolute Maximum alone is negatively infinite. . . . It cannot, in
> fact, be greater than it is, for this reason that possibility or matter
> lacks the power to extend beyond itself. . . . Since, then, nothing that
> would be a limit to the universe, by being greater than it, is able
> actually to exist, we may call the universe limitless and therefore
> privatively infinite.[2]

Apparently, Nicholas is saying that within the universe matter could only be "limited" as to position by other matter; but this other matter would be part of the universe, too. So, the universe has no physical boundary. Matter cannot be outside of the condition of matter. This does not appear to prohibit the physical expansion of the universe, although the idea seems not to have occurred to Cusanus.

Alexandre Koyré cites Descartes' letter to Chanut regarding some concerns of Queen Christina of Sweden.[3] Descartes offers Nicholas as a reference for the idea of the world's infinity "without ever being reproached by the church; on the contrary, it is believed that to make His works appear very great is to honor God." It is here, too (*De docta ignorantia* II, 1), that the notion of imprecision (as derived from the mathematical studies of the first book) is applied to the physical universe. This allows the development of the idea of infinity. Neither in movement, nor in "time and space" (*tempore et situ*), nor in music, etc., are two things equal in the material world, but only in God. Although the absolute infinity is never achieved in our universe, no limit may be set either to greatness or smallness.

It should be noted that *De docta ignorantia* was written after the work *De correctione kalendarii* from his Council of Basel days. In that work he displays familiarity with many of the historical sources in astronomy, Greek

[2] *De docta ignorantia* II, 1, #97 (h I, 64-65): "Solum igitur absolute maximum est negative infinitum; . . . (Universum) Non enim potest esse maius quam est; . . . possibilitas enim sive materia ultra se non extendit . . . et ita interminatum, cum actu maius eo dabile non sit, ad quod terminatur; et sic privative infinitum." English from *Of Learned Ignorance*, trans. Germain Heron (New Haven, 1954), pp. 70-71 (hereafter referred to as Heron). See also chap. 11 in this connection. In the passage quoted above and several others in *De docta ignorantia* II, Nicholas states that the world and individual things are as perfect (relatively to their own nature) as possible. See also "everything in everything," *De docta ignorantia* II, 5.

[3] Alexandre Koyré, *From the Closed World to the Infinite Universe* (Baltimore, 1957), pp. 6-7 and n. 8.

and Muslim as well as Western European, and discusses their varying estimates of the anomalies in the calendar. The problem is quite complex, since, in order to determine the date of Easter, several factors are involved. The length of a lunar month must be known and, for future prediction, so must the exact ratio between this and the calendar year. In fact, several cycles allow the approximation of this ratio, but none are exact. It might be said that the ratios, of day to year for example, are incommensurable, as Cusanus suspected. They are known also to vary slowly over time.

The most fundamental difficulty is that there is a slight difference between the actual year and the Julian calendar year of 365.25 days. The actual solar year is a fraction of a day shorter. Over more than a millenium and a half, the date of the actual Vernal Equinox had slipped back nearly 10 days earlier than its assumed date of March 21. This caused a discrepancy in the date of Easter, which was the point of ecclesiastical interest.[4] Many of the ancient and medieval astronomers made their own estimates of these various factors and cycles, and Nicholas recounts them. He does not discuss their observations, nor does he undertake any of his own. But he does appreciate the difficulty of accurate observations. One of the critical days

> is not to be measured without the greatest diligence and large instruments, but an error of the conjunctions of as much as a day or two may easily be seen from the sighting of the risen moon.[5]

[4] For discussions of the history and accuracy of the Julian and Gregorian calendars, see e.g., *Van Nostrand's Scientific Encyclopedia,* ed. Douglas M. Considine, 6th ed. (New York, 1983), article "Calendar," p. 490; Gordon Moyer, "Luigi Lilio and the Gregorian Reform of the Calendar," *Sky and Telescope* 64 (1982): 419. Note that the Gregorian reform was instituted in 1582 by Pope Gregory XIII, at which time 10 days were omitted from the calendar and three leap year days per 400 years were eliminated for the future. For example, the years 1700, 1800, and 1900 were not leap years, but 2000 will be. A century year is only a leap year when it is divisible by 400 as well as by 4.

[5] Nicolaus Cusanus (Nikolaus von Kues), *Die Kalenderverbesserung. De correctione kalendarii* (German-Latin ed., Heidelberg, 1955), chap. 3, p. 30: "Nec etiam ipsa dies nisi per maximam diligentiam et magna instrumenta mensuraretur, sed error coniunctionum quoad diem aut duos ex visu exortae lunae facile conspicitur." My translation. I thank my colleague, Dr. Marilyn Jahn, for reading the German version and discussing it with me. An unambiguous astronomical interpretation of this may await a more complete reading of the work. It may be said that the moon is unob-servable at "new" phase because of its proximity to the sun in the sky. It will be observable as a rising crescent a day or two (or three. . .) before new, depending on many factors. Therefore the estimation of the actual time of new moon by observation would have been difficult in Cusanus' time.

Even more important as background for this doctrine of inequality is the notion that the "supercelestial movement" may be "incommensurable with human reason," or possibly that both reason and instruments are imperfect.[6] The unboundedness of the cosmos and the inexact measurements of real things and motions would seem to imply an absence of absolute space. Indeed, for Nicholas, this is the case. However, although the universe is unbounded ("privatively infinite," as noted above), we should not attribute to Cusanus any discussion of the nature or extent of space as such, as Edward Grant makes clear in *Much Ado About Nothing*.[7]

This leads to Cusanus' much vaunted and disputed theory of the earth's motion, as well as his theory of the plurality of worlds and a common matter for the earth and stars. To recount only briefly, the following from *De docta ignorantia* II, 11 will illustrate the relativity of space and the earth's motion:

> . . . we see that it is impossible for the motor of the world to have the material earth, air, fire, or anything else for a fixed, immovable centre. In movement there is no absolute minimum, like a fixed centre, since necessarily the minimum and maximum are identical. . . .
> It is evident from the foregoing that the earth is in movement.[8]

While he does refer to observational evidence in this discussion ("from the movement of a comet . . .," etc.),[9] the very vagueness, both of the account of the motion and that of the observational grounds for the claims, indicates a man who read astronomy and studied even its mathematical aspects, but who was undoubtedly too busy to observe on his own. Indeed, one should remember that, in the *De docta ignorantia*, the purpose is always to develop wisdom in matters relating to our understanding of God.

[6] *De correctione kalendarii*, chap. 2, p. 18. The passage has to do with an oscillatory motion of the equinoctial points, called trepidation (and in fact fictitious). Cusanus cites the Arab astronomer Thebit (in Cusanus' Latin) or Tabit ibn Qurra, and mentions Tabit's doubts. Although the *De correctione kalendarii* may not count as one of Cusanus' major treatises, more work needs to be done on it, particularly in English. Even most historians of science seem to have slighted this work.

[7] Edward Grant, *Much Ado About Nothing* (Cambridge, 1981), pp. 138-140. See Pauline M. Watts' discussion in her Introduction to *Nicholas de Cusa*, De ludo globi: *The Game of Spheres* (New York, 1986), p. 18.

[8] *De docta ignorantia* II, 11, #156 (h I, 99-100): "Propter quod machinam mundanam habere aut istam terram sensibilem aut aerem vel ignem vel aliud quodcumque pro centro fixo et immobili variis motibus orbium considerantis est impossibile. . . ." *De docta ignorantia* II, 11, #159 (h I, 102): "Ex hiis quidem manifestum est terram moveri." (Heron, p. 109).

[9] *De docta ignorantia* II, 11, #159 (h I, 102).

Only in God, then, are we able to find a centre which is with perfect precision equidistant from all points, for He alone is infinite equality. God, ever to be blessed, is, therefore, the centre of the world: He it is who is centre of the earth, of all spheres and of all things in the world; and at the same time He is the infinite circumference of all.[10]

This passage must be viewed in the context of a discussion of the coincidence of opposites in God, and Cusanus' claim that God is the only true absolute. The concrete result is that the physical universe can have no physical center or boundary. Another consequence is the limitation of knowledge of the physical universe; such knowledge is never exact or absolute. This, of course, is in keeping with modern views of scientific knowledge. However, the skepticism of this viewpoint can be exaggerated, as is indicated by the following:

> Nicholas of Cusa in the fifteenth century extended this line of thought to physics. . . . None but the Divine Intelligence is capable of grasping the true essential nature and the veritable causes, . . . of any part of the physical universe whatsoever. [Human science] must content itself perforce with fictitious and hypothetical conceptions and with fictitious and hypothetical causes. By these means it may approximate indefinitely to the absolute truth, but it can never attain this goal.[11]

Theologically, we must appreciate how vastly short of exact is our knowledge of God, or indeed of his creation. Hence, "learned ignorance." However, in this state, we still attain knowledge that is useful and brings us to an appreciation of God, on the one hand, and practical (though limited and approximate) knowledge of the world, on the other. An example of the latter is the astronomical knowledge needed for the calendar reform:

> Although from all these human experiments [or observations], no certitude can be had from past to future positions of the planetary

---

[10] *De docta ignorantia* II, 11 #157 (h I, 101): "Aequedistantia praecisa et diversa extra Deum reperibilis non est, quia ipse solus est infinita aequalitas. Qui igitur est centrum mundi, scilicet Deus benedictus, ille est centrum terrae et omnium sphaerarum atque omnium, quae in mundo sunt; qui est simul omnium circumferentia infinita." (Heron, p. 108).

[11] Ralph M. Blake, Curt J. Ducasse, and Edward H. Madden, *Theories of Scientific Method: The Renaissance Through the Nineteenth Century* (Seattle, 1960), p. 25.

motions, except as the order and regularity of the motions that have been found permit future positions to be anticipated.[12]

If "certitude" means exact knowledge, then there is none. No exact ratios will enable everything to be predicted exactly. Yet the observations do permit useful predictions, and that is the essence of the modern view of science, though it may be disappointing in an epistemological sense.

Despite the theological context and purpose of this discussion, Nicholas' interest in the physical world seems real, legitimate, and well-informed for his time. For example, he was the one selected to report to the Council on calendar reform. Despite the doubts and reservations of many, it has been necessary to take account of him in many serious discussions of scientific history, as we see in the various citations here. And some of the people who admired him early in the scientific revolutions were the ones making the revolutions, such as Kepler.[13]

In *De docta ignorantia* II, 12 we see a discussion of relative observers, continuing the theme of the relative nature of the physical universe in relationship to God. But the even more interesting idea of the plurality of worlds is developed here, an idea distinctly un-Aristotelian and un-Scholastic, not only in itself, but also for its implication that there is a common materiality of the cosmos.

> On examination the body of the sun is found to be disposed like this: nearer the center there is a sort of earth, at the circumference a sort of fiery brightness and midway between them a kind of watery cloud and

---

[12] *De correctione kalendarii,* chap. 10, p. 86: "Licet ex his omnibus humanis experimentis particulariter captis nulla ex motu luminarium de praeterito certitudo ad futura habeatur nisi quantum ordo et regularitas inventorum motuum praesumi de futuris permittit." The translation is Grant's, except that I have translated *experimentis* literally instead of his "experiences." Notice that Grant omitted to translate *particulariter captis.* The passage might begin, more literally, "Although from all these human experiments *taken in particular,* no certitude . . ." Nicole Oresme, *Nicole Oresme and the Kinematics of Circular Motion,* Tractatus de commensurabilitate et incommensurabilitate motuum coeli, ed. with intro., trans., and commentary by Edward Grant (Madison, 1971), p. 143n. Grant is discussing here whether Nicholas is skeptical regarding astronomical knowledge. He concludes that "it is by no means obvious that Cusa is a complete skeptic on astronomical matters. . . ." See also Pauline M. Watts' discussion in *Nicolaus Cusanus: A Fifteenth-Century Vision of Man* (Leiden, 1982), pp. 61-65.

[13] Johannes Kepler, *Kepler's Conversation with Galileo's Sidereal Messenger,* trans. Edward Rosen (New York, 1965), p. 11, and see Rosen's discussion on p. 64, n. 56.

clearer air. Just as this earth, the sun has its own elements.[14]

So the sun has its own elements like the earth. As J. L. E. Dreyer says, "he reasons very sensibly about the nature of the heavenly bodies."[15] Nicholas goes on to claim that the "earth, then, is a brilliant [more literally, 'noble'] star having a light, heat and influence distinctly its own, . . ."[16] and even discusses the inhabitants of the celestial regions, whom he supposes to be of all types and degrees of perfection.[17]

These are not modern concepts; the elements are Aristotelian, though without the quintessence of the heavens. The earth and moon give off their own light due to their fiery upper regions, just as the sun does. And today, of course, extraterrestrial life is sought in reliable scientific investigations, but has not been found as yet. So, many regions may in fact be inhabited, though not necessarily all.

The modern critical reaction to all this varies, to say the least. Dreyer (original publication dated 1905) is interested and respectful enough to follow up a reference to an unpublished note of Cusanus describing the earth's motion and discuss it carefully. The rotation of the stars seems to be attributed both to the earth's axial rotation and to the star sphere, with discussion of other motions included. Since Nicholas purchased the manuscript in which this note is found in 1444, the note is later than the *De docta ignorantia* and demonstrates, among other things, his ongoing

---

[14] *De docta ignorantia* II, 12, #164 (h I, 105): "Considerato enim corpore solis, tunc habet quandam quasi terram centraliorem et quandam luciditatem quasi ignilem circumferentialem et in medio quasi aquiam nubem et aerem clariorem, quemadmodum terra sua ista elementa." (Heron, p. 112 [trans. of the final clause is my own]).

[15] J. L. E. Dreyer, *A History of Astronomy from Thales to Kepler* (New York: Dover, 2nd ed. 1953), pp. 284-285.

[16] *De docta ignorantia* II, 12, #166 (h I, 105): "Est igitur terra stella nobilis, quae lumen et calorem et influentiam habet . . ." (Heron, p. 113).

[17] *De docta ignorantia* II, 12, #166 (h I, 105). (Heron, pp. 115-116).

interest in the topic.[18] Dreyer concludes with more admiration for Nicholas' open mind than for any specific result:

> He was solely guided by his preconceived notion, that motion is universal to all bodies, and by thus settling the affairs of the universe out of his inner consciousness he reminds us of the early Greek philosophers, who had done the same over and over again, without being overburdened with too great a store of observed facts. All the same, he was not afraid to speculate freely on the constitution of the world without being a slave either to theology or to Aristotle, but he probably did not think his ideas ripe for publication and therefore in his books limited himself to generalities.[19]

Lynn Thorndike, in his chapter on Nicholas, is frankly disappointed, finding Cusanus' thought overrated by earlier historians of science. This chapter is little more than an occasionally witty denunciation of exaggerated scholarly claims and what McTighe calls "precursoritis."[20]

Koyré, in *From the Closed World to the Infinite Universe*, gives our Cardinal a respectful and careful hearing, but is somewhat critical of the scientific content. For example, the notions of the autonomous light of the earth and moon are "not in advance of but rather behind his time, . . ."[21] Koyré, like Dreyer, gives Cusanus credit as a speculative thinker:

> The world-conception of Nicholas of Cusa is not based upon a criticism of contemporary astronomical or cosmological theories, and does not lead, *at least in his own thinking* to a revolution in science [my emphasis]. Nicholas of Cusa, though it has often been so claimed, is not a forerunner of Nicholas Copernicus. And yet his conception is extremely interesting and, in some of its bold assertions--or

[18] Dreyer, *A History of Astronomy*, pp. 285-287. The note is more precisely located by Lynn Thorndike in *Science and Thought in the Fifteenth Century* (New York, 1929), p. 139. It is Cod. Cus. 211, fol. 55v in the Cusanus Library at Kues. The astronomical work purchased in September 1444 is apparently bound with other more astrological works. Cusanus' continuing interest in astronomy may also be seen in his purchase, also in 1444, of four astronomical instruments which are still in his library at Kues. See George Sarton, *Six Wings: Men of Science in the Renaissance* (Bloomington, 1957), p. 264. We can wonder what might have happened with regard to his contribution to astronomy if his life had been less taken up with the ecclesiastical controversies and administrative business. Of course the same might be said with regard to several branches of philosophy and theology!

[19] Dreyer, *A History of Astonomy*, p. 288.

[20] Thorndike, *Science and Thought*, pp. 133-141. McTighe, "Philosophy of Science," pp. 317-318.

[21] Koyré, *From the Closed World*, p. 19.

negations--it goes far beyond anything Copernicus ever dared to think of.[22]

Koyré concludes that

> . . . a new spirit, the spirit of the Renaissance, breathes in the work of Cardinal Nicholas of Cusa. His world is no longer the medieval cosmos. But it is not yet, by any means, the infinite universe of the moderns.[23]

This would seem to explain how we find the elucidation of Cusanus' ideas at the very beginning of Koyré's book. Notice that Koyré is exploring a change in mentality, or world view, rather than the scientific revolutions themselves. It is in this context, as we shall see, that the true value and originality of Cusanus' thought may be shown.

McTighe, too, attributes the significance of Nicholas' thought to the "theory of science":

> Nonetheless, if it is true that science is not a direct intelligible transcription of the ontological structures in the domain of sensible being, but rather a schematization whose trajectory to the sensible order is indirect and constructural, then in this respect Cusa's philosophy of science is much closer than that of the great Galileo himself to the actual conditions of the scientific enterprise.[24]

In connection with the modern scientific interest in the question of life in the universe, Steven J. Dick of the U.S. Naval Observatory, reviewing the history of the notion of extraterrestrial life, notes Cusanus' originality:

> Another crucial idea to emerge out of the late Middle Ages was extraterrestrial, even extracosmic, life. Not since Epicurus and Lucretius had mentioned in passing that the seeds of life were undoubtedly spread throughout innumerable worlds had this been a prominent concept. But Cusa stressed the point without apology: . . . Here was a view totally antithetical to Aristotle. . . . For the first time

---

[22] Koyré, *From the Closed World*, p. 8, and see n. 10.

[23] Koyré, *From the Closed World*, pp. 23-24.

[24] McTighe, "Philosophy of Science," p. 319; longer quotation, p. 337.

in history Cusa extended the scale of living being beyond the Earth and indeed into the whole universe. . . .[25]

This contrast between scientific content and scientific, or universal, world view probably accounts for the great variety of critical attitudes toward our author. Much of the previous research cited in our earlier references indicates that Cusanus was famous and widely read and respected in the succeeding two centuries. The critical assessment of whether he has any impact on the coming of "modern times" seems to depend on whether the primary concern of the critic is content or philosophy.

Two of Cusanus' scientific ideas have so far escaped mention: the work on impetus in the *De ludo globi* and the *Idiota* dialogues, particularly *Idiota. De staticis experimentis*. While Pauline Watts has discussed the subject in *De ludo globi*,[26] we will turn our attention to the *Idiota* works.

2. Experiments and the Scientific Mentality

I, too, think that Nicholas' prime contribution to the scientific age is philosophical. One of the main characteristics of the modern scientific method is experimentation. Although Cusanus is by no means the originator of the idea of gaining knowledge through experiments, his use of it, together with his popularity and prestige in the next centuries, may well have helped raise it to consciousness for succeeding thinkers.

Despite the rationalism of Greek thought in general, even Aristotle shows at least a slight empirical bent. Consider *Nicomachean Ethics* I, 8 1098b 9-13:

> We must consider it [the good], however, in the light not only of our conclusion and our premises, but also of what is commonly said about it; for with a true view all the data harmonize, but with a false one the facts soon clash [more literally, "truth soon clashes"].[27]

[25] Steven J. Dick, *Plurality of Worlds: The Origins of the Extraterrestrial Life Debate From Democritus to Kant* (Cambridge, 1982), p. 41 and notes. See also Pierre Duhem, *Medieval Cosmology*, ed. and trans. Roger Ariew (Chicago, 1985) pp. 505-510. He concludes: "The first time in Western Christianity that one heard someone speak about the plurality of inhabited worlds, it was proposed by a theologian who had spoken before an ecumenical council a few years before. . . . There can be no greater proof of the extreme liberality of the Catholic church during the close of the Middle Ages toward the meditations of the philosopher and the experiments of the physicist."

[26] *De ludo globi* I, fol. CLIIIv (Watts, *Nicholas de Cusa*, pp. 64-65).

[27] *The Basic Works of Aristotle*, ed. Richard McKeon (New York, 1941), p. 944.

I have used this passage with students to urge an observational and "scientific" approach to the study of ethics, although Aristotle was certainly aware of induction and also of the inexactness of ethics and many other subjects. Yet his position in the history of medieval science is equivocal. On the one hand, his many works of natural philosophy and his naturalistic and at least somewhat empirical approach appear to support the development of science.[28] Indeed, ecclesiastical authorities sometimes viewed his ideas as a threat to doctrines, such as that of divine omnipotence. This led, among other things, to the Condemnation of 1277. Paradoxically enough, one effect of the condemnation was to allow the theologian/scientists of the age to think some thoughts that were unthinkable to Aristotelians, such as void space, infinite space, etc.[29]

On the other hand, following the creative use of Aristotle by thinkers like St. Thomas Aquinas, the later Scholastics often accepted his ideas as authoritative, dismissing scientific or even theological ideas that appeared incompatible with those of "the Philosopher." This has led to the frequent but simplistic modern attacks on Aristotle as an impediment to scientific thought and progress.

The idea of experimental science was certainly raised during the Middle Ages. It may be seen in the Franciscan tradition of "to God through nature," and is certainly visible in the work of the Franciscan friar, Roger Bacon:

> Therefore, since all parts of speculative philosophy proceed by arguments which are based either on grounds of authority or on other grounds of argumentation, except this part which I am now investigating, that science is necessary to us which is called experimentation. And I want to explain it, as it is useful not only to philosophy but to the wisdom of God and to the guidance of the whole world, . . .
>
> This science alone, then, knows how to test perfectly by experience what can be done by nature, what by the industry of art, . . . This science alone teaches one to consider all the insanities of magicians, not that they may be confirmed but that they may be avoided, . . . I use the

---

[28] This is not the place for extensive research on the scientific method in Aristotle's philosophy, but note the brief discussion in *Introduction to Aristotle,* ed. Richard McKeon (New York, 1947), pp. xiii-xvii (in the "General Introduction").

[29] With regard to the scientific impact of the Condemnation of 219 Miscellaneous Propositions by Etienne Tempier, Bishop of Paris, in 1277, see for example Edward Grant, "The Condemnation of 1277, God's Absolute Power, and Physical Thought in the Late Middle Ages," *Viator* 10 (1979): 211-244.

example of the rainbow and of the phenomena connected with it, . . .[30]

Although it is easy for us to see beginnings of a fairly modern mentality here, it is obvious, historically, that the heyday of the empirical method was not yet, not even 200 years later. Can Nicholas of Cusa offer us anything important? After all, we have already said that he was not a rigorous observer in astronomy.

Two features of the *Idiota* dialogues appear important to me. The first is the Idiota himself, a citizen or layman, who claims to have access to wisdom, even without the books of the authorities.

> Citizen: . . . The opinion of authority has led you astray and you are like a horse who, though being by nature free, is tied with a halter to a stall and is fed only what is given to him. Your mind, bound as it is by the authority of writers, is nurtured on strange and oftimes unnatural food.
>
> Orator: If the food of wisdom is not to be found in the books of wise men, then where is it to be found?
>
> Citizen: I do not say that it is not found there but rather one does not find in books the natural food of wisdom. . . . I wish to say that wisdom cries out in the very streets and her cry is how she dwells in the highest.[31]

Here the Cardinal advocates an experiential approach, a departure from the simple acceptance of authority, and advocates it for the sake of religious wisdom itself. Later on the Idiota says,

> . . . so the taste of this wisdom cannot be acquired by hearsay but by one's actually touching it with his internal sense, and then he will bear

[30] Roger Bacon, *Opus Majus*, "On Experimental Science," excerpted in Jefferson Hane Weaver, *The World of Physics* (New York, 1987) 1:401-402; *The "Opus Majus" of Roger Bacon*, ed. John Henry Bridges (Oxford, 1897) 2:171-173.

[31] *Idiota. De sapientia* I, #2-3 (h V, 4-5; V², 4-6): "Idiota: Traxit te opinio auctoritatis, ut sis quasi equus natura liber, sed arte capistro alligatus praesepi, ubi non aliud comedit, nisi quod sibi ministratur. Pascitur enim intellectus tuus auctoritati scribentium constrictus pabulo alieno et non naturali.

Orator: Si non in libris sapientum est sapientiae pabulum, ubi tunc est?

Idiota: Non dico ibi non esse, sed dico naturale ibi non reperiri. . . . Ego autem tibi dico, quod 'sapientia foris' clamat 'in plateis'; et est clamor eius, quoniam ipsa habitat in altissimus" [Proverbia 1:20: "Sapientia foris praedicat; in plateis dat vocum suam." Ecclesiasticus 24:7: "Ego in altissimis habitavi, et thronus meus in columna nubis". Wis. 9, 17]. English trans.: *Concerning Wisdom* in *Unity and Reform: Selected Writings of Nicholas de Cusa*, ed. John Patrick Dolan (Notre Dame, 1962), p. 102.

witness not of what he has heard but what he has experimentally tasted in himself.[32]

Even wisdom must be internally experienced. This is not the primary, usual signification of "experimentally," but the usage is interesting and certainly in the spirit of the autonomous search for either wisdom or scientific knowledge.

Second, in the *Idiota de staticis experimentis* we have all kinds of much more literal experiments in specific gravity and weight based on Archimedes' principle and the ability accurately to compare weights. Even time is measured by weighing the water that flows from a clepsydra. Although the purpose is not as clearly religious as usual, the experiments are mostly only vague ideas, or thought experiments.[33] Even so, the notion of independent, experimental learning is definitely being advanced.

One of the experiments is particularly interesting because it implies the conservation of weight (mass). A hundred pounds of plants are grown in a pot containing a hundred pounds of soil by the addition of water to the seeds. The weight of the soil is not materially reduced. Even this can be recovered from the ashes if the plants are burned. Most of the weight of the plants was from the water, he concludes, illustrating the various powers of water--or, more literally, the "powers of various waters" (*aquarum variarum virtutum*)--and our ability to approach "conjectures" (*coniecturas*) of these powers.[34]

This is interesting not only because of its use of the conservation principle, but because of its practicality. Whether or not Cusanus ever performed the experiment, a later Flemish physician, J. B. van Helmont (1577-1644) seems to have done so, with a larger pot, 200 pounds of soil, and a little tree, to make one of the same points: most of the tree's weight came from the water.[35]

---

[32] *Idiota. De sapientia* (h V², 41-42): ". . . ita de hac sapientia, quam nemo gustat per auditum, sed solum ille, qui eam accipit in interno gusto, ille perhebit testimonium non de his, quae audivit, sed in se ipso experimentaliter gustavit." (Dolan, *Unity and Reform*, pp. 111-112).

[33] See Marshall Clagett, *The Science of Mechanics in the Middle Ages* (Madison, 1959), pp. 97-99. Clagett connects Cusanus "at least remotely" with the thirteenth-century Pseudo-Archimedes, *De insidentibus in humidum*, a pastiche of earlier sources on specific gravity. Cusanus "completely abandons the mathematical demonstrations characteristic of the thirteenth-century treatise; . . . his vaunted experiments are little more than 'thought' experiments."

[34] *Idiota. De staticis experimentis* #177 (h V, 129; V², 231). (Dolan, *Unity and Reform*, pp. 250-251).

[35] Stephen Toulmin and June Goodfield, *The Architecture of Matter* (New York, 1962), pp. 150-154.

Since the work of Thomas S. Kuhn, the notion that science makes progress not simply through additions but through changes of world view, or "paradigm," has become known and accepted among philosophers and historians of science.[36] If scientific world views can change, then earlier ones are not intrinsically "unscientific."[37] Kuhn's contribution is precisely this: following a paradigm change it is no longer necessary to look down on all that went before. In particular, the historian must look for the sources of the new mind set. These sources themselves will be seen differently by all those living after the revolution.

George Sarton views Nicholas as "an excellent symbol of the transition between the Middle Ages and the new age."[38] Later on he claims that, "In the middle of the fifteenth century, when the Renaissance begins, he was perhaps the greatest man in the Christian world; . . ."[39] Sarton then proceeds to sum him up scientifically in a way quite relevant to this discussion:

> The advancement of knowledge has been made possible by increasing accuracy of measurement. Cusanus did not see this as clearly as Kelvin, who lived in the nineteenth century, but in his time he was remarkable for seeing it at all. He used the balance for physical, physiological, and even mathematical investigations. He used a clepsydra to measure the frequency of the pulse and of breathing in normal and pathological conditions. He devised experiments to measure humidity and invented a bathometer (to measure the depth of water), a part of which could be released at the bottom and rise to the surface. No doubt such ideas were in the air and occurred to others (Alberti, for example); but Cusanus was the first, or one of the first, to express them. This shows his many-sidedness, for he was in fact an "idiot," i.e., a layman, in physics; by profession he was an ecclesiastical administrator. He was a prince of the Church but also a philosopher, a man of science with bold ideas, a forerunner of Erasmus.[40]

A. C. Crombie, in an important historical study, gives us a clue both to Cusanus' educational background in science and of his importance at a crucial time:

> To the theory of experiment the main contribution in the fifteenth and sixteenth centuries was made by the Paduan school. From the time of Pietro d'Abano, at the end of the thirteenth century, Padua had been a

[36] In particular, his *The Structure of Scientific Revolutions*, 2nd enlarged ed. (Chicago, 1970).

[37] Kuhn, *Structure*, p. 3.

[38] Sarton, *Six Wings*, p. 15.

[39] Sarton, *Six Wings*, p. 77.

[40] Sarton, *Six Wings*, p. 78, and notes.

stronghold of Aristotelianism and a leading medical university. Oxford methodology seems to have reached Padua at the end of the fourteenth century, and in the fifteenth century the university began to attract many of the leading scientists: Cusanus, Puerbach, Regiomontanus, Copernicus, Fracastoro; and later Vesalius, Fabrizio, Galileo, and Harvey all belonged to it, either as students or professors.[41]

Perhaps we cannot now easily understand how strange Cusanus' ideas may have sounded in his time. We shall never know when and in whom the idea of experimentation, for example, turned the corner and went from a weird new idea to one "whose time had come." Yet perhaps Cusanus, with his daring imagination, provided some of the inspiration. In particular, his work combined new or at least unusual ideas about the physical world with an interesting insistence on the value of experience, or "experiment."

To close the circle, I remark that Cusanus used science to remind us of wisdom and make us realize that wisdom itself is knowing our ignorance. This passage from one of our wisest of today's scientists, Dr. Lewis Thomas, may strike a certain resonance:

Science, especially twentieth-century science, has provided us with a glimpse of something we never really knew before, the revelation of human ignorance. We have been used to the belief, down one century after another, that we more or less comprehend everything bar one or two mysteries like the mental processes of our gods. Every age, not just the eighteenth century, regarded itself as the Age of Reason, and we have never lacked for explanations of the world and its ways. Now, we are being brought up short, and this has been the work of science.[42]

[41] A.C. Crombie, *Robert Grosseteste and the Origins of Experimental Science, 1100-1700* (Oxford, 1953), p. 297, and notes.

[42] "Humanities and Science," in his *Late Night Thoughts on Listening to Mahler's Ninth Symphony* (Toronto, 1984), p. 150.

PART THREE

DETERMINING THE POWERS AND LIMITS OF HUMAN THINKING

NICHOLAS OF CUSA'S *ON CONJECTURES (DE CONIECTURIS)*

Clyde Lee Miller

Between 1440 and 1445 Nicholas of Cusa completed *On Conjectures (De coniecturis)*, his second major theoretical work. This treatise designedly complements and extends the views proposed in his masterpiece of 1440, *On Learned Ignorance (De docta ignorantia).*[1] Even though readers limited to English have become familiar with Cusanus' name and ideas as more of his writings have been translated, the *De coniecturis* remains relatively unknown beyond the circle of Cusanus specialists.[2] Given the obscurity of the work, I will first present Cusanus' leading ideas in *De coniecturis*, then comment briefly on the extent and meaning of conjectural knowledge, and finally suggest how *De coniecturis* might count as a humanist work of the early Renaissance.

As contemporary readers, we may well be curious about the sense and

---

[1] On the date of *De coniecturis* and its connections with *De docta ignorantia*, see Josef Koch, *Die ars coniecturalis des Nikolaus von Kues* (Cologne, 1956), pp. 7-12, 31-35; also the same scholar's critical edition of *De coniecturis* (h III), p. ix; n. 38, pp. 218-219. See also the Latin-German edition of *De coniecturis*, ed. and trans. Josef Koch und Winfried Happ (Hamburg, 1971), esp. Happ's "Einführung," pp. ix-xxi. For a judicious assessment of Koch's thesis that Nicholas turned from a metaphysics-of-being in *On Learned Ignorance* to a metaphysics-of-oneness in *De coniecturis*, see Jasper Hopkins, *Nicholas of Cusa on God as Not-Other* (Minneapolis, 1983), pp. 10-11.

[2] Besides Koch's monograph mentioned in note 1, see his brief essay, "Der Sinn des zweiten Hauptwerkes des Nikolaus von Kues *De Coniecturis*," in *Nicolò da Cusa* (Florence, 1962), pp. 101-123. Other important essays on *De coniecturis:* Satoshi Oide, "Über die Grundlagen der cusanischen Konjekturenlehre," *Mitteilungen und Forschungsbeiträge der Cusanus-Gesellschaft* 8 (1970): 147-148; Peter Hirt, "Vom Wesen der konjekturalen Logik nach Nikolaus von Kues," *ibid.*, 179-198; Mariano Alvarez-Gomez, "Der Mensch als Schöpfer seiner Welt," *ibid.*, 13 (1978): 160-166; Klaus Jacobi, "Ontologie aus dem Geist 'belehrten Nichtwissens'," in *Nikolaus von Kues. Einführung in sein philosophisches Denken*, ed. Klaus Jacobi (Munich, 1979), esp. pp. 39-46; Helmut Meinhardt, "Exactheit und Mutmassungscharakter der Erkenntnis," *ibid.*, pp. 101-120. And the whole of *Mitteilungen und Forschungsbeiträge der Cusanus-Gesellschaft* 11 (1975) collects papers about Cusanus' place in the history of epistemology.

implications of "conjectures" and "conjecturing."[3] We should therefore note at the start that Nicholas' *coniectura* is not to be confused or conflated with what is ordinarily meant today by "hypothesis" in the sense of a provisional proposal or guess or hunch to be checked against evidence (usually empirical) which would verify or falsify the original hypothesis.[4] Cusanus' conjectures are provisional, not because they may be shown to be true or false, but because even true conjectures (the only ones Nicholas considers) can be revised to become more faithful to the nature of what they partially capture. This means we will not discover the correct sense of Cusanus' *coniectura* (either as a mental activity or as the content of a belief) if we merely compare it with what goes on when we surmise or make a suggestion or propose some possible lead to be investigated or examined. For Nicholas of Cusa, human knowledge, both as process and product, is tightly connected in *De coniecturis* with important metaphysical and systematic concerns. For that reason, the latter require consideration so that Nicholas' definition of *coniectura* may be understood in its proper context. Moreover, this intellectual setting and the speculative proposals of *De coniecturis* are alien enough to contemporary views to suggest that we examine Cusanus' overall doctrine as well as his teaching about conjectural knowledge.

De coniecturis provides the occasion for Cusanus to explore from a somewhat different standpoint the whole of reality already investigated in *On Learned Ignorance*: God, human beings, and the rest of creation. Once again his inquiry is inclusive and expansive rather than selective and partial. *De coniecturis* presents a vision of the whole, that totality of beings which has intrigued and engaged speculative and systematic thought in the West from the Greeks until our own time. In this work Cusanus omits the direct

[3] Books consulted which treat of *De coniecturis*: Elkehard Fränktzki, *Nikolaus von Kues und das Problem der absoluten Subjektivität* (Meisenheim am Glan, 1972), pp. 102-108; Maurice de Gandillac, *Nikolaus von Cues* (Düsseldorf, 1953), pp. 159-176, and by the same author, "Les 'conjectures' de Nicolas de Cues," *Revue de métaphysique et morale* 77 (1972): 356-364; Norbert Henke, *Der Abbildbegriff in der Erkenntnislehre des Nikolaus von Kues* (Münster, 1969); Norbert Herold, *Menschliche Perspective und Wahrheit* (Münster, 1975), pp. 42-62; Hildegund Rogner, *Die Bewegung des Erkennens und das Sein in der Philosophie des Nikolaus von Cues* (Heidelberg, 1937); Hermann Schnarr, *Modi Essendi* (Münster, 1973), pp. 40-67; Theo von Velthoven, *Gottesschau und menschliche Kreativität* (Leiden, 1977).

The best recent English translations of many of Nicholas' works are those of Jasper Hopkins (Minneapolis, various dates); many are now in second and third editions. For the *Idiota. De mente*, see my translation: *Nicholas de Cusa: The Layman about Mind* (New York, 1979).

[4] On this point see Koch, *Die ars coniecturalis*, pp. 25-26; Schnarr, *Modi*, pp. 48-49.

appeal to earlier authorities and the explicit mention of Christ and revelation which were important to *On Learned Ignorance,* but gives an account which remains no less Christian and comprehensive. This second effort to set forth the harmonious order of all things itself exemplifies the meaning of *coniectura* even as its parts spell out the conjectural character of human knowledge. In the first book of *De coniecturis* Nicholas works out the foundations of conjectural knowledge; in the second he applies this foundational exploration to the different sorts of things we know.[5] We may understand better what Cusanus achieves if we focus mainly on Book One and turn elsewhere in *De coniecturis* when it will provide insight into the meaning of conjectural knowledge or the humanist thrust of Nicholas' teaching.

1.

Book One of *De coniecturis* may be read as using arithmetic and geometry to explicate and schematize certain basic themes announced in its first chapter. Two of Cusanus' favorite theses are introduced there: (a) human knowledge is to be understood as imaging God's creative knowledge; (b) the whole of created reality is to be understood on Neoplatonic lines as issuing from its single divine source into the plurality of finite things.[6] Cusanus' extension of the traditional *imago dei* theme is decisive for his understanding of human knowing and human nature. His appeal to the Neoplatonic vision of procession from, and return to, the divine oneness now finds its counterpart in the universe of human ideas we construct as knowers. Nicholas extends and explicates these themes through the rest of Book One, proposing that they be conceptualized and imagined through arithmetical relations and geometric diagrams. These mathematical schemata are unique to *De coniecturis* (and arcane to contemporary readers), but they exemplify one meaning and use of *coniectura* even as they help articulate Cusanus' vision of the whole.

　　Chapter One of Book One opens by proclaiming that human minds image God's mind in that we produce conjectures (concepts and judgments) just as God's knowledge creates finite things. Human knowledge should be taken as "poetic" or productive to preserve its character as God's image. If we understand human knowledge as constructive and creative, we can "see

---

[5] For a more detailed outline of the work, see h III, pp. xxxii-xxxiii; Happ's "Einführung" to the German-Latin edition (n. 1 *supra);* Schnarr, *Modi,* pp. 42-43. Nicholas' prologue divides the work in terms of the commonplace into branch, flower, and fruit: h, Prologue, 4.

[6] To see how the same themes are worked out in the later *Idiota. De mente,* see my "Introduction" to *About Mind,* pp. 17-28. I give one slant on Cusanus' view of nature in "Aristotelian *Natura* and Nicholas of Cusa," *The Downside Review* 96 (1978): 13-20.

through" it, as it were, to the divine original, the model or exemplar, in whose likeness our conjectural knowledge finds its source, pattern, and goal. Cusanus sets out the parallel as follows:

> Conjectures should proceed from our mind as the real world does from the infinite divine reason. For as the human mind, the exalted likeness of God, participates in the fruitfulness of creative nature as far as it can, it puts out from itself as image of the all-powerful form rational entities *(rationalia)* in the likeness of real entities. So the human mind exists as the form of the conjectural world just as the divine [mind is form] of the real [world]. So just as that absolute divine entity is all that which is in whatever is, so too the oneness of the human mind is the being of its conjectures.[7]

Nicholas' assumptions from the Christian Platonist tradition regarding God as creator are worth noting here. His God is one, infinite, all-powerful mind, or reason. God's oneness stands as absolute and transcendent; all created things share that oneness and hence possess reality in a relative, participated way. Since human beings are creatures, our minds also participate in the divine oneness that is "all that which is in whatever is *(omne id quod est in quolibet quod est)*." But since we share God's oneness as other, or different from God, the world we create as knowers who image God is one of *rationalia*, not *realia*.

The conceptual entities we fashion mentally are no less dependent on us than the entities of the created cosmos are dependent on God. This dependence is interpreted along Platonic lines as the relation of oneness to otherness. Whatever is other than the first oneness on which it depends becomes real and one by sharing or participating in a limited way in the oneness of the first. As God's oneness is the ultimate form, or being, of whatever exists independently of us, so our mind's oneness is the source of the entities of the conceptual realm. Nicholas' original insight in *De coniecturis* is to locate the image of God's creating in human mental production of conjectures.

Our creative knowing becomes the human entry point for coming to understand God's creating and the dependence of created finite things on their infinite source. We cannot understand fully our relation to God or the point of being human and what it entails unless we search the breadth and depth of our active mental lives. Chapter One continues by proposing the goals of knowledge:

> Now God does everything for his own sake, so that he is equally intellectual beginning and end of all things. Likewise the

[7] *De coniecturis* I, 1, #5 (h III, 7-8). All translations from *De coniecturis* in the body of the paper are my own.

unfolding of the world of [human] reason, which proceeds from our enfolding mind, takes place for the sake of that fabricating [mind]. For the more acutely it [the mind] contemplates itself in the world it unfolds, the more richly fruitful does it become in itself. For its goal is the infinite reason in which it [the mind] will behold itself as it is and which alone is the measure of all reason's [works]. The more deeply we enter our own mind, of which God is the single living center, the more closely we raise ourselves to becoming like the divine mind. For this reason out of natural desire we pursue the sciences which perfect us.[8]

Knowledge is thus for the knower's sake and, if self-knowledge is our proximate goal as we "contemplate" the mental universe we construct in human knowledge, our ultimate goal is knowledge of God, "the infinite reason." But these purposes of human knowing are really not to be separated for Cusanus. Understanding ourselves as images entails some encounter with the exemplar, or ultimate measure of mind--only in contact with God's mind does the human mind "behold itself as it is." Two simultaneous movements are marked out here for human knowing: in one we move more deeply into our selves only to discover that God's mind is "the single living center" of the human mind. In the other we ascend from sense perception to intellectual vision toward the infinite reason, becoming more likened to it as we construct the mental universe out of our own resources, just as God does the real world. Ultimately the same knowing activities encompass both movements.[9]

What is worth particular notice in the above passage is that Cusanus uses the language of "unfolding and enfolding" *(explicatio/complicatio)* to describe the procession of knowledge contents from the human mind. In *On Learned Ignorance* this terminology was restricted to God's creation, as the terms had been restricted in Boethius and Thierry of Chartres from whom Nicholas inherited them. Nicholas used these concepts to gloss his under-standing of creation *ex nihilo* in Neoplatonic terms. As "enfolded" in God, all things are nothing but God's infinite oneness. As created and real in their own right, finite things are "unfolded" into the many realities other than God. In *De coniecturis* Cusanus, for the first time, takes these concep-tions over into the realm of knowledge and frames knowing in accord with the Neoplatonic conception of a dynamic universe proceeding from a single source in hierarchical stages and at the same time returning thereto.[10] The basis for this extension is his proposal that our creative knowing images the

---

[8] *De coniecturis* I, 1, #5 (h III, 8).

[9] On this process and purpose, see von Velthoven, *Gottesschau,* pp. 131-196.

[10] *Ibid.,* p. 52.

creating by God's mind. So he can speak of "the unfolding of the world of reason, which proceeds from our enfolding mind."

With this new extension of *explicatio/complicatio* we confront the second theme introduced in *De coniecturis* I, 1, the Neoplatonic vision of procession from, and return to, the source. That this theme is already required in spelling out how we are God's images as knowers (the first theme) is characteristic of Nicholas of Cusa's way of thinking. There is a simultaneity about the various aspects of Cusanus' thought that defies the linear order and analysis we expect from typically Aristotelian medieval thinkers. In this way *De coniecturis* is quite literally an intellectual vision. What Cusanus brings together here is fundamentally given and therefore to be grasped all at once. His insight encompasses concurrent and conjunctive elements--the sort of *Gestalt* of ground and figure, stage-setting and action-- we expect from visual panoply, or imagined scenario. In *De coniecturis* any and every fundamental theme may be presupposed, alluded to, echoed, or explicitly employed to help make sense of any other. His way of thinking no less than his universe is aptly characterized by the Latin slogan he adopted from Anaxagoras: *Quodlibet in quolibet*, "Everything [is] in each thing."

Cusanus' Christian inheritance enters explicitly in the final part of *De coniecturis* I, 1 where he shows how the human mind is no less trinitarian than its divine exemplar. Since the divinity comprises oneness, equality, and connection (Nicholas' terms for Father, Son, and Spirit), we will find this unitrine character paralleled in human knowing. For Cusanus what is trinitarian in human knowing is manifest in what the human mind unfolds as source and measure of the conceptual realm. Cusanus states this as follows:

> So that you may be persuaded to grasp my intention and accept mind as the principle of conjectures, notice that the first principle of all things and of our mind has been shown to be unitrine, that it is the single principle of multitude, inequality, and division among things, that from its absolute oneness proceeds multitude, from its equality [proceeds] inequality, and from its connection [proceeds] division. Likewise our mind . . . makes itself a unitrine principle of its rational constructing. For reason alone is the measure of multitude, magnitude, and composition so that if it were removed none of these would exist . . . So the oneness of mind enfolds in itself all multitude and its equality [enfolds] all magnitude, just as its connection also [enfolds] all composition. Therefore, the mind as a unitrine principle first of all unfolds multitude from the power of its enfolding unity, while multitude is generative of inequality and magnitude. Therefore in that primordial multitude, as in its first exemplar, mind hunts out magnitudes, or the different and unequal perfection of the whole [numbers]; thereupon it proceeds from both

to composition. So our mind is a principle which distinguishes, compares, and connects.[11]

Two remarks may alleviate the obscurity of this passage. The first is that Nicholas is often thinking of the whole numbers of arithmetic when he speaks of "multitude" and of the shapes of plane and solid geometry where he speaks of "magnitude" or size, and not simply of numbered things or of bodies extended in space and time. The second is that his last sentence is crucial for understanding what "unfolding" and "measuring" mean. Nicholas is referring to the mental acts required for dealing with number, size, and composition whether the objects concerned are mathematical or the spatio-temporal things encountered in sense perception.

Chapter Two of *De coniecturis* I specifies the remarks about multitude and magnitude by turning explicitly to counting and the whole numbers of arithmetic. This chapter has two important functions in the whole work. First, it underlines the significance of mathematics for understanding Cusanus' conception of mind. Second, it functions as a bridge to the rest of Book One, since Nicholas uses arithmetic and geometry as conjectural aids for understanding things outside the realm of mathematics. As he himself says,

> For reason to unfold number and to use it in constructing conjectures is nothing else than for reason to employ itself, and to fashion everything in the highest natural likeness of itself, just as God, the infinite mind, communicates being to things in the coeternal Word.[12]

What is the significance of arithmetic and geometry for understanding human knowledge?[13] For Nicholas the numbers of arithmetic are neither pre-existing Platonic forms nor Aristotelian concepts abstracted from numbered things. Rather the whole numbers are conceptual entities (Nicholas calls them *entia rationis,* "beings of reason") which the human mind constructs entirely from its own resources. ("For reason to unfold number . . . is nothing else than for reason to employ itself.")

One way our minds most closely image God's creating occurs when we construct the number series. In counting numbers we experience what Nicholas means by *explicatio,* or unfolding from oneness. Number, or "multitude," is the best parallel to the human mind's own oneness, so Cusanus terms number the mind's "first exemplar." Moreover, the numbers

---

[11] *De coniecturis* I, 1, #6 (h III, 9-10).

[12] *De coniecturis* I, 2, #7 (h III, 12).

[13] Here I follow von Velthoven, *Gottesschau,* pp. 131-196. Cf. also de Gandillac, *Nikolaus von Cues,* pp. 61-86; Karl Volkmann-Schluck, *Nicolaus Cusanus: Die Philosophie in Übergang vom Mittelalter zur Neuzeit* (Frankfurt, 1957), pp. 87-96.

of arithmetic and the figures of geometry are the sole conceptual realities he believes are *not* conjectural. Here we find an exactness and precision unavailable to human knowers in other areas. As he would later write in *Trialogus de possest*, "So if we rightly consider [the matter, we recognize that] we have no certain knowledge except mathematical knowledge. And this latter is a symbolism for searching into the works of God."[14]   What is it that human intelligence does in constructing the world of knowledge? As the last part of *De coniecturis* I, 1 suggested, it *measures*, that is to say, mind discriminates, or distinguishes, one known item from another. Our minds compare and draw parallels between objects, sizing them up, as it were, in judgments. Along with these judgments whereby we analyze and break down what we know, we also employ mind as a synthetic instrument. We are capable of joining and putting conceptions together; we discover and make connections between our ideas.

De coniecturis I, 2, #7 opens by remarking that only human animals count and employ number as "nothing else than reason unfolded." Counting is a paradigmatic activity of *ratio*. The whole number series exemplifies knowledge we fashion from our own mental resources. When we number, or count, our capacities to discriminate and relate are clearly manifest. And the mind's own oneness is mirrored in the first unit, the number one. Each succeeding number is a composite unity for Cusanus, a unitary sum of so many further units. The series of whole numbers is constructed by adding that first unit again and again and by keeping each new number separate as a distinct member of the series. Spelling out these almost automatic operations implicit in counting shows how discriminating and relating are mental functions presupposed in our understanding and use of the whole numbers in arithmetic. Reason measures each member of the series and its connection with all the others. Our ability to speak of the whole series or

---

[14] *Trialogus de possest,* #44 (h XI, 2, p. 54). I quote Jasper Hopkins' translation from *A Concise Introduction to the Philosophy of Nicholas of Cusa,* 3rd ed. (Minneapolis, 1986), pp. 119-121. It is worth noting Cusanus' explanation of this matter: "For regarding mathematical [entities], which proceed from our reason and which we experience to be in us as in their source *[principium]:* they are known by us as our entities and as rational entities; [and they are known] precisely, by our reason's precision, from which they proceed. (In a similar way, real things *[realia]* are known precisely, by the divine [intellect's] precision, from which they proceed into being.)   These mathematical [entities] are neither an essence *(quid)* nor a quality *(quale);* rather, they are notional entities elicited from our reason. Without these notional entities [reason] could not proceed with its work, e.g., with building, measuring, and so on. But the divine works, which proceed from the divine intellect, remain unknown to us precisely as they are": *Trialogus de possest* #43 (h XI, 2, pp. 52-53; Hopkins, *A Concise Introduction,* p. 119).

to select certain groupings within it bespeaks reason's capacity to put together and separate parts and whole.

Our mathematical concepts are thus non-conjectural mental constructions which best witness to our creativity as knowers. But they are also useful "in constructing conjectures," or symbolic models, for knowing things other than mathematics. *De coniecturis* I, 3, #10 proceeds at once to put number to work by discovering four numerical "unities" within the system of whole numbers.[15] These unities can then be applied conjecturally to the four "mental unities," our conceptions of the metaphysical realms which comprise all of reality. Key to discovering the four numerical unities is the fact that in the "first natural" progression (1+2+3+4=10) Nicholas finds synthesized the potential of the whole number system useful for conjecturing. A simple display of rows and columns may clarify the importance of four and ten in reaching the four numerical unities.

$$
\left.
\begin{array}{ccccccccc}
 & & & & & & 1 & & \\
1 & + & 2 & + & 3 & + & 4 & = 10 \\
10 & + & 20 & + & 30 & + & 40 & = 100 \\
100 & + & 200 & + & 300 & + & 400 & = 1000
\end{array}
\right\} 4
$$

$$
\underbrace{\qquad\qquad\qquad\qquad}_{4}
$$

(Figure 1)

By repeating the first progression for 10 through 40 and for 100 through 400, we obtain the sums of 100 and 1000 respectively. The four numerical unities thus attained are 1, 10, 100, and 1000. The first unity is the number one, itself the source of the original progression and unique in being neither root nor power of any number but itself. Ten results from the first progression and is the second unity. It is the starting point of the second progression, as well as the square and cube root of one hundred and one thousand. One hundred, the third unity, is the sum of the second progression and starting point of the third, as well as the square of ten. One thousand, the fourth unity, is the sum of the third progression and the cube of ten.

For Cusanus, each of the unities represents a stage in the mental unfolding of one (just as in Arabic notation each is represented by "1" with or without zeros added). Each unity is the origin and/or sum of the first progression three times repeated. And the four unities are more telling in Cusanus' eyes because he associates them with a parallel geometrical unfolding: the derivation of line, surface, and solid from the point. He even asserts that the numbers beyond one thousand add nothing new in that they have little

[15] On the four mathematical unities, see Koch, *Die ars coniecturalis*, pp. 26-28; Oide, "Über die Grundlagen," pp. 158-160. Figure 1 in this paper reproduces Oide's figure 3, p. 159.

utility for human conjectures in dealing with the created world or its creator.

What the human mind unfolds in non-conjectural exactness in deriving the four unities from the number one finds conjectural application in the next five chapters and, indeed, the rest of *De coniecturis* I. Chapters Four through Eight of *De coniecturis* I discuss in detail the "four unities," the hierarchically ordered spheres of being that comprise all there is. To the four numerical unities (one, ten, one hundred, one thousand) Cusanus sets in correspondence God, intelligence, soul, and body. Each represents a hierarchical stage, as well as a sphere of reality. Each proceeds in order from God's utter oneness, participates in, and images that infinite oneness in a more or less limited, or restricted, way (Cusanus' term is "contracted"). Just as the numerical unities can be understood as unfolding what is enfolded in the number one (and in the counting human mind), so the metaphysical realms are to be taken as unfolding what is enfolded in the oneness of God's mind. To each of the four metaphysical unities corresponds a level of truth and certitude. And since human beings share in the spheres of intelligence, soul, and body, there is a mode of human knowing and of human mental or verbal expression appropriate to each of the three unities after the first.[16]

Nicholas will often refer to the spheres of intelligence, soul, and body by using the human knowing capacities that parallel them: intellect, reason, and sense. This lets us see their dynamic interconnectedness in proceeding from, and returning to, God's infinite oneness. Later, in *De coniecturis* II, 16 and in the *Idiota de mente*, Cusanus conceptualizes the various knowing powers of human beings issuing from the unitary power of mind as the same sort of unfolding.[17] At the end of *De coniecturis* I, 4 Cusanus stresses again the dynamic interrelatedness of the four unities, recalling for the reader just how "everything [is] in each thing":

> Now everything in God is God, in intelligence [everything] is intelligence, in soul [everything] is soul, in body [everything] is body. This is nothing else than for mind to embrace everything either in a divine way or in an intellectual way or in the way of soul or in a bodily way . . . The first unity exists as entirely absolute; but the last, departing from all absoluteness as much as possible, is contracted. The second [unity] is highly absolute and less contracted; the third less absolute and highly contracted. Therefore, just as intelligence is not entirely divine or absolute, so the rational soul does not completely depart from sharing in divinity. And mind distinguishes and equally connects everything: in a wondrous reciprocal progression the divine

---

[16] On the four metaphysical unities, see Koch, *Die ars coniecturalis,* pp. 18-19; h III, n. 11, pp. 193-194; n. 18, pp. 200-201; n. 19, pp. 201-203; Oide, "Über die Grundlagen," pp. 161-162.

[17] *Idiota. De mente,* VII (h V, 73-79; V², 145-161).

absolute unity descends step by step into intelligence and reason and the contracted sensible [unity] mounts through reason into intelligence.[18]

As we move from God to the realm of three-dimensional bodies each unity gets more and more "contracted"--limited as unity or oneness--so that otherness and plurality appear in increasing degrees. To do this traditional Neoplatonic framework justice (it goes back at least to Proclus, while Eckhart was the most recent of Nicholas' predecessors to employ it), two complementary features must be kept in mind: each stage in the hierarchy participates in the divine oneness; all but God proceed from, and at the same time return to, the divine.

The derivation of ten, one hundred, and one thousand from the number one gives us some conjectural understanding of just how the hierarchical universe proceeds from God's oneness and yet shares that oneness in degrees of otherness. In Chapter 9 of *De coniecturis* I, and again in Chapter 13, Cusanus proposes alternative mathematical conjectures to aid our understanding of just how oneness and otherness are shared as one moves from the highest to the lowest reality. This time he employs geometrical diagrams, calling the first *figura paradigmatica*, or *P*, the second *figura universi*, or *U*. Since *P* is somewhat simpler and can exemplify Nicholas' practice, we may focus on it alone. Figure 2 reproduces Cusanus' drawing of *P*, with additions to designate where the four numerical and metaphysical unities fit in.[19]

The two overlapping triangles represented in *P* are to be imagined as two interpenetrating cones, or "pyramids of light and darkness," which symbolize the way otherness participates in oneness in every reality but God. God's utter and infinite oneness is represented as the base of the pyramid of light (on the left); utter otherness, or nothingness *(nihil)*, is pictured as the base of the pyramid of darkness. (In fact, Cusanus uses the words *quasi basis* to remind us that neither God nor *nihil* can be pictured with created things; the infinite oneness transcends all that shares its oneness.) In between are to be found all created things.

[18] *De coniecturis* I, 4, #15-16 (h III, 20-21).

[19] Regarding the figure P, see Koch, *Die ars coniecturalis,* pp. 28-30; Oide, "Über die Grundlagen," pp. 162-167; h III, n. 22, pp. 204-205. Oide shows how the *Figura universi* and figure P may be integrated, *ibid.,* pp. 167-178. Figure 2 of this paper is based on Oide's figures 6 and 7, pp. 164-165.

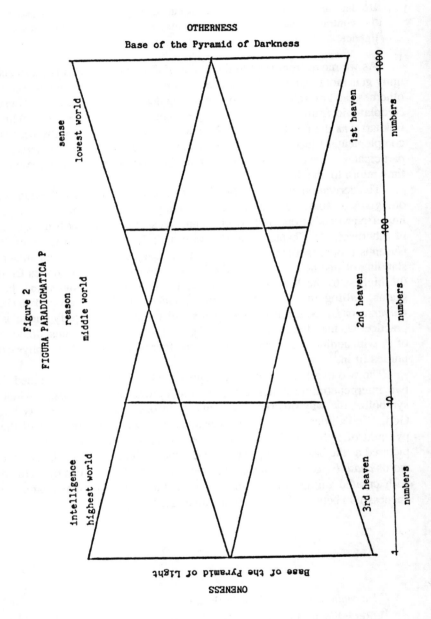

Figure 2
FIGURA PARADIGMATICA P

What the diagram captures is Cusanus' point that to have any reality at all outside of God's infinite oneness is to share oneness as more or less limited by otherness. The three-fold partition of the overlapping triangles from left to right represents the three unities that issue from God's oneness, here designated as worlds (*mundi*) or heavens *(caeli)*. These three domains are correlated with the three arithmetical unities after the number one and with the hierarchy of human knowing capacities. Moving from left to right thus takes us from more light and perfection to more darkness and less perfection, all in orderly gradation. Yet among creatures we find no highest degree of oneness or lowest degree of otherness; nowhere in creation is there oneness without otherness or otherness without oneness.[20]

This figure *P* is a good example of how Cusanus takes geometrical conceptions and applies them to understand, in an inexact and representational (and so conjectural) way, a universe that manifests participation in different degrees from more to less perfect.[21] In the second book of *De coniecturis* he again proposes it as a useful expository tool in the early chapters (II, 1-3) and takes it up explicitly in his discussions in all but five of the remaining fourteen chapters. Through this device, such topics as composition of soul and body and individual differences within a species can be schematized as matters of more and less. So, too, the knowing powers of the human mind can be interpreted as hierarchically sharing, to a greater or lesser extent, in intellectual vision. What is useful about the diagram is that it graphically presents the relation of realities less and more perfect even as its visual display orders their differences spatially to correspond to hierarchical gradations. Yet, because the diagram is conjectural, it can lend us conceptual order without pretending to capture exactly the way things are in themselves or in relation to the whole.

2.

Nicholas of Cusa's teaching about conjectures and conjecturing has to be situated within his particular reading of Christian Neoplatonism, his

---

[20] For a short summary of what Cusanus means by *alteritas,* see Koch, *Die ars coniecturalis,* pp. 19-20; for a longer treatment of the theme in Cusan thought, see Werner Beierwaltes, "Identität und Differenz. Zum Prinzip cusanischen Denkens," *Rheinisch-Westfälische Akademie der Wissenschaften.* Vorträge. Geisteswiss.: G220 (Opladen, 1977).

[21] For the principles governing the harmony and differences within and between hierarchical gradations, cf. h III, n. 19, pp. 201-203.

universe of oneness and otherness.[22]   Human knowing is a creative activity that parallels and images God's creating. As knowers, we are ultimately pursuing the divine exemplar. The quest for the ultimate pervades *De coniecturis*, as it does all of Cuasnus' writings, and it is here that he appears most Christian and most medieval. Yet precisely at this point his originality breaks through. Emphasizing the negative theology he inherited from his predecessors, Cusanus is convinced that there is no proportion between finite and infinite, that no human conceptual measure can bridge the gap between creator and creation. So he writes in the prologue to *De coniecturis*: "Our actual knowledge has no relation to that highest, humanly unattainable knowledge." As a result, our positive statements about God are "conjectures of the truth" (Prologue, 2). Conjectural knowing and its conceptual results underline the thesis that we never grasp divinity with conceptual precision, as God is in himself.

Cusanus' medieval predecessors maintained that our statements about God are "analogically" true, that in specified contexts *what* they asserted, their intelligible content, represented truly something of God's reality, without fully plumbing its depths. Yet *how* they achieved this, through limited human conception and language, was inadequate to the divine. But for Cusanus, our positive assertions regarding God cannot reach "the precision of the truth." He makes no distinction between *id quod cognoscitur* and *modus quo cognoscitur*. As human knowers, both what we know about God and how we know it, are irremediably and irretrievably limited by our ontological otherness and distance from God.[23]   This otherness prevents our adequately grasping the utter oneness that is God; "the consequence is that every human positive assertion of the truth is a conjecture."[24]

So what Cusanus explains in *De coniecturis* I should also be understood as conjectural. Drawing on traditional themes, he gives the Neoplatonic doctrine of procession and return to the One his own articulation as "unfolding and enfolding." He extends enfolding/unfolding to human cognition to designate exactly how our active fashioning of the conceptual realm images God's creation of real things. While our mathematical knowledge is non-conjectural, Nicholas explicitly calls its application to

[22] H III, n. 3, pp. 187-190, puts together the relevant quotes from *De coniecturis* referring to *coniectura,* cites passages in Cusanus' other works where the word appears as well as its sources in his predecessors, and explains its non-technical meaning in his own time.

[23] This thesis, of course, makes the initial *imago dei* theme on which *De coniecturis* hinges itself conjectural. I make more of this point in "Nicholas of Cusa and Philosophic Knowledge," *Proceedings of the American Catholic Philosophical Association* 54 (1980): 155-163, and in "Irony and the History of Philosophy," *Poetics Today* 4 (1983): 465-478.

[24] *De coniecturis* Prologue, #2 (h III, 4).

non-mathematical realities "conjecturing." So the arithmetic progression of the numbers one to four and the derivation of 10, 100, and 1000 from one parallel the unfolding of the three dependent orders of reality from God, while the geometric diagrams exhibit the participation of otherness in oneness throughout the hierarchical universe. This employment of mathematics is an apt way to articulate for thought and imagination the varied aspects of a complex and totally interconnected vision. All of *De coniecturis* can exemplify the art and secret of conjecturing since the whole treatise illustrates and expounds Cusanus' recognition of the disproportion between God's oneness and the otherness of everything else.

Conjectural knowledge, if viewed as content rather than the activity of conjecturing, covers most sectors of what we know, apart from mathematics. Our whole knowledge of God and the universe--of all that is real and independent of our knowing activity--counts as conjectural knowledge. This would include both the organized knowledge of the human and natural sciences, as well as the common-sense generalizations based on our experience. Both perceptual and conceptual knowing remain conjectural--inexact approximations to the truth of things. *De coniecturis* I, 11 provides Nicholas' reason for the thesis: the only knowledge that is not conjectural results from that knowing activity which is causally responsible for the reality of the things known. All God's knowledge is therefore non-conjectural; for human beings, only knowledge of mathematics is. In a rather obscure passage Nicholas writes:

> . . . you can understand no intelligible as it is, once you admit your intellect is a thing other than the intelligible thing itself. For an intelligible is itself understood as it is only in its own proper intellect whose being it is; in all other [intellects it is understood] in another fashion. So nothing is [cognitively] attained as it is, except in its proper truth, by which it exists. Therefore, only in the divine intellect by which every being exists is the truth of all things attained as it is. In other intellects [the truth is attained] in other and different ways.[25]

These sentences point to two fundamental separations: one between mind and knowable things, and one between human mind and divine mind. Taking the latter first, we may see that we do not penetrate to the essence of things in our knowing because we do not create extramental things but only the conceptual measures whereby we approximate them in thought. Only in the intellect, which produces or creates the knowable things, can the thing's essence or truth be comprehended on its own terms. Only there does the divine mind construct the limits and sense of the thing's reality. Humans experience this active creating in constructing mathematical concepts whose

[25] *De coniecturis* I, 11, #55 (h III, 56).

meaning and reality depend totally on human reason. For all other created things, only in the divine mind is their true measure as knowable originally set and so fully and exactly taken. All other minds understand God and what God creates not as they are, but in otherness.

There is a second distinction alluded to in the first sentence of the passage: that between the knowing mind and created knowable things. This distance, or otherness, that separates our minds from the other created things we encounter as knowers is due to the otherness intrinsic to each side. Knower and knowable both have the status of finite creatures.[26] Each is not the other, but, more fundamentally, each is not the creator, but shares in the infinite oneness of God in a limited way. Because of this limitation and otherness which distance creation from God, neither mind nor knowable created thing can perfectly fulfill its own essence. Rather each creature is merely a contracted instance of its own exemplar in the spatio-temporal universe of change. Its paradigmatic essence is identical with God's oneness. On the part of both knower and knowable there is ontological imperfection (based on what Cusanus terms "otherness"). This provides further reason why our knowledge remains inexact, approximative, "conjectural."

After Cusanus' discussion of how God's oneness can only be multiplied and shared in otherness, we should expect that the oneness of the human mind, God's image, would be multiplied and shared in otherness, not only in the varied knowing powers already mentioned, but also in the concepts and judgments that make up the content of our knowledge. Cusanus' definition of *coniectura* in *De coniecturis* I, 11 may thus be interpreted more as a corollary to his general discussion than as a thesis to be established. He says: "and so a conjecture is a positive statement which participates in truth as it is, [but] in otherness."[27] This immediately distinguishes Nicholas' conjectures from the falsifiable hypotheses or provisional hunches of later physical science. In the same chapter he writes that "the positive statements of the wise are conjectures," as if to remind us that his real emphasis is on wisdom, an account of the whole of reality in its structure, source, and goal traditional since the Greeks. This means our conjectural knowledge, while not the exhaustive or precise truth of things, does have some share in truth

[26] In Cusanus' later *Idiota. De mente,* this gap between the mind and knowable things appears as a tension between knowing as measuring and knowing as becoming like or assimilated to other things. See my "Introduction" to *About Mind,* pp. 22-27. See also F. Edward Cranz, "Cusanus, Luther and the Mystical Tradition," in *The Pursuit of Holiness,* ed. Charles Trinkaus and Heiko Oberman (Leiden, 1974), pp. 93-103, for a fascinating placing of Cusanus' ideas about knowledge.

[27] The Latin text reads: "Coniectura igitur est positiva assertio, in alteritate veritatem, uti est, participans." Both sentences quoted in this paragraph are from *De coniecturis* I, 11, #57 (h III, 58).

(ultimately in the oneness of God) but via the otherness that marks the human mind's being and knowing.

What is remarkable about Nicholas' definition of *conjectura* is that it focuses on the otherness recognized in human knowing activity rather than on that in the knowable thing. This emerges clearly in the example from perceptual experience Cusanus proposes just before he states the definition.[28]

He recalls for Cardinal Julian (Giuliano Cesarini) the cognitive experience of an audience with Pope Eugenius IV.

> While you gaze with your clear eyes upon the face of the supreme pontiff, . . . you conceive a positive statement about it which you affirm as exact in terms of sight. But when you turn to the root from which sense discrimination issues--I mean, to reason--you understand that the sense of sight participates in that power of discrimination in the otherness contracted to a sense organ. For this reason you see the deficiency of a falling off from exactness, because you gaze on his face, not as it is, but in the otherness corresponding to the angle of your eye, which is different from all the viewpoints of the others.[29]

From this example two defects are to be found in the perceptual judgment, "I see the pope's face." The first is due to the fact that reason is the basis of cognitive discrimination, even in the realm of sense. But in visual prerception what can be discerned is limited by the presentations of sight and so can be no more precise than bodily eyesight ever is. This limitation or defect is what Cusanus calls "the otherness contracted to a sense organ *(alteritas organice contracta)*."

The second limitation (an extension of the first) is that perception is always perspectival and depends on the standpoint of the viewer. So the cardinal does not see the pope's whole face, but only the part of it visible from where he stands. Cusanus terms this "the otherness corresponding to the angle of your eye *(alteritas secundum angulum tui oculi)*." Yet the perceptual judgment, "I see the Pope's face," does assert and reflect some grasp of the papal appearance. In Nicholas' words, the statement "participates in the truth as it is," but in a recognizably limited way, that is, "in otherness."

Another remarkable feature of the example is that Cusanus points out that one can assess the conjectural character of knowledge just by attending

---

[28] For a different analysis of this Cusan example, see Fräntzki, *Nikolaus von Kues,* pp. 104-106. He glosses Cusanus' description of *coniectura* thus, p. 106: "Die Mutmassung ist in der Weise eine positive Aussage, dass zugleich ihre Andersheit, d.i. Ungenauigkeit, als ihre Wesensbestimmtheit miterkannt ist, durch welche Erkenntnis allererst ihre Partizipation an der Wahrheit gegeben ist."

[29] *De coniecturis* I, 11, #57 (h III, 58).

to the "otherness" present in one's own cognitive experience *(dum autem
. . . te convertis).* Our reflective ability to recognize that our knowledge in
every area except mathematics is inexact and limited by otherness is what
enables us to see such knowledge as conjectural. The sources of this otherness are to be found in the ontological structure of knowers and knowables.
For human knowers, oneness and otherness are manifest in the varied knowing capacities each knower exhibits and employs. Other knowable things are
both independent of our knowledge and dependent on, yet other than, God.
Here we may recall how the four metaphysical realms, or "unities," are
paralleled by human knowing powers. Each successive region and power is
the "otherness" of the previous realm's "oneness." Intellect's oneness reflects
the realm of divine oneness as God's image. And our powers of intellect,
reason, and sense (with imagination) share directly in the realms of intellect,
soul, and body. So our capacities to know relate both to the oneness of
God's truth and to the otherness of all that issues from the divine.

Our own cognitive measuring is active and creative. We fashion, order,
and articulate the conceptual world of conjectures which is measured by the
oneness of the active mind. Conjectural knowledge remains provisional and
approximate, yet it can be revised and improved to become more faithful to
the true reality of finite things and God. Our ability to assess our
knowledge as conjectural by recognizing its otherness places us already
beyond the limits of conceptual knowledge and at least partially in touch
with the ideal of knowledge as complete identification of knower and
known. This ideal is only fully realized in the identity that is God's
oneness: in God all things are nothing else than God.

Cusanus calls our knowledge conjectural to contrast it with God's
knowledge. For him, God's knowledge is both aperspectival and omni-
perspectival, totally complete and utterly exact, a coincidence of knower and
known in infinite unity. We approach this ideal in seeing our present knowledge as conjectural and extrapolating beyond its limits. Our statements
about God and all the realities God creates remain partial, limited,
perspectival, approximate. To assess our knowledge as conjectural is to remain faithful to the programmatic, incomplete, and ever inadequate character
of human knowing.

In this way the doctrine of conjecture reworks the notion of "learned
ignorance" Cusanus had earlier explored.[30] Since our knowledge of God and
creatures is only provisional, its conjectural character reminds us that there
is much that we do not know. And because we see as well how our
knowing involves different powers and encounters extramental things

---

[30] For these senses of *docta ignorantia,* see von Velthoven, *Gottesschau,*
pp. 43-47; Jasper Hopkins, *Nicholas of Cusa on Learned Ignorance*
(Minneapolis, 1981), pp. 2-5.

limited by otherness, we understand why our conceptual knowledge must remain conjectural. As knowers, we do not and cannot penetrate to the true essence of other things. As for knowing God, the situation is even more drastic. Utter oneness is totally beyond the grasp of the human mind whose thought and language are limited by reason's finite status. Recognizing why we do not know and cannot know is learning at the same time that our acknowledged ignorance points beyond itself. As goal-directed activity, our knowing points beyond the limits which constrain the finite mind; God haunts what we have learned is our ignorance. As Cusanus wrote in a passage already quoted, "its [the mind's] goal is the infinite reason which alone is the measure of all reason's works and in which our mind will behold itself as it is." That our knowledge is conjectural lets us learn anew that our minds, however limited, find their "single living center" in God's mind.

3.

Learning what Nicholas of Cusa means by *coniectura* reminds us once more that human knowing is no less finite and limited than human being. But Cusanus also stresses that we are images of the divine even in our limitations. Indeed, we may well get a better sense of Nicholas' views if we recall what seems true of most Neoplatonic categorical schemes: they are much easier to penetrate sympathetically if we interpret them as synthetic frameworks extrapolated from human cognitive experience for the purpose of framing harmoniously all there is. So we must turn to the limited human mind in order to approach the divine exemplar; we must fathom the conceptual world, however conjectural, to approach an adequate account of the created world. The human knower, human knowing powers, human concepts and judgments are central to all that Cusanus accomplishes in *De coniecturis*.

Nowhere is this expressed more tellingly than in the final chapters of the treatise. In Book II, 14-17, Cusanus discusses human nature in general, the differences between individual humans, the human spirit and its knowing capacities. Finally he turns in summary to urge Cardinal Cesarini to the sort of individual self-knowledge that the art of conjecturing should evoke and effect. The tone of this long finale is set dramatically in II, 14:

> Because it [human nature] conjectures that it reaches everything either by sense or by reason or by intellect, and while it sees that these powers are all enfolded in its unity, it assumes that it can go out to all things in a human fashion. For man is God, but not absolutely, because he is man--so he is a human god. Man is also the world, but in a limited way and not all things, because he is man. So man is a microcosm, or at any rate a human world. So the very sphere of humanity embraces God and the whole world in its human power. Therefore, man can be a

human god, and as god he is capable in human fashion of being human angel, human beast, human lion or bear or anything else whatever. For within the power of human nature all things exist in its own mode.[31]

These startling proposals recall the force of Cusanus' slogan already mentioned: "Everything [is] in each thing." The passage is thus a striking extension of ideas already mentioned in part one of this essay. Human beings are microcosms, each person an epitome of the universe; as nothing but man, everything is in each man. The powers "enfolded" in the human person's unity as a knower are the basis for the ability to "go out to all things in a human fashion." In II, 15 Cusanus describes in detail how intellect, reason, and sense (plus imagination) issue from the unity of the human mind. Their hierarchical panoply reaches from the oneness of intellect to the otherness of sense. Yet our cognitive powers operate as a dynamic unity, highest and lowest mutually present and acting in concert in our encounters with the world, as well as in our active fashioning of the conjectural realm whereby we know. A few sentences after the passage quoted above, Nicholas makes human "enfolding" as extensive as human knowledge, the content known through the mind's capacities already "unfolded": "Finally, everything is enfolded in it [human nature] in a human way, since it is a human god."[32]

This encomium of human being and human knowing suggests that *De coniecturis* might count as a humanist document of the Italian Renaissance.[33] At the same time, we cannot help but note how well it continues the sort of humanism one finds everywhere in medieval thinkers after the eleventh century. They, as well as their Renaissance successors, stressed the dignity of human nature within an independent natural order. They believed that created things manifested an intelligible order open to human understanding while never forgetting that human destiny lay beyond the created in God the creator. Yet even if the origin and end of human nature transcended the natural cosmos, that world was evaluated positively and given its own autonomy and dignity, as were women and men within it. Just because they were autonomous, humans could understand their place in the cosmic order and their need to transcend it.

[31] *De coniecturis* II, 14, #143 (h III, 143-144).

[32] *De coniecturis* II, 14, #144 (h III, 144).

[33] In his classic, *The Individual and the Cosmos in Renaissance Philosophy*, trans. Mario Domandi (Oxford, 1963), Ernst Cassirer stressed Cusanus' connection with the Renaissance and later ideas. Later he admitted that "he probably overestimated the influence of Cusanus' doctrine on Italian thinkers," p. xi. For medieval humanism, see R.W. Southern, *Medieval Humanism and Other Studies* (New York, 1970), esp. the title essay, pp. 29-60.

Measured against such a summary of medieval humanism, it is clear that Cusanus' *De coniecturis* shares much of the medieval view. As he writes in II, 14, #142, speaking of human nature, "Wondrous is this work of God *(mirabile est hoc dei opificium)*." He underlines the nobility of the human in its own right but especially as God's image; he orders a Neoplatonic universe in oneness and otherness schematized perspicuously in his figures *P* and *U*. Nor did Nicholas imagine that our destiny could be fulfilled any place but in that "single living center," the divine mind to which our own knowing is fundamentally ordered. In this way we may wonder what could let this work be measured by any but medieval standards.

In spite of its positive evaluation of man's status and even the individualistic turn of its final chapter, we miss in *De coniecturis* many of the features we look for in Renaissance writing.[34] Cusanus' Latin prose is simply not up to Ciceronian standards. (Even the earlier scholastics wrote clearer Latin.) Though he later turned to the dialogue in place of the treatise, Nicholas does not emphasize literary style or form over philosophic or religious doctrines. Even when he opposes the scholasticism of his day, he does so believing it had betrayed its real theoretical purposes.

Yet on one central point Cusanus has left the Middle Ages behind and may stand as a Renaissance thinker: for him knowledge of God and the universe is a matter of conjecture.[35] Unlike the earlier medieval thinkers, he asserts that we cannot attain to knowledge of God or even to the quiddity of created things. We do encounter an independent created cosmos, but at best what we know of it is our own construction. Renaissance and later thinkers saw man's glory and dignity in his struggle to make sense of, and act in, a world that seemed more and more unintelligible. Cusanus stands half-way, as it were, between this later view and the medieval conviction that our minds can really grasp the meaning of things. For Nicholas, our position is rather one of making proposals or assertions that have their own share in God's truth since we are God's images. But the precision and certitude that might mark ideally complete knowledge are lacking to both

[34] For a typical statement of the meaning of Renaissance humanism, see S. Dresden, *Humanism in the Renaissance,* trans. M. King (New York, 1968), esp. pp. 214-237. I follow here P.O. Kristeller, "The Humanist Movement," in his *Renaissance Thought and its Sources,* ed. M. Mooney (New York, 1979), pp. 21-32. See also the monumental two-volume work of Charles Trinkaus, *In Our Image and Likeness: Humanity and Divinity in Italian Humanist Thought* (Chicago, 1970). For a view of Cusanus which locates him much nearer the Renaissance, see Pauline Watts, *Nicolaus Cusanus: A Fifteenth-Century Vision of Man* (Leiden, 1982), esp. pp. 101-116, 224-232.

[35] On this point, see Cassirer, *Individual and Cosmos,* pp. 21-23; H.G. Gadamer, "Nikolaus von Kues im modernen Denken," in *Nicolò Cusano agli inizi del mondo moderno* (Florence, 1970), pp. 39-48, esp. p. 41.

our perception and conception (except in the basic science of mathematics). If we are not blind, neither do we have God's vision.

The modification of earlier medieval confidence in our ability to know and bespeak the world and its creator as they truly are is what separates Nicholas from his predecessors, however medieval *De coniecturis* may be in every other respect. Even while he celebrates man as "a human god," Nicholas initiates in his own way a set of philosophic convictions to be paralleled in other thinkers about the lack of openness of things to human cognition. In *De coniecturis*, as in his other writings, Cusanus functions as a bridging figure between the medieval humanism that had been and the Renaissance humanism that was aborning. Our glory is to be human gods, but our knowing no less than our nature makes manifest the distance between the human image and the divine original. What is striking about *De coniecturis*, then, is that to preserve the transcendence of the medieval God Nicholas of Cusa moves toward a post-medieval view of human knowing.[36]

[36] This conclusion is similar to that of Hans Blumenberg, but it rests on the analysis of this single text rather than on an overall view of how Cusanus fits into the whole process of *Geistesgeschichte* in the West. See his *The Legitimacy of the Modern Age,* trans. R.M. Wallace (Cambridge, Massachusetts, 1983), esp. pp. 488-547.

THE LATE WORKS OF NICHOLAS OF CUSA

F. Edward Cranz

The present essay examines the late works of Cusanus, from the *De beryllo* of 1458 through the *De apice theoriae* of 1464, as an important last stage in his thought. One may divide his writings roughly into three main periods. The early period, with which we shall not be further concerned, includes the works before his "revelation" on the way back from Constantinople in 1437-38, mainly the *De concordantia catholica* of 1433 and the sermons before 1437-38. The middle period begins with the great *De docta ignorantia* of 1440 and includes as major works the *De coniecturis* of 1442-43, the *Idiota (De sapientia I and II and De mente)* of 1450, and the *De visione dei* of 1453. Finally the late period begins, as already indicated, with the *De beryllo* of 1458 and continues with the *De aequalitate* and *De principio* of 1459, the *Trialogus de possest* of 1460, the *De non aliud* of 1461, the *De ludo globi* of 1462-63, the *De venatione sapientiae* of 1462, the *Compendium* of 1464, and Cusanus' last work, the *De apice theoriae*, completed shortly before his death.

Even though it is possible to set up periods within Cusanus' thought, we must also accept his contention that in terms of his "first principle" he exhibited a fundamental unity. Thus he remarks in the *Compendium* of 1464 that if you read all his many and various writings "you will find that the first principle everywhere the same appeared to us variously and that we depicted its various showing variously."[1]

So let us first look briefly at the main characteristics of this first principle, though Cusanus will always deny the possibility of an explicit description of it. It appears in the *De docta ignorantia* as the incomprehensible which can only be grasped incomprehensibly in knowing ignorance and in darkness; we can only know that we do not know it. And in his last work he tells us that for many years he had seen that as quiddity "it must be sought beyond all cognitive power before all variety and opposition."[2]

---

[1] *Compendium* Conclusio #44 (h XI, 3, 33): ". . . et reperies primum principium undique idem varie nobis apparuisse et nos ostensionem eius variam varie depinxisse."

[2] *De apice theoriae* #4 (h XII, 119): "Cum igitur iam annis multis viderim ipsam ultra omnem potentiam cognitivam ante omnem varietatem et oppositionem quaeri oportere . . ."

Further the first principle is the ultimate ground and cause.

> Thus the absolute maximum is the one which is all things (*omnia*); all things are in it, since it is maximum. And since nothing is opposed to it, the minimum coincides with it, and hence it is in all things. And since it is absolute, it is in act all possible being. It contracts nothing from things, and from it are all things.[3]

Cusanus also realized, with the help of Pseudo-Dionysius the Areopagite, that the first principle or God is "other" in relation to our thought or knowledge and to the creatures.

> Accordingly God, who is the maximum itself, as Dionysius says in the *De divinis nominibus* "is not this while He is not something else, nor is He somewhere and not somewhere else" [*De D. N.* V, 8]. Just as He is all things (*omnia*), so also He is none of all things.[4]

Finally he formulated a dialectic which asserted both that all things are derived from the principle and also that the principle cannot be reached from any of the things derived from it.

> For the principle of all is that through which, in which, and from which all that are derived from a principle are derived; nevertheless, it cannot be reached by anything derived from a principle. It is that through which, in which, and from which every intelligible is intellected; nevertheless it is not attainable by any intellect. Likewise it is that through which, from which, and in which everything which can be said is said; nevertheless it is not attainable by saying.[5]

[3] *De docta ignorantia* I, 2, #5 (h I, 7): "Maximum itaque absolutum unum est, quod est omnia; in quo omnia, quia maximum. Et quoniam nihil sibi opponitur, secum simul coincidit minimum; quare et in omnibus; et quia absolutum, tunc est actu omne possibile esse, nihil a rebus contrahens, a quo omnia."

[4] *De docta ignorantia* I, 16, #43 (h I, 31): "Deus enim, qui est hoc ipsum maximum, ut idem Dionysius De divinis nominibus dicit, non istud quidem est et aliud non est, neque alicubi est et alicubi non. Nam sicut omnia est, ita quidem et nihil omnium."

[5] *Idiota. De Sapientia,* I, #8 (h V, 9; h V², 14): "Nam omnium principium est, per quod, in quo, et ex quo omne principiabile, principiatur, et tamen per nullum principiatum attingibile. Ipsum est, per quod, in quo, et ex quo omne intelligibile intelligitur, et tamen intellectu inattingibile. Et similiter per quod, ex quo, et in quo omne fabile fatur, et tamen fatu inattingibile."

Thus Cusanus argues, and we must agree, that the presence of the same principle, which is both ultimate ground and cause and at the same time "other" in relation to thought and knowledge, persists from the *De docta ignorantia* through his very last works. What we must try to discover, however, are the different ways in which he receives and articulates his varying experience of one and the same principle.

Let me begin with an over-simplified statement of Cusanus' position in his middle period, from the *De docta ignorantia* of 1440 through the *De visione dei* of 1453.

First, and most generally, in the middle period Cusanus' starting point is a realm of reason and intellect. From this he moves on to an awareness of what is higher and out of proportion to it. Thus the first realm is combined with what transcends it in learned, or instructed, ignorance *(docta ignorantia)*. He described this as his revelation in the epilogue to the *De docta ignorantia:*

> I was led to this, that I might embrace incomprehensibles in-
> comprehensibly in instructed ignorance by the transcending of the
> incorruptible truths which are humanly knowable.[6]

In the first realm, Cusanus can reason "objectively" about God, the universe and the mind, almost in the manner of a new *Summa*. It is typical of such a method that after discussions of geometrical figures in the *De docta ignorantia* he can speak of his conclusions in phrases reminiscent of Euclid's *Elements,* e.g., "Which was to be proven."[7]   But Cusanus also recognizes that reason and intellect cannot reach the actuality of either God or His crea-tures. Hence we must recognize our ignorance and acknowledge that it only becomes instructed as we enter the darkness of unknowing. Thus Cusanus remarks in the prologue to the *De visione dei* that his purpose is to lead the reader "by experience into the most holy darkness."[8]   He later explains:

> Who ascends beyond the end, does he not enter into what is
> undetermined and confused and thus, in relation to the intellect, into
> ignorance and obscurity? . . . Therefore the intellect must become

---

[6] *De docta ignorantia* III, Epistola auctoris #263 (h I, 163): ". . . ad hoc ductus sum, ut incomprehensibilia incomprehensibiliter amplecterer in docta ignorantia, per transcensum veritatum incorruptibilium humaniter scibilium."

[7] *De docta ignorantia* I, 13, #36 (h I, 27).

[8] *De visione dei,* ed. Jasper Hopkins, Prologue, #1, p. 112: "Conabor autem simplicissimo et communissimo modo vos experimentaliter in sacratissimam obscuritatem manuducere."

ignorant and must be established in the shadow, if it wishes to see you.
But what, o my Lord, is the intellect in ignorance? Is it not the
intellect in instructed ignorance?[9]

Second, Cusanus in the middle period continues to use the terminology
of being for both God and His creatures, and God may be called the highest
being, essence, or entity. Here are a few passages from the *De visione dei*.
"Thus you, o God, the absolute being of all things, are present to all."[10]
"You are therefore the essence of essences, giving to contracted essences that
they be what they are."[11]   "Thus, o God, your being exists in some such
way as this, that is as the being of absolute infinity."[12]

Finally, throughout the middle period, Cusanus believes himself to be
building upon and adding to the main philosophic tradition, despite some
specific criticism of particular philosophers. He does not try to distance
himself fundamentally from Plato and Aristotle as the typical representatives
of the tradition. Here are some examples of his eirenic and conciliatory
approach from the *Idiota de mente* of 1450, the last work of the middle
period in which he explicitly discusses positions held by the philosophers.
Thus early in the conversations of the *De mente* the Philosopher remarks
that the Layman (or Cusanus) has touched on all the sects, both of the
Peripatetics and of the Academics. Cusanus replies:

> All these, and however many modes of difference can be thought, are
> most easily resolved and brought into concord, when the mind raises
> itself to infinity.[13]

[9] *De visione dei* (h XIII, #53, 178): "Qui ultra finem ascendit, nonne hic
subintrat in indeterminatum et confusum et ita quoad intellectum ignorantiam et
obscuritatem, quae sunt confusionis intellectualis? Oportet igitur intellectum
ignorantem fieri et in umbra constitui, si te videre velit. Sed quid est, deus meus,
intellectus in ignorantia? Nonne docta ignorantia?" Compare *De docta
ignorantia* III, 11, #245-246 (h I, 152-153).

[10] *De visione dei* (h IV, #10, 124): "Ita enim tu, absolutum esse omnium,
ades cunctis . . ."

[11] *De visione dei* (h IX, #36, 156): "Es igitur essentia essentiarum, dans
contractis essentiis, ut id sint quod sunt."

[12] *De visione dei* (h XIV, #63, 190): "Sic se habet aliqualiter, deus, tuum
esse, quod est esse infinitatis absolutae . . ."

[13] *Idiota. De mente* II, #67 (h V, 54; V², 103): "Hae omnes et quotquot
cogitari possent modorum differentiae facillime resolvantur et concordantur,
quando mens se ad infinitatem elevat."

Cusanus can even state his own central position and then go on to find that it had been adumbrated by the philosophers.

> And all of them didn't try to say anything else, though it may be that what they said could have been said better and more clearly. All necessarily agreed that there is one infinite virtue, which we call God, in which all things are necessarily complicated.[14]

Thus in his middle period, Cusanus moves in knowing ignorance from reason and intellect to that which transcends them; he continues to make full use of the terminology of being; and he finds himself in general harmony with the main philosophic tradition, even when he moves beyond it. In his later works, however, beginning with the *De beryllo* of 1458, Cusanus gradually moves away from all these positions of the middle period, even though the movement is not completed until his last work, the *De apice theoriae* of 1464.

In the first place, and most important, he now makes it his main concern to find a new starting point in an immediate relationship, a vision of God and the first principle. As he does this the emphasis on darkness as the final stage of thought gradually disappears until it is explicitly abandoned in the *De apice*. Second, the terminology of being is not supported by the new starting point; it slowly weakens, and it too is finally rejected in the *De apice*. Finally, Cusanus begins to distance himself fundamentally from the philosophic tradition. He realizes that the ancient premises were clearly different from his own, and he works both to clarify the difference and to develop his own new position. If at the very end, he moves back to an attempted reconciliation, it is only after having taken the philosophers out of their own context and after reading them in the framework of his own new solution of the "*Posse* itself" and its appearances.[15]

Let us first notice the new program in the opening chapters of the *De beryllo*. Cusanus observes that in the past he had worked with the coincidence of opposites and with intellectual vision.[16] We should remember that beginning with the *De coniecturis* he had insisted both that God was beyond the coincidence of opposites and also that the intellect functioned

---

[14] *Idiota. De mente* II, #68 (h V, 55; h V², 104): "Et nihil aliud omnes conati sunt dicere, licet forte id, quod dixerunt, melius et clarius dici posset. Omnes enim necessario concordarunt unam esse infinitam virtutem, quam deum dicimus, in qua necessario omnia complicantur."

[15] See below, pp. 160-161.

[16] *De beryllo* I, #1 (h XI, 1, 3; XI, 1², 3).

within the realm of coincidence.[17]   Now in the *De beryllo* he uses the beryl
as a riddling coincidence of opposites by which he can move intellectually
to a new direct vision of God as the first principle: "By the intellectual
beryl one attains to the indivisible principle of all."[18]   When he has finished
his introduction, Cusanus summarizes the large program to which the *De
beryllo* and his later works will be devoted: "We wish to see God as the
indivisible principle."[19]

In analyzing the development of this program, which is completed only
with the *De apice theoriae*, we may start with Cusanus' growing awareness
of the differences between his own position and that of the philosophic
tradition which he had once largely accepted.

First, in relation to the ancient doctrine of the soul of the world,
Cusanus insists in opposition to the ancients that every creature is an
intention of God's will.

> Plato as well as Aristotle were ignorant of this. Clearly each of them
> believed that the creator intellect did everything by the necessity of
> nature, and all their error followed from this.[20]

Second, he faults the attempt of the ancients, notably Aristotle, to reach
a "third principle".

> I think that he [i.e. Aristotle] . . . and all of them failed in one thing
> most of all. Since the principles are contrary, they did not reach the
> third principle which is necessary, and this is because they did not
> believe it possible for contraries to coincide simultaneously in it.[21]

---

[17] *De coniecturis* I, 6, #22-23 (h III, 28-29); *Apologia doctae ignorantiae* (h
II, 15); *De visione dei* IX, #39, 160.

[18] *De beryllo* II, #3 (h XI, 1, 4-5; h XI, 1^2, 5-6): ". . . per eius [sc. berylli]
medium attingitur indivisibile omnium principium."

[19] *De beryllo* VII, #8 (h XI, 1, 8; XI, 1^2, 10): "Volumus autem ipsum ut
principium indivisibile videre."

[20] *De beryllo* XXIII, #38 (h XI, 1, 19; XI, 1^2, 46): "Istud ignorabant tam
Plato quam Aristoteles. Aperte enim uterque credidit conditorem intellectum ex
necessitate naturae omnia facere, et ex hoc omnis eorum error secutus est."

[21] *De beryllo* XXI, #40 (h XI, 1, 31; XI, 1^2, 45): "Arbitror ipsum [sc.
Aristotelem] quamvis super omnes diligentissimus atque acutissimus habeatur
discursor, atque omnes in uno maxime defecisse.   Nam cum principia sint
contraria, tertium principium utique necessarium non attiguerunt, et hoc ideo,
quia contraria simul in ipso coincidere non putabant possible."

A little later Cusanus explains this as a failure to reach the Spirit:

> And for this reason all the philosophers did not reach the Spirit, which is the principle of connection and which is the third person in divinity according to our perfect theology, even though many of them, and most of all the Platonists, spoke eloquently of the Father and the Son.[22]

Third, and perhaps most important, Cusanus in the *De venatione sapientiae* of 1462 criticizes the philosophers for their false starting point in all their thinking.

> The philosopher-hunters are seen in all their pursuits to have started their inquiry from this sensible world and from those things which are necessary to it, so that it might be what it is in the best manner possible, and thus they treated of God, of the heavens and their motion and of fate, of the intelligences, spirits, and ideas, and of nature itself, as if all these were necessary to this earthly world, and as if this world were the goal of all these works.[23]

Cusanus has here achieved an important insight into the nature of ancient thought, and he has also become clearer about the different movement of his own, no longer from the world to God, but from God to His creatures.

It might be useful here to note two points made in the *De principio* of 1459, though they are related specifically to Platonism rather than to the philosophic tradition in general. The immediate focus of the *De principio* is on Proclus' use of *authypostaton* or self-subsistent (*per se subsistens*). According to Cusanus, Proclus wished to apply this to the One only in so far as it is the cause of the true self-subsistents, and these are the eternal forms or ideas of Plato.[24] Cusanus in contrast regularly uses "self-subsistent" of God, and he rejects the eternal forms:

> But that there can be many things coeternal [sc. to the One], except for its three hypostases, Proclus did not say well [in asserting this].[25]

[22] *De beryllo* XXV, #42 (h XI, 1, 32; XI, 1², 48).

[23] *De venatione sapientiae* XXI, #63 (h XII, 60).

[24] *De principio* #24 (h X, *Opuscula* II, Fasc. 2, 33). I do not believe that Proclus ever says that the One is self-subsistent, and he frequently denies it (cf. the passages cited in the Heidelberg edition to the section noted). He does of course say that the One is the cause of the self-subsistents.

[25] *De principio* #25 (h X, *Opuscula* II, Fasc. 2, 35-36): "Sed quod plura possint esse sibi [sc. Uni] coaeterna tribus suis hypostasibus exceptis, non bene dixit [sc. Proclus] . . ."

Cusanus does not criticise Plato directly as he does Proclus, but he achieves the same result by reinterpreting Plato into his own very different solution.

> Plato saw how the *per se* being existed before all the beings which are different, and so for the *per se* man and the *per se* animal and so on. But did not Plato see all these things which he saw subsisting *per se* not in anything else but in himself notionally . . .[26]

Cusanus has thus read into Plato his own doctrine that man is a second God who creates beings of reason and artificial forms, as God is the creator of real beings and of natural forms.[27] By his attack on Proclus he has eliminated any intermediate realm of eternal forms and ideas.

In coordination with this denial of important philosophic assumptions, Cusanus can also move to a clearer statement of his own new position on the first principle. His central thesis is that we must take as our starting point a God who acts not out of necessity but out of will and intention. Thus, in a chapter already noted, he explains that there was no need for Plato and Aristotle to posit in addition to God a creator intellect or a soul of the world:

> For every mode of being, a first, unitrine principle is abundantly sufficient, though it is absolute and superexalted, since it is not a contracted principle like nature, which acts from necessity. The first principle is the principle of nature itself, and it is thus supernatural and free, which by its will creates all.[28]

From his notion of God as acting by will, Cusanus reaches a new statement on the relation of creator and creature. God appears as the intender, and the creatures are His intentions or meanings.

> Those things which come to be by will exist in so far as they conform

[26] *De principio* #21 (h X, *Opuscula* II, Fasc. 2, 28): "Vidit Plato, quomodo per se ens ante omnia alia et alia exsistit, ita per se homo et animal et ita de ceteris. Nonne haec omnia, quae per se subsistere vidit, non in alio, sed in se vidit notionaliter . . . ?"

[27] See, e.g. *De beryllo* VI, #7 (h XI, 1, 7; XI, 1², 9).

[28] *De beryllo* XXIII, #37 (h XI, 1, 29; XI, 1², 42-43): "Sed ad omnem essendi modum sufficit habunde primum principium unitrinum, licet sit absolutum et superexaltatum, cum non sit principium contractum ut natura, quae ex necessitate operatur, sed sit principium ipsius naturae et ita supernaturale, liberum, quod voluntate creat omnia."

to the will, and hence their form is the intention of the commander. An intention is a likeness of the one who intends, a likeness which is communicable in something else.[29]

Cusanus then uses God's intentions as a solution to the old problem of quiddity, though he will not reach his final formulation until the *De apice*. In the *De beryllo* he uses the analogy of speech as an explanation. When someone speaks to us, "if we reach the quiddity of his speech, we do not reach anything else than the intention of the speaker."[30] Later in the argument he makes the point that the cause of meaning is manifestation:

> The cause of intention is manifestation; the speaker or the creative intellect intends thus to manifest himself. When the intention has been apprehended, which is the quiddity of the word, we have "what was to be", for what "was to be" in the intellect is apprehended in the intention, just as in the completed house the intention of the builder is apprehended, which was in his intellect . . .[31]

If only Plato and Aristotle had looked to the true cause of the universe, the will of God, they would have found the true solution to all their doubts.

> What did the creator will, when he brought forth a rose from thorns? . . . What can be replied except that His marvellous intellect intended to manifest itself in this word, of how great wisdom and reason He is . . .[32]

Cusanus touches on some of the same points from a different angle in the *De non aliud* of 1461. As you will remember, he is here speaking of himself as one devoted primarily to the study of Pseudo-Dionysius, and as we shall see later in more detail, he presents the "not other" as a name for God quite agreeable to Dionysius. Throughout there is no hint of disagreement with Dionysius, but he places him, as we have seen him place Plato, in a new context of Cusanus' own.

[29] *De beryllo* XXIII, #37 (h XI, 1, 29; XI, 1², 43): "Illa vero, quae voluntate fiunt, in tantum sunt, in quantum voluntati conformantur, et ita eorum forma est intentio imperantis. Intentio autem est similitudo intendentis, quae est communicabilis et receptibilis in alio."

[30] *De beryllo* XXXI, #54 (h XI, 1, 40; XI, 1², 61): "Nam a simili, cum quis nobis loquitur, si nos quiditatem attingimus sermonis, non nisi intentionem loquentis attingimus."

[31] *De beryllo* XXXI, #54 (h XI, 1², 62).

[32] *De beryllo* XXXVI, #68 (h XI, 1, 50; XI, 1², 78-79).

In contrast to the *De beryllo*, Cusanus here uses the terminology of concept (*conceptus*) rather than of intention; he also gives more emphasis to the immediate relation of the thinker to what is absolute and to his vision of it.

In the dialogue, Petrus Balbus says he agrees with Cusanus, but that when he turns to the *non aliud*, he cannot with his mind conceive it. Cusanus replies:

> If indeed you could conceive it, it would not be the principle of all things, which in all things signifies all things. Every human concept is the concept of one something, but the *non aliud* is before any concept. . . . Therefore let the *non aliud* be called the absolute concept, which is seen by the mind but which is otherwise not conceived.[33]

In the terminology of meanings of concepts, Cusanus has thus reached a powerful characterization of God as the "absolute concept". In the continuation of the discussion, he analyzes creaturely meanings in the same context. Peter wonders whether the *non aliud* is not everything that is in any concept, and Cusanus agrees, "In every concept, the *non aliud* is whatever is conceived, while at the same time the concept which is the *non aliud* itself remains inconceivable."[34]

Peter further wonders what is the function of the "than" in such definitions as "Earth is not other than earth." Cusanus replies in terms of the general thrust of his late thought. The "than" directs the sight, and it directs it simply to the *non aliud*.[35]

We have now seen how in the late works Cusanus formulated his goal as an immediate vision of God as the first principle. In his movement toward this goal he had distanced himself from the philosophic tradition. Further he had formulated new positions dealing with God's freedom from necessity and His creation by will, or with God as absolute concept.

[33] *Directio speculantis seu de non aluid* XX (h XIII, 49): "Si quidem posses id concipere, haud utique esset omnium principium, quod in omnibus omnia significaret. Omnis enim humanus conceptus unius alicuius conceptus est. Verum ante conceptum 'non aliud' est, quando quidem conceptus non aliud quam conceptus est. Vocetur igitur ipsum 'non aliud' conceptus absolutus, qui videtur quidem mente, ceterum non concipitur."

[34] *De non aliud* XX (h XIII, 49): ". . . in omni conceptu 'non aliud' est quodcunque concipitur, manente sane conceptu, qui ipsum 'non aliud' est, inconceptibili."

[35] *De non aluid* XXI (h XIII, 50): "Quia dirigit visum . . . li 'quam' in 'non aliud' visum simpliciter dirigit."

The development of his thought is further illuminated by the new "names" for the absolute which he produces in his late works. Three are most important: 1. The *Possest* in the *Trialogus de possest* of 1460; 2. The *non aliud* in the *De non aliud* of 1461; and 3. The *"Posse* itself" *(Posse ipsum)* in his last work, the *De apice theoriae* of 1464.

In the *Trialogus de possest* Cusanus presents the first of his new names. *Possest* represents the coincidence of "to be able" *(posse)* and "to be" *(esse),* or of potentiality and actuality. It leads the one who uses and understands it into an immediate relation with God through vision.

> Accordingly this name [the *Possest*] leads the speculator above every sense, every reason, and every intellect into mystic vision, where there is the end of the ascent of every cognitive power and the beginning of the revelation of the unknown *God.*[36]

Cusanus long valued the *Possest,* even though he will brusquely reject it in the *De apice.* It appears in the *De venatione sapientiae* of 1462 as the second field of hunting, and Cusanus goes so far as to claim: "Therefore God is not to be sought in any other field than that of the *Possest.*"[37] He further notes that the philosophers ignored this field because they ignored the coincidence of opposites.

> It is clear why the philosophers, who did not enter this field, did not taste of the most delightful huntings. That which terrified them so that they wouldn't enter the field was that they presupposed that even God, as the others which follow the "to be able to become" *(posse fieri),* is to be sought this side of the difference of opposites.[38]

Cusanus presents another new name, the *non aliud* in the *De non aliud.* Like the other discoveries of his late works it leads to an immediate encounter with God, and he is persuaded that it represents an advance on anything he had seen earlier.

> Also though many names are attributed to the first principle, of which none can be adequate to Him . . . still He is seen by the eye of the mind more precisely by one mode of signification than another. Nor have I

[36] *Trialogus de possest* #15 (h XI, 2, 19): "Ducit ergo hoc nomen [sc. Possest] speculantem super omnem sensum, rationem, et intellectum in mysticam visionem, ubi est finis ascensus omnis cognitivae virtutis et revelationis incogniti dei initium."

[37] *De venatione sapientiae* XIII, #35 (h XII, 35).

[38] *De venatione sapientiae* XIII, #38 (h XIII, 37).

---

up to the present learned that any human signification leads the sight more rightly to the first [than the *non aliud*].[39]

He spells out in a little more detail what is seen, and he expresses a striking hope for a next stage of insight.

> You have rightly cast your eye (*aciem*) upon God through the *non aliud* so that you might see, as far as it is now conceded to you, all things humanly visible, as in the principle, cause or reason. . . .
>   Now moreover in this riddle of the signification of the *non aliud*, particularly since God here defines Himself, God reveals himself more clearly and fruitfully than before, to such a degree that I am able to hope that God is going at some time to reveal Himself to us without riddle.[40]

Cusanus' last "name" for God, the "*Posse* itself" *(posse ipsum)* is foreshadowed in the *Compendium* and fully affirmed in the *De apice theoriae,* and it is best presented within the general development of his thought in these final works.

In the *Compendium* Cusanus takes another important step toward his ultimate solution. We have seen that beginning with the *De beryllo* he affirmed as a new starting point the immediate vision of the first principle. He now for the first time comes to realize that the vision of the first principle or God is also the key to the visions of sense:

> There is only one object to the vision of the mind and the vision of sense; it is the object of the vision of the mind as it is in itself and of the vision of sense as it is in signs, and this object is itself the *posse,* than which nothing is more powerful.[41]

---

[39] *De non aliud* II (h XIII, 5-6): "Nam etsi primo principio multa attribuantur nomina, quorum nullum ei adaequatum esse potest, cum sit etiam nominum omnium sicut et rerum principium, et nihil principiati omnia antecedat, per unum tamen significandi modum mentis acie praecisius videtur, quam per alium. Neque hactenus equidem comperi quodcumque significatum humanum visum rectius in primum dirigere."

[40] *De non aliud* V (h XIII, 11-12): ". . . nunc autem in hoc aenigmate significati ipsius 'non aliud' per rationem potissimum illam, quia se definit, foecundius et clarius, adeo ut sperare queam ipsum Deum sese nobis aliquando sine aenigmate revelaturum."

[41] *Compendium*, Epilogus, #45 (h XI, 3, 33-34): "Tendit tota directio ad unitatem obiecti. . . . unum est obiectum visus mentis et visus sensus, visus mentis uti est in se, visus sensus uti est in signis, et est ipsum posse, quo nihil potentius." See also #47 (h XI, 3, 36).

As in the earlier works, the wish of the Absolute to manifest itself is the ultimate explanation.

> Therefore since itself the *posse,* than which nothing is more powerful, wishes to manifest itself, this is the reason why all things are.[42]

Even though Cusanus has not quite reached the name of the "*Posse* itself" *(posse ipsum),* he has already made *posse* central, and he has used the phrase "itself the *posse*" *(ipsum posse).* And as he has realized a unity within man's vision of the creator and of the creatures, the stage is set for the last movement of his thought.

Before going on to the *De apice,* it may be well to notice two positions of the middle period which long persisted in his late works despite the other changes, first his use of "being" in talking of God or of the first principle, and second his experience of darkness as the locus of ultimate religious and philosophic experience.

For the continued use of being to describe God, one can start with the *De possest.* First of all, there is the name *Possest* itself, in which being or *esse* is an important component. Early in the work Cusanus starts from the familiar text, Exodus III, 14: I AM WHO I AM *(Sum qui sum).* He explains that God is He who is and that God alone *is* perfectly and completely.[43] He later remarks "Therefore the divine essence is in all things, and it is the absolute entity which gives to all the being which they have."[44] As in earlier works Cusanus both applies the terminology of being to God and also states that God is "above being itself and not-being in every way in which these can be understood."[45] A latest instance of such use of the terminology of being is found in the *Compendium,* the next to the last work of Cusanus, where mode of being *(essendi modus)* is used of God and of that which neither sense nor imagination nor intellect can reach, since it precedes all of them. "Therefore there is no science of the mode of being,

---

[42] *Compendium* #47 (h XI, 3, 36): "Quia igitur ipsum posse, quo nihil potentius, vult posse videri, hinc ob hoc omnia."

[43] *Trialogus de possest* #14 (h XI, 2, 18).

[44] *Trialogus de possest* #65 (h XI, 2, 77): "In omnibus igitur est divina essentia quae entitas absoluta dans omnibus esse tale quale habent."

[45] *Trialogus de possest* #25 (h XI, 2, 31): The Possest is "supra ipsum esse et non-esse omni modo, quo illa intelligi possunt."

though it is most certainly seen that there is such a mode."[46]

As a second persistence from the middle period, darkness as the focus of man's awareness of God appears in the *Trialogus de possest.* Thus toward the end of the work, Cusanus tells his listener how God is to be reached.

> God as unintelligible is reached by ignorance or unintelligibly in the shade or shadow or unknowedly, where he is seen in mist and it isn't known what substance or what thing or which of beings it is.[47]

There does not appear to be any emphasis on such darkness after the *Trialogus de possest,* and one can assume that it is fading in Cusanus' thought even if it has not yet been denied.

Finally in the *De apice theoriae* all the barriers fall away; the revolution long aborning is completed and stated. Cusanus tells us that this culmination of his thought took place in meditations during the Easter festivities of 1464,[48] and he describes it in a remarkable intellectual autobiography.

Cusanus first reports what it was that he had long realized, namely that the quiddity *(quiditas)* of things lay beyond all cognitive power. We see this position clearly in the *De docta ignorantia*; it had been persistently restated ever since. Cusanus then goes on to what it was that he had never realized before these Easter festivities of 1464.

> But I had not realized that the quiddity subsisting in itself is the invariable subsistence of all substances; accordingly it is not to be multiplied nor made plural. Hence there is not one quiddity and then another of different beings, but there is one hypostasis of all. Then I saw that this hypostasis of things or their subsistence must necessarily be said to be able *(posse)* to be. . . . Therefore the *"Posse* itself" *(posse ipsum),* without which nothing can do anything, is that than which nothing can be more subsistent. Therefore it is the "what?" which has been sought, or the quiddity itself, without which

---

[46] *Compendium* I,#1 (h XI, 3, 3): "Igitur de essendi modo non est scientia, licet modum talem esse certissime videatur."

[47] *Trialogus de possest* #74 (h XI, 2, 87): ". . . sed altissimo et ab omnibus phantasmatibus absoluto intellectu omnibus transcensis ut nihil omnium quae sunt reperitur, inintelligibilis ignoranter seu inintelligibiliter in umbra seu tenebra sive incognite (attingitur). Ubi videtur in caligine et nescitur, quae substantia aut quae res aut quid entium sit. . . ." See also #31 (h XI, 2, 36).

[48] *De apice theoriae* #4 (h XII, 119).

nothing can be.[49]

Cusanus has here carried to the end the movement of thought characteristic of his late works. He has found his final name, the "*Posse* itself," for the first principle. Further, even more clearly than in the *Compendium* he recognizes that there is one solution to the problems both of the first principle and also of things. The "*Posse* itself" as first principle solves the old problem of the quiddity of things, which Aristotle had finally abandoned as insoluble and which had concerned Cusanus ever since the *De docta ignorantia*.[50] The "*Posse* itself" is the one quiddity of all things.

Peter of Ercklentz, the interlocutor of the *De apice*, wonders, since Cusanus had already said a great deal about the name *Possest* and explained it at length in the *Trialogus de possest*, why this wasn't enough. Cusanus, as already noted, rejects the suggestion, doubtless because he wishes to avoid the connection between the first principle and being (*esse*) which *Possest* emphasizes.

[49] *De apice theoriae* #4 (h XII, 119): ". . . non attendi quiditatem in se subsistentem esse omnium substantiarum invariabilem subsistentiam; ideo nec multiplicabilem nec plurificabilem, et hinc non aliam et aliam aliorum entium quiditatem, sed eandem omnium hypostasim. Deinde vidi necessario fateri ipsam rerum hypostasim seu subsistentiam posse esse . . . Ideo posse ipsum, sine quo nihil quicquam potest, est quo nihil subsistentius esse potest. Quare est ipsum quid quaesitum sive quiditas ipsa, sine qua non potest esse quicquam." Leo Gabriel in his edition: Nikolaus von Kues, *Philosophisch-theologische Schriften*, 3 vols. (Vienna, 1967) 2:364 with note 3, wrongly omits the *non* at the beginning of the quotation.

[50] Cusanus in the *De apice* when he refers to the search for the *quiditas* is echoing Aristotle, *Metaphysica* VII, 1028b2-4, a passage which had concerned him from the *De docta ignorantia*. See I, 3, #10 (h I, 9). See also *De venatione sapientiae* XII, 31 (h XII, 31-32). But in his previous works, Cusanus also speaks of many quiddities in contrast to his new assertion that there is only one. Cf. *De docta ignorantia* II, 4, #115 (h I, 74): "Et quia quidditas solis absoluta non est aliud a quidditate absoluta lunae - quoniam est ipse Deus, qui est entitas et quidditas absoluta omnium - et quidditas contracta solis est alia a quidditate contracta lunae - quia, ut quidditas absoluta rei non est res ipsa, ita contracta non est aliud quam ipsa." Cusanus makes the same point even more strongly in the *Apologia doctae ignorantiae* (h II, 33, line 20-25). For late examples of the many quiddities, see *De venatione sapientiae* XXIX, #86 (h XII, 82): "Nihil enim apprehendit intellectus quod in se ipso non repperit. Essentiae autem et quiditates rerum non sunt in ipso ipsae, sed tantum notiones rerum . . ."; #87 (h XII, 83): "Sic intellectus essentiales rerum formas et quiditates, cum sint ante notionalem suam virtutem et ipsam excedant, nequaquam attingere potest. . . ."

You will see below that the *Posse* itself, than which nothing can be more powerful or prior or better, is a much more fitting name than *Possest* or any other word, for that without which nothing can either be or live or understand.[51]

In his second statement of a major change during the Easter festivities, Cusanus declares that he has now given up his earlier view that the locus of the highest philosophic and religious experience lies in the "darkness."

I once thought that it [sc. truth] was better to be found in the shade (*in obscuro*). But truth is of great power, and in it the *Posse* itself shines brightly. . . . It most certainly shows itself everywhere easy to find.[52]

And he remarks:

Therefore the *Posse* itself is named light by certain of the saints, not the sensible or rational or intelligible light, but the light of all things which can shine, since nothing can be brighter or clearer or fairer than the *Posse* itself.[53]

The contrast is clear between the *De visione dei,* where Cusanus would lead the reader into most holy darkness and the *De apice theoriae,* where his goal is the "*Posse* itself," than which nothing could be brighter.

With these fundamental changes in hand, Cusanus can now move on to a basic position of his own which can both incorporate the newnesses of his recent meditations and also eliminate various traditional doctrines which had

---

[51] *De apice theoriae* #5 (h XII, 120): "Videbis infra posse ipsum, quo nihil potentius nec prius nec melius esse potest, longe aptius nominare illud, sine quo nihil quicquam potest nec esse nec vivere nec intelligere, quam possest aut aliud quodcumque vocabulum."

[52] *De apice theoriae* #5 (h XII, 120): "Putabam ego aliquando ipsam in obscuro melius reperiri. Magnae potentiae veritas est, in qua posse ipsum valde lucet. Clamitat enim in plateis, sicut in libello De idiota legisti. Valde certe se undique facilem repertu ostendit." Cusanus here correctly refers to the *Idiota. De sapientia* I, #3 (h V, 4-5; V², 5-6). See also #5 (h V, 6; V², 8) and #7 (h V, 8; V², 12). In the *De apice* Cusanus omits the statement of wisdom (*sapientia*) that she dwells in the highest (*in altissimis*).

[53] *De apice theoriae* #8 (h XII, 122): "Posse igitur ipsius per quosdam sanctos lux nominatur, non sensibilis aut rationalis sive intelligibilis, sed lux omnium quae lucere possunt, quoniam ipso posse nihil lucidius esse potest nec clarius nec pulchrius." In the first line the Paris edition of 1514 reads *ipsum,* and I have followed this in the translation.

become recessive in his thinking.

> I now plan to present to you this easy method *(facilitatem)*, which has not been made public before and which I regard as most secret, namely that all speculative precision is to be placed only in the *"Posse* itself" and its appearance . . .[54]

The main point to be made about this basic position of "only the *'Posse* itself' and its appearances" is that "being" at last disappears from Cusanus' thought. On the one hand "being" cannot be applied to the Posse itself:

> Nothing can be added to the *"Posse* itself". . . . Therefore the *"Posse* itself" is not the power *(posse)* to be or the power to live or the power to intellect. . . . The *"Posse"* with any addition is [only] an image of the *"Posse* itself."[55]

On the other hand, the creatures are no longer analyzed as "beings" but as appearances of the *"Posse* itself" (and we should remember that in the tradition one had always tried to rise above mere appearances in order to reach beings). In place of the older "modes of being" *(modi essendi)* Cusanus now speaks typically of modes of the appearance of the Creator, what he can also call His manifestations or His theophanies.

> Thus all things are nothing but the appearances of the *"Posse* itself".[56]

Beings lose their independent status and are reduced to appearances or manifestations of the *"Posse* itself."

[54] *De apice theoriae* #14 (h XII, 126-27): "Hanc nunc facilitatem tibi pandere propono prius non aperte communicatam, quam secretissimam arbitror: puta omnem praecisionem speculativam solum in posse ipso et eius apparitione ponendam. . ."

[55] *De apice theoriae, Memoriale,* I #17 (h XII, 130): "Ad posse ipsum nihil addi potest, cum sit posse omnis posse. Non est igitur posse ipsum posse esse seu posse vivere sive posse intelligere, et ita de omni posse cum quocumque addito. . . ."; IV, #20 (h XII, 131): "Posse cum addito est imago ipsius posse. . . ."

[56] *De apice theoriae, Memoriale,* IV, #20 (h XII, 132): ". . . ita omnia non sunt nisi apparitiones ipsius posse."

All beings (*entia*) are nothing but the various modes of appearances of the "*Posse* itself".[57]

Cusanus is no longer trying to rethink or modify a traditional doctrine of being; he is independently working out positions of his own.

Further, as a result of his solution in terms of the "*Posse* itself" and its appearances, Cusanus reaches a new statement of his relation to the philosophic tradition. As you will remember, in his middle period he had found himself in general agreement with it, though of course he intended to add new insights to it. Then in the beginning of his late period he found himself sharply critical of Plato, Aristotle, and all the rest on some main points.[58] Now at the end, but from a different perspective, he again effects a reconciliation.

After he has presented his new "easy method" of the "*Posse* itself" and of its appearances, he continues:

> . . . and all who saw rightly, tried to express this [i.e. the "*Posse* itself" and its appearances]. Those who affirmed that there is only One, looked to the "*Posse itself*."
>
> Those who said that there are One and Many, looked to the "*Posse* itself" and to the many modes of being of its appearance. . . . With such analyses (*resolutionibus*) you will see that all are easy and that every difference passes over into concord.[59]

Cusanus also suggests that a similar method of resolution can be applied to his own writings.

But if Cusanus at the end accepts almost the whole of the philosophic tradition he does so only by translating it entirely into his own new terms. The *De apice theoriae* becomes the model by which he now reads both the philosophers and also his own earlier works.

At important points the *De apice theoriae* thus registers new positions only recently achieved. At other points, equally important, the *De apice* develops to the end the program of immediacy and vision in man's relation to God and the first principle, the program first outlined in the *De beryllo*.

---

[57] *De apice theoriae* #9 (h XII, 123): "Et non videbis varia entia nisi apparitionis ipsius posse varios modos." Cusanus' typical usage in the *De apice* is to shift from the *modi essendi* of his earlier works to *modi apparitionis ipsius posse* (see #24, lines 6 and 7, h XII, 133). He can also place the *essendi modi* within the context of *apparitiones* (see #14, 22 and #15, 3, 128).

[58] See above, pp. 152-153.

[59] *De apice theoriae* #14, 5 (h XII, 127-129).

Thus the *Posse* itself is best seen through the mind or intellect which is its best image, and the vision is one which reaches beyond comprehension.

> Therefore when the mind in its power (*posse*) sees that the "*Posse* itself" because of its transcendence (*excellentiam*) cannot be grasped, then the mind sees with a vision beyond its capacity or grasp. . . . Therefore the power to see of the mind exceeds its power to comprehend.[60]

In the *Compendium,* as we noted, Cusanus saw a single vision of the mind and of the senses, and this now appears as the "simple vision" of the *De apice.*

> Hence the simple vision of the mind is not the comprehensive vision, but from the comprehensive vision the mind raises itself to seeing the incomprehensible. . . . This power of the mind to see beyond all comprehensible force (*virtutem*) and power is the supreme power (*posse*) of the mind, in which the "*Posse* itself" most manifests itself: such a power of the mind has no limits this side of the "*Posse* itself".[61]

These strands of Cusanus' thought come together in the *Memoriale* which he added to the *De apice.* He begins:

> The summit of theory or contemplation (*theoriae*) is the "*Posse* itself," the power of every power, without which nothing whatsoever can be contemplated.[62]

Cusanus is saying that God in Himself is theory and contemplation in the highest degree. As such He is both the means and the end of all Christian

---

[60] *De apice theoriae* #10 (h XII, 124): "Sed in se posse ipsum supra omnem potentiam cognitivam, medio tamen intelligibilis posse, videtur verius, quando videtur excellere omnem vim capacitatis intelligibilis posse. . . . Quando igitur mens in posse suo videt posse ipsum ob suam excellentiam capi non posse, tunc visu supra suam capacitatem videt . . . Posse igitur videre mentis excellit posse comprehendere."

[61] *De apice theoriae* #11 (h XII, 124-125): "Unde simplex visio non est visio comprehensiva, sed de comprehensiva se elevat ad videndum incomprehensibile. . . . Et hoc posse videre mentis supra omnem comprehensibilem virtutem et potentiam est posse supremum mentis, in quo posse ipsum maxime se manifestat: et est interminatum citra posse ipsum."

[62] *De apice theoriae, Memoriale* #17 (h XII, 130): "Apex theoriae est posse ipsum, posse omnis posse, sine quo nihil quicquam potest contemplari."

contemplation. And Cusanus hopes that his interlocutor Peter will through Cusanus' writings learn to become "an accepted contemplator of God."[63]

Cusanus makes this primary point again in the statement of the mission of Christ which concludes the *Memoriale*.

> By the "*Posse* itself" is signified God three and one, whose most perfect appearance is Christ. . . . Christ leads us by word and example to the clear contemplation of the "*Posse* itself". And this is blessedness which alone satisfies the supreme desire of the mind.[64]

The texts make clear that the late works of Cusanus do indeed represent an important new stage in his thinking. Beginning with the *De beryllo* of 1458 he embarks on a program aiming at an immediacy of vision in relation to the Christian God or, in other terminology, the first principle. The development culminates in the *De apice theoriae* of 1464, even though Cusanus arrived at some of his final insights only days before he wrote this last work.

His solution presents us with a Christianity which is in many ways unique. Its goal is the vision, through revelation in Christ, of the God and first principle who is not only ground and ultimate cause but also "other." It is further a vision of God both in Himself and also in His creatures or appearances. Such a statement of Christianity differs markedly from the other main forms of the late medieval and early modern periods, whether of the Reformation, of Humanism, or of the Counter Reformation. It is sad that Cusanus was given no time to develop his new insights beyond the brief scope of the *De apice theoriae*.

---

[63] *De apice theoriae, Memoriale* #16 (h XII, 130): "Eris, spero, acceptus dei contemplator . . ."

[64] *De apice theoriae, Memoriale* XII, #28 (h XII, 136): "Per posse ipsum deus trinus et unus, cuius nomen omnipotens seu posse omnis potentiae . . . significatur. Cuius perfectissima apparitio, qua nulla potest esse perfectior, Christus est nos ad claram contemplationem ipsius posse verbo et exemplo perducens. Et haec est felicitas, quae solum satiat supremum mentis desiderium."

NICHOLAS OF CUSA'S UNITY-METAPHYSICS
AND THE FORMULA *RELIGIO UNA IN RITUUM VARIETATE*

Thomas McTighe

The *De pace fidei* of Nicholas of Cusa is a remarkable work for its time.[1] It was occasioned by the fall of Constantinople in 1453. Instead of responding with bitter invective to the strife between Christianity and Islam which the event symbolized, Cusanus offers in the *De pace fidei* a message of hope. In it he argues for the unity of all religions and the possibility of peace among them once this unity is recognized. The work purports to be the account of a vision of a certain man (obviously Nicholas himself)[2] who had once visited Constantinople. The vision is of a dialogue among the representatives of all the religions, a dialogue led first by the Word of God and subsequently by St. Peter and St. Paul. Its guiding principle, enunciated by an archangel before the dialogue proper begins, is expressed in the formula: "There is only one religion in the diversity of rites (*religio una in rituum varietate*)."[3]

Needless to say, this famous formula has been the subject of controversy. Much of it centers on the meaning of the key terms "religion" and "rite," the latter a particularly vexing issue. Most, if not all, of the commentators would, however, agree that the formula is--to use the words of one of them--"supported by the weight of the Cusan unity-participation metaphysic."[4] And why shouldn't they, one might ask? Unity of religion-- diversity of rites is surely a situation that naturally lends itself to interpretation in terms of the categories of Cusanus' unity-metaphysics. James Biechler whom I quoted above, uses, at least provisionally, the language of *exemplar-imago* to explain the relationship of *una religio* to *diversitas rituum*.[5]

But an even more fundamental framework for explaining unity-multiplicity relationships is the *complicatio-explicatio* schema. According to this way of structuring such relationships, a given unity enfolds (*complicatio*) in indistinction its subordinate multiplicity. That subordinate multiplicity is, in turn, regarded as the unity unfolded (*explicatio*) into plurality, but all the while retaining its integrity as a unity. The relationship is often compared

---

[1] *De pace fidei* (h VII).

[2] See *Adnotatio* 2, p. 66.

[3] *De pace fidei* I, #6 (h VII, 7).

[4] James E. Biechler, *The Religious Language of Nicholas of Cusa* (Missoula, Montana, 1975), p. 92.

[5] *Ibid.*, pp. 81-92.

to that of the center and the radii of a circle. The multiple radii are the center pluralized, made other than itself. Yet the center retains its identity as a center and is the radii in indistinction. As Cusanus explains in the *De docta ignorantia,* all unities stand to their subordinate multiplicities in this way.[6] Thus, rest as *complicatio* enfolds within itself the serial multiplicity of the stages of motion.[7]   Time's plurality of past, present, and future is the unity of presence unfolded.[8]   And in the widest sense, the world of creation is God, absolute unity, as unfolded into multiplicity.[9]

Does Cusanus locate *una religio--diversitas rituum* within this framework? Does he regard rites as the multiple unfoldings of the complicative unity of religion? Well, the surprising fact is that he does not. Indeed, far from relating *ritus* as *explicationes* to *una religio* as *complicatio,* he seems consciously to be avoiding just such an identification. If that is the case, the obvious question is: why? There must, indeed, be pressing reasons why in so crucial a one-many situation--the situation which is at the very heart of the *De pace fidei*--he does not utilize his most fundamental philosophical schema.   Note that I am not denying the presence of the *complicatio-explicatio* schema in this dialogue. In fact, it is operative in the exposition of several doctrinal issues. Rather, I am claiming that Cusanus nowhere in the *De pace fidei* employs it or any other metaphysical structure--the *exemplar-imago* structure, e.g.--to explain *religio una in rituum varietate.*

1.

Let us consider the claims of some of the commentators before we go to the text itself. P. Naumann's interpretation makes a useful beginning. In the introduction to his translation of the *Cribratio Alcorani* he explains the formula of the *De pace fidei* thus:

> The *complicatio* of the one true religion has become unfolded in the profusion of the empirical religions. . . . All religions are only inadequate representations of the one true religion. Each of them in its own way, though only imperfectly, gives expression to the Absolute. . . .

---

[6] *De docta ignorantia* II, 3, #105-110 (h I, 69-70). This and subsequent citations of this work are to the *editio minor,* an improved version of the original Heidelberg Academy edition: *De docta ignorantia* (h VII²).

[7] *De docta ignorantia* II, 3, #106 (h I, 69): ". . . quies est unitas motum complicans, qui est quies seriatim ordinata . . ."

[8] *De docta ignorantia* II, 3, #106 (h I, 70): "Una est ergo praesentia omnium temporum complicatio."

[9] *De docta ignorantia* II, 3, #107 (h I, 70): "Deus ergo est omnia complicans in hoc, quod omnia in eo. Et omnia explicans in hoc, quod ipse in omnibus."

The Christian church, however, remains for Nicholas the religious community which comes nearest to the one true religion.[10]

Naumann's is the bluntest and, I would claim, the most consistent interpretation of Cusanus' formula if, i.e., we grant him his assumption: the assumption that the *una religio* of the *De pace fidei* is a kind of enfolding *Urreligion* which is imperfectly unfolded in the multiplicity of actual religions. In short, what Naumann says is what Nicholas would have to say if indeed he related *diversitas rituum* to *una religio* as *explicatio* to *complicatio*. But does Cusanus anywhere in the *De pace fidei* say or imply that Catholic Christianity is but one among many religions, albeit the nearest one to *una religio?* He does not. And might not the reason for this be: Cusanus' recognition that such an unacceptable consequence is inevitable if *una religio--varietas rituum* is structured according to the *complicatio-explicatio* schema?

Another commentator who interprets the formula in terms of *complicatio-explicatio* is Michael Seidlmayer. After quoting the whole passage in which the formula occurs, he continues: "It is not difficult to see that such a train of thought is rooted in the fundamental axiom of all of Cusa's *Weltbetrachtung,* in the axiom of *complicatio* and *explicatio.*"[11] He then cites a text from the letter to Rodrigo Sánchez de Arévalo as giving the most concise formulation of the *complicatio-explicatio* schema.[12] After a brief interpretation of the meaning of the schema, he concludes: "This is Cusa's fundamental law for all creatures without exception--it is also the basis of his understanding of religion . . ."[13] In support of this conclusion he cites a text from *De docta ignorantia* I, 25 where it is said that all the names of God, even those of the pagans, unfold the *complicatio* of the inexpressible name of God.[14] No text from the *De pace fidei*, however, shows that the *Grundlage der cusanischen Religionsverständnisses* is the

[10] Paul Naumann, *Cribratio Alkoran: Sichtung des Alkorans,* vol. 1 (Hamburg, 1948), p. 63.

[11] Michael Seidlmayer, *"Una religio in rituum varietate:* Zur Religionsauffassung des Nikolaus von Kues," *Archiv für Kulturgeschichte* 36 (1954): 149.

[12] Cusanus' letter of May 20, 1442, to Rodrigo Sánchez de Arévalo, Archdeacon of Treviño, is found in *Cusanus-Texte* II, *Traktate 1: De auctoritate presidendi in concilio,* ed. Gerhard Kallen, Sitzungsberichte der Heidelberger Akademie der Wissenschaften (Heidelberg, 1935), pp. 106-112. A French translation of the passage cited by Seidlmayer can be found in Maurice de Gandillac, *Oeuvres choisies de Nicholas de Cues* (Paris, 1942), pp. 172-173.

[13] Seidlmayer, *"Una religio,"* p. 150.

[14] *De docta ignorantia* I, 25, # 84 (h I, 53): "Quae quidem omnia nomina unius ineffabilis nominis complicationem sunt explicantia . . ."

complicatio-explicatio schema. Space does not allow for a consideration of Seidlmayer's lengthy treatment of the formula. Suffice it to note that though he rejects Naumann's extreme position,[15] he does claim that for Cusanus religions other than Christianity are "authentic *explicationes* or *loquutiones verbi dei.*"[16] But this introduced a puzzling shift. Instead of the other religions being *explicationes* of the *una religio*, they are now regarded as *explicationes* of the Word of God.

Still another effort to penetrate the meaning of Cusanus' famous formula is the very nuanced contribution of Josef Stallmach to the recent Trier symposium on the *De pace fidei*.[17] He begins his explanation of the formula by establishing a distinction between what he calls the "basic form" (*Grundgestalt*)[18] and the "completed form" (*Vollendungsgestalt*)[19] of religion. The former designates the essential core of religion which for Cusanus is the unity of God and the unity of human nature. The latter is the unfolding (*entfaltet*) of this essential core into the completed form of an actual religion, an unfolding which is true to the essential core and not a deformation (*Verunstaltung*) of it. Then, after a brief but accurate summary of the main ideas of Cusanus' unity-metaphysics, he asks: "to what extent do they also determine the exposition . . . of 'one religion in a diversity of rites'?"[20]

Stallmach begins his answer by turning to the very significant dialogue in Chapter Six between the Word of God and the Arab representative to the council of the wise. The exchange between the two involves, surprisingly, not the strife between Christianity and Islam, but the problem of polytheism. Using the doctrine of the primacy of unity (*ante omnem pluralitatem unitas*) the Arab and the Divine Word are able to show the polytheist that there cannot be many gods, "each of them the first cause, principle, or

[15] Seidlmayer, *"Una religio,"* p. 166, n. 67.

[16] *Ibid.*, p. 165: ". . . sind auch sie [other religions] echte explicationes oder loquutiones verbi dei und als solche neben dem Christentum werthaft und - relative - gültig."

[17] Josef Stallmach, "Einheit der Religion-Friede unter der Religionen. Zum Ziel der Gedankenführung im Dialog 'Der Friede im Glauben'," *Mitteilungen und Forschungsbeiträge der Cusanus-Gesellschaft* 16 (1984): 61-75. (Hereafter *MFCG*).

[18] *Ibid.*, p. 66: "Es gibt eine Grundgestalt von Religion, einen Wesenkern, einen gemeinsamen Grundbestand aller Religionen--weil Gott einer ist und weil . . . auch die Menschennatur eine ist . . ."

[19] *Ibid.*, p. 68: ". . . die eine Vollendungsgestalt von Religion, in der alles, was wesenschaft zum Grundbestand von Religion überhaupt gehört, entfaltet und bis zu einem Masse zur Vollendung gebracht worden ist . . ."

[20] *Ibid.*, p. 69.

NICHOLAS OF CUSA'S UNITY-METAPHYSICS

creator of the universe."[21] For, as the Arab says, "it is contradictory that there be many first principles."[22] Hence, if the polytheists can be led to a correct metaphysical reflection on the unity-multiplicity relationship, they will grasp explicit what, in fact, they admit implicity and so turn away from the worship of many gods. Stallmach terminates his discussion of this exchange with this conclusion: "In this way of looking at things . . . he [Cusanus] is able to catch sight of the One in and above all multiplicity, the *one Ur-religious in all religions* . . ." (italics mine).[23] Thus, according to Stallmach, there is a parallel between two unity-multiplicity situations: God, the absolute unity, and the multiplicity of creatures on the one hand, and on the other the unitary *Ur-religion* and the multiplicity of actual religions. And, as is clear from his next sentence, in each the unity is to its corresponding multiplicity as *complicatio* is to *explicatio.*[24]

Is Stallmach justified in establishing this parallel? I think not. His approach rests on a confusion as to the meaning of his original question. That question can be taken in two ways. In the first, the sense of the question is: to what extent do the ideas of Cusa's unity-metaphysics determine the exposition of the *object* of religion, viz., God and the relationship of creatures to God? The answer, of course, is that they are crucial to it. And Stallmach has no difficulty finding in the *De pace fidei* texts which prove this to be the case.[25] The other sense of the question is: to what extent does the unity-metaphysics determine the exposition of religion itself--religion as a *Gestalt*, to use Stallmach's own term? In other words, does Cusanus use the *complicatio-explicatio* scheme to ground the unity-multiplicity relation of actual religions (rites?) to the *una religio*?

Where in the *De pace fidei* are the texts which support *this* use of the *complicatio-explicatio* schema? Stallmach cites none because, in fact, there are none. The text which he does cite is: "The worship of gods is, therefore, an acknowledgement of the [one] divinity. And whoever says that there are

---

[21] *De pace fidei* VI, #17 (h VII, 16).

[22] *De pace fidei* VI, #17 (h VII, 16): "Nam contradicit sibi ipse plura esse principia prima. . . . Et non est possibile plura esse aeterna, quia ante omnem pluralitatem unitas."

[23] Stallmach, "Einheit," p. 70: "In dieser Sichtweise in der er [Cusanus] das Eine in und über allem Vielen, das eine Urreligiöse in allen Religionen . . ."

[24] *Ibid.:* "Wie . . . alles Viele Komplizit--Einshaft im Einen enthalten ist, so enthält andererseits alles Explizit-Viele in seinem letzten Grunde auch das Eine."

[25] E.g., *De pace fidei* VII, #21 (h VII, 21): ". . . quia in principio complicari debet principiatum . . ." Cited in Stallmach, "Einheit," p. 69, n. 43.

many gods is saying that the principle of all is antecedently one."[26] This passage will do as support for one side of Stallmach's parallel--"the One in and above all multiplicity." But it is not evidence that for Cusa there is an *Ur-religion* in and above all religions related to them as *complicatio* is to its subordinate multiplicity.

To be sure, the argument against polytheism is an argument (or, rather, part of the argument) for the unity of religion. As Stallmach rightly notes,[27] religion is one for Cusanus because the *object* of religion is one and also because the *subjects* of religion, human beings, are one in nature. But Cusanus does not utilize his fundamental metaphysical schema beyond the confines of this argument. The move to extend it to *religio una in rituum varietate* is, therefore, illegitimate, as is a similar move by Seidlmayer, who sees a parallel between Nicholas' explanation of the church (*ecclesia*) as the *explicatio Petri* (i.e., the Pope) with the many rites--one religion relationship.[28]

In the case of my last commentator, James Biechler, the same line of interpretation is offered. Cusa's formula is supported by his unity-metaphysics. Biechler, however, stresses the *exemplar-imago* relationship, not the *complicatio-explicatio* schema. Although, as he notes, the *exemplar-imago* language is not expressly applied to the formula "it would be of great significance in solving the problem of interpreting it."[29] Accordingly the relationship would be: "*exemplar* is to *imago* as *religio* is to *ritus*."[30] Rites are images marked by plurality, while *religio* as *exemplar* is a *unitas*. And the evidence offered for this equation? Exactly the same sort as the preceding commentators, a text drawn from another work. Here it is a text from the *Apologia* which related creatures to God as images to exemplar.[31] Still Biechler is the only commentator who clearly recognizes the ambiguities that result from forcing the formula into the metaphysical categories.

Surely it is significant that none of the commentators I have discussed can find a textual warrant in the *De pace fidei* itself for linking the *una religio* formula to the categories of Cusanus' unity-metaphysics. Biechler is

---

[26] *De pace fidei* VI, #17 (h VII, 16): "Cultus igitur deorum confitetur divinitatem. Et qui dicit plures deos, dicit unum antecedenter omnium principium . . ." Stallmach, "Einheit," p. 70, n. 48.

[27] See n. 18 above.

[28] Seidlmayer, "*Una religio*," pp. 186-94. See especially p. 193: ". . . die beiden Konzeptionen in einem Verhältnis der gegenseitigen Interpretation zueinander stehen."

[29] Biechler, *Religious Language,* p. 88.

[30] *Ibid.*

[31] *Ibid.* and n. 43, p. 196. The text cited is from *Apologia doctae ignorantiae* (h II, 11).

certainly right that in the *De pace fidei* "unity language occurs in nearly every paragraph."[32] But the plain fact is that nowhere in the work is the cele-brated formula: *religio una in rituum varietate* related explicitly to that lan-guage. As Biechler himself admits, there is no explicit reduction of religion and rites to exemplar and image. Indeed, even that most fundamental prin-ciple of unity-metaphysics, *ante omnem pluralitatem est unitas,* is not in-voked to explain the priority of *una religio* to *diversitas rituum.* This central tenet is called into play three times in the *De pace fidei* and each time it is cited to explain a substantive issue in Cusanus' metaphysics: the plurality of wisdoms entailing the antecedent *una sapientia,*[33] the impossibility of a plurality of eternal principles,[34] the plurality in the universe presupposing *aeterna unitas* as its principle.[35] The same is true of the *complicatio-explicatio* schema. In every case where it is invoked it explains the general metaphysical relationship of creatures to God: the Word (*verbum dei*) is the *complicatio* of all things and they in turn are the *explicatio* of the Word;[36] the promise of Christ is a *divina benedictio omne bonum in se complicans;*[37] and finally the thesis that principle and principiate are related as *complicatio* to *explicatio* is invoked to explain the triune structure of finite being as an unfolding of the Trinity.[38] There *is* one series of texts that seems to verge on making a juncture of the formula with the *complicatio-explicatio* schema, only in the end to veer off. At the end of Chapter Four the Word says: ". . . even though you were called from the different religions, all of you presuppose in all such diversity the one thing you call wisdom." Then the *Verbum* says: "Does not the one wisdom encompass (*complectitur*) all that can be said?"[39] One expects that here surely Cusanus would have the participants conclude that *una religio* as a *complicatio* is directed to the *una sapientia.* But no, the participants go on to agree that the one wisdom is the Word which "enfolds all that is infinite."[40]

[32] *Apologia doctae ignorantiae* (h I, 92).

[33] *De pace fidei* IV, #11 (h VII, 11): "Non potest esse nisi una sapientia. . . . ante enim omnem pluralitatem est unitas."

[34] *De pace fidei* VII, #15 (h VII, 14): "Non est autem possibile plures esse aeternitates, quia ante omnem pluralitatem est unitas."

[35] *De pace fidei* VII, #21 (h VII, 20-21): ". . . omnis autem multitudinis unitas est principium: quare principium multitudinis est aeterna unitas."

[36] *De pace fidei* II, #7 (h VII, 9).

[37] *De pace fidei* XVI, #57 (h VII, 53).

[38] *De pace fidei* VII, #21 (h VII, 21).

[39] *De pace fidei* IV, #12 (h VII, 13).

[40] *De pace fidei* V, #13 (h VII, 13): "Omnia enim infinita complectitur sapientia." Cusanus often uses *complecti* as a synonym for *complicare.*

At another juncture in the *De pace fidei* there is an even more striking instance of Cusanus' reluctance to invoke the technical language of the unity-metaphysics. Significantly, it occurs at the very moment when for the first time the participants discuss an actual religion, viz., polytheism. Why deal with polytheism first? Because it challenges the basis for the first half of Nicholas' formula: *religio una*. The religion of many gods raises a question not just about diversity of rites but about religion's essential unity, the unity of its object. Hence its challenges take precedence over problems of diversity among religions that accept the unity of God. Accordingly before the Arab raises the question of polytheism, the Word restates Cusanus' formula: "Therefore, for all those endowed with understanding, the religion (and worship) which lies at the bottom of (*praesupponitur*) all the diversity of rites is one."[41]   The Word, in fact, does something more than merely restate the formula. In effect He gives a commentary on the most puzzling word in the original version of the formula, viz., the word "in." One religion *in* the diversity of rites. What does "in" mean? How is the one religion "in" the multiplicity of rites?

Now, as we have seen, when it comes to unity-multiplicity relationships, Cusanus' metaphysics is in no doubt about what "in" means. A unity is "in" its subordinate multiplicity in the sense that it is unfolded into that multiplicity. The unity, all the while retaining its integrity as a unity, is resident in the multiplicity as its essence. In short, "in" means "unfolded into"--*explicatur*. But, lo and behold, the Word does *not* say: "There is one religion which is unfolded in all the diversity of rites." Instead of *explicatur* we get the more neutral, non-technical *praesupponitur*, which following the lead of Stallmach's German translation (*zugrunde liegt*)[42] I have rendered as "lies at the bottom of." The "in" of "one religion in the diversity of rites" simply registers what all rites (religions?) have in common, their *gemeinsam Grundbestand,* as Stallmach calls it.[43]   With *praesupponitur* Cusanus neatly evades the issue of an antecedent unitary religion from which all the empirical religions are unfolded.

There is, therefore, no escaping this central fact. *Pace* the commentators, the formula *religio una . . .* remains remarkably free of metaphysical interpretation. Seidelmayer cites some striking texts which assert that *tota ecclesia sit explicatio Petri* and that in Peter, and then in the pope

---

[41] *De pace fidei* VI, #16 (h VII, 15): "Una est igitur religio et cultus omnium intellectu vigentium, quae in omni diversitate rituum praesupponitur."

[42] Stallmach, "Einheit," p. 67: ". . . die aller Mannigfaltigkeit zugrunde liegt."

[43] See n. 18 above.

as successor to Peter, the church exists *complicative*.[44] If Cusanus has no hesitation in explicitly relating church and pope in terms of the *complicatio-explicatio* schema, why the odd reluctance to do so in the case of ritual diversity and unity of religion? The truth of the matter is that in *De pace fidei* Cusanus gives every indication of deliberately avoiding the location of the *una religio* formula within any sort of metaphysical categories, not within the exemplar-image structure or the *complicatio-explicatio* schema or even under the general principle, *ante omnem pluralitatem unitas*.[45] And is it not significant that the Chartrian language of *unitas* versus *alteritas* is never used to relate *religio* and *ritus*?

2.

If the foregoing analysis is correct, we are confronted with a remarkable state of affairs: Cusanus' failure to use the categories of his unity-metaphysics, especially the *complicatio-explicatio* schema, to handle that most pressing of all cases of diversity, the *tanta religionum diversitas*.[46] The reasons for the omission are not, however, difficult to determine.

Let us begin with the distinction between *religio* and *ritus*. What is *religio* for Cusanus? It seems to be this: the *cultus unius dei*.[47] Because God is one, *religio*, i.e., the *latriae cultus*, is one.[48] But what then are *ritus*? This question is far more difficult to answer. In point of fact the language of *ritus* so prominent in the early chapters is, but for one exception, put aside until Paul appears in the last chapter as the *porte-parole*. In the

---

[44] Seidlmayer, "*Una religio*," p. 186, cites a still unpublished sermon of 1454 entitled *Quomodo tota ecclesia sit explicatio Petri*.

[45] One cannot, therefore, agree with Biechler's claim (*Religious Language*, p. 84) that ". . . all external religious forms are *explicationes* of the one faith just as number is the *explicatio* of *unitas*. . ." For, if this were the case, Cusanus' own religion, Christianity, would be to the one religion as, say, the number 3 is to the monadic unit (1). Like 3 it would be a member of a multiplicity standing alongside all of the other members. It would, in short, cease to be unique and that is something Cusanus is not prepared to admit.

[46] *De pace fidei* IV, #10 (h VII, 11). As Biechler (*Religious Language*, p. 87) rightly observes, Cusanus ought not to speak of a plurality of religions. Yet, puzzlingly, he does. See also XIX, #68 (h VII, 62); III, #8 (h VII, 10); IV, #12 (h VII, 13).

[47] *De pace fidei* VII, #20 (h VII, 19): ". . . necessitatem religionis in cultu unius dei esse . . ."

[48] *De pace fidei* I, #6 (h VII, 7): ". . . saltem ut sicut tu unus es, una sit religio et unus latriae cultus." Religion is one also, because the subjects of religion, human beings, are one in nature. See XIII, #43-44 (h VII, 40-41). Cf. also Stallmach, "Einheit," p. 66, n. 28.

intervening chapters, where the discussion centers on Trinity, Incarnation, virgin birth, and the like, the talk is of *diversitas religionum.* When Paul appears, the talk is of rites, and issues such as sacraments and circumcision, not Trinity, Incarnation, etc., are discussed. This suggests that Trinity, Incarnation, etc., belong not to *ritus,* but to *religio.* Biechler, however, and also Haubst, take rites to have a wider range.[49] According to the former, rites include more than merely external practices. A rite is "a combination of doctrine and usage" and includes "dogmas as expressed in credal symbols."[50] I am not sure that this is the case. Perhaps even for Nicholas himself the distinction between *religio* and *ritus* is not altogether clear. How, for example, square *tanta religionum diversitas* with *rituum diversitas*? In any case, let us accept, at least provisionally, Biechler's account of *ritus.* Does that not mean, then, that Christianity, Judaism, Islam, and Buddhism are so many different rites, which, if Naumann and the others are correct, are *explicationes* of the *una religio?* Then Naumann's conclusion is perfectly consistent with the doctrine of *complicatio-explicatio.* There is a kind of *Ur-religion* (the one true religion) of which all the empirical religions are imperfect expressions or unfoldings.

Now the outlines of a dilemma begin to appear, the dilemma, that is, that would inevitably follow if Cusanus were to apply the *complicatio-explicatio* schema to *una religio--varietas rituum.* Either Christianity is the *Ur-religion,* the *complicatio*-religion, or it is a *ritus,* an *explicatio* of the ultimate *una religio.* But neither alternative is acceptable. If Christianity is *una religio,* that is, absolute religion, from which the others are unfolded, then orthodoxy could be saved (i.e., the uniqueness of Christianity), but this runs counter to the thesis that all things finite are *explicationes.* And Christianity is a finite form of religion. If on the other hand, Christianity is a *ritus* and therefore an *explicatio,* it is one among many. And "the rule of learned ignorance" comes into play: in the domain of *explicatio* all is *plus aut minus.*[51] Naumann confidently asserts that for Cusanus Christianity is the nearest to the absolute religion. Perhaps, but how to justify this in terms of the *complicatio-explicatio* schema? One could only measure the distance of a finite form from the absolute form, if one knew the absolute, the *complicatio*-unity. But this is impossible, since no amount of circulation through otherness ever reveals *unitas* in itself. The best one has is the conviction that all variety is polarized toward unity.

---

[49] For Haubst's view see the discussion after Stallmach's paper in *MFCG* 16 (1984): 78.

[50] Biechler, *Religious Language,* p. 90. See also Seidlmayer, *"Una religio,"* p. 177.

[51] *De docta ignorantia* I, 3 #9 (h I, 8-9) and II, 1 #95 (h I, 63): "Omnia igitur ex oppositis sunt in gradus diversitate habendo de uno plus, de alio minus . . ."

One central fact, however, sweeps away all the foregoing. As Maurice de Gandillac in the recent Trier symposium put it: "For Cusanus there is only one religion and that is the Catholic, the Christian religion."[52]   The thesis of Christianity as the *una religio* simply cannot be made to fit the metaphysical categories of *complicatio-explicatio, unitas-alteritas, exemplar-imago.* Its peculiar status as both *unique* and *finite* prevent it from being regarded as either a *complicatio* or an *explicatio.* It would and, in fact, did make sense to use these categories in the resolution of intramural problems. The different rites of the Eastern and Western Churches, of the Hussites, could be reconciled as *explicationes* of Christianity. But when the discussion is expanded to include religions outside Christianity, the metaphysics has, perforce, to be put aside in favor of vague formulas for *concordia, pax,* and the "leading back" to the *una fides orthodoxa.*[53]

In short, the *complicatio-explicatio* schema ought to apply, but cannot apply.   Ought, because it is the unique means for handling all unity-multiplicity relationships.   Cannot, because Christianity by virtue of its uniqueness as the one true religion can be neither a *complicatio* nor an *explicatio* vis-à-vis the other world religions.

Stallmach, during a discussion at the Trier symposium, made some suggestive remarks about the ambiguities in the *De pace fidei.* As he reads the situation, Cusanus' formula (*religio una in . . .*) amounts to *una ecclesia in rituum varietate.*   Cusanus, because of the difficulties in the ⨍ Council of Basel and later with the Hussites, is obsessed with the idea of *una ecclesia.*   Then under the influence of his encounter at Constantinople with other religions, he expanded the idea of *una ecclesia* to *una religio,* but "underneath, the model of *una ecclesia* still continued to operate."[54]   All of this, I think, makes good sense save the last sentence. In expanding from *una ecclesia* to *una religio* Cusanus, as I see it, understood clearly that the model of *una ecclesia,* viz., the *complicatio-explicatio* model, could not persist even surreptitiously. For the stubborn fact remains that if

---

[52] In the discussion following his own contribution to the Symposium [*MFCG* 16 (1984): 209], Maurice de Gandillac responds: "von einer Pluralität, einer Verschiedenheit der religionen keine Reden sein kann.   . . . Es gibt für Cusanus nur eine Religion, und das ist die katolische, die christliche Religion."

[53] *De pace fidei* IV, #10 (h VII, 11): ". . . in unam concordantem pacem tanta religionum diversitas conducatur . . ." Cf. also XIX, #68 (h VII, 62): ". . . ad unitatem veri cultus nationes inducant . . ."

[54] Stallmach, "Einheit," p. 308: "Ist es nicht so . . . das er dann unter dem Einfluss des Zusammenstosses verschiedener Religionen (in Konstantinopel) diese Idee zwar ausgeweitet hat zur una religio (und wenn in rituum varietate), dass dabei aber untergründig doch das Modell der una ecclesia weitergewirkt hat?"

Christianity is the one religion, and it is, then it cannot be a *complicatio* of all other religions. Nor can it be reduced to an *explicatio* alongside of other *explicationes* of some *Ur-religion*. In the end, the ambiguities in the *De pace fidei* concerning unity of religion and diversity of rites, or diversity of religions, arise not because of the presence (as some commentators claim),[55] but precisely because of the absence, of metaphysical categories.

---

[55] E.g., Biechler, *Religious Language,* pp. 88-89.

PART FOUR

CONSIDERING RELIGIOUS DIFFERENCE

THE POSSIBILITY OF DIALOGUE WITH ISLAM
IN THE FIFTEENTH CENTURY

Thomas M. Izbicki

The fall of Constantinople in 1453 drove home to Western Christendom the reality that a new age of relations with the Islamic world had begun. From the First Crusade onward, despite reverses in Palestine and the termination of the Latin empire in the East, the West, on the whole, had posssessed great advantages in political, commercial, and religious dealings with Greeks, Muslims, and Slavs. The Ottoman Turks had reversed that trend in the Eastern Mediterranean. Besides gradually destroying the Byzantine Empire, the sultans were overcoming the Christian principalities in the Balkans and threatening the last Latin enclaves in the Levant. Mehmed the Conqueror's capture of Constantinople, although not the first Turkish triumph, came as a shock to the Latins. This shock was compounded by Western Europe's collective guilt about giving so little effective aid to the embattled Greeks. Even the reigning pope, Nicholas V, had been more interested in holding out for the consumation of the union between the Eastern and Western Churches agreed to at Florence in 1439 than in sending troops and ships to the beleaguered Byzantine capital.[1]

After Mehmed had triumphed, Nicholas called for a crusade against the Turks, a summons which achieved little success. Every pope succeeding Nicholas in the fifteenth century, especially his immediate successors, Calixtus III and Pius II, espoused the same policy. Only Calixtus saw any results attend his efforts, promoting the relief of the siege of Belgrade in 1456.[2] The princes, most notably Philip the Good, Duke of Burgundy, gave varying degrees of lip service to the crusading ideal. In chivalric literature the Turk replaced the Saracen as the very image of the infidel. Despite chivalric posturing, the princes did little to combat the Turkish threat. Self-interest and the fear of the self-interest of others paralyzed even Philip the Good. At last, even Rome adopted a policy of containing the Turks, rather than overthrowing their regime.[3]

---

[1] Norman Daniel, *The Arabs and Medieval Europe,* 2nd ed. (London, 1979), pp. 305-306; Robert Schwoebel, *The Shadow of the Crescent* (New York, 1967), pp. 1-29.

[2] C.L. Stinger, *The Renaissance in Rome* (Bloomington, Indiana, 1984), pp. 106-123.

[3] Schwoebel, *The Shadow of the Crescent,* pp. 82-146.

The intellectual counterpart of the papal policy of promoting a crusade was a spate of writings intended to arouse the princes, to refute the supposed errors of Islam and, more rarely, to promote dialogue with the Islamic world. Many of these tracts, including that composed by Juan de Torquemada, merely restated traditional ideas about Islam, which was seen as a mixture of pagan sensuality and heretical Christianity. Because of such writings, the period has been dismissed by some scholars as less significant in the construction of the Western view of Islam than were the preceeding centuries, which had seen the production of such seminal works as Robert of Ketton's Latin translation of the Qur'an, the tracts of Riccoldo da Montecroce, and the eccentric missiology of Ramon Llull.[4] By comparison with these earlier works, even the tract of Dennis the Carthusian (Rickel), which allowed the Muslim some good arguments, and Pius II's famous--and unsent--letter to Mehmed the Conqueror seem like rehashes of old materials, works written more to comfort their authors and their Western readers than to bring the infidel to the faith.[5]

The exception to this negative judgment is the continued praise given John of Segovia and Nicholas of Cusa for advocating dialogue with the Islamic world. The former was a theologian, a leading conciliarist, a historian of the Council of Basel, a theoretician of missions and a student of the Qur'an. It was his discontent with Robert of Ketton's translation of the Muslim sacred text which led him to contemplate doing his own translation.[6] Nicholas of Cusa was one of the most brilliant thinkers of his age, a lawyer and theologian, a philosopher and scientist. His early conciliarist writings, which synthesized older materials into a theory of government balancing hierarchy and consent,[7] gave way to a series of speculative works unique in their own day. In the first of these, *De docta ignorantia* (1440), Cusanus wrote of the Muslims--and the Jews as well--as possessing partial

---

[4] Daniel, *The Arabs and Medieval Europe*, p. 306; idem, *Islam and the West* (Edinburgh, 1962), p. 278.

[5] Daniel, *Islam and the West*, pp. 278-279; Franco Gaeta, "Alcune osservazioni sulla prima redazione della 'Lettera a Maometto'," *Enea Silvio Piccolomini--Papa Pio II*, ed. D. Maffei (Siena, 1968), pp. 177-186 at p. 185. For a more favorable opinion of Pius II's letter, see William Boulting, *Aeneas Sylvius (Enea Silvio de' Piccolomini--Pius II)* (London, 1908), pp. 340-341.

[6] R.W. Southern, *Western Views of Islam in the Middle Ages* (Cambridge, Massachusetts, 1962), pp. 86-92.

[7] Morimichi Watanabe, *The Political Ideas of Nicholas of Cusa with Special Reference to his* De concordantia catholica (Geneva, 1963); Paul Sigmund, *Nicholas of Cusa and Medieval Political Thought* (Cambridge, Massachusetts, 1963).

truth but falling short of a complete grasp of it.[8] In 1453, in the period of shock following the fall of Constantinople, Cusanus composed *De pace fidei,* a vision of the relationship between the religions of the world as he must have wished them to be. Here again the partial truth possessed by non-Christians was emphasized as a means of leading them to the Truth, which was embodied in the Word, the interlocutor of the debate. Later, in the *Cribratio Alkorani,* Cusanus made a systematic, if less original and less conciliatory, effort to refute the errors of Islam from its holy book in order to convert Muslims to the faith.[9]

Neither of these authors possessed the deep knowledge of Arabic which became available later in the Renaissance; however, they represent the most creative approach to Islam possible in their day, when Christianity was identified with a particular visible society, which thought of itself as Christendom.[10] This, in fact, put what Cusanus called *religio* ahead of *fides,* excluding the spiritual "other" from the community nominally professing that faith. Just how creative these men were remains a matter of debate. In this age, which is ecumenical at best and relativistic at worst, there is a temptation to see in these authors, especially in Cusanus, a nearly modern man, one devoted to tolerance for its own sake. One does note the absence from *De pace fidei* of any mention of hierarchy or of such divisive slogans as *extra ecclesiam nulla salus;*[11] but Christ remains the center of the dialogue, demanding conformity to Himself as Truth. On the other extreme, one might dismiss the works of Cusanus and of John of Segovia as additional examples of the Western interior monologue about Islam, discounting them

[8] *De docta ignorantia* III, 8, #229-230 (h I, 144-145). Cesare Vasoli, "The Renaissance Concept of Philosophy," *The Cambridge History of Renaissance Philosophy,* ed. Charles B. Schmitt, Quentin Skinner, Eckhard Kessler, and Jill Kraye (Cambridge, 1988), pp. 57-74 at pp. 66-70.

[9] Southern, *Western Views of Islam,* pp. 92-94; Daniel, *Islam and the West,* pp. 276-78. On the *Cribratio,* see James Biechler, "Nicholas of Cusa and Muhammed: a Fifteenth Century Encounter," *The Downside Review* 101 (1983): 50-59.

[10] K.H. Dannenfeldt, "The Renaissance Humanists and the Knowledge of Arabic," *Studies in the Renaissance* 4 (1955): 96-117 at pp. 101-02.

[11] *De pace fidei cum epistola ad Ioannem de Segobia,* in *De pace fidei (h VII).* Yves Congar, "Salvation and the Non-Catholic," *Blackfriars* 38 (1957): 290-300 at pp. 298-300. One also notes the absence of Boniface VIII's dictum in the bull *Unam sanctam* that obedience to the pope is necessary for salvation; see J.A. Watt, *The Theory of Papal Monarchy in the Thirteenth Century* (London, 1965), pp. 129-133. In *De docta ignorantia,* too, Cusanus was concerned with faith, not structure, in his discussion of the church; see *De docta ignorantia* III, 12, #254-255 (h I, 157-158).

178   THOMAS M. IZBICKI

as serious proposals for dialogue. In this context, a salutary reminder is
Morimichi Watanabe's demonstration that Cusanus saw the possibility of
one *religio*--perhaps one church or community of faith--with a diversity of
rites, not a proliferation of sects, each with its own rite. Like Ramon Llull,
Nicholas of Cusa was confident that rational argument would bring the
Muslims into an expanded, perhaps even a transformed, Christian fold.[12]
    At this point, we should widen our horizons from the specific problem
of relations with Islam to the more general one of the possibility of
dialogue with any religious dissenter, the spiritual other, in late medieval
Europe. Needless to say, dialogue had a small place in ecclesiastical or lay
views of schismatics, heretics, Jews, Muslims, or pagans. Bernard Gui, for
example, had warned his fellow inquisitors to avoid engaging in disputes
with heretics. (One Spanish painter even turned St. Dominic, founder of
Gui's own order, the Order of Preachers, into an inquisitor, the very opposite
of his early efforts to convert the Cathars by debating with them.)[13] The
idea of disputation with the Jews, a fairly common literary device, rarely
became a reality after the debate staged by Ramon de Peñafort, another
Dominican, between one of his disciples and a rabbi, held before James I of
Aragon in the later part of the thirteenth century.[14] The humanists entered
into discussions with the Jews, particularly about the cabala; and some of
them, like Llull before them, believed that Christian cabalism would bring
the Jews to Christ. This open inquiry into Jewish mysticism, however,
brought suspicion of unorthodoxy upon Johann Reuchlin.[15]
    Ideas about dialogue with Islam were not new to the fifteenth century,
but they tended to represent a minority viewpoint. Muslims, in this matter,

[12] Morimichi Watanabe, "Nicholas of Cusa and the Idea of Toleration,"
Niccolò Cusano agli inizi del Mondo Moderno (Florence, 1970), pp. 409-418 at
pp. 411-413, 415. See also Sigmund, *Nicholas of Cusa and Medieval Political
Thought*, pp. 293-294.
    [13] *Heresies of the High Middle Ages,* ed. W.L. Wakefield and A.P. Evans.
(New York, 1969), pp. 377-378. Compare pictures of Dominic disputing with
heretics, e.g. Leonard von Matt and M.-H. Vicaire, *St. Dominic: A Pictorial
Biography* (Chicago, 1957), pl. 54, with Berruguete's *St. Dominic Presiding
Over an Auto-da-fe* in *Encyclopedia of World Art,* vol. 13 (New York, 1967), pl.
129.
    [14] Jeremy Cohen, *The Friars and the Jews* (Ithaca, New York, 1982), pp.
103-169.
    [15] Frances Yates, *The Occult Philosophy in the Elizabethan Age* (London,
1979), pp. 9-14, 17-22. In the twelfth century, Andrew of St. Victor was
criticized, even within his own abbey, for his willingness to believe that the
rabbis knew the literal meaning of the Old Testament; see Beryl Smalley, *The
Study of the Bible in the Middle Ages* (Notre Dame, Indiana, 1978), pp. 173-185.

were regarded in the same light as pagans, rather than as heretics. Their evangelization was supposed to occur by every means short of outright coercion, which could be used to restore the lapsed to the orthodox fold. The crusade was reserved to recovery of the Holy Land and other Christian possessions, whose usurpation long possession could not legitimize and whose recovery was a licit goal of a just war. Preaching to the Muslims rarely had been attempted, especially outside the crusader states in the Levant and the reconquered sections of Spain. Attacks on Muhammed in Muslim lands were more likely to lead to martyrdom than to a harvest of souls since *sharia* law forbade attacks on the Prophet's teachings and apostates were put to death.[16]   Many Christians thought martyrdom spoke louder than sermons in evangelization, and others thought that Providence would bring the sheep to the fold as history sped to its predestined close. These attitudes may help explain Christendom's endemic laxity in the deployment of missionaries.[17] Here, again, we must speculate whether a deeper cause of this failure to mount a coherent effort to evangelize the whole world was the role of Catholic Christianity as the unifying factor of Western Europe in its dealings with the internal and external "other."[18]

All of these factors would tend to suggest that the soil was poor in the fifteenth century for the tender shoot of dialogue. Nicholas of Cusa and John of Segovia, however, had seen the Council of Basel serve as the site of fruitful discussions of theological issues. Not only had that assembly promoted disputations, modeled on current academic practice, of theological and ecclesiological issues;[19] it had undertaken successful negotiations with the Hussites. In the wake of the defeat of his crusading army by the Bohemians, Cardinal Cesarini, the papal legate entrusted with the holding of the council, had led the assembly in inviting the Hussites to present their views openly at Basel. Despite the fate suffered by John Hus when he went to Constance under a safe conduct, the Bohemians chose to accept this invitation. The embassy which went to Basel included representation of all the Hussite factions, and each was represented in the group of speakers for their viewpoints of key issues. They were allowed to speak their minds and

[16] Benjamin Kedar, *Crusade and Mission* (Princeton, New Jersey, 1984), pp. 202-203.

[17] E.R. Daniel, *The Franciscan Concept of Mission in the Middle Ages* (Lexington, Kentucky, 1975), pp. 26-54, 76-100.

[18] Cohen, *The Friars and the Jews,* p. 264.

[19] A.J. Black, *Council and Commune* (London, 1979), p. 30; Gerald Christianson, "Wyclif's Ghost: The Politics of Reunion at the Council of Basel," *Annuarium historiae conciliorum* 17 (1985): 193-208; E.F. Jacob, "The Bohemians at the Council of Basel," *Prague Essays*, ed. R. W. Seton-Watson (Oxford, 1949), pp. 81-123.

to reply to the defenders of orthodoxy. Cardinal Cesarini even developed a friendship with the leader of the Bohemian delegation, Prokop the Bald. No agreement was reached on these issues; and the Bohemians had to fend off frequent requests that they take the oath of incorporation into the council. This would have bound them to accept the decisions of the council, surely to be given in favor of orthodoxy, as the authoritative pronouncements of the church. Although these debates yielded no concrete results, they opened the way for future negotiations between the Bohemians and the fathers at Basel. Eventually the council was able to capitalize on the factional divisions of the Hussites to reach an accord with the moderate Utraquist party, the so-called Compacts, which granted communion under both species, bread and wine, to that faction, in return for their partial reintegration into the Catholic fold.[20]

This accommodation never pleased the papacy. Pressure to conform to Roman standards of orthodoxy and worship became part of Rome's subsequent dealings with the Bohemians. During the reign of Calixtus III, Aeneas Sylvius Piccolomini, a former conciliarist turned papal representative, urged the Roman pontiff to tolerate the Utraquists. After succeeding Calixtus as Pope Pius II, Aeneas felt obliged, perhaps driven by reminders of his conciliarist past, to insist on undoing the work of the Council of Basel in Bohemia. He demanded the reunification of all Christendom on Rome's terms as a precondition for an effective crusade against the Turks. This yielded, instead, civil strife in Bohemia and a fresh impetus to religious dissidence.[21] The former conciliarist Aeneas Sylvius might be discerned in the letter to Mehmed the Conqueror, which attempted to deal with the threat to the frontiers of Christendom by persuasion, however feeble. The official persona of Pius II, however, functioned without reference to such pacific thoughts. There was no room in Pius' policies for dialogue with conciliarist, Hussite or Muslim. The hallmarks of the Piccolomini pontificate were the Congress of Mantua, which failed to mobilize the princes of Europe against the Turk, and the dying pope's journey to Ancona in a failed effort to inspire others to participate in a crusade.[22]

The most effective advocates of dialogue, as has been noted, were at Basel. Nicholas of Cusa had written the most brilliant, if not the most in-

[20] Otakar Odlozilik, *The Hussite King* (New Brunswick, New Jersey, 1965), pp. 110-160.

[21] R.J. Mitchell, *The Laurels and the Tiara* (London, 1962), pp. 133-163, 255-267.

[22] Watanabe, *The Political Ideas of Nicholas of Cusa*, p. 129, n. 3; Joseph Gill, *The Council of Florence* (Cambridge, 1959), pp. 77-78, 130, 147-449, 294; Gerald Christianson, *Cesarini, the Conciliar Cardinal* (St. Ottilien, 1979), pp. 1-2.

fluential, defense of conciliar supremacy, his *De concordantia catholica,* during the early years of the council. This he had dedicated to Cesarini and to Sigismund of Luxemburg, King of the Romans. Later, Cusanus and Cesarini, the one as a diplomat and the other as a statesman, were active in efforts to reunite the Latin and Greek Churches through convocation of a council of union. These efforts had helped divide the Council of Basel, the majority favoring a site for the proposed council remote from the pope, the minority a site in Italy, since it would be more acceptable to the Greeks. Eventually, the Greeks decided that the presence of the patriarch of the West, the pope, was necessary for a truly ecumenical council, which required representation of the five ancient partriarchal sees, Rome, Constantinople, Alexandria, Antioch, and Jerusalem. Thus they chose to attend the papally sponsored council at Ferrara. These diplomatic maneuvers led the minority at Basel to abandon that city for the council of union, while the majority moved to declare conciliar supremacy a dogma as a prelude to replacing Eugenius IV with a more compliant Roman pontiff. In this context both Basel and Ferrara-Florence continued the earlier effort at airing theological issues in public. The deposition of the pope was debated at length in Basel even as spokesmen for the Latin and Greek Churches were arguing the key issues dividing East and West. In the end, Eugenius, assisted by Cesarini, was able to achieve a temporary reunification of the churches even as Basel was sundering the bonds of union in the West. Cesarini himself would perish in the battle of Varna (1444), trying to bring aid to the Greeks against the Turks. The union for which he died never was consumated in full, because the Greeks had built too much of their identify on rejection of Latin doctrines. Its last vestiges died with the Greek emperor in the fall of his capital.[23]

John of Segovia had proven himself a more dedicated conciliarist. This Salamancan theologian had been involved in the same efforts, which were so divisive of institutional unity, to depose Eugenius and replace him with a pope acceptable to the Council of Basel. He saw this upheaval, however, as the suffering of Christ's body from the misdeeds of Eugenius, not as the sundering by rebels of ecclesiastical unity. At the very end, after the princes had deserted the council and its pope, Felix V, had given up the struggle, John of Segovia had acquiesced in the assembly's "election" of Nicholas V as pope before withdrawing into retirement at Haiton in Savoy. There he spent his last years studying the problem of dialogue with the Islamic world. It was to John of Segovia that Cusanus transmitted his *De pace*

---

[23] Uta Fromherz, *Johannes von Segovia als Geschichtsschreiber des Konzils von Basel* (Basel, 1960); A.J. Black, *Monarchy and Community* (Cambridge, 1970), pp. 22-29, 44-50.

fidei, perhaps in the hope that this erstwhile colleague would translate his vision of religious concord into reality.[24]

These, then, were the chief theoreticians of dialogue with the Islamic world in the fifteenth century, men who had seen earlier efforts at theological accomodation achieve at least passing success. The Utraquists had agreed to the Compacts, and the Greeks had agreed to union with the Latins. Small wonder that they hoped that persuasion and conciliation, the fruits of dialogue, were attainable. Methods that worked with the Bohemians and the Greeks just might work with the Turks.[25] Here we see less the Renaissance's search for wisdom in non-Christian sources than the attempt of Llull to bring others to the faith through argument.[26] This is the heritage of William of Rubruck, who made common cause with the Nestorians and the Muslims against the Buddhists at the Mongol court.[27] What the Renaissance gave Cusanus and John of Segovia was the urge to study the Qur'an more carefully, to search for better texts, to produce a better translation. In a later age, when the Wars of Religion had produced a need for religious tolerance within Europe, writers like Jean Bodin would look to Cusanus for inspiration.[28]

In that later period, however, the old certainties about the non-Christian world, which were part of Cusanus' intellectual millieu, were fading away. The exploration of the New World began, like the missions to the Mongols, as a quest for allies against the Muslims.[29] The Europeans, layman and cleric alike, encountered in the Americas peoples who never had heard of Jesus Christ. Eventually, efforts to fit these peoples into old theological and cultural paradigms failed. Non-Christians were coerced into baptism, despite the objections of Bartolomé de las Casas; and paternalism prevailed in the *encomienda* system, as well as at the mission station.

---

[24] One notes that the Bohemian discusses the eucharist with St. Paul, *De pace fidei* XVIII, #63-66 (h VII, 58-61).

[25] *De pace fidei*, pp. xxxvi-xl.

[26] *The Mongol Mission*, ed. Christopher Dawson (New York, 1955), pp. 191-194. Cod. Cus. 203 contains a copy of Johannes de Plano Carpini, *Liber Tartarorum;* see Jakob Marx, *Verzeichnis der Handschriften-Sammlung des Hospitals zu Cues bei Bernkastel a. Mosel* (Trier, 1905; reprint Frankfurt, 1966), p. 189.

[27] *De pace fidei*, p. xiii; Watanabe, "Nicholas of Cusa and the Idea of Toleration," p. 410.

[28] See, most recently, L.I. Sweet, "Christopher Columbus and the Millenial Vision of the New World," *The Catholic Historical Review* 72 (1986): 369-382.

[29] Lewis Hanke, *Aristotle and the American Indians* (Chicago, 1959), pp. 1-27; idem, *All Mankind Is One* (De Kalb, Illinois, 1974), pp. 159-160.

Little real effort was made to raise up a native clergy able to serve their own peoples without European intermediation with God. Missiology remained Eurocentric, even to the point of confusing Spanish mores with the dictates of natural law. The narrow cosmos of the Middle Ages, nonetheless, was gone forever. European intellectuals had to rewrite their human geography, as they did their maps and their natural philosophy, to encompass the New World, just as they had to develop a new cosmology to encompass the insights of Copernicus and the observations of Galileo.

The fifteenth century, however, did not need to take this wider world into account, although Cusanus questioned the comfortably closed Ptolemaic cosmology of his day. The unity of Latin Christendom, assailed by the Turks from without and threatened by heresy from within, remained a presupposition. Dissent on important matters of belief or practice, especially dissent based on a clear, informed conscience, was almost incomprehensible to the intellectual leaders of Europe. In this context, John of Segovia and Nicholas of Cusa represent the most creative impulse possible in dealings with the spiritual "other." They sought to make reason, rather than arms, Christendom's first line of defense. They adhered to their own faith but sought for a glimmer of truth in Islam, one they hoped to strengthen into the clear light of orthodoxy through rational argument. Whether such efforts would have yielded a harvest of souls in a context in which Islam, like Christianity, was the ideological cement of a society must be doubted. In this context, nonetheless, we must place the continued study of Cusanus' *De pace fidei*, which continues to merit attention when the tracts on Islam composed by his contemporaries, among them Juan de Torquemada, largely are ignored.

A NEW FACE TOWARD ISLAM:
NICHOLAS OF CUSA AND JOHN OF SEGOVIA

James E. Biechler

Whether or not one sides with R.W. Southern in considering the label "Renaissance of the twelfth century" a term of "sublime meaninglessness,"[1] there is not much room for doubt that substantial, even radical, innovations took inspiration during that creative century. A major factor in that inspiration was, of course, the infusion of books and treatises into European culture through the mediation of the Muslim world. Marshall McLuhan's dictum that "the medium is the message" surely finds application in this case, for along with the translations of scientific and mathematical works from the Arabic, a new appreciation of Islamic culture and, therefore, of the religion of Islam as a subject worthy of serious study, began to develop. Although that study did not always lead to results that Christians today can cite with pride, there were occasional moments of promise and insight.

The chief witness to twelfth-century concern with Islam is the so-called Toledan Collection.[2] The nucleus of the collection, completed in 1143, was Robert of Ketton's translation of the entire Qur'an, but also represented were such treatises as the *Fabulae Sarracenorum*, the *De generatione Mahumet et nutritura eius*, the *Doctrina Mahumet* and the *Risalat* attributed to al-Kindi. Although another translation of the Qur'an into Latin was made at Toledo some sixty years later, a translation more literally faithful to the Arabic, it did not attain even the comparatively sparse diffusion of Ketton's Cluniac version even though it was copied as late as the seventeenth century.[3] About the Cluniac version, John of Segovia complained in 1456 that "very few Christians have this book and it is found in very few libraries."[4] Two years earlier Nicholas of Cusa had informed him of the existence of three

---

[1] "The Place of England in the Twelfth Century Renaissance," *History* 45 (1960): 201.

[2] On the Toledan Collection cf. Marie-Thérèse d'Alverny, "Deux traductions latines du Coran au moyen âge," *Archives d'histoire doctrinale et littéraire du moyen âge* 16 (1948): 69-131; James Kritzeck, *Peter the Venerable and Islam* (Princeton, New Jersey, 1964); *Petrus Venerabilis: Schriften zum Islam*, ed. and trans. Reinhold Glei (Altenberge, 1985).

[3] D'Alverny, "Deux traductions," p. 120.

[4] *Prólogo de Juan de Segovia a su Alcorán trilingue*, in Dario Cabanelas Rodríguez, *Juan de Segovia y el problema islámico* (Madrid, 1952), p. 286. Segovia seemed unaware of the existence of the later translation.

copies of the Qur'an he had learned of during his famous legation trip
through German lands in 1450.[5]   Since Cusanus had then visited nearly
every important ecclesiastical institution in those lands and since he had
already earned a solid reputation as a bibliophile, it may be safe to conclude
that Segovia's observation about the scarcity of Latin Qur'ans has merit.[6]

The Toledan Collection provided enough material to fuel the fires of
anti-Muslim opinion for centuries, even though most of the works comprising
it were of Muslim provenance. Indeed, as Norman Daniel has demonstrated,
the image of Islam and its Prophet that was forged during the Middle
Ages has survived into modern times, and the anti-Muslim sentiment
associated with it continues to influence contemporary attitudes.[7]   There
were really very few breaks in the stream of vituperation which flowed from
the pens of medieval European thinkers and even when works were available
which portrayed Muslim religious life and values as truly pious and devoted
to God, as reported in eyewitness accounts from merchants and pilgrims, no
serious doubts about the essentially "diabolic" nature of this hostile "sect"
disturbed the common consensus.   Doubtless the Toledan Collection was
not alone responsible for the negative image of Islam but it was perhaps the
single most important factor contributing to the legitimacy and credibility
of the theological case against Islam, a case which, for Daniel, ultimately
attained the level of simple factuality:

> There developed and was established a communal mode of thought
> which had great internal coherence, and which represented the doctrinal
> unity of Christendom in its political opposition to Islamic society.
> The strength of this integral group, or series, of opinions, what we may
> call this established canon, proved to be so great as to survive the
> break-up of European ideological unity, both the division into Catholic

[5] *Epistula ad Ioannem de Segobia*, III, 6-14, in appendix to *De pace fidei* (h
VII, 101). Cusanus was not certain whether all of these were copies of the same
version. Some years later, when writing his *Cribratio Alkorani*, he did learn
that the Roermond monastery's copy was the Robert of Ketton translation and
that it was defective. Cf. James E. Biechler, "Three Manuscripts on Islam from
the Library of Nicholas of Cusa," *Manuscripta* 27 (1983): 98.

[6] Scholars differ on the diffusion of the Toledan Collection. In Ludwig
Hagemann's view, "Die zahlreichen Manuskripte, die es von ihr gibt, zeugen für
ihre weite Verbreitung in der damaligen Zeit." *Der Kur'an in Verständnis und
Kritik bei Nikolaus von Kues: Ein Beitrag zur Erhellung islamisch-christlicher
Geschichte*, Frankfurter Theologische Studien, 21 (Frankfurt a.M., 1976), p. 30.
D'Alverny, "Deux traductions," pp. 109-113, lists only fourteen MSS of the 15th
century or earlier, some incomplete, containing the Latin Qur'an. One of these
belonged to Cusanus. Two other 15th-century copies may have been copied
after the events we are discussing here.

[7] *Islam and the West: The Making of an Image* (Edinburgh, 1960), p. 8.

and Protestant, and the growth of agnosticism and atheism.[8]

The enlightened and open-minded perspective of Daniel's work suggests that its overall assessment and conclusion might have been less negative had the fifteenth century been examined more closely. Such examination would have to include the historical context in which the various writers worked, the broad intention of the work of each writer, as well as such considerations as method, and the place of each work relative to the writer's comprehensive intellectual achievement. In short, a more broadly based hermeneutic than that available to Daniel is necessary if his seminal work is to bear the fruit he obviously anticipated. As valuable and reliable as it is in its data, Daniel's survey needs hermeneutical updating and revision.

A major suggestion in that direction was given by R.W. Southern in his 1961 Harvard lectures on medieval views of Islam.[9] Under the rubric "A Moment of Vision," he discussed the views of John of Segovia, Nicholas of Cusa, Aeneas Sylvius, and Jean Germain, placing them not only within the historical context of their own time but also against the backdrop of the several preceding medieval centuries. He saw the vision of these men as "larger, clearer, and more lifelike than at any previous moment, or any later one for several centuries at least."[10] If we extend the lines of Southern's examination to include a closer inspection of the theological root systems animating the thought especially of Cusanus and John of Segovia--their work, in particular, shows an independence and freshness of approach not usually associated with medieval theologians--we shall be in a better position to understand the truth of Southern's assessment. Quite possibly we shall discover that the realism and clarity of the initiatives referred to by Southern correspond to the aptness of the theological vision espoused by each of these important thinkers.

By the mid-fifteenth century the position of Christian Europe vis-à-vis the Islamic world was substantially different than ever before. The great city of Constantinople had fallen to the Turks in 1453 and, as frightening and tragic as it was to European Christians of the time, the prospects of a unified counterattack continued to be elusive. The dying feudal order with its religion of chivalry no longer possessed the *élan vital* which animated the crusading movements of earlier times. New views of humanity and society were already well developed, and the Western church had already experienced the foreshocks of cataclysmic reformation.

Nicholas of Cusa and John of Segovia were two passionately serious

[8] *Ibid.*, p. 271.

[9] *Western Views of Islam in the Middle Ages* (Cambridge, Massachusetts, 1962).

[10] *Ibid.*, p. 103.

theoreticians who embodied the new spirit of the age and helped to give it theological credibility. Ernst Cassirer called Cusanus "the first modern thinker":

> Of all the philosophical movements and efforts of the Quattrocento, only his doctrines fulfil Hegel's demand; only they represent a "simple focal point" in which the most diverse rays are gathered. Cusanus is the only thinker of the period to look at all of the fundamental problems of his time from the point of view of *one* principle through which he masters them all. His thought knows no barriers that separate disciplines. In keeping with the medieval ideal of the whole, it includes the totality of the spiritual and physical cosmos.[11]

We should not be surprised if so significant a thinker as this should have creative theological views about Islam or that he should respond with enthusiasm to the intriguing proposal of John of Segovia, his friend of earlier years. This Salamancan theologian had come to the Council of Basel in 1433 as a supporter of the papalist position but was "converted" to the conciliarist cause and became one of its foremost theoreticians. Antony Black, in his study of conciliar theory, evaluates Segovia and his work in terms showing some resemblance to Cassirer's remarks on Cusanus:

> These doctrines and ideals received their most explicit development from John of Segovia who, like Nicholas of Cusa, paid careful attention to the underlying principles of Conciliarism. Considering himself as merely "the least of the advocates of the conciliar doctrine", he summed up better than anyone the mentality of his colleagues, and seems to express more fully what they were feeling their way towards. As in the case of Cusa, his reflections led him to expound a social philosophy which shed light both on the theology of the church and on the political theory of the state. The social ideals of the New Testament and the political norms of Aristotle were, in his work, more closely interwoven than ever, and he made perhaps the most whole-hearted attempt yet to give them constitutional embodiment. He referred frequently to historical and contemporary methods of government, as both legal and empirical evidence for his case, and so may be said to be bridging the distance between medieval and modern types of political reasoning.[12]

Thinkers as serious-minded and creative as were Cusanus and Segovia should not be expected to change their characters when confronting so important a subject as Christianity's relationship with Islam. In fact, the

[11] *The Individual and the Cosmos in Renaissance Philosophy* (New York, 1963), pp. 7, 10.

[12] *Monarchy and Community: Political Ideas in the Later Conciliar Controversy, 1430-1450* (Cambridge, 1970), p. 24.

subject of Islam seemed to play a part in the formation of their early friendship in Basel for it was this mutual interest which bridged their estrangement and afforded the magnanimous Spaniard an entree to a restoration of a friendship which political events had all but ruptured.

Nicholas of Cusa was a German canonist who had come to Basel as a conciliarist partisan, a position he probably developed as a student at Padua, but later he became one of the staunchest supporters of the papacy. The Spaniard and the German met at the council, worked together and together developed their interest in, and knowledge of Islam.[13] At Basel, Nicholas loaned Segovia his codex containing the works of the Toledan Collection and even though the two men took divergent political paths, their common views on Islam kept their relationship from disintegrating. After the fall of Constantinople each thinker earnestly returned to the problem of Christian-Muslim relations, Cusanus with his work *De pace fidei*, a fictional dialogue among adherents of the world's religions, and Segovia, with his elaborate and multi-faceted project involving a trilingual edition of the Qur'an and a bilateral conference between Christians and Muslims as an avenue toward harmonious future relations.

In some ways, John of Segovia's project strikes us as the more enlightened and practical of the two, indeed as the most promising initiative of the whole period. For, as Southern points out, Segovia's proposed *contraferentia* envisioned a multi-faceted end, one that did not necessarily

---

[13] Ludwig Hagemann's assertion (*Cribratio Alkorani, Praefatio editoris* [h VIII, p. x]) that John of Segovia introduced Nicholas of Cusa to the writings of the Toledan Collection, while it might appear plausible on the grounds that the Spaniard had closer acquaintance with actual Muslims, is not supported by Segovia's own assertion that it was from Nicholas that he obtained a copy of the work: "Etenim cum vestra concessione librum ipsum alchoran habuerim anno xxxvii. . . ." *Epistula Ioannis de Segobia ad Nicolaum de Cusa*, Cod. Vat. lat. 2923, fol. 6ᵛ; or: "Memorem quippe arbitror dominationem vestram metuendissimam quod dum Constantinopolim itura foret multo rogatu meo concessit michi ut copiari facerem librum Alchoran non continentem magis vero sectam sarracenorum sistentem." *Epistula Ioannis de Segobia ad Nicolaum de Cusa*, Cod. Vat. lat. 2923, fol. 4ᵛ, 10-14. I believe this refers to Cod. Cus. 108 which is not "comprised of" the Qur'an but also presents details about the "sect" of Islam. Cf. Jakob Marx, *Verzeichnis der Handschriften-Sammlung des Hospitals zu Cues* (Trier, 1905), pp. 107-108.

limit itself to the conversion of the Muslim.[14]   This aspect alone marks the
Segovia proposal with unique distinction. He died before his plans could
get off the drawing board. In some ways it seems not to have exerted much
influence upon those to whom it was addressed, especially Aeneas Sylvius
(later Pope Pius II). But with its fascinating irenicism and the boldness of
its overture toward Islam it should not be so readily dismissed as at least
partially influential on that fascinating letter of Pius II to Mehmed II[15]

[14] *Western Views*, p. 91. The term *contraferentia* is found only in the letter
to Aeneas Sylvius, Cod. Vat. lat. 2923, fol. 3ᵛ, 9. Cf. Cabanelas, *Juan de
Segovia*, p. 349. Rudolf Haubst, "Johannes von Segovia im Gespräch mit
Nikolaus von Kues und Jean Germain über die göttliche Dreieinigkeit und ihre
Verkündigung vor den Mohammedanern," *Münchener Theologische Zeitschrift* 2
(1951): 118. Haubst anticipated Southern's association of these three
ecclesiastics on the Islamic question and saw in Segovia's irenic approach a
carry-over of his "Basler kirchenparlamentarischen Optimismus." Southern
seems unaware of Haubst's study. On the Basel connection see also the essay by
Thomas Izbicki above.

[15] The letter is edited in Guiseppe Toffanin, *Lettera a Maometto II (Epistola
ad Mahumetem) di Pio II (Enea Silvio Piccolomini)* (Naples, 1953), pp. 108-
177. Southern is correct, I believe, in questioning the sincerity of this letter
(*Western Views*, p. 99). For a more complete evaluation of the letter and its
possible inspiration cf. Franco Gaeta, "Sulla 'Lettera a Maometto' de Pio II,"
Bullettino del'Istituto Storico per il Medio Evo e Archivio Muratoriano, 77
(1965): 127-227. Gaeta argues convincingly (pp. 163-166) for the dependence
of Pius II on John of Torquemada's treatise *Contra principales errores perfidi
Machometi*. Cf. also his "Alcune osservazioni sulla prima redazione della 'lettera
a Maometto" in *Enea Silvio Piccolomini, Papa Pio II: Atti del convegno per il
quinto centenario della morte e altri scritti*, ed. Domenico Maffei (Siena, 1968),
pp. 177-186. Torquemada's treatise will be briefly discussed below. On the letter's significance cf. also Franz Babinger, "Pio II e l'Oriente maomettano" in
Maffei, *Enea Silvio Piccolomini*, pp. 1-13; idem, *Mehmed the Conqueror and
His Time* (Princeton, New Jersey, 1978), pp. 198-201; and Robert Schwoebel,
The Shadow of the Crescent: The Renaissance Image of the Turk (1453-1517)
(New York, 1967), pp. 65-67. Norman Daniel does not question the letter's
authenticity but evaluates it as "a document that shows little originality, and of
which the latinity is not as elegant as the author's reputation might make us
expect": *Islam and the West*, p. 279. Babinger sees a heavy dependence of the
letter upon Nicholas of Cusa's *Cibratio Alkorani* although he acknowledges that
no thorough study of the matter has yet been done. He denies the letter's dependence on John of Torquemada whereas Thomas Izbicki, *Protector of the Faith:
Cardinal Johannes de Turrecremata and the Defense of the Institutional Church*
(Washington, D.C., 1981), p. 23, agrees with the thesis preferring a dependence
upon Torquemada rather than Cusanus. Babinger's denial of Torquemada's influence is based upon his judgment that the Spanish Dominican depended
completely upon Spanish data, material not evident in Pius II's letter.

urging him to submit to a few drops of baptismal water and thereby become the undisputed Christian emperor of the East.[16]

Segovia sketched the lines of his proposal in a lengthy letter to Cusanus, December 2, 1454. Recalling his experience of a dialogue with a Muslim theologian, Segovia explained to Cusanus that Muslims regard Christians as unbelievers because they worship two gods, believing that God has a son.[17] Many other misunderstandings about Christian beliefs as well as inherent weaknesses or errors in the Muslim position could be cleared up easily by face-to-face discussion on the highest level.

The dialogue approach commended itself for several reasons. First of all, Segovia wrote, the way of peace is to be preferred to the way of war.[18] That is, after all, the way of Christ himself, who differed in this respect from Muhammad who was not loath to use the sword, and it was the way the Apostles settled their differences.[19] Furthermore, experience has shown that lands won by war from the Muslims do not by that fact result in true and lasting conversions to Christianity. Even if one could succeed in the well-nigh impossible job of capturing their lands, their hatred would be such

---

[16] As for John of Segovia's impact on Aeneas Sylvius, Babinger dismisses the Spaniard's proposal as irrelevant to the actual situation because it was based upon Spanish experience: "Il fatto de credere le sue idee applicabili alla questione turca mostra che Giovanni di Segovia non era al corrente della situazione reale. In Ispagna la coesistenza cristiano-maomettana era una realta vecchia di piu secoli. Il comune sentimento spagnolo o iberico attutiva il contrasto religioso, tanto piu che la potenza dell'Islam si limitiva al piccolo principato di Granata, col quale si conviveva ottimamente." "Pio II e l'Oriente maomettano," p. 6. Cf. also Enrico Cerulli, *Nuove ricerche sul Libro della Scala e la conoscenza dell'Islam in Occidente*. Studi e Testi, 271 (Vatican City, 1972), pp. 78-86.

[17] Segovia's views on this were formed through actual experience, in discussion with a Spanish Muslim. Cf. Iohannes de Segobia *Alcoranus trilinguis, Prologus,* Cod. Vat. lat. 2923, fol. 5^r; Cabanelas Rodríguez, *Juan de Segovia,* pp. 265-266.

[18] *Epistula Ioannis de Segobia ad Nicolaum de Cusa,* Cod. Vat. lat. 2923: "Vixque inchoavi redigere scripto conceptum quem a plus xxx annis habui in corde: pace magis quam belli via fore intendendum ad exterminandam minorandamque sectam Sarracenorum" (fol. 4^v, 29-32); "Ut autem Reverendissime pater totum dicam cor meum cum iam a pluribus annis sicut praemisi cogitatio haec versata fuerit in visceribus meis pacis modo magis quam bellorum saevitiae intendendum fore ad conversionem Sarracenorum" (fol. 30^v, 31-33-fol. 31^r, 1-2). Cf. also his *De mittendo gladio spiritus in corda Sarracenorum,* Praefatio, Cod. Vat. lat. 2923, fol. 178^r, 9-19.

[19] *Epistula ad Nicolaum de Cusa,* Cod. Vat. lat. 2923, fol. 19^r-20^v.

that the people would never be converted.[20]

Among the peaceful methods there are, in his view, only three: miracle, missionary preaching, discussion. As to miracles, he finds it incomprehensible that when the Christians want to resolve a business matter with Muslims they send a delegation composed of mortal human beings to negotiate. But in the matter of religious peace, conversion of those who have submitted to the yoke of Islam, or preaching the gospel to all nations, Christians remain inert, hoping for divine intervention.[21]

Segovia's rejection of the missionary approach is truly surprising since this was the method made sacred to Christianity by the gospel admonition to go forth into the whole world preaching the good news. It had been the standard, approved, and highly praised approach to pagan and heretic alike. Segovia rejected the classical missionary method as unsuited to the special case of Islam since experience had shown that such missions generally fail. In any case, they could never succeed unless Muslim authorities give permission for such activity. Because Muslims exhibit an unusual intensity in religious matters they tend to guard against the influx of alien beliefs.[22]

The one viable approach, the *contraferentia*, nowhere developed in complete detail by Segovia in any single writing, is structured in three successive stages: first, the establishment and maintenance of peace with Muslim peoples; second, a deepening of cultural relations leading to neutralization of suspicion and antagonism and, finally, peaceful discussion of basic doctrines which separate the two ideologies. The discussions must involve both theologians and civil authorities.

Segovia was convinced that his proposal had the support of both natural law and Catholic theology as well as the experiential confirmation of history which shows that the way of peace and concord has the decided advantage over war and crusade. Among other historical examples the

[20] *Ibid.*, fol. 12ʳ, 26 - fol. 14ʳ, 6. Uta Fromherz, *Johannes von Segovia als Geschichtsschreiber des Konzils von Basel*. Basler Beiträge zur Geschichtswissenschaft, 81 (Basel and Stuttgart, 1960), pp. 42-56, gives a good summary of Segovia's project.

[21] *Epistula ad Nicolaum de Cusa*, Cod. Vat. lat. 2923, fol. 15ᵛ, 12-23: "Quoniam vero id notissimum est quod christiani tum Sarracenis super re temporali acturi inexpectato quod deus per se vel angelus illis desuper loquatur iuxta magnitudinem rerum agendarum plus minusve solemnes suos legatos vel nuncios mortales homines ad eos mittunt inducturos eos ad faciendum ea quae postulant. Magnum profecto dignumque attentione gravi offertur ante oculos nostros avisamentum. Si dum pertractandum est de pace totius populi christiani deque Sarracenorum salute sed et de gloria dei gentibus annuntianda tuenda Christi innocentia honoreque ecclesiae ac totius christianae religionis christifideles per seipsos non intendant sed expectent a deo fieri miracula."

[22] *Ibid.*, fol. 17ᵛ, 19-fol. 18ᵛ, 30.

Spanish theologian cites the case of the Hussites in which more progress was made by negotiation than by arms. Segovia himself had played an active part in those negotiations and that role had taught him to be optimistic about the dialogical approach to problem solving.

What makes John of Segovia's work on the approach to Islam so significant is his general emphasis on the points of agreement between the two religions which, in his view, should always form the starting point in discussions with Muslims. So convinced was he of the rationality of the Christian faith that even such doctrines as the Trinity and the Incarnation could, he thought, be explained to Muslims in such a way as to be convincing to them. His frequent allusion to his earlier face-to-face dialogue with a Muslim theologian, considered in the light of his striking and repeated emphasis on *experientia, praxis, practica, observatio, gesta,* and *historia* in his ecclesiological writings makes it clear that his Islam proposal had living roots deep in a more comprehensive theology that Segovia had hammered out in conflict and contemplation over several decades.[23]

Segovia's holistic view of the church in which the totality of power does not reside in any one part but in the whole itself, as well as his emphasis on "the essential pluralism of the church," correlate positively even with today's ecumenical theology. In his recent analysis of Segovia's ecclesiology, Antony Black has described the principle of collective decision-making which, Segovia insists, results in superior knowledge, more energetic resolution, and selfless love of the common good. In Segovia's words, "Out of the intermingled multitude, almost daily forced into each other's company, there is born true love for persons of all nationalities . . . so that, coming together with a certain delight, they explore more wisely the true and common good." Though Segovia was here speaking in terms of co-religionists, Black insists that the structure of the argument is metaphysical, the principle involved being derived from the natural law itself.[24]   As remarkable as Segovia's proposal for a *contraferentia* approach to Islam is in itself, its organic connection to his theology of the church marks the proposal with seriousness and with a potential for further development that look promising indeed.

Segovia knew that his political approach could bear no fruit without the participation of the leading men of the church. He therefore contacted Nicholas of Cusa, recalling their earlier friendship and their mutual interest in Islam. Furthermore, he viewed Cusanus as one sincerely dedicated to truth and to the reform of the church. He was confident that despite the papacy's call for a crusade, Cusanus could be trusted to hold his radical

[23] Antony Black, *Council and Commune: The Conciliar Movement and the Council of Basle* (London and Shepherdstown, West Virginia, 1979), p. 132.

[24] *Council and Commune*, p. 159.

proposal in confidence until the time was more politically opportune. Caution here was crucial. The general reaction to the fall of Constantinople had been to counter aggression with military force, and to that end a campaign of rhetoric had been mounted which marshalled all the skills of the new learning and of the old as well. The papacy had led the way and its position was so unqualified and its diplomatic activities were so tireless that a pacifistic stance would have been counterproductive if not foolhardy. Thus, before daring to publicize a program outlining a new direction in Christian-Muslim relations, Segovia could think of no one more likely to respond positively than Nicholas of Cusa.

One of the ironies of the Cusanus-Segovia connection is that events of the Council of Basel and its aftermath had placed these one-time collaborators on opposite sides of the papal fence. John of Segovia had been excommunicated for his support of the anti-pope, Felix V, had continued to work for the success of the council--in that capacity he actually confronted Cusanus in public debate at the Mainz Reichstag in 1444--and had remained faithful to it until the very end.[25] We may gain a better appreciation of the differences which came to disrupt their former unanimity by looking at what Antony Black has called "the essence of Baslean Conciliarism," namely, the distinction between the church as mystical body and the church as a political body. Both Cusanus and Segovia agreed on the distinction and found it important. But to understand how they differed we might, at the risk of oversimplification, see Cusanus as placing emphasis on the former, underlining the spiritual and antecedent unity of the church, while Segovia's emphasis on the latter moved him to tireless political

[25] In Cusanus' letter to Segovia, one may see a veiled illusion to their deep differences over Basel as he refers to "the bond of old friendship between us (*nexum veteris inter nos amicitiae*)": *Epistula ad Ioannem de Segobia* (h VII, 93). It is a tribute to the magnanimous character of Segovia that Cusanus' bitter animosity, confessed in a letter to Giuliano Cesarini, did not deter the Spaniard from his ideal of Christian-Muslim peace. His letter to Cusanus is as much an overture of fraternal charity as it is of interreligious concern. Cf. *De pace fidei*, *Praefatio editoris* (h VII, pp. li-lii).

activity in search of an achieved consensus.[26]   More accurately, each found great theological meaning in the notion of the *corpus Christi mysticum* and both accepted it without reservation. But Cusanus came to prefer the *mysticum* of the formula, Segovia the *corpus* term. Their differing approaches to Islam seem distinguishable precisely along the same lines.[27] Segovia's proposal, as we have seen, is an optimistic commitment to a unity to be achieved by means of discussion and dialogue. Nicholas of Cusa has quite another conception of unity and that conception understandably governs his appreciation of Christian-Muslim relations as well.

It was the horrifying news of the fall of Constantinople which stimulated Cusanus to turn his attention to the matter of interreligious harmony and to the problem of Islam in particular. His codex containing the works of the Toledan Collection shows several sets of marginalia in the Cusan hand, one set distinctly linked to the production of his *De pace fidei*, written in direct response to the tragic events in Byzantium.[28]

As the history of the Council of Basel unrolled, Cusanus had lost his enthusiasm for the principle of collective decision-making which he had so eloquently espoused in his famous conciliarist treatise, *De concordantia catholica*, written in support of the council. His subsequent abandonment of the conciliar cause and his conversion to a position of ecclesiological monarchism coincided with his conversion to a Neoplatonic metaphysics

[26] Black, *Monarchy and Community*, pp. 14-15. Black's geographic distinction is less persuasive: "[Conciliarism] drew both on the Northern piety of the type found among the Brethren of the Common Life, and on the republican spirit of the Mediterranean city-states; it was perhaps most of all Cusa who represented the former, and Segovia the latter strand." (*Ibid.*, p. 23). The association of Cusanus with the Brethren of the Common Life, although asserted in Vansteenberghe's important biography of Cusanus (listed in Black's "Bibliography") is no longer historically plausible. Cf. R.R. Post, *The Modern Devotion: Confrontation with Reformation and Humanism* (Leiden, 1968), pp. 356-357, and Gerd Heinz-Mohr, "Nikolaus von Kues und der Laie in der Kirche," *Mitteilungen und Forschungsbeiträge der Cusanus-Gesellschaft* 4 (1964): 305. The different approaches of Cusanus and Segovia might also be understood along the lines traditionally seen as dividing Plato from Aristotle. Segovia's empirical political views owed much to Aristotle. Cf. Black, *Monarchy and Community*, p. 24.

[27] For a thorough study of the ecclesiology of the two conciliarists cf. Werner Krämer, *Konsens und Rezeption: Verfassungsprinzipien der Kirche im Basler Konziliarismus*. Beiträge zur Geschichte der Philosophie und Theologie des Mittelalters, 19 (Münster, 1980).

[28] For more details on Cusanus's work on this codex cf. James E. Biechler, "Three Manuscripts on Islam."

postulating the pre-existent unity of being and truth. In this system, all the world's a hierarchy, or, as Black puts it, "'Hierarchy' was a single 'natural law' pervading cosmos and polity."[29]   In his famous *De docta ignorantia*, completed shortly after his abandonment of the Council of Basel, Cusanus articulated a theology defining the created cosmos as "the unfolding of unity."[30]   The variety characterizing our daily experience is nothing but the participation, in otherness, of the one truth. It was characteristic of Cusanus that he saw in the actual physical realities of the created world a glimpse of the *maximum absolutum* and it was this macrocosmic connection which determined the truth and value of a thing or event.[31]

In his *De pace fidei* Cusanus intellectually resolved the differences between the world's major religions in a dialogue between seventeen wise men from the various religions and regions of the world. Unlike John of Segovia who planned a dialogue with real people, Cusanus' dialogue takes place in heaven with Peter, Paul, and the Logos! Not surprisingly this ideal process arrived at the conclusion that all the world's religion is one, although it actually exists in a variety of ritual forms. Because of this intrinsic unity, it should not be too difficult, he holds, to work out the mundane details.

Not all of the participants in the heavenly dialogue discuss matters representative of their own particular traditions, but it is clear that Cusanus, who prided himself on his knowledge of Islam, made a special effort to associate the beliefs of that faith with Muslim nationalities. Thus, the

---

[29] *Monarchy and Community*, p. 60. Some authors have tried to minimize the difference between the Cusanus who composed the *De concordantia catholica*, the last great classical statement of the conciliarist cause, and the "converted" Cusanus who argued so strenuously for the monarchical papacy that he became known as the "Hercules of the Eugenians." Perhaps "conversion" is too strong a word for Cusanus' new enthusiasm for Neoplatonic thought. That he did come to a rather sudden new appreciation of these ideas is evident from his own statement: "I must confess, my friend, that at the time I received this idea from on high, I had not understood Dionysius or any of the true theologians; but after that I hurried to the writings of the doctors and there I found nothing except what had been revealed to me expressed in different ways": *Apologia doctae ignorantiae* (h II, 12). Krämer resolves the problem by placing it in a purely *political* light, choosing not to underline the ideological transformation: *Konsens und Rezeption*, pp. 281-283.

[30] *De docta ignorantia* II, 3, #108 (h I, 70).

[31] "Er bohrt sich fest in den kleinen Dingen, er sieht den Makrokosmos im Mikrokosmos reflektiert und stösst gerade so dann vor zu einer Einsicht in die Werthaftigkeit des Kleinen. . . .": Erich Meuthen, "Pius II. und Nikolaus von Kues," *Schweizer Rundschau: Monatschrift für Geistesleben und Kultur* 7/8 (1964): 440.

Turk raises the question of the crucifixion, fact for Christians but denied by Muslims, and learns that "if the Arabs would look to the fruit of the death of Christ . . . they would not take away this glory of the cross through which he merited being the most high."[32] The Persian raises the question, so difficult for Muslims, of the divine incarnation, and discovers that such a doctrine does not militate against the unity of God. Indeed, the miracles of Jesus, acknowledged by Muslims and attested in the Qur'an, demonstrate that his power is truly divine. Although it is the Jew who raises the vexing question of the Trinity, the answer is addressed to both Jew and Arab with some suggestion that the Arabs, already believing in creation and divine fecundity, are in a better position to be persuaded of this truth since it avoids the need for a multiplicity of divine creators. This argument is even better than that based upon statements that God has an essence and a soul, a word and spirit. Because the divine unity precludes God's "having" anything --He *is* identically all that He "has"--Muslims actually believe in the Trinity without adverting to it as such.[33]

Of special interest in *De pace fidei* is the comprehensive formula which Cusanus employs as expressive of the entire interreligious problematic. He introduces it in the dialogue immediately after the first two representatives, the Greek and the Italian, discuss the unitary nature of wisdom. It is the Arab who occupies the important third place in the dialogue and it is to this Muslim that the Logos makes the startling statement: "So the religion and worship of all who are intellectually alive is one and it is presupposed in all the diversity of rites."[34] The association of this formulation with the Arab is not accidental. In the *Lex sive doctrina Mahumeti* the Prophet of Islam summarized the doctrines of the prophets who preceded him by explaining that "the law or faith of all is one, but the rites of the different [prophets] were undoubtedly different." In the margin of his copy of this book Nicholas drew a pointer and noted: *fides una, ritus diversus.*[35] What is so astonishing about this formula is its neat fit with the Neoplatonic metaphysics of participation: the variety of finite being is an unfolding (*explicatio*) of the One who is the enfolding (*complicatio*) of all. Here it was the Islamic connection which gave Cusanus the key to his philosophy of religion and his solution to the intractable dilemmas of interreligious strife.

---

[32] *De pace fidei* XIV, #48 (h VII, 45).

[33] *De pace fidei* IX, #26 (h VII, 27).

[34] *De pace fidei* VI, #16 (h VII, 15): "Una est igitur religio et cultus omnium intellectu vigentium, quae in omni diversitate rituum praesupponitur."

[35] Cod. Cus. 108, fol. 25va. The Heidelberg edition cites Cusanus' note (h VII, p. 15) and reproduces the manuscript folio (facing p. xxxix).

Medieval Christians found one of the most shocking aspects of Islam in the Qur'anic description of paradise as a garden of sensuous delights. In the *De pace fidei* it is the German (*Alamanus*) who raises this sensitive question. Why, he asks, does the Qur'an condemn certain sensual pleasures which, in the life to come, it makes the substance of paradise? Medieval tradition took this inconsistency to be proof positive that Muhammad and his Qur'an were without divine authority. But the sensitive eye of Nicholas of Cusa saw even here the glint of divine truth. The intent of the Qur'an, he said, was to express to an uneducated people a vision of paradise which would be attractive to them so as to turn them away from idolatry.[36] At this point in the discussion Cusanus refers to the teaching of Avicenna who, he said, "incomparably preferred the intellectual happiness of the vision and enjoyment of God and truth to the happiness described in the Arab law, even though he was of this law."[37] Cusanus was not just engaging in the Renaissance habit of name-dropping here; he had read Avicenna's *Metaphysics* and found there a Muslim preference for joys transcending the body and its senses.[38]

Cusanus' optimism about the resolution of the Christian-Muslim problem is less evident in his later "sifting" of the Qur'an, his *Cribratio Alkorani*, although here, too, the guiding motif is his belief that the Qur'an contains the fundamental truths of the gospel and that the teaching of Muhammad is implicitly trinitarian and christological. Although he

[36] *De pace fidei* XV, #51-52 (h VII, 48-49).

[37] *De pace fidei* XV, #52 (h VII, 49).

[38] *Adnotatio* 33 in the Klibansky-Bascour edition of *De pace fidei* (h VII, 85) is erroneous here. Cusanus' marginal notation on the resurrection, Cod. Cus. 205, fol. 78[v], is nowhere near the location cited; it is to be found at Tractatus VII, c. 7 of the modern critical edition: "Oportet autem te scire quod promissio alia est quae fide recipitur, quia non est via ad probandum eam nisi credendo testimonio prophetae, sicut illa quae est de eo quod habebit corpus apud resurrectionem....Lex enim nostra quam dedit Mahometh ostendit dispositionem felicitatis et miseriae quae sunt secundum corpus. Et alia est promissio quae apprehenditur intellectu et argumentatione demonstrative, et prophetia approbat....Sapientibus vero theologis multo maior cupiditas fuit ad consequendum hanc felicitatem quam felicitatem corporum, quae quamvis daretur eis, tamen non attenderunt eam, nec appretiati sunt eam comparatione huius felicitatis quae est coniuncta primae veritati. . . ." *Avicenna Latinus Liber de Philosophia prima sive scientia divina.* Édition critique de la traduction latine médiévale, ed. S. van Riet (Louvain and Leiden, 1977-1980) V-X: 507. Unfortunately, Hagemann compounds the error by updating it in his *adnotatio* to n. 153, 2-4, *Cribratio Alkorani* (h VIII, 244-245). He cites the modern critical edition of Avicenna but, in apparent dependence upon the Klibansky-Bascour note, misplaced the Cusan marginalia by 32 pages.

finished this work several years after the death of John of Segovia, we are not wrong to place it within the entire Islamic project of their collaboration and, therefore, to consider it at this point in our discussion. Nicholas meant the *Cribratio* to be his definitive statement on Islam and, although it shows the unmistakable signs of its author's conviction that divine truth shines out wherever human enterprise occurs, this work attempts a more serious and detailed engagement with what Cusanus saw to be erroneous in the Muslim scripture. The delineation of Qur'anic "errors" does not strike the reader as unusually insightful given the long history of such polemic among medieval Christians. We are, however, struck by two notions governing the entire work and determining its spirit and objective, notions which set the *Cribratio* apart as open-minded and irenic. *Manuductio*, a theological idea with a long and distinguished pedigree, especially among Neoplatonic thinkers, refers to the method by which the human mind is guided step by step through and beyond the sensible world to a knowledge of the divine. Because the Neoplatonic cosmos is arranged in a unified but hierarchical gradation, knowledge and love must progress step by step up the ladder of being. Cusanus "sifts" (*cribrare*) the Qur'an to find those nuggets which reflect divine truth. These then serve as touchstones for his *manuductio* by which Cusanus tries "to take the Muslims by the hand to lead them to an understanding of true Christian belief."[39]   Chief among these Qur'anic truths is its teaching that Christ is the "spirit of God" (*ruholla*), which, Cusanus says, some understand as "breath," some as "spirit," some as "mind," others as "word." None of these interpretations, he says, affects the essential truth that Christ is God.[40]   From this truth about Christ, and from other truths about creativity and intellection, Cusanus develops a set of arguments designed to lead the Muslim to a grasp of Christian belief.

Interpretatio pia is another notion which marks the *Cribratio Alkorani* as radically different from the usual anti-Muslim treatise. It is Cusanus' term for a hermeneutic principle which enables him to understand the Qur'an in a sense most favorable to Christian doctrine. The phrase occurs four

[39] Hagemann, *Der Kur'an*, p. 73. Rudolf Haubst has treated the notion of *manuductio* in Cusanus. Cf. especially his *Die Christologie des Nikolaus von Kues* (Freiburg, 1956), pp. 216, 308-312. Cf. also *Sermo* XXXIII, n. 4, 8 (h XVII, 1, 58).

[40] *Cribratio Alkorani* I, 20 (h VIII, 68). In his letter to Segovia, Cusanus had used the term *ruholla*. Cf. *infra*, n. 43. The precise source of his knowledge on this point is not known. The Qur'an does not use this term in speaking of Jesus as the spirit of God. Muslim commentators on the Qur'an, however, have used the term and today all the world knows it as the name of the late Iranian leader Ayatollah Ruhulla Musavi Khomeini.

times in the text, enabling Cusanus to read Qur'anic teaching as not
antithetical to Trinitarian theology, as tacitly teaching that Christ was
actually crucified, and, finally, as not opposed to the Bible in its images of
the last judgment, paradise, and hell.[41]

Methodological motifs such as *manuductio* and *interpretatio pia*, despite
their differences from the *contraferentia* approach of John of Segovia, show
why the German idealist and the Spanish realist could find common cause
on the question of Islam. Despite their conviction that Islam seriously
deviated from the true faith, their open attitude enabled them to recognize in
it something of the divine truth they both shared.

Cusanus replied to Segovia's letter of 1454 without delay, telling him
of his own book *De pace fidei* and giving enthusiastic support to the proposal. He suggested a practical addition to Segovia's proposal recommend-
ing that the Christian side of the conference be placed in the hands of
influential laymen rather than priests because, he said, the Turks would
prefer these.[42]   He reinforced Segovia's conviction that the Christian
doctrine of the Trinity would not be an insuperable obstacle to the Muslim
once it was explained that the very perfection of the highest One essentially
involves co-relations.[43]   At the same time he suggested an approach for
convincing Muslims of the truth of the hypostatic union: it should be built
upon their own belief that "Christ is the word and son of God and *ruholla,*
that is, spirit of God."[44]   His argument here is the same as that given by
Peter to the Persian in the celestial dialogue portrayed in the *De pace fidei.*

What makes the positive and irenic approaches of John of Segovia and
Nicholas of Cusa unique is that they were conceived and articulated within
an atmosphere of supercharged anti-Muslim polemic designed to stir up
support for a crusade to recapture Constantinople. Furthermore, the sources
available to these two thinkers were all but univocal in their negative
assessment of the Prophet of Islam. Nicholas, for example, accepted it as
fact that Muhammad was uneducated, politically ambitious, pleasure-loving,
and licentious, that he had recourse to the sword when his words became

---

[41] Cf. James E. Biechler, "Christian Humanism Confronts Islam: Sifting
the Qur'an with Nicholas of Cusa," *Journal of Ecumenical Studies* 13 (1976): 13.
Even though Cusanus is clear enough about what he means by *interpretatio pia,*
some scholars have found the concept problematic. Cf. a brief discussion in
Hagemann, *Der Kur'an,* p. 72.

[42] "Non est dubium medio principum temporalium, quos Teucri sacerdotibus
praeferunt, ad colloquia posse perveniri. . . .": *Nicolai de Cusa epistula ad
Ioannem de Segobia,* December 29, 1454, Appendix to *De pace fidei* (h VII, 97).

[43] *Nicolai de Cusa epistula,* p. 98.

[44] *Nicolai de Cusa epistula,* p. 98: "Unde et ita Sarraceni fatentur Christum
verbum et filium Dei et ruholla, hoc est spiritum Dei."

ineffective, that his message was corrupted by malicious Jews, that he was instructed in Christianity by the Nestorian monk, Sergius, and that he had been a devotee of Venus. Segovia was aware of, and accepted, most of these "facts" as well. They were matters of common knowledge among theologically educated Europeans of the time, making up, as they did, a biographical portrait of Muhammad consistent with that of the stereotypical heresiarch.

That portrait was reinforced rather than challenged by the works of several contemporaries. One, a friend of Cusanus, Denys Rickel (Dennis the Carthusian), wrote his *Contra perfidiam Machometi* at the instigation of the German cardinal, who carefully read and annotated the book, and though he adopted some of its verbal formulations, its overall influence on him remained marginal. Denys also composed an imaginary dialogue between a Muslim and a Christian which, it must be admitted, does have its moments of magnanimity. But considering Denys' exalted reputation as a mystic and theologian we do not unreasonably expect a more enlightened attitude toward the Muslim faith. Although the affective element in his mystical theology is strong, it is clearly dominated by the cognitive, and when this method is applied to the Toledan Qur'an, it results in a scholastic-style, chapter-by-tedious-chapter refutation. It is serious and scholarly work but not markedly original. We hear echoes of Cusanus and Segovia in its interesting conclusion:

> Freely accept this little work, O Saracen, written with love and piety for your conversion and salvation, and consent to the truths of the Christian faith. And oh, would that the prelates and leaders of the Christians and of the Saracens would harmoniously agree that the official teachers of both sides would meet with each other and, in such a way the truth should be made clear by means of mutual discussion and those in error would be converted to the way of salvation![45]

Besides his letters against the Turks to various rulers, Denys' dialogue, incidentally, concludes with the Saracen's admission that he is now ready to embrace the law of the gospel and the Christian faith for he sees that the Qur'an is in complete disagreement with the gospel and the Mosaic law.[46] Neither Cusanus nor Segovia saw the Qur'an in quite so negative a light.

Finally, mention should be made of the work of a well-known Dominican theologian who had been with Cusanus and Segovia at the

[45] *Contra perfidiam Machometi* IV, a. 22. Cod. Cus. 107 fol. 193ᵛ; *Opera omnia, Opera minora*, vol. 4 (Tornaci, 1908), p. 442.

[46] "Video equidem Alcoranum a scripturis evangelicae ac Mosaicae legis penitus discordare": *Dialogus disputationis inter christianum et Sarracenum*, art. xix, *Opera omnia, Opera minora*, 4: 499.

Council of Basel and later was elevated to the cardinalate. John of
Torquemada's *Contra principales errores perfidi Machometi* is a step by step
refutation of the errors of Muhammad which, the cardinal writes, have been
reduced, for the sake of brevity, to forty.[47] These run the traditional gamut
from the important, e.g., denial of the divine Trinity and the Incarnation, to
the less momentous question of whether there were any palm trees where
Jesus was born (as the Qur'an asserts). Torquemada's work is character-
istically unrelieved in the relentlessness of its mission and in the rigor of its
rationalism. The same tenacity which governs his ecclesiological monarchism dominates this thoroughgoing exposé of religious fraud and error. Not
content with refutation of Muslim errors, the work concludes with an
explanation of twelve reasons why Christianity is superior to Islam, along
with a theological explanation of why various regions of the world are under
the domination of the heretical religion of Islam. Cusanus knew this work
of "lively reasons" against Islam, but he preferred a different tack. Aeneas
Sylvius (Pope Pius II) took the militant, anti-Segovian position, and
continued to the end of his life to press for a crusade. He apparently found
Torquemada's hard-line rationalism more to his liking.[48]

Our brief review of theological response to Islam in the fifteenth
century shows that on the whole it was understandably traditional, generally
following the path begun by Peter the Venerable in the twelfth century.
What surprises us is that, in the superheated anti-Muslim fervor created by
the Turkish conquest of Constantinople, the bold initiatives of John of
Segovia and Nicholas of Cusa argued for a new turn in Christian-Muslim
relations. Their initiatives revealed new possibilities for Christian
ecumenical theology, standing out in marked contrast from the contributions
of their intellectual peers and from the militant spirit of their times. Even
though he knew and respected the theological work of Denys Rickel and
John of Torquemada, Nicholas of Cusa retained a positive theological stance
toward Islam, remaining faithful to the legacy of John of Segovia. For all
their innovative appeal, the initiatives of Cusanus and Segovia had deep
theological roots and, therefore, distinct developmental potential. A variety
of factors forestalled such development, not least of which was the Lutheran
reform with its new set of theological priorities and its shocking exposure
of the pope as Antichrist in place of Muhammad.

[47] *Ioannis de Turrecrem. Cardinalis S. Sixti contra Principales errores
perfidi Machometi* (Rome, 1606), p. 47. He then goes on to enumerate only 38!

[48] Cf. *supra*, n. 14.

Portions of this essay were first presented at the Conference on Europe and
Asia 600-1600: Institutions and Ideas, University of Hawaii, January 1983. The
author acknowledges the support of the National Endowment for the Humanities
whose fellowship made this research possible.

TALKING TO SPIRITUAL OTHERS:
RAMON LLULL, NICHOLAS OF CUSA, DIEGO VALADÉS

Pauline Moffitt Watts

Ramon Llull's *Liber de gentili et tribus sapientibus* (1274-76), Nicholas of Cusa's *De pace fidei* (1454), and Diego Valadés' *Rhetorica Christiana* (1579) are all occasioned by important periods or moments of contact between Christian and non-Christian cultures. Each work also reflects a different phase in the internal history of Christian meditations on the self and spiritual others. Brief though this paper must be, I hope that it may stimulate thought regarding the different ways in which these significant incidental components contribute to the larger history of the encounters and interpenetrations of religions during the medieval and Renaissance periods.

Ramon Llull (1232/33-1316) was born on the island of Majorca, an important coordinate in the grid of western Mediterranean commercial networks. Llull lived during a period in which the hegemony of the Almohad empire in the western Mediterranean dissolved and James I of Aragon led a Christian offensive that expelled the Muslim rulers from Iberia, excepting Granada which did not fall until 1492. Concomitant with this peninsular *reconquista* was an insular one, which included the Balearic islands. Though the conqueror, James I, was Aragonese, the language and culture of the conquest was Catalan. This too was the language and culture of Llull, who apparently spent most of the first half of his life on the island of Majorca with its admixture of Muslims, Christians, and Jews from various parts of Italy, southern France, Iberia, and North Africa.[1]

As a young man, Llull was attached to the court of James I and that of his son James II and so participated in the Catalan version of the troubadour culture of Provence which the elder James imported through his conquests. According to *Vita coaetanea*, a contemporary account of Llull's life possibly dictated by him to certain Carthusian monks of Vauvert, his sensuous and unreflective life as a courtier was interrupted by a series of recurring, frightful visions of Christ upon the cross. The fifth of these led to a period of sleepless torment culminating in his discovery of his true self and mission. The following passage from *Vita coaetanea* indicates that the same "Father of

---

[1] A good brief biography of Llull and its larger historical setting is in Anthony Bonner, *Selected Works of Ramon Llull (1232-1316)*, 2 vols. (Princeton, 1985) 1:3-52. For more detail, see J.N. Hillgarth, *Ramon Lull and Lullism in Fourteenth-Century France* (Oxford, 1971), pt. 1: "Historical Background."

Lights" (James 1:17) who revealed Cusanus' mission as a philosopher and
theologian to him on the boat returning from Constantinople revealed to
Llull *his* mission as apostolate to the large numbers of recently conquered
Muslims among whom he lived:

> On the fourth occasion--or, as is more commonly believed, the fifth--
> when the vision appeared to him, he was absolutely terrified and retired
> and spent the entire night trying to understand what these so often
> repeated visions were meant to signify. . . . At last, as a gift of the
> Father of Lights, he thought about the gentleness, patience, and mercy
> which Christ showed and shows towards all sorts of sinners. And thus
> at last he understood with certainty that God wanted him, Ramon, to
> leave the world and dedicate himself totally to the service of Christ. He
> therefore began to turn over in his mind what service would be most
> pleasing to God, and it seemed to him that no one could offer a better or
> greater service to Christ than to give up his life and soul for the sake of
> His love and honor; and to accomplish this by carrying out the task of
> converting to His worship and service the Saracens who in such
> numbers surrounded the Christians on all sides.[2]

[2] The manuscript tradition of *Vita coaetanea* is complex and involves both
Latin and Catalan versions. According to both Bonner (pp. 12-13) and Hillgarth
(p. 46, n. 2; Appendix 10), the Latin version is now supposed to antedate the
Catalan, a reversal of earlier scholarship. The Latin version of *Vita coaetanea*
was likely completed in 1311 and included in the collection of Llull's works
known as the *Electorium* compiled by Thomas le Myésier. The work was translated into Catalan in the fifteenth century, probably on Majorca. A modern
edition of the Latin text has been made by H. Harada, O.F.M., *Raimundi Lulli
Opera Latina*, vol. 8, *Corpus Christianorum Continuatio Medievalis* 34
(Turnholt, 1980). The Catalan version has been edited by Francesco de Borja
Moll, *Vida Coetania del Rev. Mestre Ramon Lull segons el ms. 16432 del
British Museum* (Palma, 1933). In Harada's edition of the Latin text, the section
describing the apparitions of the Crucified to Llull is on pp. 273-274.

The English translation above is from Bonner, *Selected Works* 1:15.
Harada's Latin edition of the passage reads as follows: (273) "In quarta ergo vel
etiam quinta vice, sicut plus creditur, eadem apparitione sibi facta territus
nimium, lectum suum in- (274) travit, secum tota illa nocte cogitando tractans,
quidnam visiones istae totiens iteratae significare deberent. . . . Denique, dante
Patre luminum (Iac. 1,17), consideravit Christi mansuetudinem, patientiam ac
misericordiam, quam habuit et habet circa quoslibet peccatores. Et sic intellexit
tandem certissime Deum velle, quod Raimundus mundum relinqueret Christoque
corde ex tunc integre deseruiret. Coepit ergo intra se cogitando tractare, quod
esset servitium maxime Deo placens. Et visum est, quod melius sive maius
servitium Christo facere nemo posset, quam pro amore et honore suo vitam et
animam suam dare; . . . et hoc in convertendo ad ipsius cultum et servitium (275)
Saracenos, qui sua multitudine christianos undique circumcingunt."

Llull's revelation that he was to devote his life to the conversion of the Saracens was itself the result of a conversion experience, a turn to an heretofore unimagined "other" self. The now ruptured world of the troubadour court life left behind, Llull embarked upon a period of almost five decades of study and travel among spiritual "others."

Llull's two central goals, the foundation of training centers to instruct aspiring missionaries in the languages and culture of the infidel and the formulation of an irrefutable "Art" of persuasion, cannot be separated from the eclectic and infiltrated nature of his own thought as it developed. Put slightly differently, Llull's conversion opened him up to the influence of spiritual others in ways that distinguished him from the mainstreams of contemporary western European schooling and thinking. His idiosyncratic blendings of certain elements of Arabic science and logic, Jewish cabalism, the transmutations of Neoplatonism, his eccentric siftings of medieval philosophical and mystical traditions led to the formulations of what has been most aptly called a "frontier philosophy."[3] This "frontier philosophy" was at once adapted from, and addressed to, the borderlands, the margins of contact among the contiguous cultures of Christianity, Judaism, and Islam within which Llull lived and thought.[4]

---

[3] The formulation is in T. and J. Carreras y Artau, *Historia de la Filosofía española, Filosofía cristiana de los siglos XIII al XV*, 2 vols. (Madrid, 1939-1943) 1:635 (Cf. Hillgarth, *Ramon Lull and Lullism,* p. 13, n. 61). There are many studies of the syncretic aspects of Llull's thought, including F.A. Yates, "The Art of Ramon Lull: An Approach to it through Lull's Theory of the Elements," *Journal of the Warburg and Courtauld Institutes* 17 (1954): 115-173, and her "Ramon Lull and John Scotus Erigena," *ibid.,* 23 (1960): 1-44; R.D.F. Pring-Mill, "Grundzüge von Lulls *Ars inveniendi veritatem,*" *Archiv für Geschichte der Philosophie* 43 (1961): 23-266; E.W. Platzeck, *Raimund Lull, sein Leben, seine Werke, die Grundlage seines Denkens (Prinzipienlehre),* 2 vols. (Rome and Düsseldorf, 1962-1964). For additional references, see the bibliographies of Bonner and Hillgarth.

[4] Useful studies of the larger historical contexts include Jeremy Cohen, *The Friars and The Jews: The Evolution of Medieval Anti-Judaism* (Ithaca, New York, 1982); Benjamin Kedar, *Crusade and Mission: European Approaches toward the Muslims* (Princeton, 1984); Robert Schwoebel, "Coexistence, Conversion, and the Crusade against the Turks," *Studies in the Renaissance* 12, (1965): 164-187, and his *The Shadow of the Crescent: The Renaissance Image of the Turk* (New York, 1969). See also the AHR Forum, published in *The American Historical Review* 91 (1986): 576-624, including David Berger, "Mission to the Jews and Jewish-Christian Contacts in the Polemical Literature of the High Middle Ages" and Jeremy Cohen, "Scholarship and Intolerance in the Medieval Academy: The Study and Evaluation of Judaism in European Christendom".

It has also been called a "philosophy of combat."[5]   And indeed, we must not let our instinct to admire Llull's acquired fluency in a variety of languages and the syncretism of his thinking to mask the violent core of what he was doing. For Llull's entries into the Muslim language and thought in particular are not made in the spirit of toleration and mutual exchange but rather in that of crusading conquest. There is no more powerful an illustration of this than a story Llull tells in *Vita coaetanea*. After the conversion experience described above, Llull purchased a Muslim slave in order to learn Arabic. Some nine years later, during which time Llull had "mastered" the language of his slave, the Muslim "blasphemed" the name of Christ in Llull's absence. Here is Llull's version of what subsequently happened:

> Upon returning and finding out about it from those who had heard the blasphemy, Ramon, impelled by a great zeal for the Faith, hit the Saracen on the mouth, on the forehead, and on the face. As a result the Saracen became extremely embittered, and he began plotting the death of his master. He secretly got hold of a sword, and one day, when he saw his master sitting alone, he suddenly rushed at him, striking him with the sword and shouting with a terrible roar: "You're dead!" But even though Ramon was able, as it pleased God, to deflect his attacker's sword arm a bit, the blow nonetheless wounded him seriously, although not fatally, in the stomach. By means of his strength, however, he managed to overcome the Saracen, knock him down, and forcibly take the sword away from him. When the servants came running to the scene, Ramon kept them from killing him, but allowed them to tie him up and put him in jail until he, Ramon, decided what would be the best thing to do. For it seemed harsh to kill the person by whose teaching he now knew the language he had so wanted to learn, that is, Arabic; on the other hand, he was afraid to set him free or to keep him longer, knowing that from then on he would not cease plotting his death. Perplexed as to what to do, he went up to a certain abbey near there where for three days he prayed fervently to God about this matter. When the three days were over, astonished that the same perplexity still remained in his heart and that God, or so it seemed to him, had in no way listened to his prayers, he returned home full of sorrow. When on the way back he made a slight detour to the prison to visit his captive, he found that he had hanged himself with the rope with which he had been bound. Ramon therefore joyfully gave thanks to God not only for keeping his hands innocent of the death of this Saracen, but for freeing him from that terrible perplexity concerning which he had just recently so anxiously asked him for guidance.[6]

[5] This time the formulation is that of Hillgarth, *Ramon Lull and Lullism*, p. 13.

[6] Bonner, *Selected Works* 1:21.

It would be obdurate *not* to read much into this passage. Llull's status as the Christian pupil-conqueror and his slave's status as the Muslim conquered-teacher make it impossible for them ever to communicate as intellectual and spiritual equals, it would seem. In spite of these barriers, it appears that a human intimacy of some sort did evolve during the years the two spent studying together. Yet the Muslim slave remains deeply untouched by his master and his master's God. Indeed, he tries to destroy them both. Llull in turn welcomes his slave's death by his own hand. His God's solution releases him from his own perplexed encounter with this spiritual other. It is the same surrender to divine will that also moved the Crusaders to the bloody physical combat that marked their campaigns against the infidel in the Holy Land, giving them their famous battle cry, *Deus vult*.

It is not a coincidence that the death of the Muslim slave seems to have precipitated the illumination on the mountain in which God revealed to Llull the method of his Art. Stimulated by this illumination, Llull produced a group of seminal interrelated writings during the next fifteen years, that is, between 1274 and 1289. *Liber de gentili et tribus sapientibus* is one of this group of writings and may be associated with the contemporary polemical and apologetic works of Spanish Dominicans such as Ramon de Peñafort and Ramon Marti, and with Thomas Aquinas' *Summa contra gentiles*, though precise connections remain to be worked out. It seems likely that *Liber de gentili et tribus sapientibus* was written for the instruction of missionaries at the school Llull had founded at Miramar, that it was composed between 1274 and 1276, soon after the illumination experience, and that it takes its structure from Llull's initial formulations of the Art in works such as the *Ars demonstrativa* and *Ars compendiosa inveniendi veritatem*.[7]

Liber de gentili et tribus sapientibus is based on Llull's famous Art, the technique that he developed to convert the infidel. This Art underwent various discernible phases and permutations in the course of its creator's long life, but it does not appear that the basic metaphysic of faith that underlaid it changed. The principle of the Art--the self-diffusiveness of God --is derived from Neoplatonic metaphysics. According to Llull, God diffused Himself in sixteen attributes or Dignities. These Dignities are consubstantial with God, but they are also exemplars or universals in likeness of which the great chain of the plurality of created being that is the universe unfolds. The structure of the mind mirrors that of the created universe. Knowledge is the conscious conjoining of the realities of mind and being, worked out through the natural pairings of opposites and other combinations of vices, virtues, causes, and effects. The kaleidoscopic dynamics of the Art

---

[7] Bonner, *Selected Works* 1:17-33, 57-58; Hillgarth, *Ramon Lull and Lullism*, pp. 9-22.

and its theophanic roots thus provided Llull with a singular *via* in which a variety of spiritual "others" could be seriously entertained but also ultimately transmutated into the armaments of conversion.[8]

In *Liber de gentili et tribus sapientibus* a distraught Gentile is subjected to a popularized version of the Art, through conversation with a Christian, a Jew, and a Muslim. The ending of the piece has a strange twist which is worthy of comment in regard to Llull's talks with spiritual "others." After the Christian, the Jew, and the Muslim have taken their turns teaching the Gentile about their respective faiths, the Gentile prays to God and gives thanks. He then tells the three that he wishes to inform them which of the three faiths he has chosen. Before he can do this, two of his fellow Gentiles approach and he asks leave to tell them of the conversations and his choice before he addresses the three savants. Here comes the puzzling part.

The three wise men, somehow disinterested in the final outcome of their conversations with this "other," choose to leave the astonished Gentile without hearing of his choice. By way of explanation Llull says on behalf of the Christian, Jew, and Muslim, that "In order for each to be free to choose his own religion, they preferred not knowing which religion he would choose." This sentiment is repeated in the farewell the three proffer to the Gentile:

> . . . this is a question we could discuss among ourselves to see, by force of reason and by means of our intellects, which religion it must be that you will choose. And if, in front of us, you state which religion it is that you prefer, then we would not have such a good subject of discussion nor such satisfaction in discovering the truth.[9]

The three then depart, making arrangements to continue their discussions among themselves. Perhaps they are still talking somewhere in their garden.

At any rate, it has been supposed that this surprising ending is evidence of Llull's tolerance, his conviction that the great religions of the world could and should coexist. But if this were the case, it would in a certain sense subvert Llull's lifetime of labor on the Art and the metaphysic upon which it rested. Instead, it might well be argued that the ending is left unsaid because it is already known. There is finally only a single source of all ontological and epistemological reality: the Christian God. All thinking and being is but a diffusion or privation of that God. This *principium* is what ultimately makes Llull's Art a vehicle, not for tolerance and *convivencia,* but for conquest and conversion of spiritual "others."

[8] On the Dignities and the Art, see Bonner, *Selected Works* 1:59-70; Hillgarth, *Ramon Lull and Lullism,* pp. 9-12; and the various studies cited in note 4 above.

[9] Bonner, *Selected Works* 1:300-301.

Like Llull's *Liber de gentili et tribus sapientibus*, Cusanus' *De pace fidei* was prompted by an encounter of Christian and non-Christian other of considerable historical significance. But in the wake of the conquest of Constantinople in 1453 by the Ottoman Turks, it was the Christian world which appeared on the brink of destruction, potentially the conquered rather than the conqueror. This larger historical context informs the Cusanian dialectics of *unitas* and *alteritas* in such a way in *De pace fidei* that the result might be described as a "fortress" rather than a "frontier" philosophy.

The dialectics which buttress the fortress philosophy of *De pace fidei* derive from a number of Cusanus' earlier writings, particularly the cornerstone of his thought, the *De docta ignorantia* of 1440. In the first of the three books that comprise the work, Cusanus' speculations lead him to the conclusion that "there is no proportion between the finite and the infinite."[10]

The goal then becomes not the precision of truth as such but rather the condition of informed awareness of the parameters of one's knowledge--*docta ignorantia*:

> . . . since the desire [to know] within us is not in vain, we desire to know that we are ignorant. If we shall be able to fully attain this, then we shall attain learned ignorance. For nothing more perfect will happen to even the man most devoted to learning than to be found most learned in that ignorance itself which is peculiar to him; and he will become more learned to the extent that he knows his own ignorance.[11]

A concomitant of such "learned ignorance" is the recognition of the essential "otherness" *(alteritas)* of mind and creation in relation to God, whom Cusanus eventually will call the "not-other" *(non aliud)* in a work by that name written in 1461-62. The dichotomy between creator "not-other" and created "other" leads Cusanus to surmise in the *Apologia doctae ignorantiae* (1449) that even the two ancient Pseudo-Dionysian "sciences of God"--the *via affirmativa* and the *via negativa*--may very well finally only dissimulate rather than modify divinity:

> Truly all the likenesses that the holy men, even the most divine Dionysius, hypothesize, are wholly disproportionate and useless rather than useful to all those lacking learned ignorance--that is, the

[10] *De docta ignorantia* I, 3, #9 (h I, 8): "Quoniam ex se manifestum est infiniti ad finitum proportionem non esse."

[11] *De docta ignorantia* I, 1, #4 (h I, 6): ". . . profecto, cum appetitus in nobis frustra non sit, desideramus scire nos ignorare. Hoc si ad plenum assequi poterimus, doctam ignorantiam assequemur. Nihil enim homini etiam studiosissimo in doctrina perfectius adveniet quam in ipsa ignorantia, quae sibi propria est, doctissimum reperiri; et tanto quis doctior erit, quanto se sciverit magis ignorantem."

knowledge of this; that they [the likenesses] are wholly dis-
proportionate.[12]

The implications of such dichotomies and dissimulations for the rituals and
dogmas of any particular religion are profound. Near the end of the first
book of *De docta ignorantia*, Cusanus draws an important distinction
between what he calls the *cultura* of a religion--its public and private rituals
--and the inward experiences of its *fides*, or faith.

The *cultura* of a religion, its dogmas and rituals, is based upon the *via
affirmativa*, beliefs and actions pertaining to what God *is*. But on a higher
level, the *fides*, or faith, of a religion is based upon the *via negativa*,
meditations on what God is *not*, rather than what he is:

> . . . worship should always be guided by faith which is most truly
> attained through learned ignorance. By faith it follows that he who is
> worshipped as one is all things at once; he who is worshipped as
> inaccessible light is indeed not this corporeal light that is the opposite
> of darkness but the most simple and infinite light in which darknesses
> are infinite light; and that infinite light itself always shines in the
> darkness of our ignorance but the darknesses are not able to
> comprehend it. And thus negative theology is so necessary to af-
> firmative theology that, without it, God would not be worshipped as
> the infinite God but rather as a creature; and such worship *(cultura)* is
> idolatry, which attributes to the image that which only belongs

[12] *Apologia doctae ignorantiae* (h II, 24): "Sunt enim omnes similitudines,
quas sancti ponunt, etiam divinissimus Dionysius, penitus improportionales et
omnibus non habentibus doctam ignorantiam--huius scilicet scientiam, quod
sunt penitus improportionales,--potius inutiles quam utiles." See also Cusanus'
1453 letter to the monks of Tegernsee for a parallel passage. The text is printed
in Edmond Vansteenberghe, *Autour de la Docte Ignorance: Une Controverse sur
la Théologie Mystique au XVᵉ Siècle. Beiträge zur Geschichte der Philosophie
des Mittelalters* 14, pts. 2-4 (Münster, 1915), p. 114: ". . . tamen non est mea
opinio illos recte caliginem subintrare, qui solum circa negativam theologiam
versantur. Nam, cum negativa auferat et nichil ponat, tunc per illam revelate non
videbitur Deus, non enim reperietur Deus esse, sed pocius non esse; et si
affirmative queritur, non reperietur nisi per imitacionem et velate, et nequaquam
revelate.

Tradidit autem Dionysius in plerisque locis theologiam per disiunctionem,
scilicet quod aut ad deum accedimus affirmative aut negative; sed in hoc libello
ubi theologiam misticam et secretam vult manifestare, saltat supra disiunctionem
usque in copulacionem et coincidenciam, seu unionem simplicissimam . . ." I am
grateful to Professor F. Edward Cranz for pointing this passage out to me. For
some discussion of the ways in which Cusanus talks to and about the "other",
that is God, see my *Nicolaus Cusanus: A Fifteenth-Century Vision of Man*
(Leiden, 1982), pp. 36-61.

to the truth.[13]

In some inescapable sense then, the Christian, the Jew, the Muslim--each is *homo alienus*. God being "other" to all religions, all would-be believers are left treading a thin line between the tangible, seductive idolatries of affirmation and the ungraspable, dark *wüst* of negation. Given this, *De pace fidei* might represent a fortress against the other within Christianity as well as one against non-Christian others. The indications that Cusanus' views on non-Christian others, in contrast to Llull's, were formed mainly through readings, and exchanges with other Christian theologians, such as Juan de Segovia, seems to support this interpretation of the work. So too would his explanation that the fall of Constantinople was in part due to the Greek orthodox departure from the hegemony of the Roman church.[14]

Cusanus' search for defenses against the incursions of spiritual others from within and without the Christian faith thus makes *De pace fidei* a curiously insulated work. As James Biechler has acutely observed in his important study, *The Religious Language of Nicholas of Cusa,*

> One looks in vain for any evidence of true variety or diversity in *De pace fidei*. Its language has the curious inability to describe or discuss plurality. Rather, as soon as the subject arises, the words mysteriously

[13]   *De docta ignorantia* I, 26, #86 (h I, 54): ". . . semper culturam per fidem, quam per doctam ignorantiam verius attingit, dirigendo; credendo scilicet hunc, quem adorat ut unum esse uniter omnia, et quem ut inaccessibilem lucem colit, non quidem esse lucem, ut est haec corporalis, cui tenebra opponitur, sed simplicissimam et infinitam, in qua tenebrae sunt lux infinita; et quod ipsa infinita lux semper lucet in tenebris nostrae ignorantiae, sed tenebrae eam comprehendere nequeunt. Et ita theologia negationis adeo necessaria est quoad aliam affirmationis, ut sine illa Deus non coleretur ut Deus infinitus, sed potius ut creatura; et talis cultura idolatria est, quae hoc imagini tribuit, quod tantum convenit veritati."

[14]   The letter to Juan de Segovia wherein Cusanus formulates some of his ideas regarding the non-Christian is published in *De pace fidei cum epistula ad Ioannem de Segobia* (h VII). Worth consulting for its discussion of John of Segovia's and Cusanus' approaches to the Muslim "other" is Rudolf Haubst, "Johannes von Segovia im Gespräch mit Nikolaus von Kues und Jean Germain uber die göttliche Dreieinigkeit und ihre Verkündigung vor den Mohammedanern," *Münchener Theologische Zeitschrift* 2 (1951): 115-129. On Cusanus' analysis of the reasons for the fall of Constantinople, presented in a sermon to the Regensburg Reichstag in 1454, see James Biechler, *The Religious Language of Nicholas of Cusa* (Missoula, Montana, 1975), pp. 41-42 and notes. On the larger contemporary context of Cusanus' ideas, see Schwoebel, "Coexistence, Conversion, and the Crusade against the Turks" (n. 5 above).

direct themselves to unity and thus completely elude the political
realm, the forum of discussion and compromise, and take flight to the
realm of the metaphysical symbol so comprehensive in the embrace of
its ideal that all individuation is absorbed and neutralized.[15]

So while *De pace fidei* might on the surface appear to be a richly-hued
kaleidoscope of religions and peoples--its participants include a Greek, an
Italian, a Muslim, an Indian, a Chaldean, a Jew, a Scythian, a Frenchman, a
Persian, a Syrian, a Spaniard, a Turk, a German, a Tatar, an Armenian, a
Bohemian, and an Englishman--the differences among them are finally all
ephemeral. Subject to the Cusanian dialectics of *unitas* and *alteritas,
complicatio* and *explicatio,* the historical and cultural variables that
distinguish these peoples and their religions from one another, are only so
many refractions of the gaze of the divine *oculus,* manifestations of the
necessarily prismatic condition of human existence.[16]

It is therefore not coincidental that *De pace fidei* is, as Cusanus makes
clear at the onset of the work, the product of a *vision*:

> After the brutal deeds recently committed by the Turkish ruler at
> Constantinople were reported to a certain man, who had once seen the
> places of those regions, he was inflamed by a zeal for God and with
> many signs implored the Creator of all things that in his mercy he
> restrain the persecution which was raging more than ever because of
> different religious rites. It happened after several days--perhaps
> because of a long, drawn out meditation--a vision was revealed to this
> zealous man, and from it he inferred that of a few wise men familiar
> from their own experience with all such differences which are observed
> in religions throughout the world, a single easy harmony could be

[15] Biechler, *The Religious Language of Nicholas of Cusa,* p. 84.

[16] The Word makes this point very succinctly in dialogue with the Arab, *De
pace fidei* VI, #16 (h VII, 15): "Una est igitur religio et cultus omnium intellectu
vigentium, quae in omni diversitate rituum praesupponitur;" and VI, #17 (h VII,
16): "Omnes qui umquam plures Deos coluerunt, divinitatem esse praesup-
posuerunt. Illam enim in omnibus diis tamquam in participantibus eandem
adorant. Sicut enim albedine non existente non sunt alba, ita divinitate non
existente non sunt dii. Cultus igitur deorum confitetur divinitatem. Et qui dicit
plures deos, dicit unum antecedenter omnium principium; sicut qui asserit plures
sanctos, unum sanctum sanctorum, cuius participatione omnes alii sancti sunt,
admittit. Numquam gens aliqua adeo stolida fuit quae plures crederet deos, quorum
quisque foret prima causa, principium aut creator universi." On the theme of *una
religio in rituum varietate* in Cusanus' thinking see Biechler, *The Religious
Language of Nicholas of Cusa,* chap. 2: "Blueprint for Harmony"; Michael
Seidlmayer, *"Una religio in rituum varietate:* Zur Religionsauffassung des
Nikolaus von Cues," *Archiv für Kulturgeschichte,* 36 (1954): 145-207; and the
essays by Biechler and Thomas P. McTighe above.

found and through it a lasting peace could be established by an appropriate and true means. And so in order for this vision eventually to come to the notice of those who have the decisive word in these great matters, he has written down his vision plainly below, as far as his memory recalled it.[17]

In words that echo those of Paul's description of his enraptured conversion on the road to Damascus, Cusanus recalls how he was transported to an other-worldly, transcendental council. *De pace fidei* records its deliberations:

For he was caught up to a certain intellectual height, where, as if among those who had departed from life, an examination of this matter was thus held in a council of the highest with the Almighty presiding. The King of heaven and earth stated that the sad news of the groans of the oppressed had been brought to him from this world's realm: because of religion many take up arms against each other, and by their power men either force others to renounce their long practiced tradition or inflict death.[18]

The stately arguments which follow, orchestrated by the Word, Peter, and Paul, like those of Llull's three wise men, are somehow always other to the bitter conflicts endemic to humankind, to the agony of the choice that the Gentile must make and which his learned teachers decide not to hear. Both the frontier philosophy of Llull and the fortress philosophy of Cusanus

---

[17] *De pace fidei* I, #1 (h VII, 3): "Fuit ex hiis, quae apud Constantinopolim proxime saevissime acta per Turkorum regem divulgabantur, quidam vir zelo Dei accensus, qui loca illarum regionum aliquando viderat, ut pluribus gemitibus oraret omnium creatorem quod persecutionem, quae ob diversum ritum religionum plus solito saevit, sua pietate moderaretur. Accidit ut post dies aliquot, forte ex diuturna continuata meditatione, visio quaedam eidem zeloso manifestaretur, ex qua elicuit quod paucorum sapientum omnium talium diversitatum quae in religionibus per orbem observantur peritia pollentium unam posse facilem quandam concordantiam reperiri, ac per eam in religione perpetuam pacem convenienti ac veraci medio constitui. Unde, et haec visio ad notitiam eorum qui hiis maximis praesunt aliquando deveniret, eam quantum memoria praesentabat, plane subter conscripsit." The English translation is from *De pace fidei*, trans. H. Lawrence Bond. Concordance by James E. Biechler. Prepared for the American Cusanus Society (Philadelphia, 1986).

[18] *De pace fidei* I, #2 (h VII, 4): "Raptus est enim ad quandam intellectualem altitudinem, ubi quasi inter eos qui vita excesserunt examen huiusce rei in concilio excelsorum, praesidente Cunctipotenti, ita habitum est. Aiebat enim Rex caeli et terrae ad eum de regno huius mundi tristes nuntios gemitus oppressorum attulisse, ob religionem plerosque in invicem arma movere et sua potentia homines aut ad renegationem diu observatae sectae cogere aut mortem inferre." The English translation is by H. Lawrence Bond.

intend to promulgate the metaphysical necessity of conversion. Though both in their ways acknowledge the ambiguities, the tensions inherent in the continuing presence of non-Christian spiritual others, neither accepts the possibility that co-existence might be a human, if not a metaphysical, necessity as well.

In January of 1492, the year of Christopher Columbus' initial voyage of discovery, his monarchs, Ferdinand and Isabella of Castile and Aragon, succeeded in capturing the kingdom of Granada, the only territory on the Iberian penninsula remaining under the political control of the Muslims. In that same year, Ferdinand and Isabella issued an edict requiring the Jews of Castile and Aragon to accept baptism within four months or else to face permanent exile. These two incidents in a certain sense mark the end of an often fragile but nonetheless enduring tradition of *convivencia*, the coexistence of Christian, Jew, and Muslim in Iberia and the islands of the western Mediterranean, that had persisted since Llull's lifetime.

These events are also symptomatic of the revival of the chivalric and religious ideals of *reconquista*. And, just as the flourishing of the ideal of *reconquista* in the early thirteenth century had been accomplished by waves of religious reform, apocalyptic expectations, and the activation of inquisitorial processes, so was its late fifteenth- and early sixteenth-century counterpart.[19]

Columbus died believing that he had played a divinely ordained role in aiding Ferdinand and Isabella to fulfill their prophetic destiny of converting all the peoples of the world to Christianity and recovering Jerusalem from the infidel. He, like Llull, is said to have been buried in the robes of a Franciscan tertiary. The regular members of that order, particularly the Observants, were to play a central role in the "spiritual conquest" of the indigenous peoples of Mexico in the course of the sixteenth century. From the beginning the motivations and actions of these monks were interwoven with those of the knights of the revived *reconquista*: the conquistadors.[20]

[19] For more detailed discussions of the historical implications of these interrelated events and ideals see Marjorie Reeves, *The Influence of Prophecy in the Later Middle Ages: A Study in Joachism* (Oxford, 1969); John Leddy Phelan, *The Millennial Kingdom of the Franciscans in the New World* (Berkeley and Los Angeles, 1970); Carl Erdmann, *The Origin of the Idea of Crusade* (Princeton, 1977); Pauline Moffitt Watts, "Prophecy and Discovery: On the Spiritual Origins of Christopher Columbus' 'Enterprise of the Indies'," *The American Historical Review* 90 (1985): 73-102.

[20] On such interrelationships between Franciscans and conquistadors, see Phelan, *The Millennial Kingdom;* F. de Lejarza, O.F.M., "Franciscanismo de Cortés y cortesianismo de los Franciscanos," *Misionalia Hispanica,* 13 (1948): 43-136; J.H. Elliott, "The Mental World of Hernán Cortés," *Royal Historical Society Transactions* 17 (1967): 41-58.

The Observant Franciscan missionaries and the conquistadors were both crusaders of sorts. The conquistadors fought for material, physical control of the New World and its inhabitants and the missionaries for the hearts and minds of these spiritual "others." The first important phases of conquistador and missionary activity--Cortés' conquest of Aztec Mexico and the arrival of the famous first "Twelve" Franciscan monks--occurred within a relatively brief span of time. Cortés' expedition began in 1519, culminating in his final victory over Montezuma in 1524. The Twelve arrived in Mexico City that same year at his request and under his auspices.[21]

The spiritual "others" encountered by these missionaries were much more disturbing than those faced by a Llull or Cusanus. Their others were, in the main, members of the historically contiguous cultures of Islam and Judaism, coinhabitants of the Old World with Christians for centuries. By contrast the novelty and eccentricity of indigenous religious customs seemed to engender a kind of "culture shock" amongst some of the first missionary observers. In the earliest of their accounts, the *Historia de los Indios de la Nueva España*, Toribio de Benavente or Motolinía, one of the Twelve, described what he saw as a "transplanted hell" and went on to suggest that the Indians were subjects in an infernal kingdom ruled by the devil himself.[22]

But although the Indians appeared to be diabolical they were not on that account bestial. They possessed souls and minds and therefore could be educated and converted. To this end, the Franciscans established a sequence of schools in the early decades of their missionary work in Mexico. Among the most well-known of these schools was that of San Francisco de México, established by the famous lay brother, Pedro de Gante, to teach the sons of the indigenous elite. From these students a select group went on to study at the Colegio de Santa Cruz, founded in 1536 and designed originally to

[21] The classic account of the inception and process of the evangelization of Mexico remains Robert Ricard, *The Spiritual Conquest of Mexico: An Essay on the Apostolate and the Evangelizing Methods of the Mendicant Orders in New Spain: 1523-1572* (Berkeley and Los Angeles, 1966).

[22] Francis Borgia Steck, O.F.M., *Motolinía's History of the Indians of New Spain* (Washington, D.C., 1951), p. 96. For the original text, see Edmundo O'Gorman, *Fray Toribio Motolinía. Historia de los Indios de la Nueva España* (Mexico City, 1984), trat. 1, cap. 1, 19-20. The evangelical work done by the Franciscans among the Muslims of Granada did apparently provide some precedents for the missionaries to Mexico. On such precedents, see Antonio Garrido Aranda, *Moriscos y Indios: Precedentes Hispanicos de la Evangelization en México* (Mexico City, 1980).

prepare its graduates for the Christian priesthood.[23]

References to the Colegio and its curriculum by contemporary chronicles are for the most part sparse. The core of its faculty apparently consisted of the intellectual elite of the Franciscans then present in Mexico. It included such figures as Andrés de Olmos, composer of the first grammar of Nahuatl, the famous ethnographer Bernardino de Sahagún, and the important catechist, Juan Focher. Among its students was a *mestizo* by the name of Diego Valadés, author of a curious work entitled *Rhetorica Christiana*, which provides important information regarding the foundations and techniques of the educational program of these early Franciscan missionaries.[24]

For Valadés, in contrast to Llull and Cusanus, it is the persuading power of rhetoric rather than metaphysical necessity which provides the basis for communication with the spiritual "other." But he shares the unconscious irony of their enterprise in that he too makes fundamental use of ancient pagan sources--Cicero and Quintilian--in formulating his position. Cicero's *De inventione*, which contains a famous passage linking the beginnings of civilized life with the invention of the rhetorical arts, provided Valadés with a model for explicating the missionary endeavor amongst the Indians of Mexico. It is the *Christian* orator, equipped with the power to teach, to move, to conciliate, who will civilize these peoples; "I say that the admirable effects of this thing [rhetoric] appear more clearly than at any other time in the taming of the men of this new world of the Indies."[25]

Ancient rhetorical treatises provided Valadés and his fellow Franciscans not only with the forms and techniques for conversion, but also with the criteria needed to establish the humanity of the peoples they encountered. Here Valadés followed sections of Quintilian's *Institutio oratoria* which discussed the differences between natural and artificial rhetoric. According to

[23] On the Colegio de Santa Cruz see, in addition to the work of Ricard, Francisco Borgia Steck, *El primer colegio de America: Santa Cruz de Tlaltelolco. Con un estudio del Codice de Tlaltelolco por R.H. Barlow* (Mexico City, 1944); Miguel Mathes, *Santa Cruz de Tlaltelolco: La primera biblioteca académica de los Americas* (Mexico City, 1982); Georges Baudot, *Utopía e historia en México: Los primeros cronistas de la civilización Mexicana (1520-1569)* (Madrid, 1983), chaps. 2-3: "El Colegio de Santa Cruz de Tlatelolco."

[24] Two important modern studies of Valadés and his work are Esteban J. Palomera, S.J., *Fray Diego Valadés O.F.M. Evangelizador Humanista de la Nueva España. Su Obra* (Mexico City, 1962), and his *Fray Diego Valadés O.F.M. Evangelizador Humanista de la Nueva España. El hombre y su epoca* (Mexico City, 1963).

[25] Didacus Valadés, *Rhetorica Christiana ad concionandi et orandi usum* (Perugia, 1579), preface to the reader (unpaginated): "Huius, inquam, rei admirandi effectus, multo clarius quam unquam in Novi Indiarum orbis hominum mansuefactione apparent." Cf. Cicero, *De inventione*, 1.2.

Quintilian, illiterate peoples developed and were adept in modes of communication which did not involve writing. These modes were those of "natural" as distinct from "artificial" rhetoric. Valadés observed that certain forms of natural rhetoric were operative amongst the Indians of Mexico:

> . . . argument of this kind [based on natural rhetoric] is most efficacious in the commerce and negotiations of the Indians, who (though they do not possess nor have they possessed letters, nor the writing which is formed with them), nevertheless perform their commerce and negotiations with such skill and art, they easily lead others to admire and give assent to those things which they themselves desire.[26]

The presence of these forms of natural rhetoric certified that the Indians possessed an efficacious oral, if not written, culture.

But Valadés also knew that the Indians used systems of images and pictures for various purposes; in so doing they were engaging in a kind of "artificial" rhetoric as well:

> Moreover, an admirable example of this exists in the commercial activities and contracts of the Indians. As they are unlettered, as we have mentioned above, they make their will known to each other through certain forms and images which they are accustomed to place on panels of silk and paper sheets made from the leaves of trees. This custom in the reckoning of their accounts continues to this present day, not only among those ignorant of how to read and write but also among those capable of reading and writing correctly.[27]

In such ways, Valadés made use of the frameworks of the ancient pagan rhetorical arts to identify the oral and pictographic forms of communication used by the Indians.

---

[26] Valadés, *Rhetorica Christiana* pt. II, cap. III, 51: "Huiusmodi argumentum est efficacissimum in commerciis, et negotiationibus Indorum quae illi (quamvis sint, perpetuoque fuerint literarum, scriptuaraeque ex ipsis constatae exortes) tanta dexteritate atque arte peragunt, ut in admirationem et assensum eorum quae volent facile alios adducant." Cf. Quintilian, *Institutio oratoria* (New York, 1921), 2.17-19.

[27] Valadés, *Rhetorica Christiana*, pt. II, cap. XXVII, 93: "Huius etiam rei admirabile extat in commerciis Indorum, et contractibus exemplum qui etiam si sine literis (cuius supra mentionem habuimus) formis tamen quibusdam, et imaginibus voluntatem suam vicissim denotabant; quas gestare solent in paniculis bombycinis, papyro bibula ex foliis arborum. Ea consuetudo in hodiernum usque diem in rationum suarum tabulis remansit, non modo ab ignorantibus verum etiam recte legendi scribendique . . ."

Finally, that part of rhetorical technique known as the *ars memorativa*, provided Valadés' brethren with a means of effecting the transition from a hieroglyphic to a written system, as I have elsewhere discussed in detail.[28] Here it is sufficient to note that the Franciscans' understandings of the significations and functions of the indigenous hieroglyphics is based upon a cluster of late antique and Renaissance texts on the subject of *Egyptian* hieroglyphics. Their assumption that hieroglyphics manifest a shared symbolic language result in a "logical" absurdity: the application of Horapollo's *Hieroglyphica* to the decodification of Aztec systems. In sum, the channels of communication devised by these missionaries, themselves suffused with the alien discourses of pagan antiquity revived by the culture of Renaissance humanism, remain at the same time "other" to the true inner workings of the indigenous culture they seek to confront.

These brief considerations of three texts reflective of the ongoing history of Christian encounters with spiritual others suggest that such encounters in some way also reflect contemporaneous conflicts and tensions within the collective Christian self. Paradoxically, the projected image of the other to be conquered and/or converted mirrors the internal struggles of that apparently integral, ascendant self. The mission of the spiritual conqueror is not so much to transmit his religion and culture to that oddly inverted other as it is somehow to assimilate its chaotic presence into his own cosmic framework.

[28] Pauline Moffitt Watts, "Hieroglyphs of Conversion: Alien Discourses in Diego Valadés' *Rhetorica Christiana*," forthcoming, *Memoriae Domenicane*, Nuova Serie, 21 (1990).

EPILOGUE

THE "HERCULES OF THE EUGENIANS" AT THE CROSSROADS: NICHOLAS OF CUSA'S DECISION FOR THE POPE AND AGAINST THE COUNCIL IN 1436/1437-- THEOLOGICAL, POLITICAL, AND SOCIAL ASPECTS

Joachim W. Stieber

Nicholas of Cusa has won more acclaim in the twentieth century than he enjoyed in his own lifetime. Indeed, no other fifteenth-century thinker-- indeed no other medieval cardinal--is honored today, as is Cusanus, by societies specifically devoted to the study of his life and works, not only in his native Germany but also in the United States and Japan. Modern scholarship has focused particularly on the religious and philosophical writings of Cusanus in which he often took a new and less partisan approach to traditional disputed questions and in which he sought to reconcile dialectically opposed points of view. The modern interest in the religious and philosophical writings of Cusanus has resulted in a tendency to seek also primarily theological and philosophical motives for his decision in 1436/1437 to side with Pope Eugenius IV and against the Council of Basel. This essay is intended to redress the balance and will argue that the fundamental career decision of Cusanus in 1436/1437 can be attributed far more plausibly to motives related to his social status, his quest for benefices, and his professional training as a canon lawyer.[1] In this connection, attention will also be drawn to the fundamental continuity of outlook and conduct that links Cusanus' support of absolute papal monarchy during the conflict with the Council of Basel in the 1440's with his troubled career as Bishop of Brixen in the 1450's. In a balanced historical portrait of Cusanus, his active life as a partisan advocate of the Roman Curia and as a calculating canon lawyer who encountered the widespread hostility of his contemporaries, will have to be set against his contemplative life as an author of religious and philosophical writings that still evoke sympathy and interest in the twentieth century.

On either side of the critical year 1437, there stand two groups of Cusanus' major political-theological writings that reveal a change of perspective which may have been partly prompted by ideological, but even more, by political motives. On the one hand, there is *De concordantia*

---

[1] In exploring the motives that may have prompted Nicholas of Cusa in 1437 to throw his lot with Pope Eugenius IV rather than with the Council of Basel, this essay accepts an invitation to debate issued by Morimichi Watanabe many years ago, when he wrote, "all conjectures and guesses . . . concerning the motives behind his [Cusanus'] change of front remain open to question": *The Political Ideas of Nicholas of Cusa with special reference to his* De concordantia catholica (Geneva, 1963), p. 98.

catholica, written in 1432-ca. March 1434, followed by *De auctoritate presidendi in concilio generali* of March 1434, and on the other, the letters, treatises, and public statements written at the time of the Congress of Mainz (February/March 1441) and the Diet of Frankfurt (June/July 1442), especially the *Dialogus concludens Amedistarum errorem* (March 1441) and the letter-treatise to Rodrigo Sánchez de Arévalo (May 1442).[2] Many of Cusanus' major writings of a political-theological nature thus fall into two remarkable periods of about two years each, from late 1432 until March 1434 and from February 1441 until June/July 1442. Even if one heeds the warning of Erich Meuthen to place these writings in their context and not to

---

[2] *De concordantia catholica* (h XIV). For a carefully balanced study of *De concordantia catholica*, including an evaluation of older scholarship and a meticulous analysis of the *auctoritates* (church councils, church fathers, *Decretum Gratiani*, papal decretals, and canonists) cited by Cusanus, see Hermann Josef Sieben, "Der Konzilstraktat des Nikolaus von Kues: *De concordantia catholica*", *Annuarium historiae conciliorum* 14 (1982): 171-226; reprinted with minor changes in Herman Josef Sieben, *Traktate und Theorien zum Konzil* (Frankfurt-am-Main, 1983), chap. II: "Ein Paradigma: Nicolaus von Kues, *De concordantia catholica* (1434)" (pp. 59-109). Sieben notes that *De concordantia* is based in the main on ideas of consent previously set forth by the Council of Basel in its synodal letter *Cogitanti* of 3 September 1432 (cited in n. 11, below). Rudolf Haubst has argued that *De concordantia* contains, together with the conceptual pair *complicatio-explicatio* which describes the unifying and ministerial-governing functions of the pope as head of the priestly hierarchy, the central concepts of Cusanus' theology: Rudolf Haubst, "Die leitenden Gedanken und Motive der cusanischen Theologie", *MFCG* 4 (1964): 257-277. The other treatises are given either in full or cited in *Acta Cusana: Quellen zur Lebensgeschichte des Nikolaus von Kues,* ed. Erich Meuthen, I,1 (1401-1437); I,2 (1437–1450) (Hamburg, 1976–1983); I,2:304–320 (no. 468: letter to a community of Carthusians, ca. February 1441 and no. 469: letter-treatise to Jakob von Sierck defending the Council of Basel's translation to Ferrara, ca. before 7 February 1441), 322–325, 336–352 (no. 473, 480 and 481: Congress of Mainz, March 1441, including the reply of Cusanus to Thomas Ebendorfer's questions on the relation of the pope's authority to that of a general council, ca. 1 April 1441), 376–421, 425–432 (no. 520 and 526: Diet of Frankfurt, June/July 1442). The letter–treatise to Rodrigo Sánchez de Arévalo (20 May 1442) is appended to *Cusanus-Texte, II, Traktate,* 1: *De auctoritate presidendi in concilio qenerali,* ed. Gerhard Kallen, Sitzungsberichte der Heidelberger Akademie der Wissenschaften. Philosophisch-historische Klasse. 3. Abhandlung (Heidelberg, 1935), pp. 106–112. For an English trans. of the treatise on Presidential Authority (but not the letter to Sánchez de Arévalo) see H.L. Bond, G. Christianson, T.M. Izbicki, "Nicholas of Cusa: 'On Presidential Authority in a General Council'," *Church History* 59 (1990): 19–34.

exaggerate the differences,[3] there is a remarkable contrast between Cusanus' early years in Basel and the period when he emerged at Mainz and Frankfurt as the chief champion of Eugenius IV.

The most striking difference between Cusanus' writings in 1432-1434 and in 1441-1442 is found in the passages devoted to the question of whether the general council or the pope most fully represents the church, and who of the two therefore exercises, to the fullest extent, the power of binding and loosing which Christ entrusted to the church.[4] In 1432-1434 Cusanus had attributed this supreme power to the general council, noting that it most fully represents the unity of the infallible church, whereas individual popes have been known to err in the past.[5] By February 1441, in a letter to a community of Carthusians, Cusanus argued instead that the unity of the church throughout the world is to be found in the pope--this time pointedly omitting any reference to general councils--and then concluded bv citing a nassage from the Bull *Unam sanctam* of Boniface VIII.

[3] Cf. the remarks of Erich Meuthen in the intro. to his edition of "Der *Dialogus concludens Amedistarum errorem ex gestis et doctrina concilii Basiliensis*," *Mitteilungen und Forschungsbeiträge der Cusanus– Gesellschaft* [hereafter *MFCG*] 8 (1970): 11–114, where on p. 49 he writes with reference to *De concordantia catholica*, "Man kann diese Werke des Cusanus nicht aus ihrer politischen Situation isolieren; denn sie sind für diese Situation geschrieben, von der sie herausgefordert worden sind." In addition to the *Acta Cusana*, cited above, five of Meuthen's many other contributions to Cusanus schölarship may be cited here: *Das Trierer Schisma von 1430 auf dem Basler Konzil* (Münster, 1964); *Die letzten Jahre des Nikolaus von Kues* [1458–1464] (Cologne, 1958); the excellent epitome: *Nikolaus von Kues, 1401–1464; Skizze einer Biographie*, 5th ed. (Münster, 1982); "Neue Schlaglichter auf das Leben des Nikolaus von Kues", *MFCG* 4 (1964): 37 ff., with bibliographical references which were omitted from his earlier "Sketch"; and "Nikolaus von Kues in der Entscheidung zwischen Konzil und Papst", *MFCG* 9 (1971): 19–33.

[4] On the varieties of meaning of *repraesentare* in the writings of Cusanus, normally signifying symbolic representation, but occasionally, legal or political representation in the sense of *vices gerere*, see the synopsis in *Cusanus-Studien*, VIII. Gerhard Kallen, *Die handschriftliche Überlieferung der* Concordantia catholica *des Nikolaus von Kues*. Sitzungsberichte der Heidelberger Akademie der Wissenschaften. Philosophisch-historische Klasse. 2. Abhandlung (Heidelberg, 1963), p. 16, n. 26. See also idem, "Wort und Leitidee der *Repraesentatio* bei Nikolaus von Kues", and Werner Krämer, "Die ekklesiologische Auseinandersetzung um die wahre Repräsentation auf dem Basler Konzil", *Der Begriff der* Repraesentatio *im Mittelalter: Stellvertretung, Symbol, Zeichen, Bild*, ed. Albert Zimmermann, *Miscellanea Mediaevalia* 8 (1971): 139-162, 202-237.

[5] Cf. *De concordantia catholica* II, 18, #158 (h XIV, 194), and *De auctoritate presidendi*, pp. 24–28 (pp. 29-32 in the English trans., cited above).

Further on in the same letter, Cusanus insisted that even "if only a few support the pope" in a general council "and many oppose him," the supreme pontiff, as the successor of St. Peter, still has the final say. As precedents he cited the actions of Pope Leo I, the Great, who had challenged the decisions of the "robber council" of Ephesus (449) and of Pope Nicholas I who had rejected the decisions of a council of the Eastern church (861) which, in his judgement, had wrongfully deposed Ignatius as Patriarch of Constantinople.[6] The following year, on 20 May 1442, in a letter to Rodrigo Sánchez de Arévalo, an envoy of the King of Castile, Cusanus went even further when he referred to the pope as the *sacer princeps,* a title recalling the style of the Roman emperors. Cusanus could expect that the Castilian envoy, trained in canon law like himself, and also knowledgeable in civil law, would surely appreciate the meaning of the term *sacer princeps* which, like his earlier reference to *Unam sanctam,* suggested that the pope was indeed the *verus imperator.*[7] In the letter to Arévalo, the focus shifts to

---

[6] Cf. the letter to a community of Carthusians, dated by Meuthen as ca. February 1441, in *Acta Cusana* I,2:304–313 (no. 468), with the reference to *Unam sanctam* on p. 307, l. 36, and the reference to the pope's right to override even the majority in a general council on p. 310, l. 77–80. Josef Koch had previously published this letter, but had assigned it to the year 1439. For a discussion of the letter's significance see *Cusanus-Texte,* IV, *Briefe,* Josef Koch, *Nikolaus von Cues und seine Umwelt.* Sitzungsberichte der Heidelberger Akademie der Wissenschaften. Philosophisch-historische Klasse. 2. Abhandlung (Heidelberg, 1948), esp. pp. 23–29 which compare Cusanus' views on the status of the pope and the general council in 1433 and 1441/1442. The bull *Unam sanctam* (18 November 1302) circulated widely in the fourteenth and fifteenth centuries as one of the [*Decretales*] *extravagantes* of Boniface VIII and was often appended to the older official compilations of papal decretals. At the end of the fifteenth century, *Unam sanctam* was included by Jean Chappuis in his compilation (Paris, 1500) of the *Extravagantes communes,* liber I, tit. 8, c. 1, which became the standard edition. *Cf. Corpus iuris canonici,* ed. Emil Friedberg, 2 vol. (Leipzig, 1879; reprint Graz, 1955) [hereafter Friedberg], 2:1245-1246.

[7] On the career and legal studies of Arévalo, see Richard H. Trame, *Rodrigo Sánchez de Arévalo, 1404–1470* (Washington, D.C., 1958), pp. 11–13; idem, "Conciliar Agitation and Rodrigo Sánchez de Arévalo", *Studies in Mediaevalia and Americana: Essays in Honor of William Lyle Davis, S.J.,* ed. Gerard G. Steckler and Leo D. Davis (Spokane, Washington, 1973), pp. 89-112; Juan Maria Laboa, *Rodrigo Sánchez de Arévalo, alcaide de Sant' Angelo* (Madrid, 1973) and "Sánchez de Arévalo, Rodrigo" by B. J. Blasquez Hernandez, *Lexikon für Theologie und Kirche* 9 (Freiburg, 1964): 307-308.

the person of the pope as a symbol of church unity.[8] Although he concedes that the powers of the *sacer princeps* diminish (*exiens vires potentiae suae*) when he does not act for (reasonable) cause or necessity, Cusanus also argues that, in case of doubt, one must obey the pope.[9] Compared with Cusanus' earlier writings, the most remarkable aspect of the letter to

[8] For the letter to Arévalo, see n. 2 above. In this letter, Cusanus describes the pope's position in the church by using not only traditional theological terms, but also new expressions suggesting that the unity of the church is folded up (*complicatio*) in the pope, and is then to be unfolded (*explicatio*) in the world at large. On Cusanus' use of such new religious language, see James E. Biechler, "Nicholas of Cusa and the End of the Conciliar Movement: A Humanist Crisis of Identity", *Church History* 44 (1975): 5-21, esp. 18-19 on the letter to Arévalo. Biechler carefully delineates Cusanus' alternative religious language in his writings after 1437, but he does not claim that the new way of looking at religious issues which that language reflected was the motive or cause of Cusanus' decision for the pope and against the council in 1436/1437. As Biechler puts it, "that conversion [to the papacy] was not ideological in its motivation" (p. 11). Moreover, in his public debates with the defenders of the Council of Basel at the imperial diets of the 1440's, Cusanus continued to use also traditional theological and canonistic terminology in defending the cause of Eugenius IV. In Cusanus' writings the "new religious language" continued to coexist along with his use of traditional terms of discourse in theology and canon law, and it is with this latter predominant use that this inquiry is concerned. Not entirely convincing is Biechler's suggestion that Cusanus be considered a humanist. Sharing philosophical interests with humanists does not make one a humanist. Here it might be preferable to follow the stricter definition proposed by Paul Oskar Kristeller who insisted on a primary concern with rhetoric as the defining criterion of a humanist. Paul Oskar Kristeller, *Renaissance Thought and its Sources* (New York, 1979), 1: "The Humanist Movement" (esp. pp. 23-24) [originally published as chap. 1 of *The Classics and Renaissance Thought* (Cambridge, Massachusetts, 1955)]; and most recently "Humanism", *The Cambridge History of Renaissance Philosophy,* ed. Charles B. Schmitt (Cambridge, 1988), pp. 113-137.

[9] Cf. the relevant passages of the letter in *Cusanus-Texte* II, *Traktate* 1 (Heidelberg, 1935), pp. 111 and 110, respectively (cited in n. 2 above). Rudolf Haubst probably overemphasized the limitations upon the pope's power which Cusanus intended here when he wrote: "Wenn der Papst seine Vollmacht überschreitet, braucht man ihm nicht zu gehorchen." Cf. Rudolf Haubst, "Der Leitgedanke der *repraesentatio* in der cusanischen Ekklesiologie", *MFCG* 9 (1971): 140-165; here p. 150, n. 62. By no longer making any reference to the power of a general council, Cusanus removed the only institution which could authoritatively define that the pope has acted illegally, call him to account for his conduct in office and, if necessary, depose him. To be sure, even the most categorical defenders of papal power always conceded that a *heretical* pope would *ipso facto* be deprived of his office.

Sánchez de Arévalo is the complete omission of any reference to a general council as an authoritative gathering (*complicatio*) representing the church throughout the world (*explicatio*). Such a unifying and representative function has been taken over entirely by the pope as *sacer princeps*, unlimited (*absolutus*) by any institution that could define with superior authority whether he has acted against the law without reasonable cause or necessity, and which could call him to account for his conduct in office.

Thus by 1441-1442, Cusanus' writings leave no doubt that in the event of a disagreement between the pope and a general council, the general council would have to yield in order to preserve unity in the church. Applied to the crucial months between December 1436 and May 1437, this meant that since Eugenius IV insisted on holding the council of union with the Greeks in Italy, the Council of Basel would have to yield in order to preserve unity in the church. The majority of the council fathers, however, refused to do so, fearing that a transfer to Italy would jeopardize their independence and lead to the abrogation of their reform decrees. When the pope's representatives continued to press vigorously for a transfer to Italy, the result was acrimonious debate and "disorder" in the council. This was subsequently cited by Cusanus as a clear sign that the Council of Basel had ceased to be a true and authoritative general council. When Eugenius IV decreed the Council of Basel's transfer to Ferrara with the Bull *Doctoris gentium* (18 September 1437), he did so by invoking his authority as bishop of the universal church. Yet he also justified his action on the ground that the proceedings at Basel had been disorderly, specifically citing the precedent of Pope Leo I who had rejected the proceedings and decisions of the "robber synod" of Ephesus (449).[10] It should be noted that Cusanus had argued already in *De concordantia* (1433) that a general council can be considered legitimate and authoritative only if it is truly well ordered and marked by concord and a consensus that includes the Roman pontiff or his representatives.[11]

[10] The text of *Doctoris gentium* is in *Epistolae pontificiae ad concilium Florentinum spectantes,* ed. Georg Hofmann, pt. 1 (1418–1438) (Rome, 1940), pp. 91–99 (no. 88); the references to Pope Leo and the "robber council" of Ephesus are on pp. 94–95.

[11] Cf. *De concordantia* II, 18, #158 (h XIV, 194) for the requirement that a general synod be "well-ordered" (*ordinata*). The numerous passages in *De concordantia* in which concord and universal consent are singled out as the defining characteristics of an authoritative general council have been assembled by Meuthen in his edition of "Der *Dialogus concludens Amedistarum errorem . . . ,*" pp. 93–97, where he also gives the parallel passages in the Council of Basel's letter *Cogitanti* (3 September 1432), published in Juan de Segovia's *Gesta sacrosancta generalis synodi Basiliensis,* in *Monumenta conciliorum generalium saeculi decimi quinti* [hereafter *MC*], 2 (Vienna, 1873): 234-258.

Erich Meuthen has noted that Nicholas of Cusa continued to pay tribute to the idea of consent even in the 1440's, using it primarily in order to impugn the credibility of the Council of Basel by pointing out that almost none of the princes had recognized its deposition of Eugenius IV and subsequent election of Felix V.[12] He never presented this, however, as a primary reason for rejecting the council's legitimacy. By 1441, consent in the church had come to mean for Cusanus agreement with the divinely ordained pastors at each level of the hierarchy and, ultimately, submission to the supreme pontiff. The critical observer might ask whether one can truly speak of consent if subordinates only have a right to agree, but not a right to disagree. There can be little doubt that by 1441 Cusanus had modified the views he had earlier expressed in *De concordantia* and *De auctoritate presidendi*. His later position marked a return to a conception of the papacy's role that is comparable to that of Pope Innocent III when he convoked (1213) the Fourth Lateran Council, inviting the prelates of Latin Christendom to collaborate with him, not expecting them to disagree. In fact, Cusanus' later position may even be likened to that of Boniface VIII who, in spite of his imperial conception of the papal office, had included the principle *quod omnes tangit debet ab omnibus approbari* as a "Rule of Law" in the *Sext* (1298).[13] Like Innocent III and Boniface VIII, the older Cusanus had come to regard the quest for consent in the church primarily as a practical expedient and prudent rule of government, rather than as one of its underlying principles.

The contrast between Nicholas of Cusa's views after 1437 and his posi-tion in 1432-1434 is even sharper if we consider not only his writings but also his official conduct. When Cusanus was incorporated in the Council of Basel on 29 February 1432, he was formally joining a body that had been

---

[12] Cf. Erich Meuthen, "Konsens bei Nikolaus von Kues und im Kirchen-verständnis des 15. Jahrhunderts", *Politik und Konfession. Festschrift für Konrad Repgen zum 60. Geburtstag,* ed. Dieter Albrecht et al. (Berlin, 1983), pp. 11–29, esp. pp. 15–16.

[13] Cf. the Bull *Vineam domini* with which Innocent III convoked the Fourth Lateran Council in J.P. Migne, *Patrologia latina,* 216 (Paris, 1891): 823–825. *Quod omnes tangit* as *Regula iuris,* XXIX, is in Friedberg 2: 1122. For a discussion of *Quod omnes tangit* with reference to the government of the church and of secular society in later medieval Europe, see Yves Congar, "Quod omnes tangit, ab omnibus tractari et approbari debet", *Revue historique de droit français et étranger,* 4:36 (1958): 210– 259; reprint in idem, *Droit ancien et structures ecclésiales* (London, 1982), 3.

declared dissolved by the pope two months earlier.[14]   Moreover, Cusanus
acted at Basel as the procurator of Ulrich von Manderscheid on whose behalf
he was appealing to the council a judicial decision of the late Pope Martin
V, thereby implicitly recognizing the general council's superior jurisdiction.
For nearly two years, from his incorporation on 29 February 1432 until 15
December 1433 when Eugenius IV was finally obliged to acknowledge that
he had exceeded his authority in trying to dissolve a general council against
its will, the very participation of Cusanus in the proceedings at Basel was
an implicit recognition of the claim that Eugenius did not have the power to
dissolve or transfer a general council without its consent.

   How are we to explain the change of outlook in Cusanus' writings
between 1432-1434 and 1441-1442, separated by a clear stand with the papal
party at Basel in the crucial months from December 1436 to May 1437?
Unlike his contemporary and friend Pius II (Aeneas Sylvius Piccolomini),
Cusanus never publicly admitted that he had changed his position since the
days when he was *in minoribus agentes*.[15]   Yet it is surely no accident that
Cusanus did *not* include *De concordantia* among the works which he had
definitively copied when he assembled his literary output for posterity.   In
seeking the motives for Cusanus' decision to side with Eugenius IV against
the Council of Basel, it is not enough to accept at face value his claim--also
made by the other partisans of Eugenius IV in the 1440's--that he supported
the pope's action of transferring the council to Ferrara both because it was in
the interest of "building up the church" (*ad aedificationem ecclesiae*) and

[14] When Nicholas of Cusa was incorporated in the Council of Basel on 29
February 1432, only two weeks had elapsed since the council had formally
refused to accept its dissolution by Eugenius IV and had reaffirmed, at its second
session (15 February 1432), the decree *Haec sancta* of the Council of Constance
on the supreme authority of general councils. As procurator of Ulrich von
Manderscheid and the clergy of Trier, Cusanus, on 24 March 1432, formally
appealed a judicial sentence of the late Pope Martin V which had denied the See of
Trier to Ulrich. Cf. *Acta Cusana* I,1:50–51, 54 (no. 102–104, 109).

[15] Cf. Pius II's Bull *In minoribus agentes* (26 April 1463) in which he
retracted the conciliarist views of his youth in Carlo Fea, ed., *Pius II Pont. Max.
a calumniis vindicatus* . . . (Rome, 1823), pp. 148–164; and Gerald
Christianson, "Aeneas Sylvius Piccolomini and the Historiography of the
Council of Basel", *Ecclesia Militans: Studien zur Konzilien- und
Reformationsgeschichte*, 2 vols. (Paderborn, 1988) 1:157-184, with further
bibliography.

because he cherished unity and concord.[16]   Such an argument implies that the Council of Basel and its supporters were not motivated by the goal of "building up" the church or ideals of harmony when they urged Eugenius IV to maintain unity with the council, and it fails to do justice to their conviction that they, rather than the pope, were acting for the well-being of the church. On the contrary: in the view of the council fathers, it was Eugenius who had separated himself from the unity of the church which is most fully represented in a general council.[17]

The allegation that the council fathers at Basel cared less for concord and unity in the church than Eugenius IV and his supporters is simply not borne out by the evidence recorded in the acts of the council. Indeed, a convincing case can be made that Eugenius IV and his representatives consistently sought to undermine the council's official "Manner of Proceeding" (*Modus procedendi*) which had been designed to insure freedom of debate and a spirit of harmony and fraternal charity in arriving at the synod's decisions. In particular, the papal party had refused to accept the vote of the overwhelming majority on 5 December 1436 *not* to hold a council of union in Italy. Five months later, the pope's representatives deliberately provoked a schism in the Latin church when they insisted on the reading of their minority decree at the council's 25th session (7 May 1437) instead of accepting the

---

[16] Such a view was expressed by Josef Koch, *Nikolaus von Cues und seine Umwelt*, pp. 27–29, and endorsed by Meuthen in his article "Nikolaus von Kues in der Entscheidung", *MFCG* 9 (1971): 23, and also in *Nikolaus von Kues, 1401–1464*, pp. 77–78, where the Council of Basel and its deputations are characterized as filled with acrimonious controversy ("Debattengezänk der Ausschüsse") without taking into account that many of the sharpest controversies were deliberately provoked within the council by the pope's representatives. Among the modern biographers of Eugenius IV, Joseph Gill in his *Eugenius IV, Pope of Christian Union* (London, 1961) also makes it appear that the primary goal of the pope was unity rather than the assertion of papal claims to primacy and the restoration of papal control over benefices.

[17] Cf. the Council of Basel's letter *Ecclesiam suam Christus* (19 October 1437) in *MC* 2:1049–1060, in which the council fathers argued that Eugenius IV had separated himself from them, not they from him: "Cum enim membrum a corpore disiungitur, non totum a parte se dicitur separare, sed pars a toto segregari. Debuit quidem synodo universali ut membrum ipsius in unitate spiritus iugiter adhaerere quam etsi relinqueret, non tamen ipsa a suo vero capite Christo relinquitur." (*MC* 2:1055). The council then ended the letter with a plea for unity and harmony (*MC* 2:1059-1060). The text is also in Giovanni Domenico Mansi, ed., *Sacrorum conciliorum nova et amplissima collectio* [hereafter Mansi], 29 (Venice, 1788; reprint Graz, 1961): 289–302, esp. 296, 301-302.

will of the majority.[18]   Since Nicholas of Cusa had himself been one of the leading participants in the tumultuous events at Basel where he had supported the pro-papal minority between December 1436 and May 1437, it was therefore rather disingenuous on his part later to impugn the legitimacy of the entire council on the ground of the disordered proceedings for which he and the others of the papal minority had been chiefly responsible. Not universal concord but the defense of papal prerogatives, indeed of absolute papal monarchy, had become the chief aim of Cusanus by 1437. The conviction with which he defended absolute papal monarchy in the 1440's makes one look all the more closely at the qualifications with which he had hedged his earlier arguments in support of conciliar authority.

When Nicholas of Cusa argued in *De concordantia* and *De auctoritate presidendi* between 1432 and early 1434 that the general council possessed greater authority than the pope alone, he was defending a broad principle which had not yet been tested in a conflict between a legitimate, reigning pope and a general council. Neither he nor any one else could then foresee the specific reform program that would eventually be adopted at Basel on the basis of the council's claim to supreme authority in the church. The statements on the authority of the pope and the general council in *De concordantia* should therefore be evaluated in terms of their immediate background: the Council of Basel's reaffirmation at its first (14 December 1431) and second (15 February 1432) sessions of the decrees *Frequens* and *Haec sancta* of the Council of Constance and the carefully argued defense of these decrees in the synodal letter *Cogitanti* (3 September 1432).[19]   These statements, especially *Cogitanti,* defended the supreme authority and independence of a general council in the church not only on broad theological

---

[18] On the vote of the council fathers in the general congregation of 5 December 1436 and its public confirmation in the 25th session (7 May 1437), at which the minority departed from established procedure by insisting on the reading of its opposing decree, see the notarial protocol of Petrus Bruneti in *Concilium Basiliense* 4 (Basel, 1903; reprint Nendeln, 1971): 348–360, and the *Gesta sacrosancta generalis synodi Basiliensis* of Juan de Segovia, *MC* 2:966–969, 980–981. For an interpretation of the events see Joachim W. Stieber, *Pope Eugenius IV, the Council of Basel and the Secular and Ecclesiastical Authorities in the Empire*. Studies in the History of Christian Thought, 13 (Leiden, 1978), pp. 35–37. The extent to which the conduct of the pope's representatives at Basel violated the council's ideals of fraternal charity and consensus-building has been carefully analyzed by Josef Wohlmuth, *Verständigung in der Kirche: Untersucht an der Sprache des Konzils von Basel*. Tübinger Theologische Studien, 19 (Mainz, 1983), pp. 92–102.

[19] For the decrees issued by the Council of Basel at its first and second sessions and its synodal letter *Cogitanti,* see *MC* 2:47–62, 124–126, 234–258; and Mansi 29:3-21, 21–23, 239–267.

grounds but with reference to the urgent tasks that the council was supposed to address: to contain the Hussite heresy, to reform the church, especially to strengthen clerical discipline, to lead back (reunite) the Eastern church, and to reestablish peace among the princes of Latin Christendom. *Not* included among the openly stated aims of the council in 1432 were plans to limit or to redefine the normal role of the pope in the government of the church. Yet many of the decrees adopted by the council after 1433 would in practice have curtailed the pope's power. As a result, a number of council fathers, with Cusanus surely among them, subsequently began to distance themselves again from the principles set forth in the synodal letter *Cogitanti* which had provided the theological basis for the council's reform program.

The reform decrees published by the council fathers between 1433 and 1436 would, in fact, have transformed the papacy into a constitutional monarchy and, one can plausibly argue, it was this actual reform program which turned Cusanus against the Council of Basel. The chief reform decrees adopted were the following: the decree of the 12th session (13 July 1433) on the free election of prelates (abolishing papal reservations), the decree of the 21st session (9 June 1435) abolishing annates, the decree of the 23rd session (26 March 1436) requiring an oath of office of the pope in which he would promise to respect the authority of general councils and observe their decrees, while also strengthening the College of Cardinals. In addition to these reform decrees pertaining to the government of the church at all levels, the council had adopted a decree at its 20th session (22 January 1435) against frivolous appeals in ecclesiastical courts and, of great symbolic significance, had issued at its 24th session (24 April 1436) a plenary indulgence, the proceeds of which were to support a council of union with the Greeks under the council's auspices.[20] Taken together with the council's practice of accepting appeals from papal judicial sentences, these decrees--if implemented--would have transformed the papacy from an absolute into a constitutional monarchy. It is not surprising that Eugenius IV strongly objected to the council's proposed reforms and refused to observe them. It is not quite correct, however, to claim as some modern critics have done that

[20] The texts of the decrees are in *MC* 2:402–405, 775, 801, 847-856, 877–882; and Mansi 29:61–64, 103, 104, 110–119, 128–133.

"the council failed to adopt major reforms".[21] In fact, the prospect that the council's reforms might eventually be adopted prompted Eugenius to redouble his effort to bring the council under his control by ordering its transfer to Italy.[22] It was precisely on this issue that he found an energetic supporter in Cusanus who sided with the papal party in 1436/1437.

   Nicholas of Cusa, for his part, was also unlikely to find the Council of Basel's reform program congenial. While we can *suppose* that it ran counter to the hierarchical bent of his philosophical and religious outlook, it would *surely* not have benefited him in his professional status as a canon lawyer, nor have favored his quest for material rewards and offices in the church, for reasons that we hope to make plausible. What one can say with certainty is that Cusanus sided at Basel with the small minority that supported Eugenius IV in 1436/1437, and that by 1440 he was ready to defend Eugenius with arguments drawn from traditional theological and canonistic texts, but also with more personal arguments couched in new religious language. His political stand in 1436/1437 clearly involved relegating the authority of a general council below that of the pope. There is no evidence, however, that he acted already then on the basis of a vision of the pope's unifying role as a *sacer princeps* with unlimited powers in "building up the Church", as modern interpreters like Gerd Heinz-Mohr have argued.[23] In short, there is little evidence to support the view that Cusanus based his decision of 1436/1437 on ideological grounds.

   Nicholas of Cusa appears to have prepared his shift of allegiance from

---

[21] See, for instance, Erich Meuthen, "Nikolaus von Kues und das Konzil von Basel", *Schweizer Rundschau* 63 (1964): 377-386. Here Meuthen writes: "Zwar wurde auch eine Anzahl von Dekreten verabschiedet die das sittliche Leben und die Standespflichten des Klerus betrafen. Aber vor der grossen Reform versagte auch das Konzil" (p. 384), without even mentioning the deliberate efforts of Eugenius IV to undermine the council's reforms. A similar interpretation is given in Gerd Heinz-Mohr, *Nikolaus von Kues und die Konzilsbewegung* (Trier, 1963), p. 20: "Während die Baseler dem Aufbau der Kirche keineswegs dienten, hat Eugen IV. von seiner Vollmacht und Verantwortung rechten Gebrauch gemacht, als er um die Einheit der Kirche zu wahren und den Glauben zu mehren, das Konzil verlegte."

[22] On the motives of Eugenius IV in ordering the Council of Basel's transfer to Ferrara in 1437, see Stieber, *Pope Eugenius IV, the Council of Basel*, pp. 22-44.

[23] Cf. Heinz-Mohr, *Nikolaus von Kues und die Konzilsbewegung*, p. 20: "Als Ordnungsbegriff führt die aedificatio ecclesiae, die Aufgabe der Auferbauung der Kirche, Cusanus selbst von der Seite des Schismas auf die Seite der Einheit". See also the more fully developed presentation of the same argument in idem, *Unitas christiana: Studien zur Gesellschaftsidee des Nikolaus von Kues* (Trier, 1958), pp. 74-112.

council to pope, or at least to have considered it, since May 1435 when he began to seek confirmation of his benefices from Eugenius IV as well as from the council. Yet it was not until February 1436 that Cusanus was finally to attain greater freedom of action when the case involving Ulrich von Manderscheid was finally settled. Although the Council of Basel had upheld, on 15 May 1434,[24] the legal decision of the late Pope Martin V which had set aside the disputed election at Trier, Ulrich had not admitted defeat and had appealed this decision as well, hoping for a better settlement by direct negotiations with his adversaries. Not until December 1435-February 1436 was a final settlement reached.[25] Cusanus must have eagerly awaited the decision since, as Ulrich's procurator, he also was threatened by excommunication and the loss of his benefices. But even before Cusanus was finally able to extricate himself from Manderscheid's case, he had begun to seek contact with the papal court. As noted, he had petitioned Eugenius IV for confirmation of a provostship in May 1435.

Then, in September and October 1435, we find him cultivating the friendship of Ambrogio Traversari, the General of the Camaldolese Order, who was at Basel as the pope's personal emissary.[26] Cusanus' motives in seeking contact with the envoy were twofold: Traversari could probably help him obtain papal confirmation of his benefices and, no less importantly, Traversari was considered the foremost living authority on Pseudo-Dionysius, an author in whom Cusanus was interested throughout his life.[27] In fact, we know that a few years later Cusanus purchased the Latin translations of all Pseudo-Dionysius' works that Traversari had prepared.

[24] For the Council of Basel's decision, published on 5 May 1434, see Meuthen, *Das Trierer Schisma,* pp. 44 (no. 84), 216–219, and *Acta Cusana* I,1:156–157 (no. 226).

[25] For Cusanus' involvement in negotiations as Ulrich von Manderscheid's procurator in July 1435 and then in the final settlement between 7 December 1435 and 7 February 1436, see Meuthen, *Das Trier Schisma,* pp. 230–240, 246–253.

[26] For a supplication of Cusanus to Eugenius IV (11 May 1435), requesting confirmation as Provost of Münstermaifeld and a letter by Ambrogio Traversari to the papal referendary Cristoforo di San Marcello (24 October 1435), referring to Cusanus' efforts to commend himself, see *Acta Cusana* I,1:162 (no. 236) and 164–165 (no. 244) .

[27] Charles L. Stinger, *Humanism and the Church Fathers: Ambrogio Traversari (1386-1439) and Christian Antiquity in the Italian Renaissance* (Albany, 1977). See esp. pp. 158-162 where Stinger discusses Traversari's study and translations of Pseudo-Dionysius, and pp. 43-44, 243, n. 61 and 66 where he discusses the relations between Traversari and Cusanus, citing Cusanus' purchases of the Latin translations of all Pseudo-Dionysius' works by Traversari. A copy of one of these is still in the Hospital Library at Kues as Cod. Cus. 43.

Cusanus' relations with Traversari are thus one more instance of the interplay of material and ideological motives that characterized the gradual shift of Cusanus toward the papal side between October 1435 and December 1436. During this period, tensions between pope and council grew to such a degree that Eugenius IV and the cardinals decided to redouble their efforts to obtain the aid of the secular princes against the Council of Basel. In a memorandum prepared in June 1436, the so-called *Libellus apologeticus* of Eugenius IV, papal envoys were instructed to remind the secular princes of the pope's traditional role as the supreme judge who is entitled to "moderate" the law (that is, grant dispensations), based on his authority as Vicar of Christ.[28] While Cusanus probably did not know the actual contents of the *Libellus apologeticus*, he would have found, as a canon lawyer, many of its arguments not only familiar, but even convincing.

   Among the intellectual and material interests that were likely to incline Cusanus to the side of the pope, one must also include those related to his study of canon law at the University of Padua.[29] During his years at Padua between 1417 and 1423, Cusanus had ample opportunity to come into contact not only with students and teachers of canon and civil law but also with other scholars who had a broad interest in ancient authors. Although Cusanus appears to have been more interested in texts relating to church history and philosophy than in ancient literary works, these contacts with Italian scholars were clearly important to him, both for intellectual reasons and in some cases, such as the future Cardinal Domenico Capranica, as

[28] For the text of the *Libellus apologeticus* of Eugenius IV, see Cesare Baronio, Odorico Rinaldi, *Annales Ecclesiastici* 28 (1424-1453) (Bar-le-Duc, 1874): 194-211; the cited passage is on p. 199. For a discussion of the *Libellus apologeticus*, see Stieber, *Pope Eugenius IV, the Council of Basel*, pp. 27-34.

[29] Alois Krchnák has analyzed a codex with Cusanus' notes taken at the lectures of the Paduan professor Prosdocimus de Comitibus who taught legal procedure in ecclesiastical courts: "Die kanonistischen Aufzeichnungen des Nikolaus von Kues in Cod. Cus. 220 als Mitschrift einer Vorlesung seines Paduaner Lehrers Prosdocimus de Comitibus", *MFCG* 2 (1962): 67-84. On the study of civil and canon law at Padua in the fifteenth century, see Annalisa Belloni, *Professori giuristi a Padova nel secolo XV; Profili bio–bibliografici e cattedre* (Frankfurt-am-Main, 1986).

useful political links to the Roman Curia.[30] Moreover, the system of medieval canon law was so inextricably held together by the pope's role as supreme judge and legislator that it was rare to find a canonist who was a convinced and consistent supporter of the supreme authority of general councils. The aim of many conciliarists and reformers to limit all types of appeals to the Roman Curia would surely have reduced the need for the services of canon lawyers, a prospect few of them were likely to favor.

To the intellectual or ideological motives which may have prompted Cusanus to side with Eugenius IV rather than with the Council of Basel it is possible to add material ones that are specifically related to his social background. The known details concerning Cusanus' early life are few, but they suffice to define his social status. Nicholas' father was a prosperous merchant and respected member of the community who acted as a local magistrate and was wealthy enough to lend money to the local nobility. Like many other ambitious merchants in late medieval Europe, Nicholas' father invested in land and in a good education for his eldest son. After sound early schooling in Latin, Nicholas studied the arts at the University of Heidelberg. Only a well-supported young man could then have gone on, as Cusanus did, to the far more costly study of canon law at Padua where he earned his degree as a *doctor decretorum*. Judged by his subsequent career, Nicholas of Cusa must have been a very ambitious and hard-working young canon lawyer who was determined to make the best possible use of his knowledge of the administrative law of the church in order to secure positions that would provide him with influence and income. In the years

---

[30] On Cusanus and one of his Paduan mentors, see Gerald Christianson, "Cardinal Cesarini and Cusa's 'Concordantia'", *Church History* 54 (1985): 7-19. On the close contacts between those who combined the study of law with humanist interests, see Agostino Sottili, *Studenti tedeschi e umanesimo italiano nell' Universita di Padova durante il Quattrocento,* 1: *Pietro del Monte nella società accademica padovana (1430–1433)* (Padua, 1971). In the early decades of the fifteenth century Padua and its university were a major center of humanist studies, at which prominent humanists like Gasparino Barzizza, Vittorino da Feltre, and Guarino Veronese had either studied or taught. For an intro. see R.G.G. Mercer, *The Teaching of Gasparino Barzizza, with Special Reference to his Place in Paduan Humanism* (London, 1979). On the relations between professors of canon and Roman law and humanists in fourteenth- and fifteenth-century Italy, see Mario Ascheri, "Giuristi, umanisti e istituzioni del Tre-Quattrocento: qualche problema", *Annali dell'Istituto Storico Italo-Germanico in Trento,* 3 (1977): 43-73. The sources concerning the contacts of Cusanus with Italian humanists in the 1420's and 1430's have been assembled in Alois Meister, "Die humanistischen Anfänge des Nikolaus von Cues", *Annalen des historischen Vereins für den Niederrhein, insbesondere die alte Erzdiozese Köln* 63 (1896): 1–21; they are now edited in an exemplary manner in *Acta Cusana* I,1: *passim.*

after 1425 we find Nicholas of Cusa for a year or two as a teacher of canon law at the University of Cologne and on occasion in the service of the Archbishop of Trier, Otto von Ziegenhain. After Archbishop Otto's death in 1430, Cusanus became the procurator of Count Ulrich von Manderscheid who, as the candidate of the local nobility, sought to gain the See of Trier in the disputed election of 1430. As we have already seen, it was as Ulrich's procurator that the young Cusanus was incorporated in 1432 in the Council of Basel, then at the center of church politics in Latin Christendom.

From the very start of his public career in 1425, Nicholas of Cusa energetically pursued every opportunity to acquire ecclesiastical benefices as Erich Meuthen and, more recently, Brigide Schwarz have shown.[31] Meuthen has sought to place this quest for benefices in a more favorable light by pointing out that it was quite common at the time, and that in the medieval church there were very few bureaucratic positions in which, as an alternative, a canon lawyer could have received a regular salary for his services.[32] It is not our purpose to pass judgement on Nicholas of Cusa's acquisition of plural benefices, but merely to ask whether, or to what degree, it may have influenced his decision to side with Eugenius IV and against the Council of Basel in 1436/1437. Like most holders of plural benefices, or pluralists, Cusanus regarded his benefices primarily as sources of income. For a non-resident titular owner, the income from a benefice would, however, often consist of only a fraction of its nominal value since he was responsible for engaging a vicar to carry out the pastoral duties (*officia*) for the sake of which the benefice had been established. The actual annual yield of a benefice held in this manner might be compared to the dividend produced by a modern investment portfolio after all expenses have been deducted. The relatively modest income which many individual benefices produced for their non-resident owners often encouraged the acquisition

[31] Erich Meuthen, "Die Pfründen des Cusanus", *MFCG* 2 (1962): 15–66, is the basic study of its subject. On Cusanus as a hunter of benefices, and, later in his career, as a patron who secured benefices for his followers or clients, see Brigide Schwarz, "Über Patronage und Klientel in der spätmittelalterlichen Kirche am Beispiel des Nikolaus von Kues", *Quellen und Forschungen aus italienischen Archiven und Bibliotheken* 68 (1988): 284–310.

[32] Meuthen, "Die Pfründen", pp. 59–63.

of additional benefices.[33] It was also true, on the other hand, that the better endowed a benefice was, the greater were the chances that it would be coveted by shrewd pluralists.[34] It was at this game of seeking and managing plural benefices that Cusanus, the hard-working merchant's son and canon lawyer, excelled throughout his life.

Cusanus' first benefice appears to have been a parish church in 1425. Although it legally required him to be both a priest and in residence, he never resided in this or in any of his later benefices, nor was he ordained as a priest until about 1437.[35] It was, in fact, only through papal dispensations that Cusanus and other pluralists were able to hold benefices and to collect a substantial portion of their revenues without personally fulfilling the incumbent duties. As a skilled canon lawyer, Cusanus was his own best advocate and we find him, beginning in September 1427, but especially after October 1436 once he became a staunch partisan of Eugenius IV, requesting and receiving papal dispensations to hold two, and later even more, "incompatible benefices" (i.e., benefices each of which required residence).[36] In view of Cusanus' demonstrable determination and success in acquiring plural "incompatible benefices" by means of papal dispensations, it is not surprising that he turned in 1436/1437 against the Council of Basel which had attempted through its reform decrees to restore the greater emphasis on

[33] There are few comprehensive studies which deal not only with the acquisition of benefices by their non–resident titular owners, but also with the lives of their substitutes at the parish level. One of the best studies has been done for the diocese of Geneva which was comparable in its social structure to the diocese of Trier from which Cusanus hailed: Louis Binz, *Vie religieuse et réforme ecclésiastique dans le diocèse de Genève pendant le Grand Schisme et la crise conciliaire (1378–1450)*, 1 (Geneva, 1973). IV. "Le clergé paroissial. 2. L'absentéisme des curés" (pp. 298–337). Binz emphasizes that under the system of absentee benefice holding, the primary interest was in the revenues of the benefice rather than in the pastoral office. He has calculated that in the diocese of Geneva there was a decided increase in absentee benefice holding during the fifteenth century, going from 31% in 1411–1413, to 43% in 1443–1445, to 68% in 1481–1482, and to 80% in 1516–1518 (p. 302). It would be most interesting to have studies of other dioceses in order to compare the results with the exemplary work of Binz for Geneva.

[34] Cf. *ibid.*, pp. 312–314.

[35] Meuthen, "Die Pfründen des Cusanus", pp. 30–34, dates the ordination as priest between 1435 and 1440.

[36] Cf. *Acta Cusana*, I,1:15–16, 162, 193–193 (no. 41, 236, 284).

local self-government envisaged by the [canon] common law.[37]

Of particular relevance in this context are the reform decrees published by the Council of Basel between 1433 and 1436 which had abolished, first, papal reservation of major benefices, such as bishoprics and abbeys that traditionally had been filled by election, and then also papal reservations of minor benefices, such as parsonages or canonries that traditionally had been filled by appointment, normally by the local bishop. During most of his early career, through the 1430's, Cusanus had competed primarily for minor appointive benefices, and it is therefore appropriate to consider, initially, how the council's reform decrees would have restricted his acquisition of these benefices. One of the Council of Basel's most important measures in this respect was the decree *Et quia multiplices* of its 23rd session (26 March 1436) which had abolished the papal constitutions *Exsecrabilis* and *Ad regimen* as well as the rules of the Apostolic Chancery through which the popes had reserved to themselves the appointment to benefices.[38]   When the council abolished these papal reservations, it sought to end not only the practice of papal appointments by itself but also the pluralism which it made possible, and at the same time to reinforce its earlier abolition of the annates exacted on the occasion of papal appointments to benefices. The potential consequences of the council's action in abolishing *Exsecrabilis* can best be seen by examining how this constitution had been exploited by canon lawyers and the politically powerful since the early fourteenth century.

[37] In the fifteenth century, the term [canon] common law or *ius commune (canonicum)*, also called the written law or *ius scriptum*, referred to the *Decretum Gratiani*, the *Decretales Gregorii IX*, or *Liber Extra*, the *Liber Sextus Decretalium Bonifacii VIII*, and the *Constitutiones Clementis V* or *Clementinae*, which were collectively regarded as a codified body of [canon] law *(Corpus iuris [canonici] clausum)*, even though the *Decretum Gratiani* was, strictly speaking, only a famous teacher's private compilation. *Not* included were the Decretals which became known after 1500 as the *(Constitutiones) Extravagantes Ioannis XXII* (hence their name), the *Extravagantes (decretales) communes* or other papal constitutions issued after the *Clementinae*. For the development of this aspect of medieval canon law, see Hans Erich Feine, *Kirchliche Rechtsgeschichte. Die katholische Kirche* (Cologne, 1964), 4. "Das klassische kanonische Recht", esp. 26.V "Die Extravagantensammlungen. Das *Corpus iuris canonici*" (pp. 292–294); and Alfons Maria Stickler, *Historia iuris canonici latini; Institutiones academicae, I. Historia fontium* (Turin, 1950), esp. tit. II, c. 8: *De corpore iuris canonici* (pp. 272–276). For a discussion of the Council of Basel's attempt to reform the Latin church by restoring the norms in matters of benefices which had been in effect prior to the popes' residence at Avignon, see Stieber, *Pope Eugenius IV, the Council of Basel*, app. B: "Papal Reservations and Annates in the Fifteenth Century".

[38] The decree *Et quia multiplices* is in *MC* 2:856; and Mansi 29:120.

When Pope John XXII issued the constitution *Exsecrabilis* (19 November 1317), it appeared to be a reform measure since it was directed at plural benefice holding which was already prohibited by earlier papal legislation, though not very effectively since the practice had continued, apparently through dispensations given by bishops at the local level.[39] The novelty and significance of *Exsecrabilis* resided rather in the clauses by which the pope reserved to himself the prerogative of making new appointments to all the benefices which would become vacant as a result of this new prohibition, and in the energy with which Pope John XXII enforced the new constitution, making sure that the Camera Apostolica would also collect annates whenever he granted the benefices to new incumbents. Whatever the original intent of *Exsecrabilis* may have been, its effect over the next one hundred years was *not* to limit plural benefice holding, but rather to make it accessible only to the favored few who could obtain a papal dispensation, as opposed to a dispensation granted by a local bishop as before.[40] Even in its original form, *Exsecrabilis* had never attempted to curb the most egregious pluralists, the cardinals and the sons of kings, who were specifically exempted from its provisions. Next to this top layer of favored pluralists, all clerics who were politically well-connected, but especially canon lawyers,

[39] Boniface VIII had prohibited (1298) the holding of more than one benefice with the care of souls, *Liber sextus decretalium Bonifacii VIII*, liber III, tit. IV, c. 18, in Friedberg 2:1027. On the constitution *Exsecrabilis*, its promulgation and initial use, the best study is still Guillaume Mollat, *La Collation des bénéfices écclesiastiques à l'époque des papes d'Avignon (1305–1378)* (Paris, 1921). On *Exsecrabilis*, see pp. 25–29; on the comparable constitution *Ex debito* (15 September 1316) in which John XXII had reserved to himself the appointment to all bishoprics and abbeys whenever there was a legally moot election, p. 12. For the texts of *Exsecrabilis* and *Ex debito*, see Friedberg 2: 1207–1209 and 1240–1242. There is also an excellent overview by Guillaume Mollat, "Réserve. I Histoire", in *Dictionnaire de Droit Canonique* 7 (Paris, 1965): 635–649.

[40] On the way in which *Exsecrabilis* was used to acquire plural benefices in the 1420's, see François Baix, *La Chambre Apostolique et les "Libri Annatarum" de Martin V (1417–1431)*. Analecta Vaticano–Belgica, 14 (Brussels, 1947–1960), esp. the "Introduction", pp. clxvi–clxxvi.

continued to be in the best position to acquire plural benefices.[41] The overall effect of *Exsecrabilis* was thus not to reduce pluralism but rather to centralize it at the Roman Curia where the necessary dispensations had to be obtained and where annates were, in addition, exacted from all benefices received in this manner.

When the council fathers at Basel abolished the collection of annates and the constitution *Exsecrabilis,* they acted from a widely held perception that *Exsecrabilis* had not limited pluralism as originally intended but had made it worse. As an alternative, they wished to restore self-government to local churches, and to limit the opportunities of the servants of princes, members of the Roman Curia, and canon lawyers everywhere to acquire plural benefices. The efforts of the council fathers at Basel to curb the "execrable ambition" of the pluralists, which Pope John XXII had castigated but not brought under control, reflected a broad critical consensus of the time. The traffic in benefices, even though it was constantly being legalized by papal dispensations, was in fact regarded by many as a thinly disguised form of simony. This is how Jean Gerson had defined it in his widely read *Treatise on Simony* (1415) which insisted that a benefice should only be held by someone who also carried out the incumbent duty or office, and in

[41] A well documented example of a canon lawyer of non–noble origins who , as able to accumulate an extraordinary number of benefices by serving his prince (and himself) is Robert Auclou, *lic. in decr.,* who acquired numerous benefices during his career (first benefices ca. 1420—death in 1452). Auclou held "incompatible" benefices in Paris, Besançon, Bruges, Cambrai, Beaune, Bayeux, and elsewhere. Cf. Baix, *La Chambre Apostolique,* pp. clxxv, 279, n. 1, 434, n. 2, and *passim;* see also the Index to the "Introduction" under "Auclou". There are further references to Auclou and other beneficed clergy who served Duke Philip the Good by helping him consolidate political control through ecclesiastical benefices that included secular jurisdiction in Joseph Toussaint, *Les relations diplomatiques de Philippe le Bon avec le Concile de Bâle (1431–1449)* (Louvain, 1942). In addition to the references to Robert Auclou (pp. 25–26, n. 2, and page 164, n. 2), see those to Jean Germain, the Bishop of Nevers, and to Jean Chevrot, the Bishop of Tournai, who served their prince more than they did the church, and who were both liberally rewarded with plural benefices. It is not surprising that Duke Philip the Good of Burgundy was one of the staunchest supporters of Eugenius IV in resisting the Council of Basel's efforts to abolish the system of papal reservations and dispensations since he, his illegitimate sons, and his servants profited from it so handsomely.

which he critized the exaction of annates as a form of simony.[42] In his quest for plural benefices, Cusanus may have followed a common practice of his day, but it was a practice that was also widely criticized, and one that the Council of Basel had specifically attempted to reform.

It is unlikely that a canonist of Cusanus' intelligence and ambition would long be satisfied with the accumulation of relatively minor benefices of the kind that have been discussed thus far. There stood, however, between Cusanus and higher church office in his native diocese of Trier, and throughout the Empire, the impediment of his non-noble birth. It was most unlikely that he could ever hope to gain admittance to the cathedral chapter of Trier or of any of the other Rhenish bishoprics, let alone be elected bishop since entry was in most cases restricted to those who could prove descent from at least four noble grandparents.[43] To these formal legal bars enshrined in the statutes of the cathedral chapters, one must add the need for influential allies, usually by marriage, among the ruling noble families and territorial princes. Thus when, in one of its earliest reform decrees at its 12th session (13 July 1433), the Council of Basel abolished papal reservations of major elective benefices,[44] it in effect turned the bishoprics and abbeys of Germany even more decisively over to the nobility. Whereas in strong monarchies such as Aragon, France, or England, a king might on occasion prevail upon a cathedral chapter to elect as bishop a commoner

[42] Jean Gerson, *Tractatus de simonia* in *Oeuvres complètes,* intro., text, and notes by [Palémon] Glorieux, 6 (Tournai, 1965): xiv, 167–174 (no. 276), esp. p. 167: "in beneficio, presertim habente cura animarum, sunt hec duo, scilicet officium et beneficium. Beneficium, autem sicut dici solet et verum est, datur propter officium". Earlier in the same treatise, Gerson had insisted that the exaction of annates for granting a benefice, even by the pope, was a form of simony. Gerson therefore implicitly rejected the idea that the pope, on a *regular* basis, could dispense from the law.

[43] The classic study on the privileged role of the nobility in the German church, esp. in the later Middle Ages and the early modern period is Aloys Schulte, *Der Adel und die deutsche Kirche im Mittelalter . . . und Nachtrag zur zweiten Auflage 1922* (Stuttgart, 1910 and 1922; reprint Amsterdam, 1966). Of particular importance for Trier and the Rhineland: Wilhelm Kisky, *Die Domkapitel der geistlichen Kurfürsten in ihrer persönlichen Zusammensetzung im vierzehnten und fünfzehnten Jahrhundert* (Weimar, 1906). For a listing and discussion of the older literature, see Albert Werminghoff, "Ständische Probleme in der Geschichte der deutschen Kirche des Mittelalters", *Zeitschrift der Savigny–Stiftung für Rechtsgeschichte,* 32 [=*Kanonistische Abteilung* 1] (1911): 33–67; and also Stieber, *Pope Eugenius IV, the Council of Basel,* p. 319, n. 78.

[44] For the decree *Sicut in construenda* of the 12th session, see *MC* 2: 402–405; and Mansi 29:61–64.

who had served him well, this was very rare in the Empire and particularly unlikely in the native region of Cusanus. Only through papal reservations and appointment, based on the pope's claim to be the successor of St. Peter, on his power as *sacer princeps* as Cusanus had put it, could aristocratic privilege in the church be overruled. On the rare occasions when non-nobles had been promoted to the higher dignities in the German church, it had usually been through papal provision. Should one be surprised that in 1436/1437 Cusanus took the side of the papacy which claimed the right to set aside existing laws and to correct all Christians, kings and nobles included? In light of this, it does not seem far-fetched to compare Cusanus, the ambitious commoner and canon lawyer in the fifteenth century, with jurists from the middle classes in the sixteenth through eighteenth centuries who devoted their careers to the service of kings and princes, assisting them in building monarchies that were less constrained by the power and privileges of the nobility. It is a point to which we shall later return.

When Cusanus decided in December 1436 to vote with the papal minority in favor of a council of union in Italy, a decision he confirmed in May 1437 by agreeing to carry the minority decree to the pope for confirmation, and thence to the Greeks, the reasons for his decision were probably complex. Even if his career opportunities as a canon lawyer were more favorable if absolute papal monarchy would triumph, such a papal victory could not have been predicted with certainty in May 1437. Eugenius IV, after all, had lost his first confrontation with the Council of Basel in which the secular princes and the prelates of Latin Christendom had supported the general council. Cusanus knew that if the council won, he stood to lose the benefices he had acquired and, in fact, he lost some of his benefices in Germany during the 1440's. His decision represented a calculated risk requiring courage that may have been based on worldly ambition to be sure, but probably also on a genuine commitment to a hierarchical view of the nature and government of the church. Here his material interests, his professional training as a canon lawyer, and his orientation as a religious thinker pointed in the same direction.

Having decided to support Eugenius IV, Cusanus became one of the pope's ablest defenders in Germany where at the imperial diets of the 1440's he pleaded with the German princes to abandon their neutrality in the church conflict. During these years Cusanus fully lived up to the epithet, "Hercules of the Eugenians", which Aeneas Sylvius had bestowed upon him in 1440.[45] There is no need to rehearse here how the Roman Curia eventually undermined the Council of Basel in the Empire by offering an advantageous settlement to Emperor Frederick III and his political allies culminating in the German Concordat of 1448.[46]   In most of the meetings of princes and imperial diets of this decade Cusanus defended the pope's case not only in extensive public debates conducted in Latin where he displayed his skill in arguments drawn from canon law, but also in private negotiations with the princes and their councillors, conducted in German. Cusanus played a particularly important role in the crucial meeting at Frankfurt in September/October 1446. During the meeting the pope's envoys were able to split the united front of the German princes against Eugenius IV, making possible his full recognition as pope by Frederick III in early February 1447.[47]   Having almost achieved victory, Eugenius died a few weeks later, leaving his succesor Pope Nicholas V to reap the fruits of the papacy's diplomatic triumph which Cusanus had done so much to bring about.

The victory of Eugenius IV over the Council of Basel in Germany had not been won on the strength of the theological and legal arguments offered on the pope's behalf, but rather by offers of specific material advantages to a party of the German princes.   In fact, there is every indication that the majority of the German clergy still supported the Council of Basel and its reform decrees in 1446. Against all these odds, the papacy and its determined champions had prevailed. On 16 December 1446, a grateful Pope Eugenius rewarded his three principal negotiators at Frankfurt by naming them cardinals: Tommaso Parentucelli, then Bishop of Bologna, Juan de Carvajal, then Bishop of Plasencia, and Nicholas of Cusa, then Archdeacon of Brabant in Liège.[48]   The pope did not, however, make the elevation of Cusanus public before his own death, presumably because he did not wish to incense the anti-papal party in the Empire before the completion of the

---

[45] Aeneas Sylvius Piccolomini, the future Pope Pius II, was the first to call Cusanus "the Hercules of all the Eugenians", apparently for the first time in 1440: Pius II, *De gestis concilii Basiliensis commentariorum libri II*, ed. and trans. Denys Hay and W.K. Smith (Oxford, 1967), pp. 14-15. Since the *Gesta* were written between November 1439 and July 1440 ("Intro.", p. xxviii), they indicate that Cusanus stood out, already by 1440, as a decided partisan of Eugenius IV.

[46] These developments are examined in Stieber, *Pope Eugenius IV, the Council of Basel*, chap. 3–10.

[47] On the negotiations at Frankfurt in September/October 1446, their antecedents and the resulting settlement, see *ibid.*, pp. 278–302. See also the documents published in *Acta Cusana*, I,2:524–536 (no. 705–721).

[48] *Acta Cusana* I,2:539 (no. 727).

negotiations that would return all of Germany to the papal obedience. Fortunately for Cusanus, he was on the best personal terms with the new pope Nicholas V who only recently, as Tommaso Parentucelli, had been his colleague in the negotiations at Frankfurt. Therefore, once the church conflict had definitely been settled in the Empire through the German Concordat, Nicholas V elevated Nicholas of Cusa as a cardinal on 28 December 1448.[49]

With his elevation, Cusanus had reached a station which neither he nor anyone in his family would originally have dared aspire to. In the church, it immediately raised him above all the cathedral canons and bishops from whose closed corporations his non-noble birth excluded him. As a cardinal of the Roman church, he would have his share in the administration of the papal plenitude of power that he had defended and with which as a canon lawyer he was thoroughly familiar. The sense of personal vindication that he felt is evident in the short autobiographical statement composed in October 1449 on the occasion of a visit to his old father in Kues. After naming, in the third person, his parents and place of birth, Cusanus briefly records his doctorate in canon law at the age of 22 and his voyage to Constantinople at the age of 37 in order to bring the bishops of all the Eastern church to the council in Florence. After emphasizing that "this Nicholas defended Eugenius", he relates how the pope secretly elevated him as a cardinal and then suddenly died, and how Pope Nicholas V again elevated him as a cardinal, publicly announcing it in 1449. The statement concludes: "And indeed, the cardinal himself has ordered this account to be written to the glory of God so that all may know that the holy Roman church does not pay heed to place of birth or ancestry but is a most generous rewarder of virtuous and courageous deeds".[50]   Given this autobiographical perspective on Cusanus' career, it would be mistaken not to take very seriously his pride in his doctorate in canon law, and his sense that the Roman church would reward those who serve her, regardless of social status. It seems reasonable to suppose that hopes or expectations of this nature did play their part in his decision when, as the future "Hercules of the

---

[49] Cf. the cordial personal letter of Pope Nicholas V announcing the elevation to Nicholas of Cusa in *Acta Cusana* I,2:571-572 (no. 784).

[50] "Et ut scient cuncti sanctam Romanam ecclesiam non respicere ad locum vel genus nativitatis, sed esse largissimam remuneratricem virtutum, hinc hanc historiam in dei laudem iussit scribi ipse cardinalis . . ." The best edition of the brief autobiography: *Acta Cusana* I,2:602-603 (no. 849).

Eugenians", he stood at the crossroads in 1436/1437.[51]

Two major episodes in Cusanus' subsequent career, his "great legation" to Germany in 1451-1452 and his tenure as Bishop of Brixen, shed further light on the personal qualities and interests that affected his decision. Although Cusanus undertook his legation before turning his attention to his new diocese, his appointment as Bishop of Brixen preceded his legation and indirectly illumines it.[52] Pope Nicholas' appointment of Cusanus on 23 March 1450 as [Prince-]Bishop of Brixen has been described, with some justification, as a provocation.[53] With this unilateral action the pope violated not only the German Concordat in which he had agreed two years earlier to respect the right of the cathedral chapters in the Empire to elect their own bishops, but also disregarded a specific promise to Frederick III to consider his wishes in the selection of the next Bishop of Brixen. Moreover, the pope had acted without consulting the cathedral chapter of Brixen which had canonically elected as bishop one of its members who was, at the same time, the chancellor of Duke Sigismund in the nearby County of Tyrol.[54] There can be little doubt that Cusanus was a better qualified candidate, but this did not change the fact that he was being

[51] The image of "Hercules at the Crossroads", a topos familiar to Renaissance humanists, suggests itself since Aeneas Sylvius had bestowed the epithet "Hercules of the Eugenians" on Cusanus as early as 1440 (cf. n. 43 above). On the topos, see: Erwin Panofsky, *Hercules am Scheidewege und andere antike Bildstoffe in der neueren Kunst*. Studien der Bibliothek Warburg, 18 (Leipzig, 1930).

[52] For a recent, balanced study of Cusanus as Prince-Bishop of Brixen, see Wilhelm Baum, *Nikolaus Cusanus in Tirol: Das Wirken des Philosophen und Reformators als Fürstbischof von Brixen* (Bozen, 1983). See also, in English, Morimichi Watanabe, "Nicholas of Cusa and the Tyrolese Monasteries: Reform and Resistance", *History of Political Thought* 7 (1986): 53-72, and Pardon E. Tillinghast, "Nicholas of Cusa vs. Sigmund of Habsburg: An Attempt at Post-Conciliar Church Reform", *Church History* 36 (1967): 371-390. Watanabe gives an excellent overview of the literature on Cusanus as Bishop of Brixen. Both Watanabe and Tillinghast speak of Cusanus' reform efforts in his diocese but do not define his efforts in terms of religious or political motives, expecially with regard to his outlook and training as a canon lawyer.

[53] The letters of Nicholas V naming Cusanus as Bishop of Brixen and notifying Duke Sigismund of the nomination: *Acta Cusana* I,2:617-620 (no. 872-878). It was Hermann Hallauer who used the term "provocation" in describing the pope's nomination: *Die Schlacht im Enneberg: Neue Quellen zur moralischen Wertung des Nikolaus von Kues* (Trier, 1969), p. 5.

[54] On the election of the canon Leonhard Wiesmair, Duke Sigismund's chancellor, see Baum, *Nikolaus Cusanus in Tirol*, pp. 86-88. Baum's biography includes extensive references not only to older literature but also to unpublished archival sources, many of which will presumably be published in *Acta Cusana* II.

appointed in violation of the German Concordat and the reform decrees of the Council of Basel. In spite of all this, the pope was in fact able to force the cathedral chapter of Brixen and the neighboring Duke Sigismund to accept Cusanus as prince-bishop. On a wider stage, the pattern of Cusanus' career established in the 1430's was thus continuing, since he was winning preferment in the church through papal dispensation, in violation of the [canon] common law.

Erich Meuthen's recent study of Cusanus' legation has added many details to our understanding of this event.[55] Two observations may perhaps be added from the standpoint of this inquiry. By singling out as the two principal tasks of his legate, the promulgation of the papal jubilee indulgence of 1450 and the holding of reform synods, Nicholas V emphasized that the pope, not a general council, was the supreme authority in the church in conferring spiritual benefits and also in carrying out reform. There was a noticeable contrast between the large crowds of curious and eager German laymen and laywomen who greeted Cusanus during his legation and the undisguised hostility with which he was met at synods and gatherings of the German clergy. To the former, he appeared as a rare curiosity: a German cardinal who had risen from humble beginnings to one of the highest offices in the church.[56] To the latter, he still appeared as the

---

[55] Still useful is the itinerary of the legation published by Josef Koch, "Nikolaus von Cues und seine Umwelt", pp. 116-152 (cf. n. 5 above). Based on the forthcoming *Acta Cusana* I:3, Erich Meuthen has contributed a study which focuses heavily on Cusanus' publication of reform decrees during his legation: "Die deutsche Legationsreise des Nikolaus von Kues 1451/1452", *Lebenslehren und Weltentwürfe im Übergang vom Mittelalter zur Neuzeit: Politik - Bildung - Naturkunde - Theologie*, ed. Hartmut Boockmann, Bernd Moeller, and Karl Stackmann, rev. Ludger Grenzmann (Göttingen, 1989), pp. 421-499. For a discussion of the legation and references to the older literature, see also Stieber, *Pope Eugenius IV, the Council of Basel*, pp. 340-341.

[56] Two voices, symptomatic of the clerical dissent, may be cited: first, that of the Carthusian Vinzenz of Aggsbach who continued to see in Cusanus not a reforming papal legate but an opponent of the reforms of the Council of Basel. Cf. his letter, dated ca. February-March 1451, in Bernhard Pez and Philibert Hueber, *Codex diplomatico - epistolaris [= Thesaurus anecdotorum novissimus, 6]* (Augsburg, 1729), pp. 327-328; second, the *Avisamentum* prepared by the Dominican Hermann Talheim for submission to the diocesan synod of Mainz, dated ca. November-December 1451, which criticized the legate's claim to reform the church by delegated papal authority instead of relying on the authority of general councils, in Hermann Hallauer, "Zur Mainzer Provinzialsynode von 1451", *MFCG* 13 (1978): 253-263.

"Hercules of the Eugenians" who had undermined the Council of Basel's reforms and who continued to act as an agent of the Roman Curia which sought once more to exploit the German church through the control of taxation of clerical benefices and through other forms of papal judicial intervention.[57]

In his career as Bishop of Brixen which began in earnest in 1452 some of the same factors that had influenced his fundamental decision in 1436/ 1437 again played a role. Of particular importance was to be his hierarchical and absolutist, rather than consent-oriented, conception of authority in the church which was closely linked with the rigor and formalism of his training as a canon lawyer. At the same time, his social status as a commoner in a world dominated politically by a nobility which resented the hard-working habits and calculated demands of a merchant's son and outsider were to contribute to his political difficulties. The efforts of Cusanus as prince-bishop to recover secular rights of jurisdiction which had not been fully exercised for centuries--like his attempt to secure control of mining rights by asking the Emperor in 1452 to confirm privileges that had originally been granted in 1217--have often been characterized as outmoded and "not in keeping with the tendency of the times", since they failed to recognize the "rising" power of the secular territorial princes such as Duke Sigismund.[58]   Yet the fact that Cusanus sought to win back old feudal

---

[57] While many critics of the papacy in Germany tended to be clerics, the same group that eventually formulated the catalogue of complaints known as the "Gravamina of the German Nation against Rome", a few were also university-educated laymen such as the jurist Gregor Heimburg who criticized both Pius II and Cusanus for having turned against the Council of Basel and its reforms. On Heimburg, see the biography by Paul Joachimsohn, *Gregor Heimburg* (Bamberg, 1891), to be supplemented by the entry "Heimburg, Gregor" by Walter Kaemmerer, *Neue Deutsche Biographie* 8 (Berlin, 1969): 274-275.

[58] Hermann Hallauer writes, "Andererseits gibt die Tatsache, dass er mit seiner zähen Restaurationspolitik nicht den Zug der Zeit erkannte, zu denken. . . . Wenigstens in seinem politischen und kirchenpolitischen Denken war Nikolaus von Kues noch ganz ein mittelalterlicher Mensch": "Eine Denkschrift des Nikolaus von Kues zum Kauf der Ämter Taufers und Uttenheim in Südtirol", *MFCG* 1 (1961): 76-94, here 81. Nikolaus Grass cites this interpretation with approval in "Cusanus als Rechtshistoriker, Quellenkritiker und Jurist", *Cusanus Gedächtnisschrift im Auftrag der Rechts- und Staatswissenschaaftlichen Fakultät der Universität Innsbruck,* ed. idem (Innsbruck, 1970), pp. 102-210, here p. 136.

rights as a secular overlord was not necessarily outmoded.[59]   A typical
German bishop of the thirteenth century would probably have organized a
military expedition to recover lapsed rights. Instead, Cusanus acted as a
canon lawyer when he exploited legal precedents and as a calculating
entrepeneur when he sought to recover lost revenues. Both as a reformer of
ecclesiastical discipline and spiritual life, and as a prince-bishop, Cusanus
anticipated the policies of the reforming prince-bishops of the era of Roman
Catholic Reform and Counter-Reformation. His efforts to reassert the
superior jurisdiction of the Prince-Bishop of Brixen may be likened to the
attempt of princes in the later sixteenth century to strengthen their
supremacy of jurisdiction which manifested itself in the simultaneous
imposition of discipline and "order" in the religious, political, and social
realms.[60]

[59] Cf. Baum, *Nikolaus Cusanus*, chap. 5: "Cusanus als weltlicher Landesfürst
in Tirol", pp. 291-328, for a good overview of Cusanus' efforts to reassert his
old rights of lordship as prince-bishop. See also: *Cusanus-Texte*, V. *Brixener
Dokumente*, Erste Sammlung: *Akten zur Reform des Bistums Brixen.*
Herausgegeben von Heinz Hürten. Sitzungsberichte der Heidelberger Akademie
der Wissenschaften. Philosophisch-historische Klasse. 2. Abhandlung
(Heidelberg, 1960). Hürten comments (*op cit.*, pp. 49-50) on the "Old Testament
severity" of Cusanus' demands for full payment of the tithes even in years of bad
harvests, noting that he must have personally endorsed such rigorous
application of the relevant texts from the *Decretum Gratiani*, C. XVI, qu. 1, cc.
65-66 (Friedberg, I, coll. 783-784). This is but one more example of the strong
influence of canon law on Cusanus' outlook on church government.

[60] Only a few references to the extensive literature on the intertwined
processes of confessional politics and state-building, the imposition of
religious and social discipline, the use of lawyer-bureaucrats and of military
force, in the period 1550-1650, can be given here: Wolfgang Reinhard,
"Reformation, Counter-Reformation, and the Early Modern State: A
Reassessment", *The Catholic Historical Review* 75 (1989): 383-404; also
earlier: "Gegenreformation als Modernisierung? Prolegomena zu einer Theorie
des konfessionellen Zeitalters", *Archiv für Reformationsgeschichte* 68 (1977):
226-252; and "Zwang zur Konfessionalisierung? Prolegomena zur einer Theorie
des konfessionellen Zeitalters", *Zeitschrift für Historische Forschung* 10 (1983):
257-277. For an intro. to the financial and political aspects, see Hermann
Kellenbenz and Paolo Prodi, eds., *Fisco, religione, Stato nell' età
confessionale.* Annali dell' Instituto Storico Italo-Germanico in Trento.
Quaderni, 26 (Bologna, 1989). The processes described here from the
perspective of formal legal and political history have been placed in their broad
context of social and economic change in the excellent survey by Richard van
Dülmen, *Entstehung des frühneuzeitlichen Europa, 1550-1648* (Frankfurt, 1982),
esp. chap. 2:vi-vii and 4:ii-v on the "Society of Estates" and the "Early Modern
State", pp. 158-192 and 333-367.

NICHOLAS OF CUSA'S DECISION FOR THE POPE   249

Cusanus' simultaneous assertion of his powers as prince and bishop in his diocese of Brixen, especially his assertion of overlordship, was fully in keeping with the hierarchical conception of government in the church he had defended since 1437, and which we encountered in his writings of 1440-1441. We can go even further and note that Cusanus' training as a canon lawyer which had taught him to look upon all law as emanating from an absolute, divinely ordained source, the supreme pontiff, clearly influenced his approach to government as a prince-bishop. In short, Cusanus' outlook and his conduct illustrate Max Weber's observation that in Latin Christendom canon law and the government of the church served as guides and models of rationality for secular law and governmental practice.[61] Weber's astute observation, based on the historical legal scholarship of his day, has been amply substantiated over the subsequent decades. In particular, the role of the supreme pontiff as the first "sovereign" of Latin Christendom who claimed the power, as a free or absolute prince, to make new law or to amend and codify existing law, and to impose it on all, has been repeatedly and amply explored and demonstrated.[62] Canon lawyers and jurists trained in Roman law who served in the chanceries of secular and spiritual princes from the late fifteenth through the seventeenth centuries played a major role in bringing about this intellectual and political, and ultimately also social,

[61] Max Weber, *Wirtschaft und Gesellschaft, Grundriss der verstehenden Soziologie* (Tübingen, 1972), pp. 480-481; English trans., *Economy and Society, an Outline of Interpretative Sociology*, ed. Guenther Roth and Claus Wittich (Berkeley, California, 1968), 2:828-830.

[62] Dieter Wyduckel, *Ius Publicum: Grundlagen und Entwicklung des Öffentlichen Rechts und der deutschen Staatsrechtswissenschaft* (Berlin, 1984), 3: "Der Anteil des kanonischen Rechts an der Ausbildung staatlicher Rechsstrukturen", pp. 91-110; idem: *Princeps Legibus Solutus: Eine Untersuchung zur frühmodernen Rechts- und Staatslehre* (Berlin, 1979), esp. 4: "*Plenitudo potestatis* und absolute Herrschaftsgewalt in der Kanonistik", pp. 88-104. Wyduckel does not see in canon law the *only* source of princely absolutism, and points also to the role of Roman law and strong kings who were effective feudal suzerains in the development of the theory and practice of princely absolutism. For an account of the growth of the idea of sovereignty based largely on developments in secular law, see Helmut Quaritsch, *Souveränität: Entstehung und Entwicklung des Begriffs in Frankreich und Deutschland vom 13. Jahrhundert bis 1806* (Berlin, 1986).

transformation.[63]   Cusanus' efforts as well as his failures as Prince-Bishop of Brixen should be judged from this perspective. Seen in this light, he appears, as does most of his religious and philosophical thought, as neither entirely "medieval" nor entirely "modern", thus challenging our tendency toward an overly simplistic use of such period designations or categories.

A few selected incidents must suffice as illustrations of the thesis that Cusanus governed as prince-bishop in a manner influenced by conceptions of jurisdictional supremacy derived from canon law. The term "jurisdictional supremacy" is used in preference to "sovereignty" since the modern concept of sovereignty, as a synonym for the combined supreme executive, judicial, *and* legislative power, did not gain currency until the seventeenth century, a generation after it had been coined by Jean Bodin in his *Six livres de la République* (1576) in which sovereignty had first been defined in this sense.[64]   In his well-known conflict with Verena von Stuben, the Abbess of the Benedictine nuns of Sonnenberg, Cusanus exploited his traditional right to enforce monastic discipline to the fullest extent. Although his intervention could be justified on the ground of religious reform, Cusanus pursued it with a vigor which testifies to his determination to use the occasion to enforce his jurisdiction as a matter of general principle.[65]   This is even more true of his conflict with the Abbot Georg of the Cistercian Abbey of Stams where the issue was almost entirely one of asserting his superior jurisdiction

---

[63] On the role of jurists, many of them trained *in utroque iure,* in the development of the early modern state, see *Diritto e Potere nella Storia Europea: Atti in onore di Bruno Paradisi,* 2 vols. (Florence, 1982), esp. 1: Jean Gaudemet, "La contribution des romanistes et des canonistes médiévaux à la théorie moderne de l'État", pp. 1-36. See also Roman Schnur, ed., *Die Rolle der Juristen bei der Entstehung des modernen Staates* (Berlin, 1986). The studies in this volume, however, make it evident that not *all* jurists were promoters of absolute princely power. Among the opponents of absolute princely power, note in particular François Hotman, the author of the *Franco-Gallia* (1576) and Johannes Althusius, the author of the *Politica methodice digesta* (1614). On Althusius, see *Politische Theorie des Althusius,* ed. Karl-Wilhelm Dahm, W. Krawietz, D. Wyduckel (Berlin, 1988). On the process of late sixteenth-century "state building" from a social-historical rather than a legal-historical perspective, see the excellent study by Gerald Strauss, *Law, Resistance, and the State: The Opposition to Roman Law in Reformation Germany* (Princeton, 1986), esp. 5: "Law and Politics: The New State", and 6: "Careers and Social Place: Lawyers as a Class", pp. 136-190.

[64] Cf. the excellent study by Quaritsch, *Souveränität* (n. 58 above) which supersedes all previous studies on this question.

[65] Hermann Hallauer stresses genuine religious concerns: "Eine Visitation des Nikolaus von Kues im Benediktinerinnenkloster Sonnenberg", *MFCG* 4 (1964): 104-119.

as bishop since Cusanus had excommunicated the Abbot not because he had resisted religious reform, but because he had failed to attend the third and fourth diocesan synods conducted by Cusanus in 1456 and 1457.[66]   In excommunicating the Abbot of Stams, Cusanus went beyond the bounds of political prudence since the Cistercian abbey had traditionally been exempt from episcopal jurisdiction. Cusanus' desire to extend his jurisdictional supremacy in this instance calls to mind the comparable conduct of seventeenth-century princes. As it turned out, the Abbot of Stams success- fully appealed the issue to Pope Calixtus III, and Cusanus had to rescind his excommunication, suffering a considerable loss of prestige.

In his relations with his cathedral chapter at Brixen Cusanus' manner of government was autocratic and very much out of keeping with local traditions. Most members of the cathedral chapter hailed from noble families of the region. Moreover, it had become customary by the early fifteenth century that before proceeding to the election of a new bishop, each cathedral canon had to swear that, in the case of his election as bishop, he would adhere to an electoral capitulation which precisely regulated the powers of the bishop in his relations with the chapter. After receiving confirmation of his election, each new bishop was then expected to reiterate the promise he had made before his election.[67]   In short, the cathedral chapter was ac- customed to constitutional, not autocratic, government of the prince- bishopric. From the start, Cusanus was the outsider, replacing the cathedral chapter's choice of a bishop from within its own ranks. Moreover, since Cusanus had been named by the pope, he never swore to uphold the capitulation, and the only limits placed on his government were those defined in [canon] common law. As his subsequent actions were to show, Cusanus intended to model his style of government as prince-bishop on that of the pope. Having personally rejected the Council of Basel's attempt to impose an electoral promise or capitulation on the supreme pontiff, he

[66] On the relations of Cusanus with the Abbot of Stams, see Baum, *Nikolaus Cusanus in Tirol*, chap. 4.7: "Cusanus exkommuniziert den Abt von Stams", pp. 150-163.

[67] On the social composition of the cathedral chapter, see Leo Santifaller, *Das Brixner Domkapitel in seiner persönlichen Zusammensetzung im Mittelalter* [= *Schlern-Schriften*, 7] (Innsbruck, 1924-1925).   On the electoral capitulations of the prince-bishop, see Karl Wolfsgruber, "Die Wahlkapitulationen der Fürstbischöfe von Brixen (1418-1601)", *Festschrift zur Feier des zweihundertjährigen Bestandes des Haus-, Hof- und Staatsarchivs* 2 (Wien, 1951): 226-244.   The only capitulation surviving from the period just prior to Cusanus at Brixen is that of 1427 (pp. 226-227).   On the capitulations on the internal government of the cathedral chapter, see Leo Santifaller, "Gli Statuti del Capitolo della Cattedrale di Bressanone nel Medio Evo", *Archivio per l'Alto Adige* 22 (1927): 5-108.

would surely also resist any attempt to limit his own freedom of action as prince-bishop. The importance of the traditional capitulations at Brixen resided not only in their specific provisions, but also in their character as a symbol of constitutional government--and it is not surprising that the canons at Brixen had supported the Council of Basel throughout the 1440's.

Given the fundamental difference in political outlook between the cathedral chapter at Brixen and its new prince-bishop, it was only a matter of time before conflict would arise. Cusanus' fundamental lack of respect for the interests of his cathedral canons became evident when he insisted that his nephew, Simon von Wehlen, also an outsider from the Moselle valley, be given a position in the cathedral chapter. Cusanus insisted that his nephew should receive the canonry held by Leonhard Wiesmair, even if the latter should not succeed in establishing himself as Bishop of Chur.[68]   For Cusanus, the interests of his young nephew took precedence over those of a senior member of the chapter. By 1462, even some canons who had been brought into the chapter at Cusanus' urging had joined all the other canons in opposing their bishop whom some of them openly called a tyrant. Cusanus' style of government was resented by his cathedral canons precisely because it was in some ways not "medieval". For it could be argued that royal or princely government in later medieval Europe was by and large a government of limited princely power in which the counsel and consent of the nobility played a major role. Cusanus' government, reflecting his preference for hierarchy and the political traditions of canon law, tended to be autocratic.[69]   In its style, it looked forward to the prince-bishops of the era of Roman Catholic Reform and Counter-Reformation, and it particularly resembled the aims and efforts of the later sixteenth century popes who sought to give the Papal States a more modern form of government in order to assure increased revenues for their absolute ruler.

As Paolo Prodi has shown, the ideological roots of such a reorganization of the Papal States along the lines of absolute government were to be found in the idea of a papal plenitude of power originally elaborated by

---

[68] On the relations of Cusanus with his cathedral chapter, see Baum, *Nikolaus Cusanus in Tirol*, chap. 4.10: "Konflikte mit dem Domkapitel", pp. 223-237.

[69] This is not to deny that there was also within medieval canon law a tradition that upheld due procedure in judicial and governmental practice, but this represented a merely procedural and subsidiary strain since, as long as there was a legitimate pope, his power in matters of *discipline* was almost unlimited. The best case for the constitutional rather than absolutist tendencies within medieval canon law had been made by Brian Tierney, *Foundations of the Conciliar Theory: The Contributions of the Medieval Canonists from Gratian to the Great Schism* (Cambridge, England, 1955).

medieval canon lawyers.[69]   The transformation of the papal court from that of a bishop to that of a prince had already started with the popes of the Renaissance. Beginning with Nicholas V, the popes deliberately reaffirmed the hierocratic claims of their medieval predecessors, in part as a conscious response to the recent conciliarist challenge.[70]   Cusanus' reign as Prince-Bishop of Brixen should also be seen in the context of this ideological counter-offensive of the Renaissance papacy. From this perspective, his governmental program as prince-bishop looks much less "medieval" and seems indeed to mirror the "spirit of his times". Cusanus' failure as a Prince-Bishop of Brixen must be attributed, not to the fact that his aims were too "medieval", but rather to the fact that they were perhaps too "modern". In addition, one has to consider the personal factor of Cusanus' inability to work constructively with the traditionally dominant groups of his diocese, especially the cathedral chapter of Brixen.

Cusanus' fundamental indifference to the role of the cathedral chapter in governing his prince-bishopric is evident in his secret negotiations with the Wittelsbach Dukes Albrecht III of Bavaria at Munich (1438-1460) and Ludwig IX of Bavaria at Landshut (1450-1479) and their allied cousins, the Counts Palatine at Mosbach-Neumarkt Otto I (1410-1461) and his son Otto II (1461-1490), with whom he explored the possibility of having a Wittelsbach prince succeed Cusanus as Bishop of Brixen.[71] This project, which came to nothing, totally disregarded the traditional role of the cathedral chapter in the government of the diocese and the election of the bishop. It was clearly Cusanus' hope that a prince from the House of Wittelsbach might obtain sufficient political support from his relatives to

[69] Paolo Prodi, *Il Sovrano Pontefice* (Bologna, 1982); English trans., *The Papal Prince: One Body and Two Souls: The Papal Monarchy in Early Modern Europe* (Cambridge, 1987), esp. chap. 1: "A New Monarchy   . . .", and 2: "The Sovereign: Prince and Pastor", pp. 17-36.

[70] On the climate of opinion at the papal court in the decades after the Council of Basel, see Hubert Jedin, *A History of the Council of Trent* 1 (Edinburgh, 1957 [original publication in German, 1949]), chap. 3: "The Papal Reaction".   See also Charles L. Stinger, *The Renaissance in Rome* (Bloomington, Indiana, 1985) where the close links between the papal hierocratic claims and papal artistic patronage are emphasized. Not all these aspects of the Renaissance in Rome would probably have found Cusanus' approval.

[71] Baum, *Nikolaus Cusanus in Tirol,* chap. 5.2: "Bündnispolitik mit dem Wittelsbachern", pp. 328-344, gives extensive quotations in translations from unpublished memoranda in which Cusanus set forth his projects. See also for a number of clarifications, Erich Meuthen, "Nikolaus von Kues und die Wittelsbacher", *Festschrift für Andreas Kraus zum 60. Geburtstag,* ed. Prankraz Fried and Walter Ziegler (Kallmünz, 1982), pp. 95-113.

enable him to disregard the political power of the local nobility of the
diocese of Brixen, both in the cathedral chapter and outside it. In this
context, Cusanus must have thought especially of Duke Sigismund of the
Tyrol whom one can also regard as a nobleman rather than an incarnation of
the early modern "state".[72] Cusanus' unrealized project of a Wittelsbach
prince as the savior of the threatened rights of the prince-bishopric of Brixen
cannot fail to bring to mind that Wittelsbach princes were to play precisely
such a role at the end of the sixteenth century in the dioceses of Cologne and
Münster where they provided the political support which made possible the
full restoration of Catholicism in those ecclesiastical principalities.[73]   The
modern parallels to Cusanus' project of a Wittelsbach prince as his successor
in Brixen should not be exaggerated, yet this plan once again suggests that
one should not characterize his church politics as exclusively "medieval", for
they included conceptions of church reform and secular government that were
to shape not only Roman Catholic Reform but also secular politics in the
later sixteenth century.

    Taking as our vantage points the year 1449, when he composed his
autobiographical statement at Kues, and the 1450's when he reigned as
Prince-Bishop of Brixen, Nicholas of Cusa's fundamental decision of 1436/
1437 appears almost inevitable. Philosophical and theological considerations undoubtedly played a part, especially his interest in ideas of hierarchy,
but it also seems plausible that for a canon lawyer and a commoner, the
familiar governmental structure of a church dominated by the pope may well
have looked more appealing than the reform program of the Council of
Basel. After he had made his decision, it may, in part, have become a case
of an ever-deepening commitment to a chosen course. What distinguishes
Cusanus is the extent to which he combined the *vita activa* of a canon
lawyer involved in church politics with the *vita contemplativa* of a religious
thinker and philosopher. The breadth of his interests was reflected in his
extensive library, much of it still housed today at Kues, where codices of the
Bible and the church fathers, including the complete works of Pseudo-
Dionysius, but also numerous codices of mathematical and astronomical
treatises, are found alongside a substantial collection of fifty-five volumes

---

[72] From a conceptual standpoint, this is one of the debatable aspects of
Albert Jäger's classic study of Duke Sigismund's relations with Cusanus. See in
particular *Geschichte der landständischen Verfassung Tirols* 2 (Innsbruck, 1885;
reprint Aalen, 1970), esp. pt. 2: "Die Blütezeit der Landstände Tirols . . . 1439-
1519", pp. 134-149.

[73] The Wittelsbach prince Ernest held in the 1580's and 1590's
simultaneously the sees of Liège, Cologne, and Münster, and was succeeded by
other Wittelsbach princes at Cologne. Cf. the chap. by Franz Petri in
Rheinische Geschichte 2: *Neuzeit* (Düsseldorf, 1976), pp. 91-101, with
extensive references to the older literature.

on canon law.[74] For Cusanus the phrase "building up the church" (*ad aedificationem ecclesiae*) which he had once invoked as a key concept in justifying papal power held throughout his career a material as well as a spiritual meaning. While Cusanus has been honored modern times primarily as a religious thinker and philosopher whose spiritual writings are seemingly above the church politics of the day, it is well to remember that his life was marked by political partisanship, as he labored, a veritable Christian Hercules, on behalf of the *ecclesia militans*.

[74] Jakob Marx, *Verzeichnis der Handschriften-Sammlung des Hospitals zu Cues* (Trier, 1905; reprint Frankfurt-am-Main[p, 1966). Sec. 10 on canon law, pp. 229-268, lists 55 codices, a number of them with marginal annotations by Cusanus. See also Krchnák, "Die kanonistischen Aufzeichnungen des Nikolaus von Kues" (n. 29 above). Most, but not all, of Cusanus' library is today at the St. Nikolaus-Hospital in Kues. For a list of the manuscripts owned by Nicholas of Cusa which he left in his last will to the hospital in Kues, see Giovanni Mantese, "Ein notarielles Inventar von Büchern und Wertgegenständen aus dem Nachlass des Nikolaus von Kues", *MFCG* 2 (1962): 85-116. Most of the manuscripts listed in summary form in Cusanus' testament are still at Kues, but others found their way (mainly between 1717 and 1722) into libraries in London, Oxford, and Brussels. For the Cusanus codices now in the British Library in London and in the Bodleian Library at Oxford, see *MFCG* 3 (1963): 16-108; 5 (1965): 137-161; 7 (1969): 146-157; 8 (1970): 199-237; 10 (1973): 58-103; 12 (1977): 15-71; 15 (1982): 43-56; 17 (1986): 21-56. See in particular the last article by Hermann J. Hallauer for an account of the substantial purchases of manuscripts from the library at Kues between 1717 and 1722 on behalf of Robert Harley, Earl of Oxford. The Harleian codices of the British Library in London contain, in the main, ancient Greek and Latin authors, church fathers, medieval writers on theology, natural history and mathematics, and Renaissance commentaries. Only one of them (Codex Harleianus 3710, described in *MFCG* 12 (1977): 44-58), contains a work on law (a Commentary on the Decretals of Gregory IX, with annotations by Nicholas of Cusa). For manuscripts formerly in the St. Nikolaus-Hospital at Kues which are now in the Bibliothèque Royale in Brussels, see *MFCG* 4 (1964): 323-335; 7 (1969): 129-145; 14 (1980): 182-197. Of the Brussels manuscripts, only one (Codex Bruxellensis, 3819-20), contains material pertaining to canon law.

APPENDICES

NICHOLAS OF CUSA:

THE LITERATURE IN ENGLISH THROUGH 1988

Thomas M. Izbicki

Nicholas of Cusa's works received sporadic attention in England during Tudor and Stuart times. The portion of *De concordantia catholica* dealing with the Donation of Constantine was translated into English and published during the reign of Henry VIII. The translation was one of several works potentially subversive of papalist pretensions rendered into English to support the Tudor king's break with Rome.[1]   During the seventeenth century, Nicholas' speculative writings aroused greater interest among English scholars. Thus John Everard and Giles Randall produced English versions of Cusan tracts, not all of which were printed. Cusanus studies in English academic circles were lacking until the nineteenth century, when Lord Acton devoted an essay to Nicholas' political thought. During the following decades, other English speaking scholars, including E.F. Jacob, gave attention to Cusanus' role in Renaissance history or to his political writings. This tradition has continued to the present day, in both England and the United States, culminating in 1963 in the publication of books by Morimichi Watanabe and Paul Sigmund on Nicholas as political theorist.

Since the Second World War, even more attention has been devoted, especially in the United States, to Cusanus' speculative works. Much of

---

[1] William Marshall translated the Donation of Constantine from the Latin text by Bartholomaeus Picernus, published during the reign of Julius II. This translation and related texts by Valla, Cusanus, and Antoninus were prepared for Thomas Cromwell, for whom Marshall also rendered Marsilius of Padua's *Defensor pacis* into English. See B.W. Beckingsale, *Thomas Cromwell: Tudor Minister* (Totowa, New Jersey, 1978), p. 128. A.G. Dickens, *Thomas Cromwell and the English Reformation* (London, 1959), p. 82. The Donation also was used in the *Collectanea satis compendiosa* to show that the papacy lacked temporal power before the time of Constantine; see John Guy, "Thomas Cromwell and the Intellectual Origins of the Henrician Revolution," *Reassessing the Henrician Age: Humanism, Politics, and Reform 1500-1550*, ed. Alistair Fox and John Guy (Oxford, 1986), pp. 151-178 at p. 160. Thomas Godfray, who printed Marshall's translations concerned with the Donation, also printed an anonymous translation of Erasmus' *Epistola apologetica de interdicto esu carnium*, possibly with Cromwell's patronage; see E.J. Devereux, *Renaissance English Translation of Erasmus: A Bibliography to 1700.* Erasmus Studies 6 (Toronto, 1983), pp. 121-122, no. 18. Thomas Cranmer's library contained writings of Nicholas of Cusa; see Antonia McLean, *Humanism and the Rise of Science in Tudor England* (New York, 1972), p. 96.

this writing has been done under the influence of European scholars, including Ernst Cassirer. American scholars, besides addressing the theological and philosophical issues in Cusanus' works, have been interested in his place in the history of science. Since the time of the Second Vatican Council, Cusanus scholarship also has dwelt at length on Nicholas' ideas on the relationship between Christianity and Islam. Most recently, Cusanus' writings have been brought out of the ivory tower of scholarship into the more public area of spiritual reading, though the comprehensibility of these works in their wholeness from excerpts remains to be determined.[2]

This bibliography attempts to list all published literature in English on Nicholas of Cusa from Tudor times to the end of 1988. All translations of individual works by Cusanus are listed, including excerpts published in anthologies. So too are passages from these writings translated especially for inclusion in such a collection. All books on Cusanus, including those translated from other languages, are listed. Alternative printings, reprintings, and new editions are distinguished in most cases. Chapters or portions of them found in more general books are included when they are concerned with Cusanus in some substantive manner. Dissertations are listed only when they have been published. All articles and published abstracts of papers have been included; but book reviews have not, unless they take the form of review articles.

This bibliography is divided topically. The first part lists works concerned with the life and works of Nicholas of Cusa. Articles from certain specialized encyclopedias are entered into this section. The second part lists translations of, and studies on, individual works of Cusanus alphabetically by title. Under each title, translations appear first, listed in chronological order. Excerpts taken from translations are noted in conjunction with the original bibliographic record for that version. Studies of the works are listed following the translations in alphabetical order by author. Although the compiler has tried to examine every work listed, the assignment of studies to this section remains a difficult decision. The third section deals with doctrines. It has been subdivided into studies of Cusanus' speculative thought, including theology, philosophy, and science; his doctrine on relations with non-Christians; his ideas on reform; his political and ecclesiological teachings; and his influence on later writers. A brief fourth section deals with manuscripts from Cusanus' library and editions of his works. A final section lists bibliographic sources which might be consulted by interested research-

---

[2] See the work of Yockey listed above in Part IIIA, which does not attempt a systematic translation of any work or of any substantial portion of one. See also, more recently, the posthumous publication of Nicholas of Cusa, *Dialogue about the Hidden God,* trans. Thomas Merton (New York: Dim Gray Bar Press, 1989).

ers. Other sources which might be consulted, online or in print, include *Philosopher's Index, Religion Index*, and *Historical Abstracts*.

The following texts are available, entirely or in part, in English translation. These translations are listed in chronological order by date of publication under the following titles in Part II below:

Apologia doctae ignorantiae
De concordantia catholica (excerpts)
De dato patris luminum
De docta ignorantia
De ludo globi
De non aliud
De pace fidei
De visione dei
Idiota (entire text and individual books)
Sermones (two texts)
Trialogus de possest.

Limitations of space and time prohibit inclusion of publications from 1989 and 1990, including the translation by my colleague in the American Cusanus Society, Mark Führer: Nicholas of Cusa, *The Layman on Wisdom and the Mind*, trans. M.L. Führer. (Ottawa: Dovehouse Editions, Inc., 1989). Such must remain for periodic supplements of this bibliography in the future.

I. General Studies of Life and Works

"Aeneas Sylvius and Nicholas de Cusa: Symbols of the Renaissance," *Dublin Review* 139 (1906): 267-276.

Bado, Walter, "In Honor of Nicholas of Cusa, 1464-1964," *The Modern Schoolman* 42 (1964): 1-2.

Bartos, F.M., "Cusanus and the Hussite Bishop M. Lupac," *Communio Viatorum* 5 (1962): 35-46.

Beck, Hans-Georg *et al., From the High Middle Ages to the Eve of the Reformation*, trans. Anselm Biggs. History of the Church 4. (New York: Seabury Press, 1980), pp. 585-594, c. 59, Theology in the Age of Transition.

Bett, Henry, *Nicholas of Cusa*. Great Medieval Churchmen. (London: Methuen & Co., 1932). Reprinted: (Merrick, New York: Richwood Publishing Co., 1976.)

Bilaniuk, Petro B.T., "Nicholas of Cusa and the Council of Florence," *Proceedings of the Patristic, Medieval and Renaissance Conference* 2 (1977): 59-75.

Reprinted: idem, *Studies in Eastern Christianity*, ed. Isabel A. Massey. vol. 2. (Munich: P.B.T. Bilaniuk, 1982), pp. 113-128.

Bond, H. Lawrence, "Nicholas of Cusa," *Abingdon Dictionary of Living Religions,* ed. Keith Grim, Larry D. Shinn, and Roger A. Bullard. (Nashville: Abingdon Press, 1981), p. 539.

Duclow, Donald F., "Nicholas of Cusa," *The Encyclopedia of Religion,* ed. Mircea Eliade. vol. 10. (New York: Macmillan, 1987), pp. 430-431.

Hagen, J.G., "Nicholas of Cusa," *The Catholic Encyclopedia,* ed. Charles G. Herbermann *et al.,* vol. 11. (New York: Robert Appleton Co., 1911), pp. 60-62.

Hillgarth, J.N., *Ramon Lull and Lullism in Fourteenth-Century France.* (Oxford: At the Clarendon Press, 1971), pp. 270-274, c. 7, Epilogue, The Place of Paris in Later Lullism: The Influence of Le Myésiers's Works.

Hopkins, Jasper, "Nicholas of Cusa (1401-1464)," *Dictionary of the Middle Ages,* ed. Joseph Strayer *et al.,* vol. 9.   (New York: Charles Scribner's Sons, 1987), pp. 122-125.

Janssen, Johannes, *History of the German People at the Close of the Middle Ages,* trans. M.A. Mitchell and A.M. Christie. (London: Paul, Trench, Truebner and Co., 1900), pp. 1-6, Introduction. Reprinted: (New York: AMS Press, 1966.)

Joda, Robert, "Nicholas of Cusa: Precusor of Humanism," *Renaissance and Reformation in Germany,* ed. Gerhart Hoffmeister. (New York: F. Ungar Publishing Co., 1977), pp. 33-50.

Koch, Josef, "Nicholas of Cusa," *New Catholic Encyclopedia.* vol. 10. (New York: McGraw-Hill Book Co., 1967), pp. 449-452.

Maurer, Armand, "Nicholas of Cusa," *Encyclopedia of Philosophy.* vol. 5. (New York: Macmillan, 1967), pp. 496-498.

Riedel, John O. *et al., A Catalogue of Renaissance Philosophers (1350-1650).* (Milwaukee, Wisconsin: Marquette University Press, 1940), pp. 31-34, c. XXII, The *De docta ignorantia* Controversy.

Vespasiano da Bisticci, *Renaissance Princes, Popes, and Prelates: The Vespasiano Memoirs, Lives of Illustrious Men of the XVth Century,* trans. William George and Emily Waters. intro. Myron P. Gilmore. (New York: Harper & Row, 1963), p. 156, Cardinal Cusano--a German (1401-1464). (Reprint of the translation, first published by Mac Veagh in 1926, with a new introduction.)

Walsh, James J., *Catholic Churchmen in Science.* 3rd series. (Philadelphia: American Ecclesiastical Review, 1917), pp. 85-114, c. 3, Cardinal Nicholas of Cusa. Reprinted: (Freeport, New York: Books for Libraries Press, 1966.)

II. Individual Works

Apologia doctae ignorantiae

Nicholas of Cusa's Debate with John Wenck: A Translation and an Appraisal of "De ignota litteratura" and "Apologia doctae ignorantiae" ed. & trans. Jasper Hopkins, 1st ed. (Minneapolis: A.J. Banning Press, 1981). 2nd ed. (Minneapolis: A.J. Banning Press, 1984). 3rd ed. (Minneapolis: A.J. Banning Press, 1988.) (Translated from the Leipzig edition.)

Cribratio Alchorani

Burgevin, Frederick H., *Cribratio Alchorani: Nicholas Cusanus' Criticism of the Koran in the Light of His Philosophy of Religion.* (New York: Vantage Press, 1969).

De beryllo

Lutz, Cora E., *The Oldest Library Motto and Other Library Essays.* (Hamden, Connecticut: Archon Books, 1979), pp. 33-37, The Mystical Symbol of the Beryl. (Plate from Yale University MS 334 facing p. 33.)

Trinkaus, Charles, "Protagoras in the Renaissance," *Philosophy and Humanism: Renaissance Essays in Honor of Paul Oskar Kristeller,* ed. Edward P. Mahoney. (New York: Columbia University Press, 1976), pp. 190-213.

De concordantia catholica

Excerpt translated in *A treatyse of the Donation or Gyfte and Endowment of Possessyons, Gyuen and Graunted ynto Sylvester, Pope of Rhome, by Constantyne, Emperour of Rome. . . . The Sentence and Mynde of Nycolas of Cuse of the Tytle of Saynt Peter ad Vincule Cardynall Whiche He Wrote Unto the Counsell Holden at Basyle of the Sayd Donation and Gyfte of Constantine. . . .,* trans. William Marshall. (London: Thomas Godfray, 1534). (The Donation with the opinions of Lorenzo Valla, Cusanus and Antoninus of Florence.)[3]

Excerpts translated in Coker, Francis W., *Readings in Political Philosophy,* rev. ed. (New York: Macmillan, 1938), pp. 257-73, c. 10, Nicholas of Cusa (1401-1464). (Lib. 2 cc. 12, 13, & 14, Lib. 3 cc. 4, 12, 25, 35, 36, & 37 translated from the Paris edition.)

Excerpts translated in *The Portable Renaissance Reader,* ed. James B. Ross and Mary M. McLaughlin. (New York: The Viking Press, 1949), pp. 624-630. (Translated by McLaughlin from the Heidelberg Academy edition.)

[3] See above n. 1.

Excerpts translated in Lewis, Ewart, *Medieval Political Ideas*. vol. 1 (London: Routledge & Kegan Paul, 1954), pp. 190-192, 314-320. (Lib. 2 cc. 19 & 34. Lib. 3 cc. 32-33, 35, & 41).

* * * * *

Coleman, Christopher B., *Constantine the Great and Christianity. Three Phases: The Historical, the Legendary, and the Spurious.* Studies in History, Economics, and Public Law. (New York: Columbia University Press, 1914), pp. 188-191 with Latin text of Lib. 3 c. 2 at pp. 228-237. Latin text of Lib. 3 c. 2. (Reprinted: New York: AMS Press, 1968.)

(See also Watanabe, Morimichi in III C. below.)

De dato patris luminum

Hayes, T. Wilson, "A 17th-century Translation of Nicholas of Cusa *De dato patris luminum,* " *Journal of Medieval and Renaissance Studies* 11 (1981): 113-136. (Prints John Everard's translation from Folger Shakespeare Library MS v. q. 222.)

Hopkins, Jasper, *Nicholas of Cusa's Metaphysic of Contraction.* (Minneapolis: A.J. Banning Press, 1983). (Latin text from the Heidelberg Academy edition accompanying Hopkins' translation of *De dato patris luminum.*)

* * * * *

Führer, Mark L., "The Metaphysics of Light in the *De dato patris luminum* of Nicholas of Cusa," *International Studies in Philosophy* 18 no. 3 (1986): 17-32.

De docta ignorantia

Of Learned Ignorance, trans. Germain Heron. intro. D.J.B. Hawkins. (London: Routledge & Kegan Paul, 1954). Reprinted: (Westport, Connecticut: Hyperion Press, 1979).

Excerpts printed in Santillana, Giorgio di, *The Age of Adventure: The Renaissance Philosophers.* The Great Ages of Western Philosophy 2. (Boston: Houghton Mifflin, 1957), 47-63. (Reprinted several times.)

Excerpt printed in *Unity and Reform: Selected Writings,* ed. John P. Dolan. (Notre Dame, Indiana: University of Notre Dame Press, 1962), pp. 55-98. (Lib. 3).

Excerpt printed in Happold, F.C., *Mysticism: A Study and an Anthology.* (Harmsworth: Penguin, 1963), pp. 340-341. (Lib. 3 c. 11).

Excerpt printed in Wippel, John F. and Allan B. Wolter, *Medieval Philosophy: From St. Augustine to Nicholas of Cusa.* (New York: The Free Press, 1969), pp. 457-463, c. 8, Nicholas of Cusa. (Lib. 2 cc. 2 & 3).

Revised excerpts printed in Fallico, Arturo B. and Herman Shapiro, *Renaissance Philosophy.* vol. 2, *The Transalpine Thinkers, Selected*

Readings from Cusanus to Suarez. (New York: Random House, 1969), pp. 3-24, Part 1 c. 1, Nicholaus of Cusa (Cusanus). (Lib. 1 cc. 1-12).

Excerpt translated in *The Portable Medieval Reader,* pp. 667-675. (Translated by Ross from the Bari edition.)

Reprinted in *Late Medieval Mysticism,* ed. Ray C. Petry. Library of Christian Classics 13. (Philadelphia: Westminster Press, 1957), pp. 360-366. Reprinted: (London: SMC Press, 1957) and (Philadelphia: Westminster Press, 1962 & 1980).

Hopkins, Jasper, *Nicholas of Cusa On Learned Ignorance: A Translation and an Appraisal of "De docta ignorantia".* (Minneapolis: A.J. Banning Press, 1981). (From the Heidelberg Academy edition.)

* * * * *

McGreal, Ian P., "Of Learned Ignorance," *Masterpieces of World Philosophy in Summary Form,* ed. Frank N. Magill and Ian P. McGreal. vol. 1. (New York: Salem Press, 1961), pp. 343-347. Also: (New York: Harper, 1961); (London: G. Allen & Unwin, 1963); and (New York: Harper, 1966).

Reprinted in *World Philosophy: Essay Reviews of 225 Major Works,* ed. Frank N. Magill and Ian P. McGreal. vol. 2. (Englewood Cliffs, New Jersey: Salem Press, 1982), pp. 743-752 with review of literature by Keith E. Yandell. Also: (Epping: Bowker, 1982).

De ludo globi

De ludo globi: The Game of Spheres, trans. & intro. Pauline M. Watts. Janus series 11. (New York: Abaris Books, 1986). (Text from the Paris edition facing Watts' translation.)

* * * * *

Miller, Clyde L., "Nicholas of Cusa's *De ludo globi:* Symbolic Roundness and Eccentric Life Paths," *Text and Image,* ed. David W. Burchmore. Acta 10. (Binghamton, New York: The Center for Medieval and Early Renaissance Studies, State University of New York, 1986), pp. 135-148.

De non aliud

Nicholas of Cusa on God as Not-other: A Translation of "De li non aliud", trans. & intro. Jasper Hopkins. (Minneapolis: University of Minnesota Press, 1979). 2nd ed. (Minneapolis: A.J. Banning Press, 1983). 3rd ed. (Minneapolis: A.J. Banning Press, 1987). (From the Heidelberg Academy edition.)

De pace fidei

Translated in *Unity and Reform,* pp. 185-237. (Translated by Dolan from the Paris and Basel editions.)

De pace fidei, trans. H. Lawrence Bond. Concordance by James E. Biechler. (Philadelphia: American Cusanus Society, 1986). (From the Heidelberg Academy edition.)

*   *   *   *   *

Burr, George L., "Anent the Middle Ages," *American Historical Review* 18 (1912-13): 710-726.

Pelikan, Jaroslav, "Negative Theology and Positive Religion: A Study of Nicholas Cusanus *De pace fidei,*" *Prudentia,* supplement (1981): 65-77.

Sweetman, J. Windrow, *Islam and Christian Theology: A Study of Theological Ideas in the Two Religions.* Part II. (London: Lutterworth Press, 1954), vol. 2, pp. 159-178, Part 2, c. 2, Nicholas of Cusa.

De visione dei

The Single Eye: Entituled the Vision of God Wherein is Infolded the Mistery of Divine Presence, trans. Giles Randall. (London: Printed for John Streater, 1646).

The Vision of God, trans. Emma G. Salter, intro. Evelyn Underhill. (London: J.M. Dent and Sons, 1928). Reprinted: (New York: Ungar Publishing Co., 1960.)

Reprinted in *Unity and Reform,* pp. 128-184.

Excerpts reprinted in Happold. *Mysticism: A Study and an Anthology,* pp. 336-340, cc. 9, 10, 12, & 13.

Excerpts reprinted in Grant, Patrick, *Mysticism in Western Tradition.* (New York: St. Martin's Press, 1983), pp. 24, 70-71, & 74.

Excerpts reprinted in *Late Medieval Mysticism,* ed. Petry, pp. 367-384, cc. 19-25.

Nicholas of Cusa's Dialectical Mysticism: Text, Translation and Interpretive Study of "De visione Dei", ed., tr., and intro. Jasper Hopkins. (Minneapolis: A.J. Banning Press, 1985). 2nd ed. (Minneapolis: A.J. Banning Press, 1988). (Edition and translation by Hopkins facing.)

*   *   *   *   *

Certau, Michel de, "The Gaze of Nicholas of Cusa," *Diacritics: A Review of Contemporary Criticism* 17 no. 3 (1987): 2-38.

Cowley, Patrick, "The Gaze of God," *Theology* 53 (1950): 218-223.

Miller, Clyde L., "Nicholas of Cusa's the Vision of God," *An Introduction to the Medieval Mystics of Europe,* ed. Paul Szarmach. (Albany, New York: State University of New York, Press, 1984), pp. 293-312.

Panofsky, Erwin, "Facies illa Rogeri maximi pictoris", *Late Classical and Mediaeval Studies in Honor of Robert Mathias Friend, Jr.,* ed. Kurt Wietzmann. (Princeton, New Jersey: Princeton University Press, 1955), pp. 392-400.

Idiota

The Idiot in Four Books: The First and Seconde of Wisdome, the Third of the Minde, the Fourth of Statick Experiments, or Experiments of the Ballance, trans. John Everard. (London: William Leake, 1650).
Reprinted: intro. William R. Dennis. Reprint Series 19. (San Francisco: California State Library, 1940).
* * * * *
Führer, Mark L., "Wisdom and Eloquence in Nicholas of Cusa's *Idiota De sapientia* and *De mente*," *Vivarium* 16 (1978): 142-155.
Hayes, T. Wilson, "John Everard and Nicholas of Cusa's *Idiota*," *Notes and Queries* 28 (1981): 47-49.
Schultheisz, Emil, "On the Beginnings of Quantitative Thinking in Medicine (Nicholas of Cusa and the Idiot)," *Advances in Physiological Sciences: Proceedings of the 28th International Congress of Physiology. Budapest 1980,* ed. Emil Schultheisz. History of Physiology 21. (Oxford: Pergamon Press, 1981), pp. 1-7.

Idiota, Lib. 1-2: *De sapientia:*

Translated in *Unity and Reform,* pp. 99-127. (Translated by Dolan from the Paris and Basel editions.)
Idiota, Lib. 3: *De mente:*
Idiota de mente. The Layman about Mind, trans. & intro. Clyde L. Miller. Janus Series 7. (New York: Abaris Books, 1979). (Text from the Paris edition facing Miller's translation.)
* * * * *
Miller, Clyde L., "Metaphor and Simile in Nicholas of Cusa's *Idiota de mente*," *The Late Middle Ages,* ed. Peter Cocozzella. Acta 8. (Binghamton, New York: The Center for Medieval and Early Renaissance Studies, State University of New York at Binghamton, 1981), pp. 47-59.

Idiota, Lib. 4: *De staticis experimentis:*

Veits, Henry, "*De staticis experimentis* of Nicolaus Cusanus," Annals of Medical History 4 (1922): 115-135 (trans. by D. D. Kirkaldy Ellis). Reprinted: Idem, *"De staticis experimentis" of Nicolaus Cusanus* (New York: Henry Veits, 1922).
Translated in *Unity and Reform,* pp. 239-60. (Translated by Dolan from the Paris and Basel editions.)

Sermones

No Uncertain Sound: Sermons that Shaped the Pulpit Tradition, ed. Ray C. Petry. (Philadelphia: Westminster Press, 1948), pp. 289-91, From a Sermon on the Eucharist, & pp. 292-294, Where is He Who is Born King of the Jews. (From the Heidelberg Academy edition.)

Reprinted in *Late Medieval Mysticism,* ed. Petry, pp. 385-388 & 389-391.

* * * * *

Petry, Ray C., "Emphasis on the Gospel and Christian Reform in Late Medieval Preaching," *Church History* 16 (1947): 75-91 at pp. 88-90.

O'Malley, John W., *Praise and Blame in Renaissance Rome: Rhetoric, Doctrine, and Reform in the Sacred Orators of the Papal Court, c. 1450-1521.* (Durham, North Carolina: Duke University Press, 1979).

Trialogus de possest

A *Concise Introduction to the Philosophy of Nicholas of Cusa,* trans. & intro. Jasper Hopkins. (Minneapolis: University of Minnesota Press, 1978). 2nd ed. (Minneapolis: University of Minnesota Press, 1980). 3rd ed. (Minneapolis: A.J. Banning Co., 1986). (Text from the Paris edition facing Hopkins' translation.)

III. Doctrines

A. Speculative Thought

Bado, Walter, "What is God: An Essay on Learned Ignorance," *The Modern Schoolman* 42 (1964): 3-32.

Beck, Lewis W., *Early German Philosophy: Kant and His Predecessors.* (Cambridge, Massachusetts: The Belknap Press of Harvard University Press, 1969), pp. 56-71, c. 4, Nicholas of Cusa.

Biechler, James E., *The Religious Language of Nicholas of Cusa.* (Missoula, Montana: Scholars Press, 1975).

Blumenberg, Hans, *The Legitimacy of the Modern Age,* trans. Robert M. Wallace. (Cambridge, Massachusetts: MIT Press, 1983), pp. 483-547, pt. 2, c. 2, The Cusan: The World as God's Self-Restriction.

Blystone, Jasper, "Is Cusanus the Father of Structuralism," *Philosophy Today* 16 (1972): 296-305.

Bond, H. Lawrence, "Nicholas of Cusa and the Reconstruction of Theology: The Centrality of Christology in the Coincidence of Opposites," *Contemporary Reflections on the Medieval Christian Tradition: Essays in Honor of Ray C. Petry,* ed. George H. Shriver. (Durham, North Carolina: Duke University Press, 1974), pp. 81-94.

Cassirer, Ernst, *The Individual and the Cosmos in Renaissance Philosophy,* trans. Mario Domandi. (New York: Barnes and Noble, 1963), pp. 7-45, c. 1, Nicholas Cusanus & pp. 46-72, c. 2, Cusanus and Italy.

Chudoba, B., "Four Medieval Sketches on the Meaning of Time," *St. Vladimir's Theological Quarterly* 16 (1972): 72-82.

Collins, James D., *God in Modern Philosophy*. (Chicago: Henry Regnery Co., 1959), pp. 2-11, pt. 1, c. 1, Cusanus and the Method of Learned Ignorance.

Conger, George P., *Theories of Macrocosms and Microcosms in the History of Philosophy*. (New York: Columbia University Press, 1922), pp. 54-55, c. 3, Microcosmic Theories in Early Modern Reactions from Scholasticism. Reprinted: (New York: Russell & Russell, 1967.)

Cope, Jackson, *The Theatre and the Dream: From Metaphor to Form in Renaissance Drama*, (Baltimore: Johns Hopkins University Press, 1973), pp. 14-28, c. 1, Platonic Perspectives: Structural Metaphor from Cusa to Ficino.

Copleston, Frederick C., *A History of Philosophy*, vol. 3. *Ockham to Suarez*. (Westminster, Maryland: The Newman Press, 1960), pp. 231-247, c. 15, Nicholas of Cusa. (First published in 1946; multiple reprintings.)

idem, *Medieval Philosophy*. (London: Methuen & Co., 1952), c. 11, Speculative Mysticism: Nicholas of Cusa. Also (New York: Harper & Row, 1952.) Reprinted: (New York: Harper & Row, 1961.)

Coulton, George G., *Studies in Medieval Thought*. (London: T. Nelson & Sons, 1945), 200-216, c. 16, Nicholas of Cues. Reprinted: (New York: Russell & Russell, 1965.)

Cousins, Ewart H., "Bonaventure, the Coincidence of Opposites and Nicholas of Cusa," *Studies Honoring Ignatius Charles Brady, Friar Minor*, ed. Romano S. Almagno and Conrad L. Harkins. Franciscan Institute Publications, Theology Series 6. (St. Bonaventure, New York: The Franciscan Institute, 1976), pp. 177-198.

Cranz, F. Edward, "Saint Augustine and Nicholas of Cusa in the Tradition of Western Christian Thought," *Speculum* 28 (1953): 297-315.

idem, "The Transmutation of Platonism in the Development of Nicolaus Cusanus and of Martin Luther," *Nicolò Cusano agli inizi del mondo moderno: Atti del Congresso Internazionale in Occasione del V Centenario della Morte di Nicolò Cusano. Bressanone, 6-10 settembre 1964*. (Florence: G.C. Sansoni, 1970), pp. 73-102.

idem, "Cusanus, Luther and the Mystical Tradition," *The Pursuit of Holiness in Late Medieval and Renaissance Religion. Papers from the University of Mighican Conference*, ed. Charles Trinkaus and Heiko A. Oberman. Studies in Medieval and Reformation Thought 10. (Leiden: E.J. Brill, 1974), pp. 93-102.

idem, "1100 A.D.: A Crisis for Us?," *De litteris* (1982): 84-108 at pp. 95-106.

Damon, Phillip, "History and Idea in Renaissance Criticism," *Literary History and Historical Understanding: Selected Papers from the English Institute,* ed. Phillip Damon. (New York: Columbia University Press, 1968), pp. 25-51.

Duclow, Donald F., "Pseudo-Dionysius, John Scotus Eriugena, Nicholas of Cusa: An Approach to the Hermeneutics of the Divine Names," *International Philosophical Quarterly* 12 (1972): 260-278.

idem, "Gregory of Nyssa and Nicholas of Cusa: Infinity, Anthropology and the *via negativa," The Downside Review* 92 (1974): 102-108.

idem, "The Analogy of the Word: Nicholas of Cusa's Theory of Language," *Bijdragen: Tijdschrift voor Filosofie en Theologie* 38 (1977): 282-299.

idem, "The Dynamics of Analogy in Nicholas of Cusa," *International Philosophical Quarterly* 21 (1981): 295-301.

idem, "Anselm's *Proslogion* and Nicholas of Cusa's Wall of Paradise," *The Downside Review* 100 (1982): 22-30.

Duhem, Pierre M.M., *Medieval Cosmology: Theories of Infinity, Place, Time, Void and the Plurality of Worlds,* ed. & trans. Roger Ariew. (Chicago: University of Chicago Press, 1985), pp. 505-10, c. 13, The Plurality of Worlds in Fifteenth-Century Cosmology.

Eby, Charles T., "Nicholas of Cusa and Medieval Cosmology: An Historical Reassessment," *Proceedings of the Patristic, Mediaeval and Renaissance Conference.* 11 (1986): 83-90.

Emery, Kent, Jr., "Twofold Wisdom and Contemplation in Denys of Ryckel (Dionysius Carthusiensis)," *Journal of Medieval and Renaissance Studies* 18 (1988): 99-134.

Forbes Liddell, Anna, "The Significance of the Doctrine of the Incarnation in the Philosophy of Nicholas of Cusa," *Actes du XIème Congrès International de Philosophie* vol. 11. (Amsterdam: North-Holland Publishing Co., 1953), pp. 126-131. Reprinted: (Nendeln: Kraus Reprint, 1970.)

idem, "Man and Nature in the Philosophy of Nicholas of Cusa," *Atti del XII. Congresso Internazionale di Filosofia.* vol. 11 (Florence: Sansoni, 1960), pp. 281-284.

Führer, Mark L., "Principle of *contractio* in Nicholas of Cusa's Philosophical View of Man," *The Downside Review* 93 (1975): 289-296.

idem, "Purgation, Illumination and Perfection in Nicholas of Cusa," *The Downside Review* 98 (1980): 169-189.

idem, "The Evolution of the Quadrivial Modes of Theology in Nicholas of Cusa's Analysis of the Soul," *American Benedictine Review* 36 (1985): 325-342.

idem, "Ulrich of Strassbourg and Nicholas of Cusa's Theory of Mind," *Revue Danoise de Philologie et d'Histoire* 36 (1985): 225-239.

Gandillac, Maurice de, "Neoplatonism and Christian Thought in the Fifteenth Century (Nicholas of Cusa and Marsilio Ficino)," trans. Mary Brennan. *Neoplatonism and Christian Thought,* ed. Dominic J. O'Meara. Studies in Neoplatonism, Ancient and Modern 3. (Albany, New York: State University of New York Press, 1982), pp. 143-165.

Gane, Erwin R., "The Intellect-Will Problem in the Thought of Some Northern Renaissance Humanists: Nicholas of Cusa," *Andrews University Seminary Studies* 12 (1974): 83-93.

Gay, John H., "Four Medieval Views of Creation," *Harvard Theological Review* 56 (1963): 243-273.

Gilson, Etienne, *History of Christian Philosophy in the Middle Ages.* (London: Sheed & Ward, 1955), pp. 534-540, Pt. 11 c. 4, Journey's End. (Multiple reprintings.)

Grant, Edward, *Much Ado About Nothing: Theories of Space and Vacuum from the Middle Ages to the Scientific Revolution.* (Cambridge: Cambridge University Press, 1981), pp. 139-140, c. 6, Late Medieval Conceptions of Extracosmic ("Imaginary") Void Space.

Harries, Karsten, "Cusanus and the Platonic Idea," *The New Scholasticism* 37 (1963): 188-203.

idem, "The Infinite Sphere: Comments on the History of a Metaphor," *Journal of the History of Philosophy* 13 (1975): 5-16.

Hay, W. H., "Nicholas Cusanus, the Structure of His Philosophy," *The Philosophical Review* 61 (1952): 14-25.

Hopkins, Jasper, "A Detailed Critique of Pauline Watts' *Nicolaus Cusanus: A Fifteenth-Century Vision of Man,"* *Philosophy Research Archives* 9 (1983): microfiche supplement, 26-61.

Hoye, William J., "The Meaning of Neoplatonism in the Thought of Nicholas of Cusa," *The Downside Review* 104 (1986): 10-18.

Hujer, Karel, "Nicholas of Cusa and His Influence on the Rise of New Astronomy," *Proceedings of the Twelfth International Congress of the History of Science. Paris 1968.* vol. 3A. (Paris: Blanchard, 1970-1971), pp. 87-92.

Ingegno, Alfonso, "The New Philosophy of Nature," *The Cambridge History of Renaissance Philosophy,* ed. Charles B. Schmitt, *et al.* (Cambridge: Cambridge University Press, 1988), pp. 236-263.

Jacob, Ernest F., "Cusanus the Theologian," *Bulletin of the John Rylands Library* 21 (1937): 406-424.

Reprinted: idem, *Essays in the Conciliar Epoch.* 1st ed. (Manchester: Manchester University Press, 1943), pp. 154-169. 2nd ed. (Manchester: Manchester University Press, 1953). 3rd ed. (Manchester: Manchester University Press, 1962).

Jaspers, Karl, *The Great Philosophers*. ed. Hannah Arendt. trans. Ralph Manheim. vol. 2. A. Helen and Kurt Wolff Book. (New York: Harcourt, Brace & World, 1962), pp. 116-272, Nicholas of Cusa.

Reprinted: idem, *Anselm and Nicholas of Cusa*. Harvest Book 289. (New York: Harcourt, Brace, and Jovanovich, 1974).

Katsaros, Thomas and Nathaniel Kaplan, *The Western Mystical Tradition*. (New Haven, Connecticut: College and University Press, 1969), pp. 294-298, c. 16, From Wycliffe to the Renaissance.

Keefer, Michael H., "The World Turned Inside Out: Revolutions of the Infinite Sphere from Hermes to Pascal," *Renaissance and Reformation* 12 (1988): 303-311.

Klibansky, Raymond, *Continuity of the Platonic Tradition During the Middle Ages*. (London: The Warburg Institute, 1939). Reprinted: (London: The Warburg Institute, 1950.)

New edition in idem, *The Continuity of the Platonic Tradition During the Middle Ages* and *Plato's "Parmenides" in the Middle Ages and the Renaissance*. (Munich: Kraus International Publications, 1981.) Also: (Milwood, New York: Kraus International Publications, 1982.)

idem, "Plato's *Parmenides* in the Middle Ages and the Renaissance," *Mediaeval and Renaissance Studies* 1 (1943): 1-55.

Reprinted: idem, *The Continuity of the Platonic Tradition during the Middle Ages*, pp. 81-335.

idem, "Nicolas of Cues," *Philosophy in the Mid-Century, A Survey, Contemporary Thought in Eastern Europe and Asia*. vol. 4. *History of Philosophy*, ed. Raymond Klibansky. (Florence: Nuova Italia, 1959), pp. 88-94.

Koenigsberger, Dorothy, *Renaissance Man and Creative Thinking: A History of Concepts of Harmony 1400-1700*. (Atlantic Highlands, New Jersey: Humanities Press, 1979), pp. 100-147, c. 3, The Infectious Imagination of Nicholas of Cusa.

idem, "Universality, the Universe and Nicholas of Cusa, Untastable Foretaste of Wisdom," *European Historical Quarterly* 17 (1987): 3-33.

Koyré, Alexandre, *From the Closed to the Infinite Universe*. Publications of the Institute of the History of Medicine, the Johns Hopkins University, 3rd Series: the Hideyo Noguchi Lecture 7. (Baltimore: Johns Hopkins University Press, 1957), pp. 5-27, c. 1, The Sky and the Heavens, Nicholas of Cusa and Marcellus Paligenius. Reprinted: (New York: Harper & Brothers, 1958.)

Kraye, Jill, "Moral Philosophy," *The Cambridge History of Renaissance Philosophy*, pp. 303-386.

Lai, Tyrone, "Nicholas of Cusa and the Finite Universe," *Journal of the History of Philosophy* 11 (1973): 161-167.

Levao, Ronald, *Renaissance Minds and Their Fictions: Cusanus, Sidney, Shakespeare.* (Berkeley: University of California Press, 1985).

Lohr, Charles H., "Metaphysics," *The Cambridge History of Renaissance Philosophy,* pp. 537-638.

Long, Pamela O., "Humanism and Science," *Renaissance Humanism: Foundations, Forms, and Legacy,* ed. Albert Rabil Jr., vol. 3. (Philadelphia: University of Pennsylvania Press, 1988), pp. 486-512.

Longeway, John L., "Nicholas of Cusa and Man's Knowledge of God," *Philosophy Research Archives* 13 (1987-1988): 289-313.

Lovejoy, Arthur O., *The Great Chain of Being.* (Cambridge, Massachusetts: Harvard University Press, 1936), pp. 112-115, c. 4, The Principles of Plenitude and the New Cosmography.

McTighe, Thomas P., "The Meaning of the Couple *complicatio-explicatio* in the Philosophy of Nicholas of Cusa," *Proceedings of the Catholic Philosophical Association* 32 (1958): 206-214.

idem, "Nicholas of Cusa as a Forerunner of Modern Science," *Proceedings of the Tenth International Congress of the History of Science. Ithaca 1962.* (Paris: Hermann, 1964), pp. 619-622.

idem, "Nicholas of Cusa's Theory of Science and Its Metaphysical Background," *Nicolò Cusano agli inizi del mondo moderno,* pp. 317-338.

idem, "Thierry of Chartres and Nicholas of Cusa's Epistemology," *Proceedings of the Patristic, Medieval and Renaissance Conference* 5 (1980): 169-176.

Martin, Vincent, "The Dialectical Process in the Philosophy of Nicholas of Cusa," *Laval Théologique et Philosophique* 5 (1949): 213-268.

Matsen, Herbert S., "Jasper Hopkins on Nicholas of Cusa," *International Studies in Philosophy* 14, no. 2 (1982): 77-84.

Maurer, Armand, *A History of Medieval Philosophy.* (New York: Random House, 1962), pp. 310-324, c. 20, Nicholas of Cusa.

Meschkowski, Herbert, *Ways of Thought of Great Mathematicians: An Approach to the History of Mathematics* (San Francisco: Holden-Day, Inc., 1964), pp. 25-31, Nicholas of Cusa.

Meyer-Baer, Kathi, "Nicholas of Cusa on the Meaning of Music," *Journal of Aesthetics and Art Criticism* 5 (1947): 301-308.

Milbank, John, "Man as Creative and Historical Being in the Theology of Nicholas of Cusa," *The Downside Review* 97 (1979): 245-257.

Miller, Clyde L., "Aristotelian *natura* and Nicholas of Cusa," *The Downside Review* 96 (1978): 13-20.

idem, "Nicholas of Cusa and Philosophic Knowledge," *Proceedings of the American Catholic Philosophical Association* 54 (1980): 155-163.

idem, "Cusan Treasure," *Cross Currents* 32 (1982): 366-369. (An essay reviewing Hopkins' translations.)

idem, "Irony in the History of Philosophy," *Poetics Today* 4 (1983): 465-478.

idem, "A Road Not Taken--Nicholas of Cusa and Today's Intellectual World," *Proceedings of the American Catholic Philosophical Association* 57 (1983): 68-77.

Miller, D.L., "Kingdom of Play: Some Old Theological Light from Recent Literature," *Union Theological Seminary Quarterly* 25 (1979): 343-360.

Monfasani, John, "Pseudo-Dionysius the Areopagite in Mid-Quattrocento Rome," *Supplementum Festivum: Studies in Honor of Paul Oskar Kristeller.* (Binghampton, New York: Medieval and Renaissance Texts and Studies, 1987), pp. 189-219.

Nebelsick, Harold P., *Circles of God: Theology and Science from the Greeks to Copernicus.* Theology and Science at the Frontiers of Knowledge 2. (Edinburgh: Scottish Academic Press, 1985), pp. 183-190.

Randall, John H., Jr., *The Career of Philosophy from the Middle Ages to the Enlightenment.* vol. 1. (New York: Columbia University Press, 1962), pp. 177-190, c. 6, The Nature Enthusiasts: Nature as a Spectacle and as a System of Useful Forces.

Rasmussen, Dennis F., "God as Ground and Measure," *The Personalist: An International Review of Philosophy* 52 (1971): 717-734.

Rice, Eugene F., Jr., "Nicholas of Cusa's Idea of Wisdom," *Traditio* 13 (1957): 345-368.

idem, *The Renaissance Idea of Wisdom.* Harvard Historical Monographs 37. (Cambridge, Massachusetts: Harvard University Press, 1958), pp. 19-27, c. 1, The Medieval Idea of Wisdom.

Romani, Romano, "Natural Man and His Soul," trans. Herbert Garrett. *Soul and Body in Husserlian Phenomenology: Man and Nature,* ed. Anna-Teresa Tymieniecka. Analecta Husserliana 16. (Dordrecht: D. Reidel Publishing Co., 1983), pp. 129-151.

Rose, Paul, *The Italian Renaissance of Mathematics: Studies on Humanists and Mathematics from Petrarch to Galileo.* Travaux d'Humanisme et Renaissance 145. (Geneva: Librarie Droz, 1975), pp. 26-75, c. 2, Patrons, Collectors and Translators: Humanist Origins of the Mathematical Renaissance.

Scott, Wilson L., "The Philosophical Significance of Rigidity in Physical Science," *XIVth International Congress on the History of Science.* Proceedings no. 2. (Tokyo: Science Council of Japan, 1975), pp. 313-315. (Cusanus and Newton.)

Struever, Nancy S., "Metaphoric Morals: Ethical Implications of Cusa's Use of Figure," *Archéologie du Signe.* ed. Lucie Brind'Amour & Eugene Vance. Papers in Medieval Studies 3. (Toronto: Pontifical Institute of Medieval Studies, 1982), pp. 305-334.

Taylor, Henry O., *Thought and Expression in the Sixteenth Century,* 2nd ed. revised, vol. 2. (New York: The Macmillan Company, 1930), pp. 267-290, c. XXX, The Scholastic Aristotle, Platonism, and Nicholas of Cusa.

Thorndike, Lynn, *A History of Magic and Experimental Science.* vol. 4. (New York: Columbia University Press, 1934), pp. 387-393, c. 46, Humanism in Relation to Natural and Occult Science.

idem, *Science and Thought in the Fifteenth Century,* (New York: Columbia University Press, 1929), pp. 133-141, c. 7, Nicholas of Cusa and the Triple Motion of the Earth, & 296-297, Appendix 15, An Astronomical Note by Nicholas of Cusa. Reprinted: (New York: Hafner, 1963.)

Vasoli, Cesare, "The Renaissance Concept of Philosophy," *The Cambridge History of Renaissance Philosophy,* pp. 57-74.

Watts, Pauline M., *Nicolaus Cusanus: A Fifteenth-Century Vision of Man.* Studies in the History of Christian Thought 30. (Leiden: E.J. Brill, 1982).

idem, "Pseudo-Dionysius the Areopagite and Three Renaissance Neoplatonists, Cusanus, Ficino & Pico on Mind and Cosmos," *Supplementum Festivum,* pp. 279-298.

Whittaker, T., "Nicholas of Cusa," *Mind* 34 (1925): 436-454.

Wind, Edgar, *Pagan Mysteries in the Renaissance.* (New York: W.W. Norton and Co., 1968), pp. 178-188, c. 14, The Concealed God.

Yockey, James F., *Mediations with Nicholas of Cusa.* (Santa Fe, New Mexico: Bear, 1987). (Excerpts in translation arranged topically.)

B. Ecumenism

Biechler, James E., "Christian Humanism Confronts Islam: Sifting the Qur'an with Nicholas of Cusa," *Journal of Ecumenical Studies* 13 (1974): 1-14.

idem, "Nicholas of Cusa and Muhammad: A Fifteenth-Century Encounter," *The Downside Review* 101 (1983): 50-59.

Borelli, John, "Coincidence and Harmony of Religions in the Thought of Nicholas of Cusa and Vijñánabhiksu," *Bulletin--Secretariatus pro Non Christianis* 61 (1986): 36-46.

Corless, Roger G., "Decalogus de numine non pleno: A Buddhist-Christian Conference at the Highest Level," *Dharma and Gospel: Two Ways of Seeing,* ed. Garry W. Houston. Biblioteca Indo-Buddhica 13. (Delhi: Sri Satguru Publications, 1984), pp. 21-34. (Cusanus is one of the interlocutors.)

idem, "Speaking of the Unspeakable: Negation as the Way in Nicholas of Cusa and Nágárjuna," *Buddhist-Christian Studies* 2 (1982): 107-117.

Herring, Herbert, "Unity in Plurality," *Spiritual Perspectives: Essays in Mysticism and Metaphysics,* ed. Tellavaram M.P. Mahadevan. (New Delhi: Arnold Heinermann, 1975), pp. 112-118.

Lecler, Joseph, *Toleration and Reformation,* tr. T.L. Westow. vol. 1. (New York: Association Press, 1960), pp. 107-110, Book 2, c. 1, pt. 1, Nicholas of Cusa (1401-1464).

Martinez Gomez, Luis, "From the Names of God to the Name of God: Nicholas of Cusa," *International Philosophical Quarterly* 5 (1965): 80-102.

Norman, Julie C., "Nicholas of Cusa, Apostolate of Unity," *The Downside Review* 99 (1981): 59-74.

Parsons, Richard, "Ecumenicity in the Fifteenth Century," *Church Quarterly Review* 159 (1958): 365-372.

Pearson, Samuel C., "Comprehending Religious Diversity: a Pre-Enlightenment Irenic Tradition," *Encounter* 39 (1978): 233-256. (Llull, Cusanus, and Bodin.)

Rescher, Nicholas, "Nicholas of Cusa on the Qur'an: A Fifteenth Century Encounter with Islam," *The Muslim World* 55 (1965): 195-202.

Schwoebel, Robert H., "Coexistence, Conversion and Crusade against the Turks," *Studies in the Renaissance* 12 (1965): 164-187.

Southern, Richard W., *Western Views of Islam in the Middle Ages.* (Cambridge, Massachusetts: Harvard University Press, 1962), pp. 92-94, c. 3, The Moment of Vision.

Watanabe, Morimichi, "Nicholas of Cusa and the Idea of Tolerance," *Nicolò Cusano agli inizi del mondo moderno,* pp. 409-418.

C. Reform of the Church

Biechler, James E., "Nicholas of Cusa and the End of the Conciliar Movement: A Humanist Crisis of Identity," *Church History* 44 (1975): 5-21.

Bond, Robert R., *The Efforts of Nicholas of Cusa as a Liturgical Reformer.* Pontificium Athenaeum Internationale "Angelicum." (Salzburg: Nonntal, 1962).

Brann, Noel L., "Pre-Reformation Humanism in Germany and the Papal Monarchy: A Study in Ambivalence," *Journal of Medieval and Renaissance Studies* 14 (1984): 159-185.

Janelle, Pierre, *The Catholic Reformation.* (Milwaukee: The Bruce Publishing Co., 1963), pp. 21-23, c. 2, Early Reactions Against the Disease.

Nagler, Arthur W., "A Potential Luther of the Fifteenth Century," *Methodist Review* 104 (1921): 192-203.

idem, "Nicholas of Cusa, Cardinal and Reformer," *Church Quarterly Review* 62 (April 1906): 62.

Sullivan, Donald L., "Nicholas of Cusa as Reformer: The Papal Legation to the Germanies, 1451-1452," *Medieval Studies* 36 (1974): 382-428.

idem, "Apocalypse Tamed: Cusanus and the Traditions of Late Medieval Prophecy," *Journal of Medieval History* 9 (1983): 227-236.

Tillinghast, Pardon E., "Nicholas of Cusa vs. Sigmund of Hapsburg: An Attempt at Post-Conciliar Church Reform," *Church History* 36 (1967): 371-390.

Watanabe, Morimichi, "The Episcopal Election of 1430 in Trier and Nicholas of Cusa," *Church History* 39 (1970): 299-316.

idem, "Duke Sigismund and Gregor Heimburg," *Festschrift Nikolaus Grass zum 60. Geburtstag,* ed. Louis Carlen and Fritz Steinegger. vol. 1. (Innsbruck: Universitätsverlag Wagner, 1974), pp. 559-574.

idem, "Humanism in the Tyrol: Aeneas Sylvius, Duke Sigismund, Gregor Heimburg," *Journal of Medieval and Renaissance Studies* 4 (1974): 177-202.

idem, "Nicholas of Cusa and the Tyrolese Monasteries: Reform and Resistance," *History of Political Thought* 7 (1986): 53-72. Also in *The Politics of Fallen Man: Essays Presented to Herbert A. Deane.* (Exeter: Imprint Academic, 1986), pp. 53-72.

Weiler, Anton. "Nicholas of Cusa on the Reform of the Church," trans. David Smith. *Election and Consensus in the Church,* ed. Giuseppe Alberigo and Anton Weiler. Concilium 77. (New York: Herder and Herder, 1972), pp. 94-102.

D. Political and Ecclesiological Thought

Acton, John E.E.D. Acton, Baron, "Nicholas of Cusa," *The Chronicle* (Sept. 7, 1867): 565-567.

Reprinted: idem, *Essays on Church and State,* intro. Douglass Woodruff. (London: Hollis and Carter, 1952), pp. 246-250. Also (New York: Viking Press, 1953). Reprinted: (New York: Thomas Y. Crowell, 1968.)

Black, Antony, *Council and Commune: The Conciliar Movement and the Fifteenth-Century Heritage.* (London: Burns & Oates, 1979), pp. 51-54, c. 3, Formation of Basle Conciliarism (1431-4).

Christianson, Gerald, "Cardinal Cesarini and Cusa's *Concordantia,*" *Church History* 54 (1985): 7-19.

Dunning, William A., *A History of Political Theories, Ancient and Mediaeval.* (New York: Macmillan, 1935), 270-276, c. 10 pt. 4, Nicholas of Cusa and the Council of Basel.

Jacob, Ernest F., "Nicholas of Cusa," *The Social and Political Ideas of Some Great Thinkers of the Renaissance and the Reformation,* ed. Fossey J. C. Hearnshaw. (New York: Brentano, 1925), pp. 32-60. Also (London:

Harrap, 1925); (New York: Barnes & Noble, 1925). Reprinted: (New York: Barnes & Noble, 1949 & 1967.)

Morrissey, Thomas E., "Cardinal Zabarella and Nicholas of Cusa. From Community Authority to Consent of the Community," *Mitteilungen und Forschungsbeiträge der Cusanus-Gesellschaft* 17 (1986): 157-176.

Oakley, Francis, "Natural Law, the *corpus mysticum* and Consent in Conciliar Thought from John of Paris to Matthias Ugonius," *Speculum* 56 (1981): 786-810.

Pelikan, Jaroslav, *Reformation of Church and Dogma (1300-1700).* The Christian Tradition 4. (Chicago: University of Chicago Press, 1984), pp. 98-110, c. 2, One, Holy, Catholic, Apostolic.

Petry, Ray C., "Social Responsibility and the Late Medieval Mystics," *Church History* 21 (1952): 3-19.

Sigmund, Paul E., "Cusanus' *Concordantia:* A Re-interpretation," *Political Studies* 10 (1962): 180-197.

idem, "The Influence of Marsilius of Padua on XVth Century Conciliarism," *Journal of the History of Ideas* 23 (1962): 392-402.

idem, *Nicholas of Cusa and Medieval Political Thought.* Harvard Political Studies. (Cambridge, Massachusetts: Harvard University Press, 1963).

idem, "Hierarchy, Equality and Consent in Medieval Christian Thought," *Equality,* ed. J. Roland Pennock and John W. Chapman. Nomos IX. (New York: Atherton Press, 1967), pp. 134-153.

idem, "The Concept of Equality in the Political Thought of Nicholas of Cusa," *Nicolò Cusano agli inizi del mondo moderno,* pp. 507-521.

Tierney, Brian, *Religion, Law and the Growth of Constitutional Thought, 1150-1650.* Wiles Lectures 1979. (Cambridge: Cambridge University Press, 1982), pp. 66-71, c. 4, Popular Sovereignty, Federalism and Fundamental Law: Azo to Althusius.

Ullmann, Walter, "The Papacy and the Faithful," *Gouvernés et Gouvernments.* Recueil de la Societé Jean Bodin pour l'Histoire Comparative des Institutions 25. (Brussels: Imprimerie des travaux publics, 1965), pp. 7-45.

Reprinted: idem, *Jurisprudence in the Middle Ages: Collected Studies.* (London: Variorum Reprints, 1980), Section VIII.

Watanabe, Morimichi, *The Political Ideas of Nicholas of Cusa with Special Reference to His "De concordantia catholica".* Travaux d'Humanisme et Renaissance 58. (Geneva: Librarie Droz, 1963).

idem, "Nicholas of Cusa as a Canon Lawyer," *Yearbook of the American Philosophical Society 1965* (1966): 642-644.

idem, "Authority and Consent in Church Government: Panormitanus, Aeneas Sylvius, Cusanus," *Journal of the History of Ideas* 33 (1972): 217-336.

E. Influence on Later Thinkers

Bruno, Giordano, *Five Dialogs by Giordano Bruno: Cause, Principle and Unity,* trans. & intro. Jack Lindsay. (New York: International Publishers, 1962), pp. 18-21, Introduction, pt. 3.

Duhem, Pierre M.M., *To Save the Phenomena: An Essay on the Idea of Physical Theory from Plato to Galileo,* trans. Edmund Dolan and Chaninah Maschler. intro. Stanley L. Jaki. (Chicago: University of Chicago Press, 1969), pp. 47, 57-60, c. 4. The Renaissance Before Copernicus. (Cusanus' influence on Lefèvre d'Étaples and Luiz Coronel.)

Emery, Kent, "Mysticism and the Coincidence of Opposites in 16th-Century and 17th-Century France," *Journal of the History of Ideas* 45 (1984): 3-23. (Lefèvre d'Étaples, de Bovelle, Clichtove, and others as channels of Cusanus' influence.)

Hayes, T. Wilson, "Nicholas of Cusa and Popular Literacy in 17th-Century England," *Studies in Philology* 84, no. 1 (1987): 80-94. (John Everard.)

Heller, Henry, "Nicholas of Cusa and Early French Evangelism," *Archiv für Reformationsgeschichte* 63 (1972): 6-21.

Hoff, Hebbel E., "Nicolaus of Cusa, Van Helmont and Boyle: The First Experiment of the Renaissance in Quantitative Biology and Medicine," *Journal of the History of Medicine and Allied Sciences* 19 (1964): 99-117.

Horvitz, Joseph, "A Criticism of Shmuel Hugo Bergman's Account of Nicolaus Cusanus," *Grazer Philosophische Studien* 24 (1985): 95-113.

Hughes, Philip E., *Lefèvre: Pioneer of Ecclesiastical Renewal in France.* (Grand Rapids, Michigan: William B. Eerdmans Publishing Co., 1984), pp. 44-47, Nicholas of Cusa.

Jantz, Harold S., *Goethe's Faust as a Renaissance Man: Parallels and Prototypes* (Princeton, New Jersey: Princeton University Press, 1951), especially pp. 36-45, c. 3, Faust's Intellectual Position: Cusanus, Pico de Mirandola, and Others, & pp. 117-123, c. 7, Cusanus and the Unity of Faust. Reprinted: (New York: Gordian Press, 1974.)

Kalivoda, Robert, "The Significance of J.A. Comenius for Modern Philosophy," *Communio Viatorum* 28 (1985): 59-66.

McTighe, Thomas P., "Nicholas of Cusa and Leibnitz's Principle of Indiscernibility," *The Modern Schoolman* 42 (1964): 33-46.

Morse, J. Mitchell, "Burrus, Caseous, and Nicholas of Cusa," *Modern Language Notes* 75 (1960): 326-334.

Payne, John B., "Erasmus and Lefèvre d'Étaples as Interpreters of Paul," *Archiv für Reformationsgeschichte* 65 (1974): 54-83. (Cusanus' influence on Lefèvre's exegesis.)

Rice, Eugene F. Jr., "Jacques Lefèvre d'Étaples and the Medieval Christian Mystics," *Florilegium historiale: Essays Presented to Wallace K. Ferguson,* ed. J.G. Rowe and W.H. Stockdale. (Toronto: University of Toronto Press, 1971), pp. 89-124.

Sanders, P.M., "Charles de Bovelle's Treatise on Regular Polyhedra (Paris, 1511):" *Annals on Science* 41 (1984): 513-566. (De Bovelle wrote on Cusan themes while his mentor Lefèvre was editing Cusanus' works.)

Victor, Joseph M., "The Revival of Lullism at Paris, 1499-1516," *Renaissance Quarterly* 28 (1975): 504-34. (Lefèvre read Llull in the light of Cusanus' doctrines.)

IV. Manuscripts, Editions and Library

Biechler, James E., "Three Manuscripts on Islam from the Library of Nicholas of Cusa," *Manuscripta* 27 (1983): 91-100.

Kibre, Pearl, "The Intellectual Interests Reflected in Libraries of the Fourteenth and Fifteenth Centuries," *Journal of the History of Ideas* 7 (1946): 257-297.

Kristeller, Paul O., "A Latin Translation of Gemistos Plethon's *De fato* by Johannes Sophianos Dedicated to Nicholas of Cusa," *Nicolò Cusano agli inizi del mondo moderno,* pp. 175-193.

Lefèvre d'Étaples, Jacques, *The Prefatory Epistles of Jacques Lefèvre d'Étaples and Related Texts,* ed. Eugene F. Rice Jr., (New York: Columbia University Press, 1972), pp. 342-348, no. 109, Preface to the Works of Nicholas of Cusa (1514).

Nordenskiöld, Adolf E., *Facsimile-atlas to the Early History of Cartography: With Reproductions of the Most Important Maps Printed in the XV and XVI Centuries.* trans. Johan A. Ekelof and Clements R. Markham. (Stockholm: P.A. Norstedt, 1889), pp. 16-18, no. 8; p. 25, plate 13. (First copper-print map of Central Europe, published in a Rome 1507 *Planisphaerium Ptholomaei,* probably is a copy of a map owned by Cusanus.) Reprinted: (New York: Kraus Reprints, 1961); (Nendeln: Kraus Reprints, 1970); (New York: Dover Publications, 1973.)

Ullman, Berthold L., "Manuscripts of Nicholas of Cues," *Speculum* 13 (1938): 194-197.

Reprinted: idem. *Studies in the Italian Renaissance.* (Rome: Edizioni di Storia e Letteratura, 1955), pp. 357-363. 2nd ed. Storia e Letteratura, Raccolta di Studi e Testi 51. (Rome: Edizioni di Storia e Letteratura, 1973), pp. 357-364.

V. Bibliographic Sources

American Cusanus Society Newsletter. (1983-   ) .

International Medieval Bibliography. (1967-   ).

Danzer, Robert, "Cusanus-Bibliographie, Fortsetzung (1961 bis 1964) und Nachträge," *Mitteilungen und Forschungsbeiträge der Cusanus-Gesellschaft* 3 (1963): 223-237.

Kaiser, Alfred, "Cusanus-Bibliographie, 4. Fortsetzung (1972-1982) mit Ergänzungen," *Mitteilungen und Forschungsbeiträge der Cusanus-Gesellschaft* 15 (1982): 121-147.

Kleinen, Hans and Robert Danzer, "Cusanus-Bibliographie (1920-1961)" *Mitteilungen und Forschungsbeiträge der Cusanus-Gesellschaft* 1 (1968): 95-126.

Kohl, Benjamin, *Renaissance Humanism, 1300-1550: A Bibliography of Materials in English.* (New York: Garland Publishing Company, 1985).

Trout, Wolfgang and Manfred Zacher, "Cusanus-Bibliographie, 3. Fortsetzung (1964-1967) und Nachträge," *Mitteilungen und Forschungsbeiträge der Cusanus-Gesellschaft* 6 (1967): 178-202.

Vázquez, Mario, "Cusanus-Bibliographie, 3. Fortsetzung (1967-1973) mit Ergänzungen," *Mitteilungen und Forschungsbeiträge der Cusanus-Gesellschaft* 10 (1973): 207-234.

The author is grateful to Professor Morimichi Watanabe, President of the American Cusanus Society, and to other members of the Society, particularly to Professor H. Lawrence Bond, for their assistance in the compilation of this bibliography. Professors F. Edward Cranz, Donald Duclow, Thomas McTighe, and Clyde Lee Miller provided lists of their own publications, while Professors Gerald Christianson and Pauline Watts provided offprints of articles listed here. Professor Hans Gerhard Senger provided an invaluable list containing several additional entries.

CURRICULUM VITAE

Morimichi Watanabe

Education

Hogakushi (LL.B.), Faculty of Law, University of Tokyo, 1948
University of Tokyo, 1948-1950
Princeton University, 1950-1952
Columbia University, 1954-1961
M.A., Columbia University, 1956
Ph.D., Columbia University, 1961

Positions Held

Meiji Gakuin Junior College, Tokyo
Lecturer, 1948-1950
Professor, 1950
Meiji Gakuin College, Tokyo
Instructor, 1949-1951
Lecturer, 1951-1954
Kansas State College of Pittsburg
Visiting Assistant Professor, 1960-1961
Queens College, City University of New York
Instructor, 1961-1963
C.W. Post Campus, Long Island University
Assistant Professor, 1963-1966
Associate Professor, 1966-1971
Professor, 1971-
Faculty of Law, University of Tokyo, Tokyo
Visiting Professor, 1976 (Summer)
Faculty of Law, Keio University, Tokyo
Visiting Professor, 1976 (Summer)
Faculty of Law, Himeji Dokkyo University, Himeji
Visiting Professor, 1989 (Fall)

Memberships

American Political Science Association
American Historical Association
Medieval Academy of America
Renaissance Society of America
American Catholic Historical Association
American Society of Church History

Memberships (cont.)

University Seminar on the History of Legal and Political
          Thought, Columbia University (Chair: 1983-1985)
University Seminar on the Renaissance, Columbia University

Awards and Honors

Dean's Recognition Award
          C.W. Post College, Long Island University, 1976

Research Grants
          American Philosophical Society, 1964
          American Council of Learned Societies, 1966
          Foundation for Reformation Research, 1970
          American Philosophical Society, 1970
          C.W. Post Campus, Long Island University, 1974
          Council on International Educational Exchange, 1976
          American Philosophical Society, 1977
          C.W. Post Campus, Long Island University, 1984
          The Trustee Award for Scholarly Achievement,
                    Long Island University, 1981

President

American Cusanus Society, 1983-

Editor

American Cusanus Society Newsletter, 1984-

Other Positions

Wissenschaftlicher Beirat (Academic Advisory Board),
          Cusanus-Gesellschaft, Member, 1968-
Nihon Kuzanusu Gakkai (Japanese Cusanus Society),
          Honorary Adviser, 1983-

BIBLIOGRAPHY

The Works of Morimichi Watanabe

Book

The Political Ideas of Nicholas of Cusa with Special Reference to his De concordantia catholica, Travaux d'Humanisme et Renaissance 58 (Geneva, 1963).

Translation

Paul Oskar Kristeller, *Runessansu No Shiso* (Renaissance Thought) (Tokyo, 1977).

Articles

"An Inquiry into the Study of Medieval Political Thought," *Meiji Gakuin Review* 19 (September, 1950): 33-51.

"Puerto Rico: The Caribbean Crossroads," *Meiji Gakuin Review* 28 (February, 1953): 101-114.

"A Study of the 1952 American Presidential Election," *Meiji Gakuin Review* 29 (June, 1951): 87-109.

"The American President as Maker of Foreign Policy and Commander-in-Chief," *Meiji Gakuin Review* 33 (December, 1953): 67-80.

"Eight Philosophers of the Italian Renaissance," *Bibliothèque d'Humanisme et Renaissance* 27 (1965): 539-541.

"The Life and Thought of Nicholas of Cusa," *Journal of Theology* 28 (Tokyo, 1965): 114-120.

"Nicholas of Cusa as a Canon Lawyer," *Year Book of the American Philosophical Society 1965* (1966), pp. 642-644.

"A Note on the Two International Cusanus Congresses of 1964," *Journal of Philosophical Studies* 43 (Kyoto, 1966): 845-853.

"Nikolaus von Kues--Richard Fleming--Thomas Livingston," *Mitteilungen und Forschungsbeiträge der Cusanus-Gesellschaft* 6 (1967): 167-177.

"The Episcopal Election of 1430 in Trier and Nicholas of Cusa," *Church History* 39 (1970): 299-316.

"Nicholas of Cusa and the Idea of Tolerance," *Nicolò Cusano agli inizi del mondo moderno* (Florence, 1970), pp. 409-418.

"Jurisprudence and Humanism: A Critical Study of Gregor Heimburg (ca. 1400-1472)," *Year Book of the American Philosophical Society 1971* (1972), pp. 688-689.

"Authority and Consent in Church Government: Panormitanus, Aeneas Sylvius, Cusanus," *Journal of the History of Ideas* 33 (1972): 217-236.

"Humanism in the Tyrol: Aeneas Sylvius, Duke Sigmund and Gregor Heimburg," *Journal of Medieval and Renaissance Studies* 4 (1974): 177-202.

"The Lawyer and Conscience," *U P* (a publication of The University of Tokyo Press) 24 (October, 1974): 8-13.

"Duke Sigmund and Gregor Heimburg," *Festschrift Nikolaus Grass zum 60. Geburtstag,* ed. L. Carlen and F. Steinegger, vol. 1 (Innsbruck, 1974), pp. 559-573.

"Gregor Heimburg and Early Humanism in Germany," *Philosophy and Humanism: Renaissance Essays in Honor of Paul Oskar Kristeller,* ed. Edward P. Mahoney (Leiden, 1976) pp. 406-422.

"Political Theory in the Late Middle Ages: The Fourteenth and Fifteenth Centuries," *Aufstieg und Niedergang der römischen Welt,* pt. 3, ed. Wolfgang Haase (Berlin and New York, in press).

"The Growth of the Hierocratic Theory of Church Government", "The Decline of Papal Authority," and "The Conciliar Movement and Nicholas of Cusa," *Foundations of European Political Theory* (Tokyo, 1977), pp. 96-101.

"Imperial Reform in the Mid-Fifteenth Century: Gregor Heimburg and Martin Mair," *Journal of Medieval and Renaissance Studies* 9 (1979): 209-235.

"Humanism, Law and Reform: Reflections on Fifteenth-Century Lawyers," *Ventures in Research,* Series 8, 1979 (1981): 7-35.

"Natural Law, Professor Boissonade and Japan," *Vera Lex* 3 (Summer/Fall, 1982): 6-7, 21.

"Luther Research in America and Japan", *Concordia Theological Quarterly* 48 (1984): 39-54.

"Cusanus Research in the United States," *Report of the Japanese Cusanus Society* 5 (March, 1985): 7-17.

"Cusanus, Roman Law and Humanism: In Comparison with Gregor Heimburg," in *Nikorausu Kuzanusu Kenkyu Josetsu* (Essays on Cusanus) (Tokyo, 1986), pp. 289-310.

"Lutherforschung in Amerika und Japan" (with Lewis W. Spitz), *Lutherische Theologie und Kirche* 33 (N.F. 9) (1986): 121-135.

"Nicholas of Cusa and the Tyrolese Monasteries: Reform and Resistance", *The Politics of Fallen Man: Essays Presented to Herbert A. Deane* (Exeter, 1986): 53-72; also published in *History of Political Thought* VII, 1 (Spring, 1986): 53-72.

"The Influence of Italian Humanism on Martin Luther", *Luther Studies* 2 (Tokyo, 1986), pp. 57-87.

"Luther's Relations with Italian Humanists, with Special Reference to Baptista Mantuanus," *Luther-Jahrbuch* 54 (1987): 23-47.

"Political Theory, Western European: After 1100", *Dictionary of the Middle Ages,* ed. Joseph R. Strayer and published under the auspices of the American Council of Learned Societies, vol. 10 (New York, 1988), pp. 18-26.

Reviews

Paul E. Sigmund, *Nicholas of Cusa and Medieval Political Thought* (Cambridge, Massachusetts, 1965) in *Bibliothèque d'Humanisme et Renaissance* 27 (1965): 335-337.

Francis Oakley, *The Political Thought of Pierre d'Ailly: The Voluntarist Tradition* (New Haven, 1964) in *Bibliothèque d'Humanisme et Renaissance* 28 (1966): 491-493.

Felice Battaglia, *Metafisica, Religione e Politica nel Pensiero di Nicolo da Cusa* (Bologna, 1965) in *Bibliothèque d'Humanisme et Renaissance* 29 (1967): 274-275.

C. Iwasaki and S. Oide, trans., *Nikorausu Kuzanusu* (Nicolaus Cusanus): *Chi aru Muchi* (De docta ignorantia) (Tokyo, 1966) in *Mitteilungen und Forschungsbeiträge der Cusanus-Gesellschaft* 7 (1969): 170-172.

Nicholai de Cusa Opera omnia, vol. 14: *De concordantia catholica,* ed. Gerhard Kallen (Hamburg, 1959-1968) in *The Catholic Historical Review* 55 (1969): 460-464.

288   WATANABE BIBLIOGRAPHY

A. J. Black, *Monarchy and Community: Political Ideas in the Later Conciliar Controversy, 1430-1450* (Cambridge, 1970) in *Church History* 40 (1971): 485.

S. Oide and T. Sakamoto, trans., Nicolaus Cusanus: *Kakuretaru Kami* (Deus absconditus) (Tokyo, 1972) in *Mitteilungen und Forschungsbeiträge der Cusanus-Gesellschaft* 10 (1973): 240-241.

Nicolai de Cusa Opera omnia, vol. 16, 1: *Sermones* 1 (1430-1441), Fasciculus 1, ed. R. Haubst *et al.* (Hamburg, 1970) in *The Catholic Historical Review* 59 (1974): 657-658.

Walter Brandmüller, *Das Konzil von Pavia-Siena, 1423-1424*, 2 vols. (Münster, 1968-1974) in *Church History* 44 (1975): 403-404.

Nikolaus von Kues als Promotor der Oekumene, ed. Rudolf Haubst (Mainz, 1971) in *The Catholic Historical Review* 61 (1975): 79-81.

Barbara Frank, *Das Erfurter Peterskloster im 15. Jahrhundert: Studien zur Geschichte der Kloster-reform und der Bursfelder Union* (Göttingen, 1973) in *The Catholic Historical Review* 63 (1977): 149-150.

James E. Biechler, *The Religious Language of Nicholas of Cusa* (Missoula, Montana, 1975), in *The Catholic Historical Review* 64 (1978): 462-463.

Erich Meuthen and Herman Hallauer, eds., *Acta Cusana: Quellen zur Lebensgeschichte des Nikolaus von Kues,* vol. 1, pt. 1, ed. Erich Meuthen (Hamburg, 1976), in *Mitteilungen und Forschungsbeiträge der Cusanus-Gesellschaft* 12 (1977): 155-158.

Martin Bodewig, Josef Schmitz, and Reinhold Weier, eds., *Das Menschenbild des Nikolaus von Kues und der christliche Humanismus* (Mainz, 1978) in *The Catholic Historical Review* 67 (1981): 77-78.

Itzhak Galnoor, ed., *Government Secrecy in Democracies* (New York, 1977) in *The Journal of Politics* 40 (1978): 1114.

Quentin Skinner, *The Foundations of Modern Political Thought*, 2 vols. (Cambridge, 1978) in *The Historian* 42 (1980): 652-655.

Jasper Hopkins, *A Concise Introduction to the Philosophy of Nicholas of Cusa,* rev. ed. (Minneapolis, 1980) and *Nicholas of Cusa on God as Not-Other* (Minneapolis, 1979) in *Renaissance Quarterly* 34 (1981): 557-560.

Young C. Kim, *Japanese Journalists and their World* (Charlottesville, 1981) in *The Journal of Politics* 44 (1982): 1169.

Ernst H. Kantorowicz, *The King's Two Bodies: A Study in Medieval Political Theology* (Princeton, 1957; paperback ed., 1981) in *Church History* 52 (1983): 258-259.

Brian Tierney, *Religion, Law and the Growth of Constitutional Thought, 1150-1650* (Cambridge, 1982) in *Church History* 52 (1983): 499.

Pauline Moffitt Watts, *Nicolaus Cusanus: A Fifteenth-Century Vision of Man* (Leiden, 1982) in *Church History* 53 (1984): 92-93.

Wilhelm Baum, *Nikolaus Cusanus in Tirol: Das Wirken des Philosophen und Reformators als Fürstbischof von Brixen* (Bozen, 1983) in *Church History* 54 (1985): 104.

Erich Meuthen and Herman Hallauer, eds., *Acta Cusana: Quellen zur Lebensgeschichte des Nikolaus von Kues,* vol. 1, pt. 2, ed. Erich Meuthen (Hamburg, 1983), *Mitteilungen und Forschungsbeiträge des Cusanus-Gesellschaft,* 17 (1986): 263-266.

Addresses

"The Lawyer in an Age of Political and Religious Confusion", an address delivered on the occasion of the twentieth anniversary of C. W. Post College of Long Island University, May 9, 1975.

"Nicholas of Cusa as a Reformer," Medieval Studies Council Lecture, Smith College, October 5, 1987.

"Nicolaus Cusanus as an Ecclesiastical Reformer," Plenary Address, Annual Meeting of the Japanese Cusanus Society, Doshisha University, Kyoto, Japan, November 10, 1989.

Papers

"Nicholas of Cusa and the Idea of Tolerance," Congresso Internazionale Nicolò Cusano, Bressanone, Italy, September 9, 1964.

"Archdiocese of Trier and Nicholas of Cusa: His Early Career as a Lawyer," Fourth Biennial Conference on Medieval Studies, Western Michigan University, March 14, 1968.

"Episcopal Election of 1430 and Nicholas of Cusa: His Activities as a Canon Lawyer," Columbia University Seminar on the Renaissance, May 7, 1968.

"Nicholaus de Tudeschis, Nicholaus Cusanus, and Aeneas Silvius Piccolomini on Authority and Consent in Church Government," Columbia University Seminar on the History of Legal and Political Thought, May 19, 1970.

"Humanism in the Tyrol: Aeneas Sylvius Piccolomini and Gregor Heimburg," Columbia University Seminar on the Renaissance, May 16, 1972.

"The Problem of Imperial Reform in the Mid-Fifteenth Century: Gregor Heimburg and Martin Mair," Reformation Seminar, Graduate Center, City University of New York, April 13, 1973.

"Professors, Lawyers, and Churchmen in the Conciliar Movement," The Medieval Study, Graduate Center, City University of New York, March 9, 1976.

"Gregor Heimburg and Humanism: The University of Padua in the Fifteenth Century," Queens College. City University of New York, February 27, 1979.

"Humanism, Law, and Reform: Reflections on Fifteenth-Century Lawyers," Ventures in Research, C.W. Post Campus, Long Island University, February 28, 1979.

"Han Fei (d. 233 B.C.), Legalist of Ancient China, and Machiavelli," Columbia University Seminar on the History of Legal and Political Thought, April 26, 1979.

"Nicholas of Cusa, Gregor Heimburg, and the University of Padua," Columbia University Seminar on the Renaissance, October 21, 1980.

"Nicholas of Cusa, Gregor Heimburg, and the University of Padua," Seventeenth International Congress on Medieval Studies, Western Michigan University, May 6, 1982.

"Cusa, Luther, and Humanism," Nineteenth International Congress on Medieval Studies, Western Michigan University, May 11, 1984.

"The Origins of Modern Cusanus Research: Before and After the Heidelberg Edition," Twenty-First International Congress on Medieval Studies, Western Michigan University, May 9, 1986.

"Nicholas of Cusa as Bishop of Brixen," Twenty-Second International Congress on Medieval Studies, Western Michigan University, May 8, 1987.

"Nicholas of Cusa, the Council of Florence, and the *Acceptatio* of Mainz (1439)," Twenty-Fourth International Congress on Medieval Studies, Western Michigan University, May 4, 1989.

"Nicolaus Cusanus the Political Theorist Reconsidered," Kansai Association for the Study of Western Political Thought, Konan University, Kobe, Japan, December 9, 1989.

"Nicholas of Cusa and his Political Ideas," Faculty of Law, Himeji Dokkyo University, Himeji, Japan, January 22, 1990.

Symposia

Internationaler Cusanus-Kongress, Brixen, Italy, September 6-10, 1964, delivering a paper.

Symposium, "Nikolaus von Kues in der Geschichte des Erkenntnisproblems," Trier, West Germany, October 18-20, 1973, serving as commentator.

Conference, "Approaches to the Study of Chinese and Japanese Political Thought," York University, Toronto, Canada, April 2-3, 1977, serving as commentator.

Fourth Annual Meeting of the Northeast American Society for Eighteenth-Century Studies, C.W. Post Campus, Long Island University, October 16-18, 1980, serving as Chair of Session 1: "Literature and the Law."

Symposium, "Der Friede unter den Religionen nach Nikolaus von Kues," Trier, West Germany, October 13-15, 1982, representing the American Cusanus Society.

Sixth International Congress for Luther Research, Erfurt, East Germany, August 14-20, 1983, serving as discussion leader in Part A, Session 2 ("Luther's Knowledge of Italian Humanism") of Seminar 5 ("Luther and Humanism").

Symposium: "Das Sehen Gottes nach Nikolaus von Kues," Trier, West Germany, September 25-27, 1986, representing the American Cusanus Society.

International Symposium of the Cusanus-Gesellschaft: "Weisheit und Wissenschaft: Cusanus im Blick auf die Gegenwart," Bernkastel-Kues and Trier, West Germany, March 29-31, 1990, representing the American Cusanus Society.

American Cusanus Society Newsletter
Editor and Publisher

Vol. 1, no. 2	July 1984
Vol. 2, no. 1	January 1985
Vol. 2, no. 2	July 1985
Vol. 3, no. 1	February 1986
Vol. 3, no. 2	September 1986
Vol. 4, no. 1	March 1987
Vol. 4, no. 2	September 1987
Vol. 5, no. 1	February 1988
Vol. 5, no. 2	September 1988
Vol. 6, no. 1	March 1989
Vol. 6, no. 2	August 1989
Vol. 7, no. 1	June 1990

INDEX

Persons

d'Abano, Pietro, 114.
Acton, Lord, 5, 259.
Aggsbach, Vinzenz of, 246 n.
d'Ailly, Pierre, 21.
Alan of Lille, 89-100.
Albert (of Bavaria), 74, 79, 83.
Albert III (see Albrecht III).
Albert the Great, 8, 39, 45-56, 69.
Alberti, 114.
Albrecht III of Wittelsbach, Duke, 74, 253.
Althusius, Johannes, 250.
Anaxagoras, 124.
Andrew of St. Victor, 178 n.
Anselm, 8, 62, 93, 96.
Antoninus, 259 n.
Archimedes, 13.
Archimedes (Pseudo-), 113 n.
Arévalo, Rodrigo Sánchez de, 163, 222, 224.
Aristotle, 7-8, 32, 68, 106, 108-111, 115, 124-125, 144, 146, 149, 158, 188, 195 n.
Ascensius, Jadocus Badius, 24.
Auclou, Robert, 240 n.
Augustine, 8, 63.
Averroes, 46, 47.
Avicenna, 198.

Bacon, Roger, 101, 111.
Baeumker, Clemens, 31.
Balbus, Petrus, 150.
Barzizza, Gasparino, 235 n.
Baur, F.C., 21 n.
Baur, Ludwig, 32 n., 39.
Bernardino de Sahagún, 216.
Berruguete, 178 n.
Bessarion, Cardinal, 6.
Bett, Henry, 5.
Biechler, James, 161, 166-167, 170, 211.
Biel, Gabriel, 7.
Birck, Maximilian, 24.
Black, Antony, 188, 193-194, 196.

Blumenberg, Hans, 7-8, 250.
Bodin, Jean, 182, 250.
Boethius, 123.
Bonaventure, 72-73, 83, 85, 89, 97.
Boniface VIII, 223, 224 n., 227, 239 n.
Bruneti, Petrus, 230 n.
Bruno, Giordano, 27.
Burckhardt, 34.
Buridan, 8.

Calixtus III, 115, 180, 251.
Capranica, Cardinal Domenico, 234.
Carvajal, Juan de, 243.
Casas, Bartolomé de las, 182.
Cassirer, Bruno, 27, 29.
Cassirer, Eduard, 28.
Cassirer, Ernst, 6, 25, 28-33, 34, 41, 188, 260.
Cassirer, Heinrich, 33.
Castile, King of, 224.
Cesarini, Cardinal Giuliano, 135, 137, 179-181.
Chanut, 102.
Chappuis, Jean, 224 n.
Chevrot, Jean, 240 n.
Christina of Sweden, Queen, 102.
Cicero, 139, 216.
Clamanges, Nicholas de, 21.
Clemens, F.J., 22, 24.
Cohen, Hermann, 25-29, 31.
Columbus, Christopher, 214.
Comitibus, Prosdocimus de, 234 n.
Constantine, 259.
Constanzi, Enrico, 17.
Copernicus, 7, 101, 108-109, 115, 183.
Cortés, 215.
Crammer, Thomas, 259 n.
Crombie, A.C., 114.
Cromwell, Thomas, 259 n.

Daniel, Norman, 186-187.
Dante, 72, 92.

Places
(in the career of Cusanus and related figures)

Citations to Cusanus' Works